Voting and Faithfulness

Catholic Perspectives on Politics

Edited by Nicholas P. Cafardi

Paulist Press
New York / Mahwah, NJ

Cover design by Mark Lo Bello
Book design by Lynn Else

Library of Congress Cataloging-in-Publication Data
Names: Cafardi, Nicholas P, editor.
Title: Voting and faithfulness : Catholic perspectives on politics / Nicholas P Cafardi.
Description: New York : Paulist Press, 2020. | Summary: "Fifteen essays aimed at voters on a variety of topics such as faithful citizenship, how Catholics perceive and talk about issues such as war, life issues, character issues, and how our bishops teach. Includes discussion questions for each essay"— Provided by publisher.
Identifiers: LCCN 2019028362 (print) | LCCN 2019028363 (ebook) | ISBN 9780809154906 (paperback) | ISBN 9781587688867 (ebook)
Subjects: LCSH: Christianity and politics—Catholic Church. | Catholics—Political activity. | Catholic Church—Doctrines.
Classification: LCC BX1793 .V68 2020 (print) | LCC BX1793 (ebook) | DDC 261.7088/28273—dc23
LC record available at https://lccn.loc.gov/2019028362
LC ebook record available at https://lccn.loc.gov/2019028363

ISBN 978-0-8091-5490-6 (paperback)
ISBN 978-1-58768-886-7 (e-book)

Published by Paulist Press
997 Macarthur Boulevard
Mahwah, New Jersey 07430
www.paulistpress.com

Printed and bound in the
United States of America

Contents

Preface

That seems a strange topic, doesn't it, *Voting and Faithfulness*? We don't normally think of those two concepts at the same time. What could their joinder possibly mean? The premise of this conjunction is that voting, although we do not normally think of it that way, is an action that has a moral value. Voting can involve morally acceptable or morally unacceptable choices. Voting can be a good deed or an evil deed. And, very importantly, when we vote, we should try to be faithful Catholics doing good. Our faith should inform this action as it informs all our actions.

This is the position of the American bishops. Starting in 2007, preceding the 2008 presidential election, and again in 2011 and 2015, always preceding the presidential election by one year, the United States Conference of Catholic Bishops has issued an official document, *Forming Consciences for Faithful Citizenship*, instructing Catholics on how the beliefs and values of our faith should help us to form our consciences before we vote in the national elections.

In their June 2018 meeting, however, the bishops' conference chose to deviate from their quadrennial practice and decided not to revise their document *Forming Consciences for Faithful Citizenship* for the 2020 federal election cycle. Instead they voted overwhelmingly to supplement the most recent 2015 version with a brief letter and some videos. A floor amendment requires that these additional materials incorporate the teachings of Pope Francis.

You will see that title, *Forming Consciences for Faithful Citizenship*, sometimes shortened simply to *Faithful Citizenship*, frequently in this volume. It is the key document when contemplating the moral values that Catholics should bring to their electoral choices, so it is natural that a volume of essays on voting and faithfulness would refer often to that work of the U.S. bishops.

This concept also provides our work with its title, *Voting and Faithfulness*. How do I, as a faithful Catholic, apply the teachings of my faith to the act of voting? There are fifteen essays in this volume on five different themes by respected Catholic theologians and professors that discuss the riches of church teaching that faithful American Catholics should consider in order to inform their conscience before they vote. That conscience, once informed, is the highest moral authority that an individual can look to. That informed conscience is the goal of this work.

Too often, the teachings of our church are reduced to sound bites, usually by those who wish to distort those teachings for their own purposes, political or otherwise. But our two thousand-year-old faith, beginning with the divine revelation of the Gospels, Acts and the letters of the Apostles, then all of the teachings of the early fathers, the medieval outburst of theological speculation that culminated in St. Thomas Aquinas, the reformation of that faith when challenged by its members, the social justice encyclicals of the popes starting in the 1800s and running to current times, and the great gift of the Second Vatican Council, whose teachings are still being received in the church, is not a matter easily reduced to simplistic nostrums. It is a faith of phenomenal sophistication and wisdom, both a challenge and a comfort to its adherents.

So, this book, if it meets its goal, will be an exercise in conscience formation for Catholics who wish to be faithful when they vote, taking into account the great wealth of the church's teachings, and attempting to apply them to the political issues that confront us as faithful Catholics and as American voters.

The first section of this volume presents an overarching Catholic perspective on current political issues. Bishop John Stowe of Lexington, Kentucky, in his essay, "The Interrelatedness of Life Issues," writes about the inescapable relationship of pro-life issues to each other. Starting with the March for Life to protect the unborn, he focuses on the vast content of Catholic social justice teaching which should inform our political actions as Catholics. In the U.S. bishops' recent letter on racism and in the approach of Pope Francis who has turned the church's attention to the peripheries, to the care of the most vulnerable, and to a care for our common home, Bishop Stowe sees the protection of life across a spectrum of political issues as a unified whole in Catholic teaching. On the same theme, Dr. Nicholas P. Cafardi, Dean Emeritus of Duquesne University Law School, in his essay "Reforming *Faithful Citizenship*," considers what a revised version of *Faithful Citizenship* might look like if the bishops had decided to completely rewrite their document from the pro-life perspectives of Pope Francis.

The second section deals with how we think and talk about political issues from a Catholic frame of reference. In his essay, "The Roots of Catholic Polarization in the United States," Robert G. Christian, III, cofounder and editor of *Millennial*, deals with how an undue political partisanship has taken hold within the American church, the deleterious effects it has had on Catholic comity, and what some potential remedies for this polarization might be. Dr. David DeCosse from Santa Clara University writes about the freedom of the conscience in *"Faithful Citizenship* and the Theology of Conscience: A Reflection on Grace, the World, and the 2020 Election." He compares the theology of conscience used in *Faithful Citizenship* with the theology of conscience of John Courtney Murray, where human freedom is understood in terms of human rights in a democracy; he also compares it with the theological concept of the *sensus fidelium*, the understanding of the faith by the faithful. Dr. Nancy Dallavalle of Fairfield University writes in "Our 'First Freedom'? Sex, Gender, and Sexuality in Religious Freedom Claims" that sex and gender language haunts modern presentations of religious freedom. She sees this as the result of a clash between a "soft" millennialism and a "dogmatic" secularism, each claiming the priority of conscience, but with different interpretations of what conscience means. She cautions against those who would use the primacy of the conscience and the banner of religious freedom to resist the rights of others, especially in the areas of sex and gender. Dr. Bernard Prusak of King's College, in his essay, "How to Speak to Nones and All: Integrity about Religious Liberty," examines why the nones and the millennials decline participation in both organized religion and organized politics and what might be done to address that declining participation. As an effective way to engage them in both, he suggests a politics of integrity, a style of engagement in the public square rooted in a person's core identity and in the recognition of the integrity of others.

The third section of this volume deals with individual life issues. Dr. Charles Camosy of Fordham University contributes his analysis of "Shifting Abortion Politics," explaining in a detailed historical retelling how one's position on the right to an abortion has become such a defining element in American politics. He does see a possible end to this debate for those courageous enough to cease the endless villainizing of the other side and claim the common ground where most Americans appear to agree. Dr. Gerald J. Beyer, of Villanova University, deals with "Worker Justice as a Pro-Life Issue." He examines the church's social justice teachings on the rights of workers and then discusses how justice for workers might play out as a pro-life issue in our political life as Catholics. Dr. Lisa Sowle Cahill of Boston College, in her essay, "Ending War Is a Priority for Pope Francis: How about U.S. Voters?" examines the Catholic tradition of the just war, and how papal teaching since the Second Vatican Council has moved away from a just war analysis to a nonviolent approach as emblemized in the teachings of Pope Francis. She then examines whether this part of papal teaching has made its way into the pews of American churches, the hearts of American Catholics, and our voting booths. Dr. Tobias Winright of St. Louis University in his essay, "Conscience and the Military," writes about Catholic just war theory. He explains that, when it comes to issues such as our nation's wars, Catholics tend to bifurcate their faith from their lives. He then enters an examination of Catholic just war theory and its historical development, and how it might be time to consider an alternative theory of "just peacemaking."

In our fourth section, our authors deal with concerns of character in politics. Dr. Tina Astorga of the University of Portland in Oregon in her "The Rise of Populism: A Theo-Ethical Critique," deals with the phenomenon of populism as exemplified by the current U.S. president, but through the analytical lens of Christ cleansing the temple as an example of what someone who was a true populist, with the best interests of others (the populace) at heart, would look like. Dr. Cathleen Kaveny from Boston College questions how we assess candidates for political office in her essay, "Voting as a Moral Act: Candidates, Issues, and Election Guides." With new issues certain to emerge during an elected official's term of office, she questions whether the candidate's character would not be a better judgment tool in assessing suitability for office than what the candidate says about individual issues, because while issues change, character does not. Author John Gehring from Faith in Action writes about the misuse of faith in "Reclaiming Catholic Identity in the Trump Era." He deals with the issues of racism, nativism, and nationalism that gained a certain prominence in the last elections and examines how the church has historically dealt with these issues in its attempts to form a truly Catholic character.

Our fifth section deals with the bishops and their relationship to the laity on political issues. Prof. Angela C. Carmella of Seton Hall University addresses "An Informed Laity: Understanding the Church's Political and Legal Advocacy," examining what effect the tactics of our bishops in lobbying and lawsuits on abortion, gay rights, and contraceptive mandates has had on the faithful. In this regard, she explains that civil law has its limits. It must seek the common good of a common society, which may require a different type of moral-political advocacy. Dr. Massimo Faggioli from Villanova University writes of "The Transatlantic Catholic Gap: Pope Francis and the U.S. Catholic Church." In this essay, he brings an international and global perspective to the reception of Pope Francis's pontificate in the United States and questions how our politics have entered the American church to the point where papal teaching is now freely challenged or rejected by some of our bishops for what appear to be partisan reasons.

Each of these essays is followed by questions for further reflection, provided by the editor, to increase your understanding of and engagement with the important issues that the authors address. Although they all appear in the same volume, it would be a mistake, with such a distinguished and varied group of scholars, to think that they share all the opinions of their co-contributors expressed in this book. Similarly, the universities and organizations mentioned above are used for author identification purposes only. Each essay, each author speaks for her/himself, not another author, not an institution, and, as noted, the questions for further reflection are the editor's, not the author's.

If we have met our collective responsibility, then at the end, you will put this book down with a renewed enthusiasm for putting our Catholic faith into action when you enter the voting booth, with a fully informed conscience and with a renewed perspective on the richness and relevancy that our Catholic faith brings to questions such as, "For whom do I vote and why?"

Nicholas P. Cafardi
Editor

PART I

Rewriting
Faithful
Citizenship

1

The Interrelatedness of Pro-Life Issues

Bishop John Stowe

The March for Life

The annual March for Life in Washington, DC, draws tens of thousands of people to demonstrate their support for the sanctity of human life near the January 22 anniversary of the Supreme Court's 1973 *Roe v. Wade* decision. The actual march is preceded by Masses, vigils, and other prayerful events that are designed to emphasize the youthful participation in the fight to end abortion on demand as a constitutionally protected right in the United States. Long processions of bishops and a homily by a prominent prelate are featured in a Mass at the National Shrine of the Basilica of the Immaculate Conception. Busloads of young people who call themselves the "pro-life generation" arrive from across the country; many are chartered by Catholic schools and dioceses. The lack of attention from the secular media to this sizable annual event is frequently lamented in Catholic circles. But the spread of a viral video featuring Catholic high school students in what appeared to be a face-to-face confrontation with a Native American in the aftermath of the march, along with the subsequent controversy about the video's context, brought plenty of attention to the march in 2019.

The video clip seen far and wide features a young student, wearing a red baseball cap emblazoned with President Donald Trump's signature "Make America Great Again" slogan, face-to-face with a Native American elder who continues to chant with his rhythmic drumbeat. Unfortunately, this became the iconic snapshot of the 2019 march. Reaction to the video drew further attention to the partisan politics that have so bitterly divided the country and infected the church. Bishops who initially condemned the behavior of the students in the video were vehemently chastised by those who claimed that the students themselves were the victims of racist and anti-Catholic bias. Interpretations of the video clip were largely dependent upon the viewer's politics and worldview. More importantly, the video and the surrounding controversy raise serious questions about the alignment of the Right to Life movement with a president whose policies do little to affirm the dignity of the human person. That moment provided an opportunity for U.S. Catholics to consider how support of the most basic right, the right to life itself, has become separated from the fundamental value of the dignity of each human person. It drew attention to the uncritical alliance of much of the Catholic pro-life movement with the Republican party because of the shared goal of ending abortion, at a time when that party is headed by a leader who has no qualms about insulting immigrants from nonwhite countries, boasting of his sexual exploitation of women, and repeatedly distorting the truth for self-serving purposes.

Donald Trump, having never held any public office, began his campaign for the U.S. presidency with a speech denigrating immigrants from Mexico and broadly categorizing them as rapists and murderers. This was not only extremely offensive to the immigrants themselves, but should have elicited vociferous protests from the church that has consistently called for comprehensive immigration reform for decades and which counts the Latino population, largely from Mexico, as a positive influence and a major source of the church's growth in this country. As president, Trump has considerably lowered the standard of rhetorical decorum and did not shy away from using offensively vulgar terms to describe the nations of origin of African and Caribbean refugees and immigrants. He has publicly stated his preference for increasing the number of immigrants from countries like Norway as opposed to creating a more generous immigration policy for those fleeing hunger, violence, and suffering in their materially impoverished and dangerous homelands. The president who is celebrated by some as a champion

4

of the pro-life movement because he appointed staunchly antiabortion judges to the Supreme Court is the same president whose administration created and enforced policies that kept little children penned up in chain-link cages at the U.S.-Mexico border and who presided over the separation of young immigrant children from their parents in custody.

In recent years, video messages from the president and the live presence of the vice president of the United States have given the March for Life the feel of a campaign rally for the president. It is quite expected that the president would highlight his contributions to the antiabortion cause and his friendliness to the movement, but subjecting students sponsored by Catholic institutions to the partisan rhetoric and divisive politics advocated by this presidential administration should not be left unchallenged.

Catholic leaders should ask whether the students of the "pro-life generation," now exposed to the partisan rhetoric at the March for Life, have been taught about the peace activists at the origins of the pro-life movement for whom opposition to abortion was a natural extension of opposition to all forms of violence. Juli Loesch, who had trained with César Chávez and the United Farm Workers to protect the rights of migrant workers, was instrumental in creating an organization called "Mobilization for Survival" whose members emphasized a consistent pro-life ethic in the immediate aftermath of *Roe v. Wade*. These activists were equally committed to the end of the nuclear arms race and the abolition of abortion because they were both threats to the sanctity of human life. Loesch joined forces with Benedictine Sister Mary Lou Kownacki during the formative period of what is today Pax Christi USA, the national chapter of the international Catholic Peace movement.

Catholic Social Teaching

Catholic social teaching has rich content and a long history of defending the right to life of the unborn within the framework of an overall reverence for the dignity of the human person. Today's young Catholic pro-life activists may not be aware of how, in the decade preceding the *Roe v. Wade* decision, priests, nuns, and clergy of various traditions stood shoulder-to-shoulder with Dr. Martin Luther King Jr. and marched for civil rights. Do they know that in the 1980s the U.S. bishops wrote Pastoral Letters calling for an end to the threat of nuclear devastation and promoting world peace? These teachings, consistent with a reverence for human life, were not always well received by the political partisans who agreed with the bishops on the evils of abortion. In the same decade, the bishops wrote a letter advocating economic inclusion of the marginalized and suggesting that the morality of the economy was to be judged on the impact it has on the poor. This too was promoted within an overall teaching of the value of human life and dignity. The pro-life movement and its constituent reverence for the sanctity of human life must include the promotion of all that is necessary for human beings to flourish. A "pro-life generation" should be familiar with all the life issues that have made the Catholic community homeless among the political parties.

Throughout the decades since *Roe v. Wade*, the Catholic Church's opposition to abortion has been steadfast. Lamentably, the "seamless garment" approach to the interconnectedness of the life issues, so forcefully articulated by the late Cardinal Joseph Bernardin, has become less prominent within the American hierarchy. Showing the interconnectedness of all the life issues came to be seen by some in the hierarchy as detracting from the singular importance of the basic right to life itself. Gradually abortion has become a stand-alone issue for many in the church. Single-issue voters can find great support among fellow Catholics and some Catholic organizations to justify their votes for candidates who are steadfastly against abortion even though they have appalling records concerning the care of the poor, the environment, global human rights, and use of destructive force.

Pope Francis

From the beginning of his papacy in 2013, Pope Francis, who describes himself as having been chosen from the ends of the earth, has tried to turn the church's attention to the peripheries. By the peripheries, the pope means those farthest from the centers of power, that is, the most vulnerable. He clearly and repeatedly includes the unborn in his descriptions of the marginalized. But Pope Francis sees the lack of reverence for life in the womb as the consequence of a consumerist culture that has come to consider human beings to be just as disposable as our outdated products. The same attitude that would permit aborting a child allows for the careless indifference to the elderly and the handicapped and even the disposal of the terminally ill. He has decried, in homilies and apostolic exhortations alike, the "globalization of indifference," which allows the powerful to ignore the suffering and deaths of the poor even when this occurs regularly on a massive scale. Pope Francis would find it hard to justify support for an administration intent on building walls to keep out human beings considered undesirable, that has fought for a policy that intentionally seeks to exclude refugees on the basis of their profession of Islam, and that has been slow and equivocal in its questionable condemnation of racially incited violence. He would find it inconceivable to consider such an administration to be "pro-life."

Pope Francis describes the interrelatedness of pro-life issues in his 2018 apostolic exhortation *Rejoice and be Glad*, a reflection on the universal call to holiness. He says, "Our defense of the innocent unborn, for example, needs to be clear, firm and passionate, for at stake is the dignity of a human life, which is always sacred and demands love for each person, regardless of his or her stage of development. Equally sacred, however, are the lives of the poor, those already born, the destitute, the abandoned and the underprivileged, the vulnerable infirm and elderly exposed to covert euthanasia, the victims of human trafficking, new forms of slavery, and every form of rejection" (*Gaudete et exultate* 101).

Open Wide Our Hearts

In November 2018, in the context of increasing hate crimes, violence against people of color, and a surge of white nationalist demonstrations that have coincided with the Trump candidacy and presidency, the U.S. Catholic bishops issued *Open Wide Our Hearts*, their first Pastoral Letter on racism since 1979. This letter speaks of the structural kind of racism that has worked itself into the fabric of our nation. It describes the unspeakable sins from the slave trade in which the church was itself complicit as well as the sins of national policies that forced Native Americans off their lands, harmed their traditional cultures, and threatened their very livelihood. The Pastoral Letter inserts racism in its rightful place as a "life" issue. The legacy of slavery, the Jim Crow era of enforced segregation, and unofficial policies that kept people of color from certain neighborhoods, jobs, and educational opportunities have contributed to the systematic racism about which the people in the dominant culture can be blindly naive. Our pro-life catechetical and educational curriculum needs to include a critical look at our culture and national history, which have threatened the dignity and sanctity of whole categories of human lives. Pro-life students must grapple with this history and ask themselves how they are going to live differently. Those students who come from the dominant cultures must learn why the slogan "Make America Great Again" can be seen as offensive, especially when the word *again* for many refers to a more racially segregated and stratified period of history.

The bishops' letter on racism also helps point the way toward a comprehensive pro-life ethic: "Our individual efforts to encounter, grow, and witness, to change our hearts about racism must also find their way into our families. We urge each person to consider the dignity of others in the face of jokes, conversations, and complaints motivated by racial prejudice. We can provide experiences for children that expose them to different cultures and peoples" (*Open Wide Our Hearts*, 26–27).

Intercultural encounters, opportunities for immersion experiences in the inner city or at the southern border, mission trips, and service projects with the appropriate accompanying theological reflection as well as opportunities for dialogue with other religious traditions can all help younger people overcome prejudice and fear of the other while growing in reverence for human dignity. As our parishes become more diverse, we will find opportunities for overcoming the globalization of indifference right within our own congregations that span across categories of race, nationality, and immigration status. The church's service to migrants and refugees can also help form these values in the next generation.

The Care of Creation

A genuinely pro-life agenda must also include an emphasis on the care of creation. Our young people are quite aware of the environmental danger that threatens their future. The near unanimity of the scientific community has established that major catastrophic consequences will face the inhabitants of the earth because of climate change and that the idea of the planet becoming uninhabitable for greater numbers of human beings is not at all far-fetched. How can this not be of concern to those intent on preserving human life in the womb? The presidential administration that so solemnly addresses the March for

Life has withdrawn the United States from the Paris climate agreement and has steadily and eagerly reversed many of the environmental regulations set in place by the previous administration. More than merely partisan reversals, the catastrophic consequences for the air, water, and soil that will result from these reversals threaten the quality of human life, especially for populations that do not have access to the private goods and services that can lessen the effects of environmental degradation for some.

Building on the attention his immediate predecessors gave to environmental concerns, Pope Francis's 2015 encyclical, *Laudato si'*, enshrines the care of creation within the official body of Catholic social teaching. Pope Francis takes the name of this encyclical and the spirituality incorporated throughout from his namesake, Francis of Assisi. In his famous "Canticle of the Sun," St. Francis celebrates a familial interconnectedness among all of creation. Pope Francis takes note of the alarming condition of the planet and the disproportionate consequences for the poor from ecological devastation, the destruction of their homelands and the means of their livelihood, which results in armed conflict and mass migration. The pope insists on the dignity of the human person, whose dominion over creation, paired with responsibility, is asserted in the Scriptures and at the same time offers a critique of an excessive anthropocentrism that would diminish human responsibility for the care of other creatures and elements of creation. "When we fail to acknowledge as part of reality the worth of a poor person, a human embryo, a person with disabilities—to offer just a few examples—it becomes difficult to hear the cry of nature itself; everything is connected" (*Laudato si'* 117). Pope Francis demonstrates that an attitude of reverence toward human life requires a sensitivity and reverence toward all life and all creation. The destruction of the environment and its effects on the human community cannot be ignored; a fully consistent pro-life attitude will include care for what Pope Francis describes as our common home.

Conclusion

The pro-life movement claims that its ultimate goal it is to make abortion unthinkable; this is substantially more than making abortion illegal. This noble aim involves not just a political and legal strategy, but

9

an effort to bring about real conversion in a society that views everything as disposable. Regarding issues as diverse as the reform of church structures to transforming the global economy, Pope Francis has stated that a change of structures without the corresponding conversion of hearts will lead to the eventual corruption of whatever new structure is set in place; how much more this conversion is needed regarding the basic dignity of the human person. The energy, vitality, and creativity of the thousands of young people who consider themselves part of the pro-life generation have so much to contribute to the overall conversion necessary to make abortion unthinkable. If they can cultivate an understanding of the interrelatedness of all creation, consider how best to address the economic pressures that make abortion appear as a viable option to women in crisis pregnancies, recognize how the degradation of women is connected to their sexual exploitation and the possibility of unwanted pregnancies, and see how insulting cultures and races of people is incompatible with a reverence for life, this youth-led movement can be prophetic. The alignment of the movement with a narrow focus on the rights of the unborn, without the larger concerns of the overall flourishing of human life, and a continued uncritical alliance with a partisan leader, will result in further division that in the end is not really pro-life at all.

Questions for Further Reflection

1. Have you ever attended the annual March for Life in Washington, DC? Did you think it was a religious event? A political event? Did you see the video of the Catholic high school students and the Native American elder that the author mentions? What did you think when you first saw it? Did your impressions change when you learned more about the context?

2. The author thinks that our current president has been inconsistent on life issues. How does he justify that characterization? Do you agree or disagree?

3. What does the author explain were the peace activism roots of the pro-life movement? Did you know about these origins? Does

knowing them make you see the pro-life movement in a different light? Why or why not?

4. The author says that Catholic social teaching has a long history of defending the dignity of the human person. What examples does he give of this? Were you aware of this history?

5. The author mentions "the seamless garment" approach to life issues. Have you ever heard of that approach? What does it entail?

6. The author contrasts this approach with considering abortion as a stand-alone issue. What does he see as the difference between these two approaches? Which approach do you prefer yourself? Was your answer based on your faith or your politics? Explain.

7. What does Pope Francis's outreach to those in the peripheries entail? Are these geographic or economic peripheries, or both? How is outreach a life issue? What does Pope Francis mean by the "globalization of indifference"? Is this a life issue? How would a Catholic voter combat this "globalization of indifference"?

8. What does Pope Francis say about the lives of the poor in his apostolic exhortation *Rejoice and Be Glad*? Do the lives of the poor need as much protection as the lives of the unborn? Are these rights in opposition to each other or are they part of the same Catholic ethic? Explain. How does your answer affect how you would vote?

9. Were you aware of the U.S. bishops' letter *Open Wide Our Hearts*? If not, why not? What is this letter about? Have you taken the time to read it? Why do you suppose the bishops found it necessary to issue such a letter in 2018?

10. What ways does the author suggest as ways for young people to overcome prejudice and fear of others? Do you agree or disagree with this approach?

11. What roles does the care of creation play in a pro-life agenda? How is the care of creation being affected by current politics? What role does Pope Francis's encyclical *Laudato si'* play in your views of a Catholic rationale for protecting creation? Would a care for creation affect the way you vote? Why or why not?

12. The author says that a true pro-life movement would require not just a change of structures but a change of heart. What structures is he talking about here? What changes of heart? How could you help such changes come about?

2

Reforming *Faithful Citizenship*

Nicholas P. Cafardi

Introduction

The American bishops' document *Forming Consciences for Faithful Citizenship* has remained basically the same from its initial version in 2007, although there have been some minor changes in subsequent versions. For example, the 2015 version interpolated, without really integrating, some quotes from the teachings of Pope Francis. That version was a matter of some heated discussion among the bishops at their 2015 meeting. A few bishops were very unhappy, and said so in their public discussions, that the thoughts of Pope Francis were quoted but not really reflected in the thrust of the document; that the 2015 document still pretty much reflected the same faulty analytical tools as the previous versions; that the sea change that Pope Francis had caused in the Catholic world was not well reflected in the bishops' 2015 document.

After three election cycles, and after their bitter 2015 debate, the bishops appear to understand that their quadrennial revisions of *Faithful Citizenship* are not working, and so they have jettisoned that process for the 2020 national elections, leaving us with the inadequate 2015 version of *Faithful Citizenship* and whatever supplemental materials the USCCB's staff comes up with.

Intrinsic Evil

What are those analytical tools of the previous versions of *Faithful Citizenship* that some bishops were complaining about? The basic analytical tool that *Faithful Citizenship* uses is the concept of "intrinsic evil." That is a rather heavy term, "intrinsic evil." The very words seem to connote a "great and contaminating" evil, an all-encompassing evil, the kind that must be avoided at all costs, the kind of evil that devours souls.[1]

The concept of intrinsic evil is not evangelical; it does not come from the Gospels, the words of Christ as reported to us by the evangelists. Rather, its roots are in the moral theology of St. Thomas Aquinas in the thirteenth century and got a boost in St. John Paul II's 1993 encyclical, *The Splendor of Truth*, where he talks about it in number 80.

What does that theological concept, *intrinsically evil*, mean? It does not mean seriously or gravely evil, as you might expect, even though it sounds that way. Rather, intrinsic evil means that there are some actions that are always morally wrong no matter what the circumstances, and that a faithful Catholic can never do them or directly assist in doing them without objective moral fault. In Catholic theology, intrinsic evil encompasses acts such as lying, contraception, masturbation, fornication, adultery, and homosexual acts. Oddly, it does not encompass murder, because murder, in Catholic theology, is not always morally wrong, as for example, when you kill someone in self-defense.

But, despite these systematic weaknesses, intrinsic evil is the major analytical tool that the bishops chose, back in 2007, to deal with the moral act of voting. Catholics may not use their votes in order to advance a political agenda that encompasses intrinsic evil, the bishops say in that first and every recurring version of *Faithful Citizenship*.

What are some of the acts that the bishops in *Faithful Citizenship* identify as intrinsically evil? The most recent version, from 2015, lists eleven acts as intrinsically evil: (1) abortion, (2) euthanasia, (3) human cloning, (4) embryonic stem cell research, (5) genocide, (6) torture, (7) wartime targeting of noncombatants, (8) racism, (9) treating workers as mere ends, subjecting them to subhuman living conditions, (10) treating the poor as disposable, and (11) same-sex marriage. That, by the way, is the order in which the bishops list them in *Faithful Citizenship*.

These actions are intrinsically evil. There is no situation in which it is morally acceptable to do any of them. Because of this, *Faithful Citizenship* says no Catholic may perform or directly help to perform any of these actions by voting for a candidate who favors such intrinsic evils. It is that second alternative that enters into our politics, because *Faithful Citizenship* says that if a Catholic votes for a candidate who favors any of these intrinsic evils, with the intent of advancing this evil by their vote, then the Catholic is participating in that moral evil by helping to perform that intrinsically evil act, and they have incurred moral culpability. So it follows that Catholics may not vote, without moral fault, for a candidate who favors abortion, euthanasia, human cloning, embryonic stem cell research, genocide, torture, wartime targeting of noncombatants, racism, treating workers as mere ends, subjecting them to subhuman living conditions, treating the poor as disposable, or same-sex marriage if the Catholic shares that same goal and is voting for that candidate in order to accomplish that intrinsically evil result.

It is obvious, however, that each of our main political parties, Democrats and Republicans, favors some of what the bishops say are intrinsic evils. In the 2016 presidential election, the Democratic candidate favored eliminating the Hyde amendment. It was in the Democratic platform and the candidate mentioned it in a number of speeches. The Hyde Amendment, which has been a part of every federal budget since 1976, prohibits the use of federal taxpayer dollars for any abortions, except in case of rape or incest. In other words, the Democratic candidate and her party favored the use of federal tax dollars to fund abortions. So it is fair to say that voting for the Democratic candidate was a way to advance abortion rights. And abortion is first on the bishops' list of intrinsic evils.

The Republican candidate vilified Mexicans and Muslims and sought support from Breitbart News, famous for being the "home of the alt-right," a euphemism that describes a loose coalition of white supremacists and those with similar views. While not being so obtuse as to directly espouse racism, the Republican candidate used a number of racial memes to indicate where he stood on the issue. During the campaign, he also said that he favored torture and the targeting and killing of both ISIS and their families. His exact phrase was "I am going to bomb them to hell." This sounds to me like favoring the intrinsic evils of racism, torture, and the targeting of noncombatants. So it is fair to say that voting for the Republican candidate was a way to advance those intrinsic evils.

Then who do Catholics vote for? The candidate who favors abortion rights or the candidate who promotes racism, torture, and targeting noncombatants? All of these are intrinsically evil acts that Catholics may not support, as *Faithful Citizenship* clearly states.

Or do we not vote at all? Or do we support a harmless third-party candidate, basically throwing our votes away?

The analytical tool of intrinsic evil does not easily answer this dilemma. The term is at the same time both under-inclusive and over-inclusive. How is it under-inclusive? Well, it does not include, for example, waging war. War is not an intrinsically evil act. Why not? Because Catholic theology recognizes that some wars are morally justifiable. What kinds of wars would those be? Certainly, a defensive war is morally justifiable. A nation is attacked, and it must defend its people, so it sends its army to war. That would be what Catholic theology calls a just war. But unlike defensive war, preemptive war is much more difficult, if not impossible, to justify morally. For example, St. John Paul II, in his January 13, 2003, address to the diplomatic corps, said that America's war against Iraq was not a just war. That war, of course, was a preemptive war. America attacked Iraq without being attacked itself. But such acts, even though they are morally wrong as St. John Paul said the Iraq war was, do not fall into the category of intrinsic evil. They may be evil, but they are not intrinsically evil. In this sense, the bishops' analytical tool in *Faithful Citizenship* is under-inclusive.

But the term *intrinsic evil*, besides being under-inclusive, is also over-inclusive. Lying, for example, is an intrinsic evil. It is morally wrong at all times and in all situations to lie. But would you hesitate to lie if you were living in occupied Europe in the 1940s and the Gestapo asked you if you were sheltering Jewish people in your home? I hope that you would not hesitate. You would not think twice. You would lie. This example indicates how the bishops' analytical tool of intrinsic evil is over-inclusive.

This does not even take into consideration that lying is the mother's milk of politics. The old saw—How can you tell when a politician is lying? When his or her lips are moving—almost like the concept of intrinsic evil, is true for all times and in all places for all politicians. Do

Catholic voters help to advance intrinsic evil when they vote for a candidate who is a consistent liar?

These are the problems with the bishops' use of *intrinsic evil* in *Faithful Citizenship*. First, it implies serious, grave evil, which is not what the term means, so it is analytically ambiguous. Second, it is at the same time both under- and over-inclusive. In American constitutional law, classifications that are either too broad or too narrow are invariably found to be an improper basis for laws. If the bishops' classification were held to this analysis, it would fail. It would be an improper basis for evaluating the moral value of voting.

The third, and I think the greatest, problem with intrinsic evil as an analytical tool is that it emphasizes what we Catholics should be against, not what we should be for. We should be against candidates for political office who favor abortion, euthanasia, human cloning, embryonic stem cell research, genocide, torture, wartime targeting of noncombatants, racism, treating workers as mere ends, subjecting them to subhuman living conditions, treating the poor as disposable, or same-sex marriage.

The Problems with a Negative Framework

This negative framework has led to those lists you see from those self-appointed Catholic voter organizations at election time about what issues and which candidates Catholics must vote against. These ads appear in Catholic newspapers and in pamphlets at the back of our churches and on car windshields in church parking lots during Sunday Mass. These pamphlets are famous for containing lists of things usually referred to as the Catholic nonnegotiables. These usually come in a list of five: abortion, euthanasia, embryonic stem cell research, human cloning, and same-sex marriage.

There are a few things we could say about such lists. First, they leave off a big part of the bishops' list—namely genocide, torture, wartime targeting of noncombatants, racism, treating workers as mere ends, subjecting them to subhuman living conditions, and treating the poor as disposable, and so are a misrepresentation of Catholic teaching.

Second, it is impossible not to note that the abbreviated list seems unduly slanted toward sexual sins, all involving either human reproduction or human sexuality, with the addition of euthanasia. This puts me in mind of Pope Francis's comment in his September 2013 *Civilta Cattolica* interview with Father Spadaro when he said that the church had to stop obsessing about abortion, gay marriage, and contraception. Listing these five things as the Catholic nonnegotiables certainly lends itself to Pope Francis's characterization of obsession with sexual issues. And the point of the pope's characterization was that this was a mischaracterization of the church, that it left out too much of what the church was for. He said that it elevated dogma over love, and emphasized moral doctrines over serving the poor and the marginalized.

Third, it is impossible not to note that by talking primarily about sexual sins and completely omitting sins against social justice, these lists of Catholic nonnegotiables favor a right-wing agenda, at the expense of the wealth of Catholic social justice teaching. Note that what the so-called Catholic nonnegotiable list omits from the bishops' list in *Faithful Citizenship* are racism, unjust treatment of workers, and treating the poor as disposable. Are these not just as important to oppose in our politics as the "nonnegotiables"? Of course they are. But adding these to the list leads to the inevitable conclusion, noted above, that neither the parties nor their candidates are four-square with Catholic teaching, while the shortened list favors, as I said, a more right-wing agenda and a more right-leaning political party.

But the problem with either list, the semifraudulent one that omits social justice issues, or even the longer, more complete one of the bishops in *Faithful Citizenship*, is that they are statements of what the church opposes. You see, when you talk about what you oppose, you're talking about what you would reject or even punish. It makes our faith an instrument of negativity. It defines us by saying what we are against.

To my mind, the worst thing about such a negative list is that it encourages identity politics. You can't be a good, practicing Catholic if you do or favor or support these things. And in identity politics, there is no compromise. You need to be completely against these things to be a good Catholic. It is either right or wrong, no in between, no compromise. But one of the reasons, perhaps the major reason, why our politics are in the mess they are in today, is identity politics. Identity politics undermines the common bonds that we share, and, most importantly, makes politics, which requires the seeking of common ground, an impossible task, as we are seeing these days. And yet seeking the common good as the proper end of political participation is a clear teaching of the church, or at least St. John Paul II says so in number 42 of *Christifideles laici*, his 1988 apostolic exhortation at the end of the Synod on the Laity.

What Are Catholics For?

It is not enough simply to say what we Catholics are against. What are we for? Now hopefully the logicians among you will have an insight and say, that's easy. Just take the inverse of the bishops' list of intrinsic evils and you will know what the church is for. If it were only that easy.

Let's take abortion. The church is firmly against it. What is the opposite of being against abortion? For too many people, the opposite of being against abortion is simply to be in favor of the child being born. But this is only being pro-birth. Being against abortion must mean more than that for Catholics. Pope Francis said as much in September 2017 on board his plane leaving Colombia after his five-day visit to South America. He said, "I have heard it said that the president of the United States presents himself as a man who is pro-life, and if he is a good pro-life [man], then he will understand that the family is the cradle of life and that it must be defended as a unit."

So the opposite of being against abortion is not being pro-birth, it is being pro-life, pro-family in all of its aspects. It's easy for politicians to cut off funding for abortion agencies and claim to be pro-life; but for some reason, it is much more difficult for them to provide public funds so that a pregnant mother who can't afford it has good prenatal care, so that the child, once born, has good medical care, enough to eat, a decent place to live, and as he or she grows, a good education. Cutting off funds is easy; providing them is less so. The last Congress allowed the funding for the Children's Health Insurance Program (CHIP) to expire for a time, thus potentially depriving millions of poor youngsters in our country of necessary medical care. How can these same politicians claim a pro-life label? No politician can say they are pro-life and fail to do these things, fail to guarantee that the poorest among us, especially the children, do not suffer in their health-care needs because they are poor. Simply being against abortion, and only that, certainly does not meet the Holy Father's definition of pro-life, nor should it meet any Catholic's definition of pro-life.

So taking the list of intrinsic evils and turning them around does not really tell us what Catholics should vote for. And shouldn't *Faithful Citizenship* tell us what the bishops think we should vote for, not just against? Conscience formation can't just be limited to rigid moral prohibitions, which then lead easily to negative criteria—the Catholic nonnegotiables—which are readily misused in political debate and, as I have said, lead to the identity politics that divide us as a nation.

The bishops had a real opportunity to do this in their 2019 version of *Faithful Citizenship*, but they have evidently decided to take a pass. It is an understatement to say that our bishops' conference has lost credibility and contact with many of our people and has stumbled into irrelevancy. Their focus on the culture wars has pleased some, especially their emphasis on Catholic religious freedom, particularly in their fight against providing contraception as part of health-care coverage. But it has also disappointed many, especially the young. The bishops' almost unilateral focus on pelvic issues, especially in the context of how they themselves have mishandled the clergy child sexual abuse crisis, seems hypocritical and disproportionate to true gospel values. They have frittered away their stature and believability in the larger culture, and perhaps, worst of all, they find themselves in a branch of Catholicism cut off from its Roman roots. Peter is not where the American bishops are.

How We Should Practice Politics

What should they do? Let's start with the fact that our political system in the United States is broken. Our politics have become vicious and polarizing, and I am not sure that the bishops do not bear part of the blame, or my even greater fear, that these political divisions are seeping into the church itself, in the shape of pro- and anti-Francis forces among the American bishops.

The list of inherent evils in *Faithful Citizenship* implies that those who support candidates whose positions might admit of what the bishops call intrinsic evil are themselves evil. That is not a very big step for some Catholic political commentators and bloggers to take. This, in turn, allows our politics to become nasty and unchristian. After all, evil deeds and the evil persons who do or who encourage evil deeds deserve vilification or worse.

So the bishops can't just talk about intrinsic evil; they can't just talk about these negative moral principles as the 2015 version of *Faithful Citizenship* does, the version that the bishops have decided to leave unchanged, and stop at that. Rather, the bishops should first talk about the process of politics that has become so bitter. The bishops need to say that in pursuit of Catholic principles, no Catholic may demonize the other side of the political debate. They need to say phrases like "pro-abort" and the "Party of Death" in the mouths of Catholics are sinful. They need to come down and come down hard, with all the moral authority that remains to them, against so-called Catholic websites and broadcast networks—of the right and left—that are more about partisan politics than they are about the gospel.

They need to say that politics will always be a matter of compromise. They need to say that Catholics have an obligation to unite, not divide. They need to see politics as it is—not the accomplishment of the ideal, of the perfect, but the best compromise possible on the imperfect. Even when the popes ruled, their government was far from perfect. Absolutizing moral principles under the guise of intrinsic evil helped get us to the current polarization, and lets the church, and even worse, lets the cross, be used as a political tool. The application of moral principles to politics always has and always will require prudential judgment where rational persons may disagree and those who disagree with us are not, for that reason, evil, or even bad Catholics or anti-Catholics. The instrumentalization of the cross can never, ever be a Catholic value. The Lord who owns that cross, after all, told us to love our enemies.

The bishops need to regain their equilibrium and re-earn the moral authority that they once had in our country. Focusing first on the "how" of our politics, before they focus on the "what" of our politics can do that. Let's start with what the goal of politics should be in the Catholic view. Theologian after Catholic theologian, including as I pointed out before, St. John Paul II, has said that the proper goal of politics is the common good, not the good of one part of society over another, not the good of the victors over the losers, but the good of all. In today's turbulent politics, the moral voice of the church saying this is needed more than ever. The bishops need to say that working together is a Catholic value; helping each other is a Catholic value; taking care of each other is a Catholic value. They also need to say that government is not our enemy, that there are societal problems so great, problems of inequality so unjust, and so built into the system, that only government can address them.[2] They need to say that the denigration of government is destructive to the common good, and that government is no more than what we all decide to do together, with each other and for each other. This is nothing more than Lincoln at Gettysburg. How much would our politics benefit if our bishops were to say this in the version of *Faithful Citizenship* that ought to be, and if our Catholic politicians were to actually hear them? We can only hope, for our democracy, that the age of miracles endures.

And then, after our bishops say how Catholics (and other people of good will) should practice politics, without the rancor, without the spite, without the destructive one-upmanship, without an allegiance to party or to identity groups that they would place above the common good of the country, then they can get into the substance of what our priorities as Catholics should be in deciding how to vote. And in this part of the *Faithful Citizenship* that ought to be, they can't just interpolate some thoughts from the Holy Father, they need to make those thoughts of Pope Francis come alive in the document. And they need to avoid negatives, what Catholics are against. They need to say what Catholics as faithful citizens of the American republic stand for, what our political goals should be, and they need to say and do this in terms of the Gospels and the words of Christ.

The Positive Pro-Life Issues

The first issue must, of course, be life. Catholics are pro-life. We accept the words of Jesus in Scripture that, "Whatever you to do the least, the littlest, the poorest among you, you do to Me." But please note: Being pro-life does not simply mean being antiabortion. Pro-life is more than being pro-birth. As I have already mentioned, that child whom we Catholics hold so precious in the mother's womb needs prenatal care, for the child, for the mother. Once the child is born, it will need adequate nutrition, housing, health care, and education. A politician cannot be pro-life and then turn around and vote for a federal or state budget that slashes prenatal care programs, the WIC program, the CHIP program, school lunch programs, Head Start programs, or after-school programs for these children. These two positions are completely antithetical, and the politicians who pursue the Catholic vote, claiming to be pro-life, and who then cut these vital programs that support life are hypocrites. And the bishops who allow them to get away with this are hypocrites. This is not pro-life, not in any true Catholic sense of that term.

Since human life begins at conception, when the divinely oriented soul enters the embryonic human body, the bishops' disdain of human cloning and embryonic stem cell research makes complete sense. Such procedures conjure images of the sorcerer's apprentice. While seeming perhaps to be harmless, they create forces we humans cannot control. There is a wisdom, a pro-life wisdom, in teaching, as the church does, that human life is not a laboratory animal to be experimented with. But why not express it as a positive? God, the Creator, is the master of life. We humans are not, and we delude ourselves and have the potential to do great harm when we pretend that we are.

We cannot forget that euthanasia is also a pro-life issue. Right now euthanasia is legal in six American jurisdictions and the movement is growing. We need to persuade our fellow citizens that there are other answers to the problems of the end-of-life. But persuade does not mean to decree. And we can't just be against euthanasia. We have to be for something here, namely seeing that the terminally ill, no matter how poor they are, receive the health care and the palliative care that they need and deserve, even at our expense or government expense. The witness of Catholic nursing homes and Catholic hospice care is our best argument here. As St. Francis of Assisi is reputed to have said, "Preach the gospel always, and if you have to, use words."

In this same context, we cannot forget that health care is a human right that government—all of us together—must guarantee to each other. St. Pope John XXIII said this in his encyclical *Pacem in terris* in 1963,[3] but it is a lesson that we Catholics have yet to learn. The right to health care is a Catholic issue, is a pro-life issue.

Here, the Jimmy Kimmel test is a quite valuable Christian tool: no one should die in this country because they are poor. There is no way to hear Jesus's parable about the Good Samaritan and think or act otherwise. The priest and Levite who passed the wounded man by undoubtedly said or thought, "Well, I will pray for him." No, the Lord said, that is not enough; and St. James says the same thing in his epistle: "Be doers of the word, and not merely hearers who deceive themselves" (1:22), and in the same letter, "If a brother or sister is naked and lacks daily food, and one of you says to them, 'Go in peace; keep warm and eat your fill,' and yet you do not supply their bodily needs, what is the good of that? So faith by itself, if it has no works, is dead" (2:15–17).

I am not endorsing the Affordable Care Act here, nor am I saying that the bishops should, but the bishops do need to say that Catholics cannot vote for candidates who would strip the poor and the elderly of the health care or the medicines necessary to keep them alive. And saying let the private sector, let private charity, take care of them, is basically what the priest and the Levite said when they passed the wounded man in the road: let someone else take care of him. The United States is the only wealthy nation that doesn't guarantee essential health care and affordable medicines for all. We also have a much higher poverty rate than our economic peers, especially among children, and a much higher infant mortality rate, despite the sophistication of our medical system. Why? The answer, of course, comes down to politics: we Americans are uniquely unwilling among developed nations to take care of our fellow citizens. How Christlike is that?

We can spend a lot of time, and the bishops do spend a lot of time in the 2015 *Faithful Citizenship*, talking about things that Jesus never mentioned. But this is something that he did mention, this need to care for each other, and he mentions it way more than once in the gospel stories that we have of his life on earth.

To be fair to the bishops, the recent statements on the right to health care of the U.S. Bishops' Committee on Domestic Justice and Human Development have been very strong. These statements need to find their way into the version of *Faithful Citizenship* that ought to be, since they are sorely missing in the 2015 version that is and will remain unchanged for the next national elections.

And we cannot forget that the care of our common home, the earth, is also a pro-life issue. Pope Francis's first encyclical on his own, *Laudato si'*,[4] teaches that care for mother earth is the common responsibility of us all. Clean air is necessary to human life, clean water is necessary to human life, preventing pollution and remedying it when it happens is necessary to human life. These are all a part of the care of our common home. Catholics ought not to avoid or soft pedal these concerns when they vote. If the care of the earth was an important enough concern for Pope Francis's first encyclical, then it ought to be an important enough concern for Catholics when they vote for political candidates. On that care literally depend our lives, the lives of our children and grandchildren, the future of our human species. No politician who would ignore these pro-life concerns and allow the rape of mother earth for financial profit merits a Catholic's vote and the bishops should clearly say so in the version of *Faithful Citizenship* that ought to be.

This brings me to another pro-life issue: the economy. Pope Francis in his visit with the community of Villa Nazareth in Rome in June 2016 said that ours is an economy that kills.[5] That statement upset a lot of people, primarily those who profit from the modern economy, but Pope Francis is not the first pope to say this. Pope Pius XI, in his encyclical *Quadrigesimo anno* in 1931, said, "In the first place, it is obvious that not only is wealth concentrated in our times but an immense power and despotic economic dictatorship is consolidated in the hands of a few....This dictatorship is being most forcibly exercised by those who, since they hold the money and completely control it, control credit also and rule the lending of money. Hence they regulate the flow, so to speak, of the lifeblood whereby the entire economic system lives, and have so firmly in their grasp the soul, as it were, of economic life that no one can breathe against their will."[6] And of course, if you cannot breathe, you die.

So Pope Francis is not saying anything new in papal teaching here. St. John Paul and Benedict XVI said similar things as did Pius XI.[7] On his first trip outside the Vatican, after his election as pope, Francis went to the Italian island of Lampedusa, a small island, south of Sicily, where the bodies of so many African refugees have washed up from the Mediterranean. There, he spoke of the "globalization of indifference."

On his second visit outside the Vatican, to speak to unemployed workers on the Italian island of Sardinia, he said, "It is a form of suffering, the shortage of work—that leads you—excuse me if I am coming over a little strong but I am telling the truth—to feel that you are deprived of dignity! Where there is no work there is no dignity! And this is not only a problem in Sardinia—but it is serious here!—it is not only a problem in Italy or in certain European countries, it is the result of a global decision, of an economic system which leads to this tragedy; an economic system centered on an idol called 'money.'" In his 2013 apostolic exhortation, *Evangelii gaudium*, Pope Francis says, "Today everything comes under the laws of competition and the survival of the fittest, where the powerful feed upon the powerless."[8]

Our own bishops used to be quite good on this, before so many of their heads were turned by wealthy donors and their money. In 1986, our bishops wrote in their Pastoral Letter, *Economic Justice for All*, that our tax system "should be continually evaluated in terms of its impact on the poor."[9] They also took the position that the tax system "should be based on three criteria: those below the poverty line should pay no taxes at all, burdened enough by the costs of basic needs; the system should raise enough revenue to pay for the public needs of society, especially to meet the basic needs of the poor; and, in order to reduce inequalities of income and wealth in our country, it should be structured according to the principle of progressivity, so that those with relatively greater financial resources pay a higher rate of taxation."[10] Nothing in the current, not-to-be revised *Faithful Citizenship* is that clear, nothing. The bishops tried to pass another statement on the economy in 2012, but it failed to get the required majority, primarily because the draft document omitted references to the rights of workers to organize, which has been a key teaching of the church since Leo XIII and *Rerum novarum* in 1891.

The right to work and the right to organize as workers is also a pro-life issue. As Pope Francis said on Sardinia, without work there is no personal dignity. You will recall the list of intrinsic evils in the current *Faithful Citizenship*. They include treating workers as mere ends, subjecting them to subhuman living conditions, treating the poor as disposable. This is exactly what happens to workers when they do not have the right to organize, and when their employers can instrumentalize them to create more wealth for themselves. The right of workers to organize is a bulwark against an economy that kills. In a June 2017 talk to the Delegates of the Italian Confederation of Trade Unions, Pope Francis said, "Unions are an expression of the *prophetic profile* of society. Unions are born and reborn each time that, like the biblical prophets, they give a voice to those who have none, denounce those who would 'sell the needy for a pair of sandals' (cf. Amos 2:6), unmask the powerful who trample the rights of the most vulnerable workers, defend the cause of foreigners, the least, the rejected." He also said, in that speech, that "The capitalism of our time does not understand the value of trade unions, because it has forgotten the *social nature of economy*, of business. This is one of the greatest errors. Market economy: no. Let us say '*social market economy*,' as Saint John Paul II taught: social market economy."

And, as Francis said on Lampedusa, immigration is also a pro-life issue. Referring to the dead migrants who ended up on that island, the Pope said, "[We say] it's not our responsibility, and with that we feel reassured, assuaged. The culture of comfort, which makes us think only of ourselves, makes us insensitive to the cries of other people, makes us live in soap bubbles which, however lovely, are insubstantial; they offer a fleeting and empty illusion which results in indifference to others; indeed, it even leads to the globalization of indifference. In this global-ized world, we have fallen into globalized indifference. We have become used to the suffering of others: it doesn't affect me; it doesn't concern me; it's none of my business!" But the global immigration crisis is our business. Yes, of course, we have to have safe borders. Every nation does. But that does not have to mean we have to have closed borders. The Lord told us, in no uncertain terms, to welcome the stranger (Matt 25:35). How do we do that if all of our country's doors and windows are closed?

Migration in Pope Francis's eyes is closely linked to racism. If you have seen the sorry pictures of bodies on the beach at Lampedusa that Pope Francis visited, they are the bodies of our black brothers and sis-ters, fleeing the poverty and wars of Africa. Europe is turning its back on them and they are dying. Speaking on the issue of migration, Pope Francis said, "Many people forced to emigrate suffer, and often, die tragically....Many of their rights are violated, they are obliged to sepa-rate from their families and, unfortunately, continue to be the subject of racist and xenophobic attitudes."[11]

But, unfortunately, racism is not just extraterritorial to the United States. It exists as much here as it does on Lampedusa and every place where the color of a person's skin determines what human rights they have. Racism, in the Mediterranean, in the United States, kills. As our bishops say in their November 2018 Pastoral Letter, *Open Wide Our Hearts: The Enduring Call to Love; A Pastoral Letter Against Racism*, opposing racism is a pro-life cause. No one in our country should be deprived of any human right, to a job, to a decent place to live, to health care, to education, because of their race. And those politicians who allow, per-mit, or, worse, encourage such discrimination are not pro-life, and do not merit a sincere Catholic's vote.

And after Sandy Hook, Charleston, Orlando, Las Vegas, Souther-land Springs, Santa Fe, Pittsburgh, and Thousand Oaks, how can any concerned Catholic think that the prevention of gun violence is not a pro-life issue? Our bishops clearly do. The American bishops, in their 2013 statement after Sandy Hook, called on all Americans, but especially legislators, "to address national policies that will strengthen regulations of firearms." They also, at the same time, signed onto a statement with forty-five other religious groups advocating that Congress require universal background checks for all gun purchases, limit civilian access to high-capacity weapons and ammunition magazines, and make gun trafficking a federal crime.[12] None of these pro-life measures, other than a passing mention, are dealt with in the last, not-to-be-revised version of *Faithful Citizenship*. They need to be emphasized in the version of *Faithful Citizenship* that ought to be. Catholics cannot, with their votes, advance the cause of denying the reasonable regulation of firearms. That, as it should be self-evident, is the opposite of pro-life. It is pro-death. And our bishops need to say so in the *Faithful Citizenship* that ought to be. "[This is] the urgency of the great choice we face as a species: will we choose to continue to affirm a culture of systemic violence—or will we build a culture of active, creative, and liberating nonviolence so that we can not only survive but thrive?"[13]

To this point, I have covered the entire list of what the bishops call "intrinsic evils" in the 2015 version of *Faithful Citizenship*, except for same-sex marriage, and I have recharacterized all of the bishops' negative "You must nots" as positive, pro-life "You musts." As God told his people in Deuteronomy: "I have set before you today life and… death….Choose life" (Deut 30:15–19). This is a must. I believe that such a positive approach to these issues is a true reflection of our Holy Father's thought, his approach of accompanying people rather than lecturing at them. And, to be fair, I should tell you that, toward the end of their 2015 *Faithful Citizenship*, the bishops do get around to a positive list, but it's not the heart or methodology of the document, as it should be.

The bishops' last intrinsic evil, same-sex marriage, is difficult, for me at least, to see as a purely pro-life issue. Yes, I know, it is through marriage that future lives are created. But the church has never required fertility to make a marriage valid. I see this issue, rather, as many people (especially the young) do, as a remnant of the culture wars that divide our country along partisan lines. It is also one of those things that Pope Francis said the church need not keep harping on. An unfortunate aspect of the church's opposition to same-sex marriage in the civil forum is that it carries aspects of intolerance. Yes, I realize that the opposite is true. The church could just as easily say that those pushing same-sex civil marriage on those of us who, because of our faith, reject it are also intolerant of our religious beliefs. But in the scales of intolerance, the weight will always go against those who would prevent rather than those who would permit.

My answer has been to distinguish civil law marriage from matrimony.

Civil marriage is a creature of the state and belongs to the state. The sacrament of matrimony, on the other hand, belongs to the church. The state has never defined civil marriage the same way that the church defines matrimony, if for no other reason than that the state allows divorce and matrimony is indissoluble. After having lived for so long with state laws on marriage that do not reflect our Catholic teaching on matrimony, I am reluctant to see the bishops go to the mat on this issue. So in the *Faithful Citizenship* that ought to be, if the bishops feel compelled to deal with same-sex marriage, perhaps they should simply say that Catholics oppose discrimination against people with a same-sex attraction, but they also oppose discrimination against those who do not, for religious reasons, accept same-sex marriage and leave it at that. That is not a culture war issue. That is simply a request for a nondiscriminatory civil society to respect our religious beliefs.

Conclusion

I would like to end this essay with a meditation from a follower of St. Francis, the Franciscan friar Fr. Richard Rohr, that puts me much in the mind of Pope Francis on political issues:

> How is it that after two thousand years of meditation on Jesus Christ we've managed to avoid everything that he taught so unequivocally? This is true of every Christian denomination, even those who call themselves orthodox or doctrinally pure. We are all "cafeteria Christians." All of us have evaded some major parts of the Sermon on the Mount (Matthew 5–7): the Beatitudes, Jesus' warning about idolizing "mammon," his clear directive and example of nonviolence, and his command to love our enemies being the most obvious. Jesus has always been too much for us. He is the only true "orthodoxy" as far as I can see.
>
> In fact, I have gone so far as to say, if Jesus never talked about it once, the churches will tend to be preoccupied with it (abortion, birth control, and homosexuality are current examples), and if Jesus made an unequivocal statement

about it (for example, the rich, the camel, and the eye of a needle, [turn the other cheek, welcome the stranger, care for the poor as if they were him], we tend to quietly shelve it and forget it. This is not even hard to prove.

Because most of the church has refused to take Jesus' teaching and example seriously, now much of the world refuses to take Christians seriously. "Your Christianity is all in the head," they say. "You Christians love to talk of a new life, but the record shows that you are afraid to live in a new way—a way that is responsible, caring, and nonviolent. Even your 'pro-life movement' is much more pro-birth than pro-life."

Like it or not, the church is finally becoming much more universal in its teaching. Marginalized and oppressed groups have a wealth of insights to offer us in reading the Gospel. The New Testament is being rediscovered by altogether different sets of eyes, raising very different questions and perspectives that we just never thought about before. We are just beginning to honor the voices of women, minorities, and many groups that have not had access to the power, privilege, and comforts of past theologians. Frankly, they represent the peoples who first heard the Gospel and allowed it to radically change their lives.[14]

Our bishops have decided to stick with their inadequate 2015 version of *Faithful Citizenship*, rather than consider a revision for the 2020 elections. This is an unfortunate choice because our bishops' reliance on their list of intrinsically evil "do nots" from medieval theology that pervade their 2015 statement has not served them, the nation's Catholics, or the nation very well. It has reduced them to partisan irrelevance, when what they have available to preach is the most relevant notion of all time, the words of the Lord. What we need from our pastors is not a list of political "must nots," but a gospel-based list of voting "musts" that exalt the positive values of the Gospels, the values of caring for each other, the entire spectrum of the values of life, in all of its stages, and in all of its places, that are the approach of Pope Francis. And then, maybe then, our bishops might be on track to redeem themselves from irrelevancy, to change some lives, to save some souls, and perhaps even to help save our nation as well. *Adiuva nos, Domine.*

NOTES

1. See M. Cathleen Kaveny, "Intrinsic Evil and Political Responsibility: Is the Concept of Intrinsic Evil Helpful to the Catholic Voter?," in *Voting and Holiness: Catholic Perspectives on Political Participation*, ed. Nicholas P. Cafardi (New York: Paulist Press, 2012).

2. "The threshold of basic respect for human life is being crossed, and brutally at that, not only by instances of individual conduct but also by the effects of societal choices and structures." Pope Francis in his Letter to the Pontifical Academy for Life on its 25th Anniversary.

3. *Pacem in terris* 11.

4. *Laudato si'* is the second encyclical issued under his name, on May 24, 2015. The first encyclical to bear his name was *Lumen fidei*, issued on June 29, 2013, which was his completion of a draft by his predecessor, Benedict XVI.

5. The pope was quoting himself. He said much the same thing in his Apostolic Exhortation *Evangelii gaudium* 53.

6. Nos. 105–6.

7. St. John Paul in his encyclical *Centesimus annus*, 1991; Benedict XVI in his encyclical *Caritas in veritate*, 2009.

8. No. 53.

9. No. 202.

10. Kevin Clarke, *America*, October 5, 2017.

11. Message to participants of Mexico-Holy See Colloquium on Migration and Development, July 15, 2014.

12. Faiths United to Prevent Gun Violence, January 15, 2013 Statement.

13. John Dear, *The Nonviolent Life* (Pace e Bene Press, 2013), x, cited in Richard Rohr, *Non-Violence: Taking Jesus Seriously*, September 17, 2017.

14. Rohr, *Non-Violence: Taking Jesus Seriously*, September 17, 2017.

Questions for Further Reflection

1. What criticisms did some bishops make of the 2015 version of *Faithful Citizenship*? How did the bishops' conference respond? What will the 2019/2020 version of *Faithful Citizenship* look like?

2. Explain the concept of intrinsic evil. Where does it come from? What does it mean? What are some things that Catholic teaching says are intrinsically evil? Does the author think that this concept is a good analytical tool in the political context? Why or why not? Do you agree or disagree? Explain.

3. What are some of the things that the 2015 version of *Faithful Citizenship* says are intrinsically evil? Do you agree with this list? Are there some things that you would omit? Why? Are there some things that you would add? Why?

4. The author says that in the 2016 elections both major parties endorsed positions that were intrinsically evil. What positions were those? Do you agree with the author's conclusion that these acts are intrinsically evil? Does this mean that both political parties are themselves evil?

5. The author thinks that a negative focus on issues can lead to identity politics. Explain his argument here. Do you agree or disagree? Why? Do you think that identity politics is a bad thing?

6. The author says that the opposite of being against abortion is not simply to be in favor of the child's birth. How does he justify this statement? Do you agree or disagree? Why?

7. The author says that our political system in the United States is broken. What does he mean by this? How is it broken? How does he say that our bishops may have played a role in this?

8. The author thinks that our bishops should focus on the "how" of politics before they focus on the "what" of politics. What does he mean by this? What does he think will be achieved by such a change in focus? Do you agree or disagree? Explain.

9. The author lists a number of pro-life issues that should affect the way a Catholic votes. What are they? Do you agree with all of them? Some of them? None of them? Which ones do you agree with and why? Which ones do you disagree with and why?

10. What reason does the author give for treating same-sex marriage differently than the other intrinsic evils listed in *Faithful Citizenship*? Is this a cop-out or do you buy the distinction that the author is making? Do you agree with the author's solution? If you don't agree, what would your solution be?

PART II

How Catholics Perceive and Talk about Issues

3

The Roots of Catholic Polarization in the United States

Robert G. Christian, III

Introduction

To talk about the political polarization of Catholics in the United States, it is necessary to begin more broadly by talking about overall political polarization in the United States. The reason for this is simple: most American Catholics do not have Catholic worldviews. The primary reason for this is that many American Catholics, perhaps most, have little to no knowledge of Catholic social teaching—which sadly remains the church's "best kept secret" here in the United States—or the underlying philosophical and theological assumptions that shape it. As a result, many Americans let their political ideology or partisan identity shape their faith and political behavior, setting aside Christianity's radical, countercultural demands.

Polarization and Partisanship in the United States

It is also important to examine what polarization is and what it is not. Among Catholics, there are divisions over doctrinal issues and liturgical matters. There are also racial, ethnic, and socioeconomic divides. All these stand in the way of greater unity for the church. But perhaps no form of polarization is more widespread, divisive, and toxic than political polarization.

There are two primary types of political polarization in our democracy: polarization among elected officials and other political party elites and polarization among voters or the public. High levels of polarization exist when a high percentage of officials or the public have noncentrist views, coalescing around certain ideological poles. In our country right now, there are two major poles: liberal and conservative. Low polarization is when voters or elites are more closely clustered around the center of the political spectrum. Asymmetrical polarization occurs when one pole is at a far greater distance from the center than the other pole, as a result of a recent widespread change in the views of voters or public officials.

Sometimes the term *polarization* is used when people are actually discussing *partisanship*. Partisanship is not focused on one's theoretical views or ideology, like polarization, but on one's loyalty to his or her party. Periods of high partisanship exist when there is a great deal of loyalty or conformity to one's party. In periods of low partisanship, elected officials and voters are more likely to vote across party lines. Negative partisanship is when the driving force is not support of one's own party but opposition to the other party.

Polarization is also sometimes confused with acrimony or enmity across party or ideological lines. Polarization and partisanship can foster the use of harsh language and a growing number of bitter exchanges between liberals and conservatives, or Democrats and Republicans, but these possible effects are not polarization itself. This is a critical distinction, because some proposed solutions to polarization, such as promoting more polite or friendly behavior, are more about reducing enmity than polarization, which has structural causes.

Neither polarization nor partisanship is inherently bad in a democracy. Grave injustices have been preserved untouched during periods of low polarization, while important ideas have arisen and important advances have occurred in highly polarized times. At the same time, elite polarization can lead to disastrous stalemate, gridlock, and stagnation, particularly during periods of divided government, where simple compromises are difficult to achieve, and the government consequently fails to act on critical matters. This is the situation we have faced in recent years.

We are currently experiencing high levels of both polarization and partisanship (including negative partisanship)—both among the public and public officials (though polarization among the public is lower than among elites). The polarization has been asymmetrical, with Republican officials moving significantly farther from the center than Democrats—though Democrats have moved left on social issues in the last decade and may be poised to move left on economics following the 2018 midterm elections. Importantly, not only are the country and our government deeply divided, but they are also close to evenly split in many ways. This combination contributes heavily to the very high levels of frustration and enmity that we are experiencing as a society.

The various costs of polarization have led many to grow concerned about the rising polarization we are experiencing. But for Catholics with a sincere commitment to Catholic social teaching, elite polarization is acutely problematic because neither major pole is aligned with church teaching. Both contemporary American conservatism and liberalism are rooted in an individualism that is incompatible with the church's understanding of the human person and community. As a result, contemporary liberalism's social libertarianism and conservatism's economic libertarianism are radically at odds with the Catholic commitment to the common good. Those who share the church's pro-life and pro-social justice communitarian approach are grossly underrepresented in Congress and among leaders in both parties.

As many U.S. Catholics take their cues from the ideology of their preferred political party, a great deal of dissent from church teaching exists on both the left and the right. Dissent on the left mirrors the dissent of others in the West, most notably in its support for legal access to abortion. Support for extreme free market beliefs and policies, meanwhile, are a far bigger problem in the United States than anywhere else in the world. This is in part because laissez-faire theories and social Darwinism have done more to shape the conservative economic ideology of the Republican Party than more communitarian approaches, in contrast to conservative Christian Democratic parties around the world that were instead heavily influenced by Catholic social teaching.

Various Catholic Democrats have sometimes tried to defend their support for abortion on demand by declaring their personal opposition to the sin of abortion, while claiming they do not want to push their religious beliefs on others by translating that into legal restrictions on access to abortion. This ignores the church's understanding that the protection of unborn life is a matter of social justice and human rights, rather than simply an effort to prohibit a sin.

Numerous Catholic Republicans, meanwhile, have tried to relativize church teaching on economic and social justice by distorting and stretching concepts like subsidiarity and prudential reasoning to justify an economic ideology that the church has called a "poisoned spring." They have tried to create new holes in our already incomplete social safety net, while redistributing wealth to the richest Americans by claiming that such transparently unethical and imprudent measures might somehow be prudent or by conflating subsidiarity with stripping the federal government of its ability to carry out responsibilities that only it can perform. Some go so far as to say Christianity requires only charitable giving, ignoring the need to create more just social structures.

Both polarization and partisanship have grown tremendously in the past few decades. As Democrats lost ground in the South and Republicans grew weaker in the Northeast, the major parties have developed greater ideological cohesion. The ideological sorting of the parties has strengthened liberalism in the Democratic Party and conservatism in the Republican Party. At the same time, there has been a significant increase in the number of Independents, with over 40 percent of the public identifying as Independents in many recent polls. Many of these Independents lean strongly toward one party or the other, but the absence of these voters—who are often not doctrinaire liberals or conservatives—in the party infrastructure and their inability to vote in many primary elections has allowed ideologues of the left and right to gain even greater influence within their respective parties.

This process has been intensified by gerrymandering. The use of gerrymandering to create a very high percentage of safe seats that are not competitive in the general election has increased the ideological purity of candidates, as candidates whose party is a strong majority in a district are far more concerned about losing in the primary to a more right-wing or left-wing candidate than losing in the general election.

The rise of the Tea Party movement accelerated this trend, challenging very conservative members of Congress from the right in primaries. At the same time, shifting populations have created more imbalanced voting districts and imbalanced states. Geographic clustering has occurred, in which many people have moved to areas where their neighbors are more likely than not to share their values and lifestyle. This self-sorting is a major contribution to political polarization.

Another key factor in rising polarization is the way campaigns are financed and the rising cost of getting elected. The dominant role played by special interest groups in our elections is the product of a system that gives the wealthy disproportionate influence. This influence is used to ensure ideological conformity on issues from abortion to taxation, where candidates feel compelled to embrace the extreme positions of their donors, ignoring their constituents and the larger public's preference for more middle-of-the-road policies. As a result, the wealthiest members of each party have far greater influence than the average party member.

This is occurring at a time when economic inequality has exploded. We are living in the Second Gilded Age. When plutocracy advances, democracy and real political participation are eroded. A number of political scientists have found that widening economic inequality itself produces higher levels of polarization.

Talk radio, cable news, and social media have also contributed to polarization. Many Americans are now in silos or bubbles, closed off from alternative perspectives and constantly being fed narratives that align with the interests of their party or ideology. This includes the dissemination of fake news on social media. Polarization is not just a difference of opinion at this point, but often a disagreement over the veracity of basic facts.

Another critical part of our country's divisions has been the growing polarization on the Supreme Court and increased politicization in the nomination and confirmation process. An argument can be made that *Roe v. Wade* and the response it generated have made this polarization on the Supreme Court inevitable (though there are a variety of factors behind it). Unlike other controversial opinions that resulted in dramatic shifts in public opinion, the country remains deeply divided over the wisdom of the ruling. And the pro-life and pro-choice movements have made appointments to the Supreme Court the central focus of their efforts. There are a sizable number of single-issue voters on this issue, compared to others, and many view the Court and potential nominees primarily through the prism of how they will rule on abortion. As the parties became more polarized and special interest groups gained more influence, the old norms surrounding Supreme Court nominations have collapsed. Those seeking to advance other ideological objectives through the Court have also used this central culture war clash to promote more ideological nominees who can achieve unrelated policy objectives that are deeply unpopular with the public. The Court is losing legitimacy with this increased politicization and the collapse of certain long-standing norms.

Polarization and Partisanship in the U.S. Church

The average American Catholic has been shaped by these changes. Catholic institutions and media have also contributed to this greater polarization. Like the secular press, the Catholic press is largely divided between left-wing and right-wing outlets. "Pro-life Catholics" can get their news and tailor their social media feeds from loyal Republicans and conservatives, while "social justice Catholics" can do the same from liberals and Democrats.

Likewise, the middle-of-the-road Catholic outlets have engaged in "both-sidism," where all sides are treated as equally responsible, valid, and reasonable on a subject (when they are not). Certain approaches to civility and dialogue (often facilitated by vocal opponents of polarization) are intensifying polarization by providing yet another forum to ideologues and failing to maximize the influence of Catholics who put church teaching above their party and ideological preferences. Thus, they reinforce and strengthen a status quo that has many Catholics feeling "politically homeless."

Both Catholic institutions and the press have also engaged in false balance—allowing right-wing dissenters to claim they are orthodox and giving them a forum to distort and discreetly attack church teaching and spread their ideology. Left-wing dissenters, who are typically open about their dissent, are often excluded from these same panels, periodicals, and other forums. The result is that right-wing dissent is stronger in the U.S. Catholic Church than anywhere else in the world.

The "libertarian invasion" that Pope Francis has warned about is being aided by Catholic institutions and media. Certain ideologues are given strong incentives to hide their true motives behind the rhetoric of Catholic social teaching. If the Francis Effect does come to the United States, this false balance would be overturned in favor of a consistent commitment to Catholic social teaching and equal treatment of those who wish to challenge it.

Until recent years, this is what polarization looked like in the United States and how it divided American Catholics and distorted the faith. With the rise of Donald Trump, however, populist nationalism—another ideology deeply at odds with church teaching—has become increasingly important among both elites and the public.

One consequence has been the rise of what many are calling alt-Catholicism. Alt-Catholics in the United States have set up their own alternative magisterium, one that permits them to reject church teaching on a range of subjects. The term is fitting because many of these ideological positions align with positions held by the alt-right: anti-Semitism, anti-Muslim bigotry, hostility to refugees and other migrants, hostility to racial justice, sexism, support for far-right strongmen and democratic backsliding, isolationism, and sectarianism. Other priorities include support for the death penalty and for the church to take a more hard-line anti-gay approach. Some seek to discredit church teaching on economic and environmental justice, as well. To be clear, it is common for alt-Catholics to reject some alt-right positions, while embracing others, and to even openly condemn the alt-right so they will not be associated with white supremacists.

The United States has become the epicenter of anti-Pope Francis right-wing dissent. Some of this comes from mainstream Republicans who are opposed to Francis's social justice agenda. Some of it mirrors the anti-immigrant and anti-Muslim populism that is surging around the West. Some of it comes not from polarization, but partisanship, and a greater commitment to Donald Trump than to the pope. Finally, some opposition comes from opponents of Vatican II, who reject much of the last 125 years of church teaching, including its affirmation of universal human rights and commitment to genuine participation in government, instead favoring integralism, monarchism, antidemocratic paleoconservatism, or other traditionalist ideologies.

These alt-Catholic individuals who claim to be more orthodox and more Catholic than the pope, despite publicly dissenting from clear church teaching, have used social media (including troll armies filled with anonymous accounts) and the Catholic press to magnify their favorite narratives and conspiracy theories, despite the small number of U.S. Catholics (and miniscule number of global Catholics) who embrace this approach. Even the mainstream Catholic media, prone to an "all sides matter" mentality and blinded by the distorted reality of the Catholic social media bubble, has confused social media popularity with real world support and magnified their influence.

So as the church faces the problem of overcoming the big divide in American Catholicism between conservatives and liberals, it must now also contend with a small group of militant, far-right dissenters who distort and damage the U.S. church on a daily basis.

All of this comes at a crisis point for the U.S. church with yet another sexual abuse crisis damaging the church's credibility in the eyes of many. Further, attempts have been made to hijack the most recent crisis by those who are seeking to advance a separate ideological agenda. The anti-pope faction, which includes alt-Catholics and opponents of economic justice, has threatened civil war and schism, while attempting to engineer a coup. This has only intensified polarization, and unless faithful Catholics begin to act, we are likely to see polarization increase further.

Potential Remedies for Catholic Polarization in the United States

Those hoping for a quick fix to the problem of Catholic polarization are sadly out of luck. Reducing Catholic polarization will almost certainly require reducing overall political polarization in the country, a difficult challenge. At the same time, the church can and should act to convince more U.S. Catholics to embrace Catholic ideals and support the countercultural approach of Catholic social teaching. This will, in part, require reducing partisanship among Catholics. But if Catholics remain divided by party and polarization does not drop dramatically, it is important to consider how we might work to reduce acrimony and enmity among American Catholics across party and ideological lines.

Catholic polarization is intrinsically problematic. It undermines the effort to build communion among U.S. Catholics, which is at the very heart of the faith and the church's mission. There will always be disagreement within the church, but the large chasms that exist are bound to generate great disunity and discord. It also undermines Christian witness. People are not just turned off by the infighting, but by the failure to live gospel values. When the church is not a poor church for the poor but filled with people who justify the abandonment of the weak and vulnerable, few will find this witness compelling. And in a secular age, the power of witness is vital for keeping people, especially young people, in the church and for adding converts.

Polarization, particularly as it is manifested on social media and in the Catholic press, has also resulted in some Catholics attempting to capitalize on the sexual abuse crisis to advance their ideological or liturgical agenda. Traditionalists, supporters of an unfettered free market, and alt-Catholics even attempted to orchestrate a coup against the pope, failing spectacularly, as they were unable to provide evidence to back up numerous key claims. It is no surprise that the anti-pope faction is overwhelmingly American, given the amount of dissent and polarization present in the U.S. church. In a less dramatic way, some on the left have tried to use the crisis to advance their own preexisting goals for church reform. A more unified church would be in a far better position to respond to this crisis by focusing on its real causes and effective solutions.

Reducing polarization is therefore an important goal, but it is far from the only important one. If we want greater unity, it must not be at the cost of human dignity or protecting the poor and vulnerable, or failing to confront racism and other forms of bigotry. It cannot be achieved by setting aside core Catholic values to appease warring ideological camps. At the same time, reducing polarization can help to advance the common good, bring greater unity to the church, and empower pro-life, pro-social justice Catholics who feel alienated as voters and citizens. And church leaders cannot foster unity by "rising above polarization"— simply ignoring it and what is driving it.

Structural Political Reform

A primary consideration should be advocating for structural political reform. Campaign finance reform is essential for redemocratizing our system of government and ensuring the type of authentic participation

43

that Catholic social teaching demands. A system that is dominated by economic elites will not be motivated by a preferential option for the poor and vulnerable, as they will continue to prioritize economic libertarianism in the Republican Party and social libertarianism in the Democratic Party. Nothing would do more to undermine special interest groups, which play a key role in fostering polarization in our politics, than diminishing the power of money in elections.

Redistricting reform cannot make every race competitive, particularly given demographic trends, but it can reduce the behavior that has intensified polarization and make representation more closely reflect the views of the public. The creation of independent commissions or other more neutral mechanisms for drawing districts is a far better approach than allowing politicians and other ideologues to draw district lines in which they use computers to choose favorable sets of voters.

If many Independents were to join the major political parties, the influence of doctrinaire liberals and conservatives would be reduced. The current dominance of these figures, however, is deterring many from joining these parties. Catholics should join a party and work to reverse efforts aimed at ensuring ideological cohesion. At the same time, primary reform would help to reduce polarization by allowing these voters to participate earlier in the process. Open primaries or nonpartisan blanket primaries are two possible approaches.

Increasing access to the ballot and stopping new efforts at voter suppression would also create a more democratic system and help in reducing polarization. Black Americans, Latinos, and the poor are the primary targets of voter suppression efforts. These groups are disproportionately likely to oppose the abortion litmus test of wealthy white liberals and efforts to redistribute wealth to the rich while cutting programs for the poor. By helping these citizens to increase their influence, polarization can be diminished.

If economic inequality increases polarization, working for greater social and economic justice will reduce it. Once again, standing up for Catholic social teaching and the common good will have the secondary effect of reducing polarization. And a large middle class has long been considered the backbone of strong, stable democracies, an important consideration given domestic and global trends.

Addressing polarization on the Supreme Court requires addressing the thorough politicization of the Court. The Court has a constitutional role as a countermajoritarian force in safeguarding fundamental rights, even if public opinion has suddenly become hostile to such rights. A polarized Court of ideologues, however, that simply mirrors the dominant ideologies in the political branches is largely unable to play that role. Radical reforms, such as the direct election of Supreme Court justices or the creation of term limits, for instance, should be considered if this role is seen as no longer viable.

Catholics should refuse to analyze the Court through the prism of just one issue. They should support potential nominees who would show proper deference to the political branches, respect the traditional role and purpose of the Court, and safeguard fundamental rights. They should in turn oppose the placement of new justices on the Court who are left-wing judicial activists that favor the creation of new rights with little pretext and right-wing textualists or originalists whose strict constructionist approaches are designed to advance the goals of small government ideologues. This may be a lonely fight and it requires taking on special interest groups that have played an increasingly important role in picking nominees, but the legitimacy of the institution itself is collapsing. Reducing the number of ideologues on the Court can help to reverse this.

A Unified Vision for the Church

Support for this type of structural political reform is vital, since these structural factors have been critical in generating and sustaining Catholic polarization. It is also essential, however, for the church to look inwardly and examine how we should behave toward our fellow Catholics and as a community.

Step one in confronting Catholic political polarization should be to unite against all forms of bigotry and those seeking to undermine our democratic system. We must not forget the lessons of the 1930s and allow brutal ideologies to become mainstream among American Catholics. Essentially, this is about preventing a new pole—one more toxic and antithetical to Christian values than the existing poles. A failure to arrest rising alt-Catholicism would make Catholic polarization far worse—creating new obstacles to communion, jeopardizing souls, pulling the U.S. church away from the global church, and badly damaging Christian witness. It is perhaps the gravest threat to Catholicism in the United States.

But we also need a positive vision for what the church in the United

States should look like and the contribution it can make to the common good. There is no better approach to reducing Catholic polarization than in following Pope Francis's lead at all levels of the church. The U.S. bishops, individually and collectively, should embrace the pope's agenda of ending the throwaway culture and replacing it with a culture of solidarity. Disunity among the bishops, prioritizing pet issues above the gravest threats to the common good, and thinking more about institutional considerations than living the gospel will only exacerbate polarization. Given the very limited knowledge the average Catholic has of Catholic social teaching, increasing knowledge, understanding, and support of Catholic social teaching must be a top priority. This requires teaching people to understand what a Catholic worldview looks like in a culture that is often hostile to it in its embrace of extreme individualism and libertarianism. And it requires inspiring them to be a Catholic first. Rather than caving to the ambient culture or succumbing to polarization themselves, bishops should be clear about the countercultural approach Catholics of every party are required to take. They can emphasize the different paths Catholics may take in seeking to promote the common good, but also the limits of what Catholic social teaching permits, so that these Catholic principles are not so easily stretched and distorted by those with ulterior motives.

With greater unity among bishops, we might hope that Pope Francis's approach would begin to shape our dioceses and parishes much more than it has thus far. The unwillingness of some church bureaucrats to accept the pope's leadership has limited the "Francis Effect" that could be revitalizing our church. Meanwhile, getting priests to promote the fullness of Catholic teaching and encourage parishioners to fight for the unborn and the poor, for strengthening marriage and the social safety net, for the religious freedom of Catholics and non-Catholics, and for every other Catholic principle, regardless of partisan divides, is vital for generating change in the pews and reducing polarization.

The United States Conference of Catholic Bishops currently advocates for this communitarian approach. But it must resonate from the top to the bottom in the church, and this message needs to be spread with verve and passion. U.S. Catholics must not seek merely cosmetic change on the face of society but a real revolution of solidarity. Catholic leaders should try to rally Catholics behind a *whole life* approach that confronts the gravest threats to human life and dignity in our society and around the world.

This will profoundly challenge both major political parties. Yet Catholics should join a party, even a third party if they feel it is the most suitable way to advance the common good. For an everyday Catholic, joining a party almost always maximizes his or her influence. Being an Independent may give one a sense of purity, separated from the messiness of party politics, but too often it means inactivity until one is deciding which flawed candidate they will support in the general election. Membership in a party does not need to lead to the abandonment of one's principles. Being in a party does not signal agreement with the entire platform, particularly in a two-party system. Practically, the parties will not change without the pressure of internal reformers and/or a powerful, organized movement outside of the party, such as a strong third party that threatens its viability. Joining a party and sticking to one's Catholic beliefs is therefore a key way to reduce polarization. Ultimately, Catholics are called to stand up for their values and to support or oppose specific legislation that will promote or harm the common good, regardless of their party allegiance. Catholics are called to examine their well-formed consciences in deciding for whom they should vote, as they consider all the important issues that affect the common good. They can do this in a party, if they refuse to be partisans before Christians.

More Responsible Political Engagement and Discourse

A third essential element in confronting polarization is more responsible political engagement and discourse. The incredibly harmful impact of social media on democracy is not just the product of nefarious antidemocratic actors, but the irresponsible behavior of users. The failure to check sources, show caution before spreading false information, and consider who is writing a post or article and why is pervasive. Even some of the smartest Catholic thinkers recklessly retweet and elevate the most hateful and toxic voices on social media if that individual happens to agree with them on a random subject. Reducing polarization requires carefully considering what one is sharing and doing the research required to make sure that one is behaving responsibly in what they share. This requires a refusal to promote those who disseminate hate, nonsense, and false narratives that intensify polarization and enmity. It requires the discipline to find the best sources and share articles from these sites rather than those that lack credibility and a moral compass. Being responsible also means carefully considering whether one is engaged in partisan or cliquish behavior that leads to intellectual sloppiness or unfair attacks on others. And it means making sure that one is not posting for the rush of endorphins they might get from generating likes, shares, and new followers. Vile racists and partisan hacks flourish on sites like Twitter, which often reward bad behavior. Catholics must remember being virtuous is more important than being popular.

Being more responsible in how we use and consume media, and social media should go along with how we interact with others offline. Authentic dialogue can help to reduce partisanship, polarization, and unnecessary hostility. Dialogue is possible when the desire for it is mutual and sincere. There is no such thing as unilateral dialogue, though we should never treat someone in a way that ignores their worth and dignity as a person. But dialogue is possible when there is a mutual willingness to listen to one another, to take in new information and be open to modifying one's views based on that information, and to attempt not to coerce but to persuade the other person. This type of dialogue is critical in a democracy. Its absence is one reason why our democracy is short-circuiting. And it has the potential to draw people away from the bumper sticker slogans of popular ideologies and partisan rhetoric.

But this does not mean that one must engage in dialogue with everyone. Some forums, like social media, are not well suited for engaging in this type of dialogue. It is perfectly fine to avoid certain conversations and to block people on social media if their tactics or dehumanizing views are causing distress or irritation. Many of these individuals have no interest in dialogue. Engaging with them will simply be a waste of time. And it is not necessary to have a relationship with everyone that one runs across in real life or online. It may even be necessary for some people to move on from relationships that already exist, if they are no longer worth the costs associated with maintaining them.

In evaluating politicians and their rhetoric, Catholics should be neither naive nor cynical. Some people argue that it's best to assume that everyone has good intentions. But they do not. And it is extremely reckless as a citizen to assume that politicians have good intentions when their records show otherwise. It harms democracy. There is no Christian responsibility to believe lies and there is no shortcut to prudence. When the evidence shows a disconnect between a politician's actions and rhetoric, it is not wrong to attempt to evaluate their intentions rather than assume they are entirely benign. Further, intentions are not everything. They are relevant for a politician's eternal soul, but not nearly as important for a voter as the concrete impact of the politician's behavior and voting record. Likewise, engaging with fellow citizens does not require assuming they are interested in sincere dialogue or the flourishing of all people. Ideally there would be some level of trust between public servants and voters, as well as between two Catholics discussing the best way to advance Catholic principles, but this trust must be rooted in reality.

We also need more responsible behavior by the Catholic media in the United States, which too often has been deeply irresponsible and helped to fuel Catholic polarization. Some Catholic outlets engage in openly partisan behavior and put their political ideology above church teaching. Some of these completely distort church teaching to advance their ideological objectives. Most disturbingly, a number have become rabidly opposed to the pope and staunch defenders of the throwaway culture, bigotry, and a toxic alt-Catholicism. No Catholics should support these alt-Catholic publications in any way. Church leaders should warn everyday Catholics about how hostile they are to Catholic values. Catholics should also be aware of the other outlets' biases. These outlets can still have worthwhile content, but readers must be responsible so that they can discern what is worthwhile and sincere and what is not.

The middle-of-the-road Catholic outlets have also engaged in irresponsible behavior. Some have shown more interest in the status or name of the writer than the quality and integrity of their argument. They have provided a forum to bigots who do not deserve a forum anywhere in mainstream media. One of the biggest problems is that these media outlets have often further empowered ideologues, providing doctrinaire liberals and conservatives with yet another forum, while those who are both pro-life and pro-social justice are given less space to defend church teaching and the pope's agenda, something that is already very limited in the broader media landscape. Catholic periodicals that are run by religious orders or those that profess to uphold Catholic teaching or claim to be "Catholic first" should almost certainly be posting very little that opposes church teaching and nothing that distorts it. Those that do wish, in the name of open-mindedness or the desire to reflect the views of the larger population, to promote the writing of Catholics with non-Catholic worldviews or those who dissent from core Catholic principles should again refuse to run articles that distort church teaching or cloak their dissent. But they should also eschew false balance. By permitting dissent on something like economic justice, but not on a topic like abortion, these outlets are legitimizing one form of dissent, which is one reason why this dissent is a bigger problem in the United State than anywhere in the world. Catholic social teaching, as Pope Francis has said, is all nonnegotiable. Outlets that create a special set of "nonnegotiables," against the direction of the pope, while taking an otherwise relativistic approach, are deeply harming the church. False balance by the press and Catholic institutions, where those who are orthodox on one side are treated the same as dissenters on the other side of the political aisle, makes polarization more prevalent, problematic, and bitter. If an outlet wants to have a wide-open approach, it should be done sincerely and fairly. If it cannot or will not, it should cease to provide special treatment to pernicious forms of dissent.

Reducing Animosity across Party and Ideological Lines

The changes required to reduce polarization are considerable and not very easy to achieve. We can expect polarization to persist in the immediate future. It is therefore worthwhile to consider how we might reduce enmity in such a polarized environment.

Authentic dialogue can be a means of persuading others to move away from their ideology toward Catholic social teaching or to embrace parts of Catholic social teaching that they reject, but it can also be a way to come to a greater understanding with those who continue to hold different views.

It is important to remember that Catholics without a Catholic worldview or who publicly dissent are still Catholic. We should not want them to leave the church. We should want to persuade them to embrace a fully Catholic worldview, which is a lot easier if they do not feel they are being pushed out of the church. While some dissenting ideologues seek to expel people from the church in order to remake it in their ideological image, this approach is fundamentally contrary to the Christian mission. These ideologues have often been the champions of the weaponization of the sacraments. But as Pope Francis has made clear, sacraments are not a prize for the most virtuous or just. One way to reduce enmity is to firmly reject such approaches and affirm that Catholics are still Catholic.

Another way to reduce the enmity so often generated by polarization is to love people with *terrible* political opinions. That means not letting politics dominate everything or trying to create a bubble where one is only surrounded by those who meet the most exacting standards of wisdom and virtue. Many people have little understanding of the nuances of policy debates and are easily swept up by bumper sticker slogans and propaganda. Our lives can still be enriched by their presence. Another downside of social media has been that people broadcast toxic views so frequently, it can be hard to compartmentalize that part of them and preserve a relationship. But preserving relationships with family and friends is conducive to both our flourishing as persons and reducing polarization. There will be times when it is exceptionally frustrating, but it is often in these relationships where people will be exposed to new ideas and information that lead to the evolution of their views.

Of course, that does not mean we must stay friends with everyone or place ourselves in conversations and situations that continually bring us misery. For someone who believes in human dignity, it can be hard to be around someone who thinks sick children don't have a right to health care or that unborn children are better off dead than raised in poverty. And sadly, millions of Americans believe these types of things. This is particularly true if one has experienced certain forms of dehumanization firsthand. If someone is propping up structural racism or treating a politician who brags about sexual assault like he is a great role model, no one should criticize those who have experienced this racism or been subject to sexual assault for not feeling comfortable in the presence of a person who holds such views. Scolding people for not wanting to be around those spouting such rhetoric, particularly if it is in a hostile way, is wrong. At the same time, it is possible to be friends with those who have radically different worldviews, and this is a great foundation for dialogue and learning how to live together in a pluralistic society.

One critical way to reduce enmity is for American Catholics who are publicly dissenting from church teaching to be honest about their dissent. Catholics should not overstate their knowledge of church teaching or their commitment to it. They should not distort it—intentionally or through neglect. And they should never downplay it or undermine it, making it seem optional by twisting concepts like intrinsic evil or the need for prudential reasoning. They should describe church teaching in a way that is clear and fair, having examined it with the desire to fully understand and accept it. If ultimately, having looked at church teaching in its best light, they feel that core Catholic principles and factual reality point to a different conclusion than what is spelled out in papal encyclicals, for instance, and they wish to discuss this publicly, they should be honest and clear about it and explain precisely why. The Catholic press should likewise set such standards for those who wish to write in Catholic publications or appear on a Catholic television network, if they publish or broadcast dissent. Efforts to hide dissent undermine trust. Dishonesty generates hostility. To reduce animosity, U.S. Catholics should approach public dissent with honesty and integrity.

These are three ways to reduce enmity and conflict, but there are times when a confrontational approach is appropriate. It can be contentious to consistently defend the dignity of all people, particularly when a careful, thoughtful approach is met with hostility. There are times when conflict is necessary. In a democracy, where verbal jousting can be a substitute for violence when ideas and interests clash, this can be viewed as a peaceful means for resolving conflict. But it is also clear that at other times, arguments and debates can be a total waste of time. Often there are more fruitful ways to spend one's time. On social media, it is often wise to block trolls and those looking to pick fights. It is often a waste of time to hate-read simplistic hot takes. Most people would be better off spending their time reading a limited number of good, thoughtful writers, rather than a wide range of superficial op-eds by writers feigning expertise. And responsible citizens should be willing to put in the time to find genuine experts if they wish to make definitive statements on exceptionally complex policy matters and to read books, white papers, and other resources that take the subject seriously. We might also hope that Catholic outlets will favor precise, thoughtful, nuanced articles by competent writers and commentators over sensationalism, hot takes, and clickbait. Real dialogue can reduce enmity, but it requires responsibility and work. In the absence of these, enmity too may grow worse before it starts getting better.

Questions for Further Reflection

1. Do you think the author is correct when he says that many Catholics in the United States have little or no knowledge of Catholic social teaching? Why do you think this is? How do you think this situation might be effectively remedied?

2. How does the author define *polarization*? What are its different types? How is polarization different from partisanship?

3. What does the author mean when he says that both contemporary American conservatism and liberalism are rooted in an individualism that is incompatible with church teaching? How is the individualism of conservatism incompatible with church teaching? How is the individualism of liberalism incompatible with church teaching? What examples does the author give of these? Can you think of any other examples?

4. What political effect has the rise of independent voters had on both major political parties according to the author? How has gerrymandering intensified this effect?

5. What other factors does the author identify as intensifying our political polarization?

6. On what basis does the author say that Catholics are politically homeless? Do you agree or disagree? Explain.

7. What does the author mean by *alt-Catholicism*? What has been the political effect of alt-Catholicism? What has been its religious effect, specifically regarding the teachings of Pope Francis? Why do you think this is? Is it okay for Catholics to challenge papal teaching for political reasons?

8. What does the author think have been the effects of political polarization on the church? Can you think of any other effects? Have you personally seen or been affected by these? Which ones? How?

9. What ideas does the author give for reducing Catholic polarization? Can you think of any others? How real are such suggestions, that is, are they likely to work?

10. The author says that Catholics should work for political reforms. What kind and why? Can you think of any other types of political reforms that Catholics should work toward? Why?

11. What does the author say has been the effect of the politicization of the U.S. Supreme Court? What is his remedy for this? Should the Catholics on the U.S. Supreme Court consider Catholic social teachings in their judgments? Why or why not? Pope Francis has recently changed the *Catechism of the Catholic Church* to say that the death penalty is no longer acceptable, yet the Catholic majority on the U.S. Supreme Court rather consistently votes to uphold every death sentence that comes before them. Can they do this and still describe themselves as Catholics? What reasons do you think they would give to justify their death penalty positions?

12. What does the author mean by a unified vision for the church? What would this unified vision look like? What role would the common good have in such a solution? What role would the "Francis Effect" have in such a solution? What role would the United States Conference of Catholic Bishops have in such a solution?

13. Why does the author think that Catholics should not be political Independents? Do you agree or disagree? Why?

14. What conduct does the author say that social media plays in responsible political discourse? How would you apply the author's suggestions in your own conduct?

15. What kind of dialogue does the author say is necessary in a democracy? How likely is it that this type of dialogue can occur? What could you do to make such dialogue possible?

16. What role does the author say that Catholic media outlets should play in reducing polarization? How likely is this to happen? What could you do to help make it happen?

17. What suggestions does the author give for reducing animosity among Catholics along party and ideological lines? How likely do you think the author's suggestions are to succeed? What could you do personally to reduce this animosity?

4

Faithful Citizenship and the Theology of Conscience

A Reflection on Grace, the World, and the 2020 Election

David E. DeCosse

Introduction

Iintend in this essay to evaluate the theology of conscience in the document called *Forming Consciences for Faithful Citizenship: A Call to Political Responsibility*, issued every four years by the United States Conference of Catholic Bishops (USCCB). What is the theology of conscience in the current document, a holdover from the bitter 2016 election? What should be the theology of conscience in the next iteration of the document, now no doubt already on the minds of bishops and likely to be approved—whatever form it takes—at the November 2019 meeting of the USCCB? And I note the phrase "whatever form it takes" because it's neither clear that past iterations of the document have been all that effectual[1] nor that in the age of Twitter and YouTube the best means of communicating with the social-media-saturated people of God is dry, discursive text. But in whatever form the bishops deploy Catholic teaching in the certain maw of the 2020 American election, there will have to be implicitly or explicitly a theology of conscience playing a crucial role in the effort.

Here are the three steps to my argument. First, the theology of conscience in the next iteration of *Faithful Citizenship* should be consistent with recent work by Pope Francis on conscience, aptly described by James Keenan as setting conscience free "to be fully itself."[2] Second, the theology of conscience should detach itself from an overly self-referential concept of the freedom of the church and instead be reconnected with the mission of the church articulated by John Courtney Murray: that the freedom of the church "stands or falls" with the freedom of the people—where the freedom of the people is understood especially in terms of the human rights that are essential for the common good of constitutional democracy.[3] And, third, the theology of conscience of the next iteration of *Faithful Citizenship* should be connected clearly to the concept of the *sensus fidelium* and to the related idea of our shared mission in Christ—grace at work in the world—understood in terms of the baptismal imagery of priest, prophet, and ruler.

Of course, Pope Francis has boldly affirmed the importance of respecting the conscience of the laity. "We have been called to form consciences, not to replace them," he famously said in *Amoris laetitia*.[4] When he added in *Gaudete et exsultate* that the "lives of the poor, those already born, the destitute, the abandoned and the underprivileged, the vulnerable infirm and elderly exposed to covert euthanasia, the victims of human trafficking, new forms of slavery, and every form of rejection" are "equally sacred" to the "innocent unborn," he not only argued against the prioritization given in *Faithful Citizenship* to issues of "intrinsic evil" like the opposition to legalized abortion. But he also advanced a theology of conscience less attuned to abstract propositions about acts and more attuned to the concrete person in need sitting at the kitchen table, knocking at the front door, waiting even now in some holding pen along the border.[5] Indeed, Francis embeds conscience in history, relationship, and complexity. He qualifies the orientation of conscience to conceptual absolutes. Instead, the one absolute to which conscience is oriented—an absolute that, in any case, is always mediated—is our experience of the relationship of God's love in Christ through the Spirit.[6] Thus, for Francis, conscience signals the singularity of a person—but it is always a person in relation and especially in relation to the mystery of divine love.[7] As such, conscience is a capacity that allows men and women to make moral and spiritual sense of the limits and complexities of a changing life. And conscience is oriented to truth and the moral law—but also more clearly embedded in a world of embodiment, emotion, freedom, value, and grace. Where Joseph Ratzinger anchored conscience in the ontological memory of anamnesis, Francis complements this by orienting conscience to the change and growth that redemptive grace makes possible—and thus to the One who opens up a once-closed future and whom Francis calls the "God of surprises."[8] Finally, Francis's respect for the consciences of the laity blends well with his emphasis on the *sensus fidelium* or the gift of the Holy Spirit to the whole church for receiving and applying God's self-revelation.[9] In particular, he calls for the formation of conscience consistent with the sense of faith informed by the experience of the poor.[10]

But what are the signs of these deeply troubling political times to which such developments should respond in the next iteration of *Faithful Citizenship*?

I think the times demand that we focus on the relationship of the gospel to the political as such. I mean by saying this that economic and cultural concerns are crucial but that the most fundamental challenge that we face—in terms of the focus of *Faithful Citizenship*—pertains to the liberal democratic political order in itself. I have no illusions about the imperfections of such a political order. But for the sake of core principles of Catholic social thought—freedom of conscience and religious freedom, human dignity and the common good, subsidiarity and solidarity—this order is worth preserving. And I have hopes for the continuing reform of such an order—on the basis, among other things, of a far less individualistic, far more situated understanding of freedom. But at bottom I agree with the argument of *Washington Post* columnist E. J. Dionne: "If liberal democracy does not survive and thrive, every other problem we face becomes much more difficult."[11] The threat is global: the emergence of "strong man" authoritarian and usually populist governments in the United States, Russia, China, Turkey, India, Egypt, Congo, Venezuela, Hungary, Poland, and the Philippines (among other countries). Some of these governments preserve a veneer of democratic freedoms. But all of them—at least in terms of their current leadership—are in principle hostile to an unambiguous defense of the classic constitutional political freedoms and related human rights. And most of these governments are committed to an ethnic or racial or religious nationalism as a matter of principle and as a means by which to stoke resentment and solidify power.

Cathleen Kaveny has argued that *Faithful Citizenship* has been too focused on issues alone and not enough on the character of politicians. After all, she said, the actual choice before voters always involves assessing the capacities of a particular politician to effectuate change on certain issues. She has also argued that it is important to distinguish issues as fundamental, and/or urgent, and/or amenable to improvement.[12] I think Kaveny's suggestions point toward a better way of reflecting on conscience and political choices. I also think her suggestions are especially helpful in the present fraught political moment in which we are often shockingly if no longer surprisingly confronted by the authoritarian vices of the president and by repeated political developments that threaten our constitutional order. Accordingly, I believe a theology of conscience at this time should be especially attuned to the virtues, vices, practices, norms, culture, and structures—and related fundamental and urgent issues—that pertain to the endurance and renewal of the liberal democratic order in the United States.

Setting Conscience Free to Be Fully Itself

Given developments in the theology of conscience and the challenge of these political times, what are steps to be taken in the integration of a theology of conscience into the revision of *Faithful Citizenship*?

The first step is to set conscience free to be fully itself. The idea here is severalfold: to associate conscience more clearly with its own capacity for moral truth; to embed that capacity in a concrete world; and by these steps to set conscience free to respond to grace at work in the world. The need for these steps arises from the deficiently ratifying nature of conscience in *Faithful Citizenship*. To be sure, the bishops state in the document that they are not telling Catholics how to vote.[13] They also acknowledge the importance of the link of conscience and prudence, with the moral virtue accorded a distinctive and even courageous role in applying the truth of unchanging moral principles to the circumstances facing a voter.[14] But the weight of *Faithful Citizenship* falls on the side of constraining the conscience to vote in ways that the bishops consider consistent with the "whole truth in authentic love"[15]—a consistency especially evident in the rejection of law and policy construed to support actions falling in the category of intrinsic evil. By putting things in this way, the bishops affirm that conscience derives its dignity from its correspondence with the truth manifest especially in certain universal, negative commandments. These negative norms bear the objective weight here: The conscience of the Catholic voter plays a ratifying, functional role. One attains truth by accepting the universal, negative norm in all its apparent applicability—or dallies with subjectivism by deciding otherwise.

But this is too cut-and-dried a way of thinking about conscience and truth. Michael Lawler and Todd Salzmann, commenting on Pope Francis's theology of conscience, have argued that objective norms assist conscience in the moral assessment of particular situations. But, Lawler and Salzmann note, conscience plays its part as well in this process. Each person relies on what they call the "objective orientation of conscience" to assess the relevance of the norm to all of the circumstances of a particular historical or cultural context. This process leaves us with complementary objectivities provided by the norm and conscience from which emerges moral truth.[16] These observations pertinent to fundamental theology complement work in political theology relevant to conscience by Kaveny who, for instance, offers a Thomistic account of the complexity of moving from conscientious conviction to actual legislation. To acknowledge such complexity is not a concession to evil but recognition of the incarnate, concrete reality amid which conscience should seek to shape good laws that lead people to virtue.[17]

In light of such theological developments, I think it can be helpful to reimagine the meaning of the striking image offered years ago by theologian Timothy O'Connell: that conscience kneels before the truth.[18] Everyone agrees that this should be the case. But what can this phrase mean in a way that vindicates the potential for agency and objectivity and relationality of the conscience of the one kneeling? The work of Australian theologians Tom Ryan and Daniel Fleming puts flesh on the bones of the kneeling conscience. Ryan draws on the work of John Paul II and *Gaudium et spes* to argue that we should think of the fundamental intuitions of conscience toward the true and the good less in terms of clear, discursive principles of practical reason and more in terms of moral intuitions arising from visceral encounters with others and with the concrete and natural world. Thus, for Ryan, our primary moral awareness is anchored in embodiment and relationship—with all of the associated vulnerabilities, emotional complexities, and possibilities of bias.[19] Fleming, then, builds on Ryan's articulation of such a primordial conscience to argue that conscience is best understood as kneeling first before our awareness of the call of responsibility toward others—and only on the basis of that experience then is able accurately to move toward the discernment of moral truth.[20]

Vaclav Havel, no stranger to difficult political times, at the height of the Cold War beautifully evoked a picture of such a primordial conscience set free to be fully itself and thus to be ready to engage with politics. He said,

> Our "I" [or conscience] primordially attests to [the] world and personally certifies it; that is the world of our lived experience, a world not yet indifferent since we are personally bound to it in our love, hatred, respect, contempt, tradition, in our interests and in that pre-reflective meaningfulness from which culture is born. That is the realm of our inimitable, inalienable, and nontransferable joy and pain, a world in which, through which, and for which we are somehow answerable, a world of personal responsibility. In this world, categories like justice, honor, treason, friendship, infidelity, courage, or empathy have a wholly tangible content, relating to actual persons and important for actual life. At the basis of this world are values which are simply there, perennially, before we ever speak of them, before we reflect upon them and inquire about them.[21]

Conscience, Religious Freedom, and the Freedom of the People

The first step, then, is to free conscience to be fully itself. But free for what? Here it is important to connect conscience to mission, referenced in *Faithful Citizenship* but far more emphasized by Pope Francis as the very heart of his papacy. I'd like to speak of conscience and mission in light of two related theological themes: first, religious freedom, and, in the next section, the *sensus fidelium*. A theology of conscience is inevitably affected by how these related theological themes are understood.

How does the theology of conscience in *Faithful Citizenship* connect to religious freedom, understood in part as the freedom with which the church pursues its mission to the political order? *Faithful Citizenship* is clear on the centrality of mission: "We are called to participate in public life in a manner consistent with the mission of our Lord," the bishops say at the outset of the document.[22] But it is important to see two problems with the document's conception of mission, both having to do with ways *Faithful Citizenship* portrays religious freedom and both having important implications for the theology of conscience. First, the document adverts in its closing pages to grounding the right to religious freedom in human dignity.[23] But more often and more prominently, the document bases the right to religious freedom in religion itself.[24] In doing so, *Faithful Citizenship* shares in a mode of argument with moral theories that situate the right to religious freedom within a more fundamental set of basic goods to which practical reason is oriented—and with one of the chief among these basic goods being religion itself.[25] In this view, the good has priority over the right, and the right to religious freedom and its connection to human dignity is seen as necessary but functional, not so much an exigency flowing from human nature but more a means by which the truth of religion may be pursued. In a similar fashion, *Faithful Citizenship* renders the right to religious freedom more as a matter belonging to the church and less as a right belonging to human beings as such. What is at stake in many matters of religious freedom, the document argues, is the Catholic conscience but not so much the conscience of a Catholic or a Muslim or an atheist or a woman seeking contraception in her health insurance plan or a gay couple seeking a wedding cake.

Call it what you will—the basic good of religion, truth, the corporate identity of the church—these categories provide the better part of the justification of religious freedom in *Faithful Citizenship*. And they correspondingly provide the content that informs the document's vision of the church's mission to the political order. In one section of the document, the bishops speak of religious freedom insofar as religion is a leaven to society because it provides moral qualities having their basis in God's will.[26] In other sections, the bishops note that it is "central to the mission of the Church" to "teach truths in public life."[27] Indeed, more than anything, in *Faithful Citizenship* the Catholic conscience in union with the hierarchical church is on mission to the political order by witnessing to the "whole truth in authentic love."[28]

I think there is a better way for the theology of conscience in the next iteration of *Faithful Citizenship* to be integrated with the concepts of religious freedom and mission. First, conscience should be connected more specifically to human dignity as the ground of the right to religious freedom. This would conform more specifically to the letter of the *Declaration on Religious Freedom*.[29] But doing so would also allow conscience to be connected more closely to the historical and relational sense of conscience in the theology of Pope Francis. In a commentary, John Courtney Murray argued that human dignity in the *Declaration on Religious Freedom* "consists formally in a person's responsibility for self and the world" and that the "primordial demand" of dignity is that a person acts by one's own counsel, in freedom, and moved internally by the risk of one's whole existence. Murray also argued that dignity was at once ontological and social and thus that a crucial dimension of dignity like conscience could not be isolated from history and relationship.[30] By more persuasively associating conscience with dignity and freedom, these arguments more clearly extend the rights of conscience to everyone within and outside the church. Also, by associating conscience with a more historical notion of dignity, it is possible to see conscience more clearly situated in a world of conflicting claims, difficult balancing acts, and hard trade-offs.

By turning to human dignity, we can also conceive more broadly of the mission of the church to which conscience is oriented. Here I think, for instance, of Murray's observation that the word *dignity* has a personal and political reference. On the one hand, it refers to the ground of the right to religious freedom and thus to the moral basis for juridical limits on the power of the state. On the other hand, dignity is associated with "popular constitutionalism: that is, that the people, not the state, are the main agents of the ethical direction of society, including the definition of the proper constitutionally limited role of government."[31] On the basis of such assumptions, Murray argued on behalf of understanding the mission of the church in terms of the "conjoining of the Church's freedom to exercise its rightful concern for the common good with the people's…freedoms [with such freedoms, Murray argued, understood especially as the 'interrelated and interdependent individual democratic rights']."[32] "The two freedoms [of the Church and the people] are inseparable," Murray said, "in fact, they are identical.

They stand or fall together."[33] In his 2015 speech at Independence Hall in Philadelphia, Pope Francis spoke of religious freedom in terms similar to the arguments advanced by Murray. Francis primarily referred to religious freedom in terms of the concept of human dignity. And he also pointedly connected the religious freedom of the church with the religious freedom of other religious traditions: of all such religions, he said, "At the heart of their spiritual mission is the proclamation of the truth and dignity of the human person and human rights."[34] In putting things in this way, conscience is both freed to be fully itself and to be on mission in service to the freedom of the people understood especially in terms of constitutional and human rights.

Conscience, the *Sensus Fidelium*, and Mission to the Political Order

For the next iteration of *Faithful Citizenship*, it will also be important to connect the theology of conscience to mission understood in terms of the *sensus fidelium*. Of course, Pope Francis has recovered an emphasis on this ancient doctrine, understood as the "supernatural sense of faith of the entire people of God."[35] And he has made this emphasis theoretical and pastoral, discussing the doctrine in various texts and vivifying it through the open dialogue of deliberative synods.[36] At the least, the recovery of the *sensus fidelium* calls into question the reliance on the more heavily hierarchical, teaching-and-learning model of the church favored to date by *Faithful Citizenship*. The next iteration of the document surely should draw more on the insights of all of the faithful.

In his recent writing on conscience, James Keenan has called specifically for a deeper integration of the theology of conscience with the *sensus fidelium*. Such integration has been slow in coming, he said, because theology has generally paid little attention to conscience or to the *sensus fidelium* and because many in the hierarchy haven't been very interested anyhow in such matters.[37] Moreover, he adds, the Catholic Church in the United States has had an especially difficult time integrating the *sensus fidelium* and conscience into its thought and practice. On the one hand, since the Second World War the American church has favored a strong sense of obedience to the hierarchy—a disposition in tension both with the integrity of conscience and with the horizontal emphasis of the *sensus fidelium*. On the other hand, the prevailing postwar American view of conscience has centered almost entirely on individual freedom of conscience from imperious law or command—think of the Evangelical Christian Colorado baker refusing to make a wedding cake for two gay men intending to marry. To be sure, the prophetic image of the uncompromising witness of conscience to the moral law in the face of coercive power has its time and place: the examples of St. Thomas More and St. Oscar Romero ring down the ages. But, Keenan argues, this lonely, heroic image of conscience has often become in American culture a stunted, individualistic simulacrum of the actual heroic conscience. Keenan calls this stunting the "arrested development of the American conscience"[38] and sees it manifested in such vices as the radical individualism that negates an appropriate sense of individuality; in the blindered rejection of solidarity with the poor and with the natural world; and by the rashness that reaches for the nearest gun instead of the courage that faces the racist American past erupting unredeemed into the present.[39]

How might *Faithful Citizenship* integrate conscience and *sensus fidelium* in a way that responds to the "arrested development of the American conscience"? I would like to suggest the reimagination of conscience and *sensus fidelium* in terms of the multifaceted imagery of being baptized into mission as priests, prophets, and rulers. Such imagery would respond to Keenan's concern about the narrowcasting of conscience in the American church: The prophetic model of conscience as witness could be retained but complemented with conscience rendered in a priestly and ruling key. Moreover, such imagery would also connect conscience more clearly to the *sensus fidelium*. In a recent article, theologian Anthony Ekpo argued for the recovery of the *sensus fidelium* precisely in the key of sharing in the threefold office of Christ. *Lumen gentium*, he noted, refers to the participation of the people of God primarily in Christ's prophetic office. This is true, so far as it goes. But, Ekpo argues, the singular focus on sharing in the prophetic office suffers from an ambiguity in the conciliar document about how precisely the whole people of God and the magisterium share in this charism. And this ambiguity, Ekpo says, allows the reflexive return of the problematic model of the teaching and learning church. By turning instead to the imagery of the threefold office, we can see conscience disposed to participate more fully in the grace of Christ's prophetic—and priestly and ruling—mission.[40]

What, more specifically, might the appeal to such imagery in a theology of conscience oriented to mission look like in a future version of *Faithful Citizenship*? First, regarding the prophetic office: The document should draw on the insight of the whole people of God and especially the poor. Moreover, the document should pair its appropriate reluctance to tell the Catholic laity how to vote with an outspoken, prophetic advocacy for the right to vote (among many other matters of political practice about which to be prophetic). There is no justification whatsoever for the voter suppression tactics now being practiced throughout the United States. By taking such a stand, the document would signal that conscience is not only implicated in intraecclesial matters but also in the arbitrary denial by law of voting as an expression of the dignity of conscience on the part of each voter and as a right that is an inalienable freedom of the people.[41]

What of the priestly mission of conscience toward the freedom of the American people? Here I think especially of the priestly, mediating, and even sacrificial or expiatory mission to the greatest sign of our stunted American conscience: the way we have been misshaped by our history of slavery, Jim Crow, lynching, mass incarceration, police shootings, and birtherism. Such a mission could involve in particular, as Keenan suggests, fostering an indispensable virtue of conscience: humility before the truth of this past and present.[42] Thus it would be a humility ever ready to say with the Psalmist amid the apparent certitude of our conscience, "Cleanse thou me of my unknown faults."[43] And it would be conscience disposed toward the humility associated with Christ's redemptive mission. In his discussion of the American conscience, Keenan has argued that when we discover our sinfulness, we discover our freedom: we discover sinfulness and redemption together because it is only by being redeemed that we can know our sinfulness.[44] Who knows how a priestly, mediating effort by the church in the United States to face the sins of our past—a sorely needed event of grace at work in our world—might lead to a renewal of the meaning of the freedom of the people?

Finally, what of the ruling nature of conscience on mission to the freedom of the people? Here thinking of conscience in the key of "rule" suggests that the next iteration of *Faithful Citizenship* should address what John Courtney Murray called the "constitutional consensus" by which we *rule* ourselves and become a people. In a recent speech, Bishop Robert McElroy described the consensus as "the glue which held America together, through common moral and spiritual values rather than ties of blood or nationalism." But, McElroy added, the consensus has been shattered and "our national soul has truly been hollowed out."[45] What to do to restore this? McElroy argues that the renewal of the consensus should be founded on solidarity understood as the recognition in light of grace that we are all debtors of the society of which we are a part. Accordingly, we should foster the formation of conscience in terms of the beliefs, norms, practices, and institutions that have been handed on to us and by which our democratic society of self-rule is able to exist at all. Here I think of civil dialogue and shared truth, the rejection of tribalism, the separation of powers, the independence of the judiciary, the significance of scientific research, and more.[46] To take on such tasks in the next iteration of *Faithful Citizenship* would be an instance of the ruling conscience on mission to the freedom of the people.

Conclusion

I am aware of the range of church-state positions from the sectarian to the establishmentarian. But I have argued here in a different key: that the church, while respecting the autonomy of the political order and seeking no favors from it, could nevertheless take on itself a spirit of mission toward the beliefs, practices, and institutions of politics itself.[47] We are at a time when theology needs to reimagine the relationship of the church and politics amid a crisis of the nation-state; a pluralism from which there is no turning back; and the emergence at the Second Vatican Council of a more cosmopolitan, less nationalistic brand of Catholicism.[48] There are resources in the Catholic tradition to assist this project of reimagination—including the documents of the Second Vatican Council and untapped strains of medieval and early modern ecclesiastical thought and practice that played a part in the emergence of modern liberal democracy.[49] It is time to draw on such resources to reimagine the theology of conscience for our political times.

NOTES

1. Cathleen Kaveny, "Voting and Faithful Citizenship," in *Law's Virtues: Fostering Autonomy and Solidarity in American Society* (Washington, DC: Georgetown University Press, 2012), 189–218, at 189.

2. James F. Keenan, "Receiving *Amoris Laetitia*," *Theological Studies* 71, no. 1 (2017): 193–212, at 203.

3. John Courtney Murray, "The Problem of Religious Freedom," *Theological Studies* 25 (1964): 503–75, at 555. (Murray is commenting here on the efforts of John XXIII to link the freedom of the church not simply to the "human quality of society" but also to the modern, civil freedoms that are the primary safeguard of the common good.) See *Pacem in terris* 60 and Leon Hooper, *The Ethics of Discourse: The Social Philosophy of John Courtney Murray* (Washington, DC: Georgetown University Press, 1986), 135–36.

4. *Amoris laetitia* 37.

5. *Gaudete et exsultate* 101.

6. "Letter to a Non-Believer: Pope Francis Responds to Dr. Eugenio Scalfari, Journalist of the Italian Newspaper *La Repubblica*," September 4, 2013, http://w2.vatican.va/content/francesco/en/letters/2013/documents/papa -francesco_20130911_eugenio-scalfari.html. Pope Francis wrote to Scalfari: "You ask me whether it is erroneous or a sin to follow the line of thought which holds that there is no absolute, and therefore no absolute truth, but only a series of relative and subjective truths. To begin with, I would not speak about "absolute" truths, even for believers, in the sense that absolute is that which is disconnected and bereft of all relationship. Truth, according to the Christian faith, is the love of God for us in Jesus Christ. Therefore, truth is a relationship."

7. Pope Francis, "A Big Heart Open to God: An Interview with Pope Francis," Antonio Spadaro, *America*, September 30, 2013, https://www .americamagazine.org/faith/2013/09/30/big-heart-open-god-interview -pope-francis.

8. "Big Heart Open to God" and Joseph Ratzinger, "Conscience and Truth," in *Crisis of Conscience*, ed. John M. Haas (New York: Crossroad, 1996), 1–20, at 12–15.

9. "Big Heart Open to God," and *Evangelii gaudium* 119–20.

10. *Evangelii gaudium* 198.

11. E. J. Dionne, "The most consequential question facing the world," *The Washington Post*, August 23, 2017, https://www.washingtonpost.com/opinions/ the-most-consequential-question-facing-the-world/2017/08/23/3d2f5514 -7eb3-11e7-83c7-5bd5460f0d7e_story.html?utm_term=.0220217c382d. By "liberal democracy" I am referring to what Christopher Insole calls "constitutional liberalism," which he identifies primarily with a set of practices like the "restriction of the use of coercive public power to sustaining peace and justice (giving to each their due), rather than to enforcing ultimate truth or unity of belief; the protection of individuals within a framework of rights and liberties; the separation of powers (between the lawmakers, law-enforcers and those who interpret the application of the law), and the mixed constitution (elements of rule of the one, the few and the many." See Insole, "Theology and Politics:

The Intellectual History of Liberalism," in *Theology, University, Humanities*, eds. Christopher Craig Brittain and Francesca Aran Murphy (Eugene, OR: Cascade Books, 2011), 173–93, at 174–75.

12. Kaveny, "Voting and Faithful Citizenship," 199–206.

13. *Faithful Citizenship* 7.

14. *Faithful Citizenship* 19.

15. *Faithful Citizenship*, introduction.

16. Michael G. Lawler and Todd A. Salzman, "In *Amoris Laetitia*, Francis' Model of Conscience Empowers Catholics," *National Catholic Reporter*, September 7, 2016, https://www.ncronline.org/news/theology/amoris-laetitia -francis-model-conscience-empowers-catholics.

17. Kaveny, preface, *Law's Virtues*, xi–xii. Virtuousness and justice alone are not enough for good law. Rather, drawing on Aquinas's use of seventh-century Isidore of Seville's philosophy of law, Kaveny argues that good law should be virtuous, just, possible to nature, attuned to the custom of a country, suitable to time and place, necessary, useful, clearly expressed, and framed for no private benefit but for the common good.

18. Timothy O'Connell, *Principles of Catholic Morality* (New York: Harper Collins, 1990), 91.

19. Tom Ryan, "Conscience as Primordial Moral Awareness in *Gaudium et spes* and *Veritatis Splendor*," *Australian e-Journal of Theology* 18, no. 1 (April 2011): 83–96, at 86–88, 96.

20. Daniel Fleming, "Primordial Moral Awareness: Levinas, Conscience, and the Unavoidable Call to Responsibility," *Heythrop Journal* 56 (2015): 604–18, at 612.

21. Vaclav Havel, "Politics and Conscience," UNIV, accessed November 11, 2019, http://www.univforum.org/sites/default/files/HAVEL_Politics %20Conscience_ENG.pdf. A note accompanying the posting of the speech online explains, "In February 1984, Václav Havel wrote this speech on the occasion of receiving an honorary doctorate from the University of Toulouse. He was unable to deliver the speech on May 14, 1984 and was represented by English playwright Tom Stoppard. The essay first appeared in Czech in *Přirozený svět jako politický problém: eseje o člověku pozdní doby* (The Natural World as Political Problem: Essays on Modern Man), ed. Václav Bělohradský (Prague: Edice Expedice, 1984). Erazim Kohák and Roger Scruton translated it into English for the *Salisbury Review*, no. 2 (January 1985). This translation is used here.

22. *Faithful Citizenship* 1.

23. *Faithful Citizenship* 72.

24. *Faithful Citizenship* 4.

25. See, for instance, Robert P. George, "Religious Liberty: A Fundamental Human Right," in *Conscience and Its Enemies: Confronting the Dogmas of*

Liberal Secularism (Wilmington, DE: ISI Books, 2013), 115–25, and Christopher Tollefsen, "Conscience, Religion, and the State," *American Journal of Jurisprudence* 54, no. 1 (January 1, 2009): 93–115.

26. *Faithful Citizenship* 4.

27. *Faithful Citizenship* 11.

28. *Faithful Citizenship*, introduction.

29. *Declaration on Religious Freedom* 2.

30. John Courtney Murray, "Arguments for the Human Right to Religious Freedom," Woodstock Theological Library, accessed November 26, 2019, https://www.library.georgetown.edu/woodstock/murray/1968.

31. Leon Hooper, *The Ethics of Discourse*, 132. See also Murray, "The Problem of Religious Freedom," *Theological Studies* 25 (1964): 503–75.

32. Leon Hooper, *The Ethics of Discourse*, 135.

33. Murray, "The Problem of Religious Freedom," 555.

34. "Pope Francis' remarks during meeting for religious freedom at Independence Hall," *Crux*, September 26, 2015, https://cruxnow.com/papal-visit/2015/09/26/pope-francis-remarks-during-meeting-for-religious-freedom-at-independence-hall-english/.

35. *Lumen gentium* 12.

36. See, for instance, "A Big Heart Open to God"; *Evangelii Gaudium* 119–21; and International Theological Commission, "*Sensus Fidei* in the Life of the Church," 2014, http://www.vatican.va/roman_curia/congregations/cfaith/cti_documents/rc_cti_20140610_sensus-fidei_en.html.

37. James F. Keenan, "Redeeming Conscience," *Theological Studies* 76, no. 1 (2015): 129–47, at 131.

38. James F. Keenan, "The Arrested Development of the American Conscience in Moral Decision Making," *America*, December 22, 2016, https://www.americamagazine.org/arts-culture/2016/12/22/arrested-development-american-conscience-moral-decision-making.

39. Keenan, "Redeeming Conscience," 134–36.

40. Anthony Ekpo, "The *Sensus Fidelium* and the Threefold Office of Christ: A Reinterpretation of *Lumen Gentium* no. 12," in *The Sensus Fidelium and Moral Theology: Readings in Moral Theology No. 18*, eds. Charles E. Curran and Lisa A. Fullam (Mahwah, NJ: Paulist Press, 2017): 91–112. Ekpo's article first appeared in *Theological Studies* 76, no. 2 (2015): 330–46.

41. For a discussion of the moral nature of voting, see Kaveny, "Voting and Faithful Citizenship," 191, 211; and Maureen O'Connell, "Can You Sin When You Vote?" in *Voting and Holiness*, 197–214. The *Compendium of the Social Doctrine of the Church* says of the values informing an act like voting and democracy more broadly, "An authentic democracy is not merely the result of a formal observation of a set of rules but is the fruit of a convinced acceptance of the values that inspire democratic procedures: the dignity of every human

person, the respect of human rights, commitment to the common good as the purpose and guiding criterion for political life. If there is no general consensus on these values, the deepest meaning of democracy is lost and its stability is compromised." See *Compendium* 406–8; http://www.vatican.va/roman_curia/pontifical_councils/justpeace/documents/rc_pc_justpeace_doc_20060526_compendio-dott-soc_en.html#Values%20and%20democracy.

42. Keenan, "Arrested Development."

43. Psalm 19. See also Ratzinger's use of this phrase from Psalm 19 in his discussion of the possibility of the justified conscience of a member of the Nazi SS. "Conscience and Truth," 5.

44. Keenan, "Arrested Development."

45. Robert McElroy, "Religious Freedom Today," Speech Given at Georgetown University, November 16, 2017. Text provided by Bishop McElroy.

46. McElroy, "Religious Freedom Today."

47. For taking this approach in this essay, I am indebted to Clement Majawa, "Church as Conscience of the State: Christian Witness in Politics for the Transformation of Africa," *African Ecclesial Review* 56, nos. 2–3 (2014): 151–81.

48. See Massimo Faggioli, *Catholicism and Citizenship: Political Cultures of the Church in the Twenty-First Century* (Collegeville, MN: Liturgical Press, 2017), xxi, 44, 58–9, 63, 102, and 112.

49. See Insole, "Theology and Politics," 183–87.

Questions for Further Reflection

1. The author says that *Faithful Citizenship* should be consistent with the thought of Pope Francis on the conscience. How has Pope Francis described the role of the church in forming consciences? How does the concept of intrinsic evil, so critical to the current version of *Faithful Citizenship*, jibe with Pope Francis's theology of the conscience?

2. How does Pope Francis's theology of the conscience relate to Pope Benedict XVI's theology of the conscience? Does the author think that they are at odds or complementary to each other? Explain.

3. The author says that the times require that we focus on the relationship of the gospel to the political. To what political times is he

referring? Do you agree with his description of those times? Why or why not?

4. The author cites Kaveny on the importance of the character of politicians, which *Faithful Citizenship* does not mention. Should the bishops have discussed the character of political candidates in *Faithful Citizenship*? How would such a consideration further the analysis of how Catholics should vote in good conscience?

5. In this regard, the author again mentions a "theology of the conscience." What exactly does he mean by this? Is this a useful concept in a political analysis of competing candidates? How? Do you see yourself using such a method of analysis? Why or why not?

6. How does the author say that we set conscience free? Does this mean that the church/the bishops have no role in our conscience formation? If they do have a role, what is it? What should it be?

7. The author says that "conscience kneels before the truth." What does that mean? What is the source of this truth? Does it come from the teachings of the church or from some other sources?

8. What is the primordial conscience set free to be fully itself? How does Vaclav Havel evoke this concept?

9. Once a conscience is free to be fully itself, what is the next step? How does this concept relate to religious freedom? How does it relate to the *sensus fidelium*? Does *Faithful Citizenship* say/imply anything about this?

10. The author says that *Faithful Citizenship* roots the right to religious freedom in religion itself. What are the strengths/weaknesses of this argument according to the author? Do you agree or disagree with the author's analysis here? In the final analysis, what does the author propose as a better root for the right to religious freedom?

11. The author says that dignity has a personal and a political reference, citing John Courtney Murray. What did Murray mean by this? How does the author apply it to the formation of conscience?

12. What does *sensus fidelium* mean? How does Pope Francis understand this concept? Does the *sensus fidelium* reflect the magisterial style of *Faithful Citizenship*?

13. How does the author say that the theologian James Keenan would integrate a theology of conscience with the *sensus fidelium*? How does this relate to the "lonely, heroic image of conscience" and the

stunted development of American conscience? How does it relate to racism?

14. How does the author say that *Faithful Citizenship* could use the concepts of freedom of conscience and *sensus fidelium* to reimagine itself? What would such a version of *Faithful Citizenship* look like? What concepts would it emphasize? What concepts would it reject?

15. What is John Courtney Murray's "constitutional consensus"? What does the author say is the status of this consensus? Does it exist? If not, why not and how could it be restored?

16. What role does the author think that such a consensus should play in *Faithful Citizenship*?

5

Our "First Freedom"?

Sex, Gender, and Sexuality in Religious Freedom Claims

Nancy A. Dallavalle

Introduction

As Catholics across the United States go to the polls in November 2020, will their public actions be informed by their faith? Current patterns tell us that Catholics vote much like others in the United States, whether these are millennial Latinas in the Bronx, agribusiness farmers in Lincoln, or retirees in Dallas and Phoenix. Early data from the 2016 presidential election seemed to indicate that a slim majority of Catholics voted for the Republican presidential candidate, while a later study indicated that Catholics slightly favored the Democratic candidate.[1] Others have argued that the split was statistically even. Is there an identifiable "Catholic bloc"? Not in this day.

Forming Consciences for Faithful Citizenship, a voting guide offered by the United States Conference of Catholic Bishops (USCCB), illustrates the dilemma.[2] Catholics are called to be sober and prudential in their political engagement. They are called to uphold the dignity of the human person in all cases. They are called to create a just and humane social order. And they are called to uphold religious freedom, "not only

73

to secure the just freedom of the church and the faithful here but also to offer hope and an encouraging witness to those who suffer direct and even violent religious persecution in countries where the protection is far weaker."[3] As neither political party maps onto the bishops' vision, one might conclude that Catholic voters would be evenly split on these issues.

Yet there are some interesting patterns within the Catholic vote. While of necessity Catholics end up voting for one party or another, Mark Gray of the Center for Applied Research in the Apostolate notes that in that 2016 election, 42 percent of Catholic voters were "unaffiliated," in that they were not strongly identified with either party.[4] Surveying the range of Catholic concerns as voters go to the polls— abortion, yes, but also gun control, immigration, the environment, and the role of government in alleviating poverty—this large unaffiliated group tended not to vote as the church would advise on the issue of abortion, but was strongly supportive of church positions on all the rest of these issues. Those Catholics who affiliated more clearly with a political party, whether Democratic or Republican, were somewhat less supportive of these issues, with one exception: "Republicans [were] more consistent with the church's position on the legality of abortion than any other group."

Thus the Republican party seems to fit "the Catholic vote" in spite of the wide disagreement of the Republican party with the range of issues the church puts forward, benefiting from popular sense that "the Catholic vote" is most faithfully exercised in an opposition to legalized abortion (and same-sex marriage), an association that also drives partisan fundraising—on both sides of the aisle. Despite efforts by many bishops to broaden this perspective to include related issues such as euthanasia and the death penalty, opposition to abortion and same-sex marriage remain the litmus test (with the social acceptance of transgender persons now also at issue). A conservative independent (not church-sanctioned) organization called "Catholic Vote" exemplifies this reduction of Catholic concerns to issues of sex and gender. In their presentation, the values of *Faithful Citizenship* are overturned: immigration is addressed only as "legal immigration," environmental concerns must reflect the priority of private property, and a discussion of the government's role in supporting families and children says nothing about policies for daycare or parental leave (its proposal consists of a "family tax credit," which would hardly support those who are low-income). Most strikingly, the important Catholic notion of the common good is deemed "dangerous," because it is used to justify support for broad public programs of public benefit rather than programs that support "individuals and families."[5]

How can this misrepresentation stand? Evidently, they get away with this because of their support for the USCCB's position on abortion and same-sex marriage. In the popular mind, a complex story put forward by the U.S. bishops consistently defaults to questions about sex and gender as the "nonnegotiables" for Catholics, as if Catholicism could readily be explained as an elaborate system for policing sexual behavior. Yet this one-sided presentation is neither the position of the USCCB, nor is it characteristic of various statements of pastoral concern and teaching authority issued by individual U.S. bishops, taken as a whole. Yet it persists and, I suggest, the ghost of these questions of sex and gender continues to haunt the entire religious freedom "cause" as this has been presented since the late twentieth century.

Of course, the partisan divide in question is focused on the contemporary U.S. context, a caveat that must be kept in mind when considering a global religion like Catholicism. With Vatican II's Declaration on Religious Freedom, Catholics consider religious freedom to be the civil right for everyone, one that should be protected by law: "Therefore government is to assume the safeguard of the religious freedom of all its citizens, in an effective manner, by just laws and by other appropriate means."[6] Just as the protection of religion has a specific political dynamic in this country, this claim meets a far different fate elsewhere, as the U.S. Catholic bishops are well aware. They insist that the struggle for this freedom in the United States offers an important point of reference for those for whom it is not assured, asking the faithful to uphold religious freedom here as a message to those elsewhere. On the one hand, this sense of common cause is appropriate, as the United States has, at its best, stood as a beacon for freedom and liberty for other countries. On the other hand, the sense of urgency about serious violations of religious freedom in some other contexts is occasionally used to stifle careful analysis of precisely which "religious freedom" claims in our own country the U.S. bishops are trying to protect.[7]

Religious Freedom and Conscience Protection

The notion that the state cannot compel or coerce religious belief depends on the claim that individuals possess an inner norm called conscience, a personal "rudder" of sorts that guides judgement and action. These are intertwined; the public square and private conviction cannot be neatly separated—one's actions in public are always, to some extent, "expressive" of one's personal beliefs. The reverse is also true, that is, those inner convictions always have a social context—the "privacy" of an inner life does not exist in splendid isolation. In other words, our private thoughts and public context are always in dialogue; we have no "pure" inner self, nor do we engage in public as "neutral" actors.

The right to religious freedom is a right that recognizes this interplay. From the adoption of the First Amendment until now, however, the interpretive context for this interplay has shifted, requiring that any claims and analysis of this freedom include a historical perspective. Indeed, political scientist Stephen F. Schneck tells us that the notion of a stable concept called "freedom of religion," which we need only to cite and apply, misreads history: "Far from anything like a consensus agreement among the Framers about the proper role for religion in public life, they [the Framers] were in fact bitterly divided on the issue." There is no "singular and settled consensus" to be retrieved.[8] Schneck identifies four models that describe various positions on religion and public life, all of which were in the air during the eighteenth century. At that time two of the four shaped the dominant competing visions: "civil religionists" saw religion as a helpful tool of the state, as it provided language for "civic virtue" and a sense of common cause; while "religious separationists" held that a "wall" between church and state was necessary for the integrity of each. Today, however, the current culture war debates are driven more by the two models that were present but less influential at the time of the "Framers:" "millennialism," which identifies the American project with the fulfillment of salvation history, putting the state in service to Christianity as its proper fulfillment; and "secularism," which completely dismisses religion as dogmatic and irrational. Schneck finds it surprising that today's public discussion is dominated by these two previously marginal frameworks for religion in public life, as if these were the only options.[9]

This foregrounding of a clash between a "soft" millennialism and a rather "dogmatic" secularism—both to some extent products of opposing minority extremes—does indeed shape the conversation about religious freedom in the popular media and in the minds of many voters. Both perspectives are easily co-opted by identity politics on the right and left, and both are easily caricatured by the opposite perspective. The noise of this conflict today seems to have driven away a public consideration of the other options. For the soft millennialist, the question of religion is intellectually inseparable from the question of patriotism and the national agenda. Traditional norms of governing, rooted in the careful discourse of checks and balances and policies and procedures, seem, to this mind, to obscure the importance of Christian zeal in service of national destiny. For the "dogmatic" secularist, religious affiliation is incompatible with responsible citizenship. For these, the claims of religion can be, at most, a hobby, but it is always one with dangerous pretensions, as these claims are nothing more than equal parts irrationality and nostalgia—the latter tantamount to a taste for fascism.

What is striking is that each of these collapse the social scaffolding of church and state in favor of an appeal to a self untethered to history in the first case, and to the social world in the second. Both movements are dominated on the popular stage by male voices (whether preachers or "new atheists"), yet both movements claim to be the champion of women, whether as protectors of a cult of "true womanhood" or as the "real" liberators of women from history and embodiment (and religion). The first would completely privatize claims about sex and gender, under the banner of care for "our" women. The second would claim that sex and gender are merely interchangeable aspects of being human (and opponents will charge that this perspective seems to suggest that masculinized secularity is the proper female future). Both would claim the priority of conscience, but this would be a conscience subsumed into the transhistorical triumph of Christ on the one hand, or the highly subjective interiorized conscience of the individual on the other. Neither is inclined to learn from history, build coalitions, or engage dialogically in the public square.

Catholic Christianity, on the other hand, has regarded religion and conscience to be intertwined, in the sense that Catholic formation was understood to provide conscience formation for its adherents, building a framework for reflection around a more general innate sense of "right and wrong." Particularly after Vatican II's reflection on conscience in its

Declaration on Religious Freedom, the conscience of an individual believer was to be privileged, with the understanding, however, that the believer had a "formed conscience." "Wherefore every man has the duty, and therefore the right, to seek the truth in matters religious in order that he may with prudence form for himself right and true judgments of conscience, under use of all suitable means….It follows that he is not to be forced to act in a manner contrary to his conscience. Nor, on the other hand, is he to be restrained from acting in accordance with his conscience, especially in matters religious."[10]

The banner under which this operates in the public sphere is that of "religious freedom." Yet, at the same time that Vatican II was opening the way for a ringing affirmation of religious freedom and the right to follow one's conscience, secularizing and liberalizing currents in the industrialized West were challenging the underpinning of the newly privatized domestic church of family and hearth.[11] While "conscience" was factored into public issues such as participation in war, for most Catholics "conscience" was a private forum in which Catholic teaching about sex, sexuality, and gender met the logic of the sexual revolution. These domestic considerations shaped Catholics' approach to the public square, as "traditional" and "progressive" labels began to refer almost exclusively to a place on a continuum between sexual restriction and permissiveness. (It is not surprising that the increasing practice of "living in sin" did not refer to the cohabitation of thieves.)[12]

The Culture in Flux: The Religious Freedom Restoration Act

In 1993, responding to Supreme Court decisions that were seen as infringing upon the proper exercise of religious freedom, the Religious Freedom Restoration Act (RFRA) was passed, with bipartisan support. Reflecting its then-broad appeal, it was supported by both the American Civil Liberties Union (ACLU) and the National Conference of Catholic Bishops (NCCB, now known as the USCCB). These were able to join forces, according to medical ethicist Luke Gatta, in large part because the articulation of "the exercise of religion" was so ambiguous that "both the ACLU and the USCC understood the RFRA according to their own definition of religious exercise."[13] But the developing polarization about the notion of "conscience," in models similar to those identified by Schneck for "religious freedom," meant that these two would eventually diverge.

On the one hand, the U.S. bishops and the ACLU were able, at first, to agree to protect religious liberty as it "protects the internal expression of conscience," free "from coercion by government."[14] For the USCCB, however, religious freedom *must also* recognize that persons are inherently social; to sunder a person's public actions from their private conscience ignores what it means to be human. Thus, the USCCB would later take the side of the business owners in the Hobby Lobby case, who claimed "the liberty to externalize their conscience in the workplace, even if to do so limited access to contraception for their employees."[15]

The ACLU disagreed with this position, now opposing the RFRA, given the Hobby Lobby case. What changed? For the ACLU, gender norms for traditional Christianity and gender norms for a new progressive sensibility were now in irreconcilable conflict: "As our society has moved toward greater equality for racial minorities and women, it has been less willing to accept religion as a justification for discrimination."[16] Religious norms about sex and gender were now not private, for the ACLU, if their exercise by one party meant the denial of the full public exercise of differing norms for sex and gender by another party. Gatta's evaluation of the ACLU's position is blunt.

> The ACLU decision to wash their hands clean of the bill represents an interpretation that the Free Exercise Clause protects a person's conscience only in private matters, where it can safely be exercised without potential friction. In this view, the external expression of one's conscience is hastily mistranslated as paternalistic. Its exercise outside the religious community, should it affect another individual's autonomous expression, is cheaply equivalent to the proselytizing of one's theocratic pretensions. In this secularized worldview, churches, synagogues, and mosques are able to grow and shrink with the ebb and flow of the population that fills them, but not contribute to the public conscience. Outside the religious institution, the public sphere should be sterilized of any religious expression....The heart of the RFRA

debate is the prerogative to externalize one's conscience in a pluralistic society.[17]

Indeed, Catholics have an obligation to have their faith impact their public lives. This is not merely a directive to "live my faith in public," it is a claim that there is a constitutively public dimension to belief. This is not merely in the publicly embraced value of the love of neighbor, the concern for "healing of the world" that is shared with the other Abrahamic faiths. It is also a sense that there is a social dimension to belief that, while never imposed on others, must remain as a public witness. Thus, the clash over employer-sponsored health plans that offer contraceptives, or the refusal of the Catholic agency to accept gay and lesbian couples as adoptive parents.

Legal scholar Cathleen Kaveny recognizes this conundrum: "The bishops are dealing with the difficult problem of finding a *modus vivendi* with a fast-evolving moral consensus that conflicts with traditional Catholic teachings." Catholics see this as a secular society infringing on its beliefs by not allowing the public exercise of its norms about sex and gender and the dignity of the human person. But for a "secular" public, Kaveny points out, these are not religion questions, they are *discrimination* questions. "Atheist Charities would be refused a license, too, if it made the same decision—or if it refused to place a child with Catholics, for that matter."[18] Furthermore, Kaveny argues, the U.S. bishops' rhetoric on these topics does not reflect *Dignitatis humanae*'s recognition that rights language should be put forward in "a framework of competing rights and duties, particularly the duty to promote the common good." This requires that "rights claims" be accompanied by the relevant "relational responsibilities." In contrast, she observes, "the most striking aspect of the bishops' claims about religious liberty is the absolute nature of their assertions."[19]

In the United States, such "absolute" claims about what is central to Catholicism are most likely to be about issues of sex, sexuality, and gender. The freedom to pray, to gather for worship, to proclaim the Nicene-Constantinopolitan creed, to reject Arianism, to venerate the Blessed Virgin—none of these are the focus of the concerns about religious freedom in the United States. Instead, abortion, same-sex marriage, and access to contraception dominates the dialogue. Nor would ordinary Catholics be surprised that sexual issues are the focus of the USCCB as, for many Catholics as well, the "bottom line" for the practice of the faith (whether observed or not) tends to be adherence to sexual norms and attendance at Sunday Mass.

In other words, the social imaginary of being Catholic, for many in the pews, for most of the twentieth century, was captive to obedience issues of Mass attendance (at which the revealed truths of faith were simply affirmed), regular penance, and the restriction of sexual activity to sacramentally married heterosexual couples, activity that would avoid any form of birth control. Almsgiving was considered important, but negotiable, direct service to the poor, heroic. In this "social imaginary," the practice of the Catholic faith was private and domestic, with the parish church the venue for its affirmation, particularly as it offered sacraments only to those whose adherence to these norms was documented in parish records. As the public conversation about sex and gender norms liberalized, however, in the last decades of the twentieth century, the need for a "restoration" of "religious freedom" became imperative.

Religious Freedom as "The First Freedom"

In the First Amendment, the prohibition on establishing a particular religion and the right to the free exercise of religion appear first in a list of claims. In that same sentence, there follows the assertion of the freedom of speech, of the press, of assembly, and the right to "petition the Government for a redress of grievances." What constituted a "religion" and how it was exercised in a "free" fashion, was, of course, specific to the time of the Constitution. If, at that time, the project of colonialism shaped the understanding of religion found in this amendment, the twentieth century witnessed, in the United States, the gradual encroachment of the notion of religion as a private exercise of conscience, a development that tracked the mainline Protestant Christianity that dominated elite U.S. culture. Today, while the notion of "religion" is increasingly associated with expressive individualism, the other freedoms named—of the press, of assembly, and so on—have not undergone a similar transformation. On the contrary, these freedoms are still generally recognized as public goods, functioning in a way that is similar to the way they did at the time of the amendment's adoption (although one might argue that the freedom of the press is under attack, the meaning of a "free" press has not changed significantly).

But the notion of "religion" itself, as we hear it, is a product of a framework for the study of religion that emerged nearly a century after its assertion as a "right" in the U.S. Constitution, modeled on Western Christianity. That would be different from the understanding of "religion" by the Framers and, most importantly, it continues to be a term in flux. How to relate this freedom with those mentioned in tandem with it?

A recent understanding was articulated by Vice President Mike Pence in remarks on religious freedom in the summer of 2018:

> The American Founders enshrined religious freedom as the first freedom in the Constitution of the United States…the most fundamental of freedoms. When religious liberty is denied or destroyed, we know that other freedoms—freedom of speech, of press, assembly, and even democratic institutions themselves—are imperiled….In America, we prove every day that religious freedom buttresses all other rights.[20]

How does this "buttressing" work? A *New York Times* editorial raised questions about Vice President Pence's assertion. Several weeks after the Vice President's remarks, the *Times* editorial board called attention to the shifting arguments now employed in the discussion of religious freedom.[21] It observed that President Obama saw a correlation between a country's support for religious rights and its support for human rights. But, the *Times* observed, those who are putting forward the "first freedom" framework, as does Mr. Pence, sever this connection in practice and in policy, saying that rights for sexual minorities, for example, are "political" (and in the current political climate, it is clear that President Trump intends to frame the other rights in the First Amendment as "political" as well).[22] In this reading, being gay or lesbian is a political choice, not an expression of something fundamental to the person, such as religious faith. "Religion," for the Vice President, is framed in the worldview of "millennialism," a Christian narrative tied deeply to the narrative of the United States. Unlike the other freedoms, religious freedom is not "political," in this telling, it is "quasi-natural" and therefore not to be analyzed as are the rights claims of a secular public (assertions of those rights are "political" [read: partisan] acts).

It is thus not surprising that the issues that most need the protection of religious freedom in the United States generally involve gender and sexual morality, which are privileged as "religious claims," and thus removed from public scrutiny.

"Catholic Vote" would agree.[23] Its agenda also demonstrates that issues of sex and gender and sexuality are seen as the key religious beliefs that need to be protected. In other words, it views the maintenance of traditional religious norms about sex as a protected freedom, against those who argue for "politicized" rights. Any attempt to legislate in favor of protections for gays or lesbians or transgendered persons, or to provide birth control, is seen as an intrusion by an overreaching government. And, having wrapped traditional religious norms about sex and gender so tightly in the cloak of religious freedom, those norms, like religious belief itself, are now *beyond question*, they are simply foundational.

This should be problematic to Catholics for two reasons. Theologically, we do not understand Catholic teaching on human sexuality to be in the category of "revealed" truth, as would be, for example, the teaching that God is triune, or that Jesus Christ rose from the dead. These are claims of faith; we do not attempt to explain these "scientifically." The Catholic opposition to abortion as well as its opposition to some forms of contraception, however, are based on publicly available evidence, they are part of the order of "the natural," not "the supernatural." Catholic positions that engage social norms about marriage involve claims about faith as well as about the social order—there is a role for public discourse here as well, not least about engaging recent studies of gender norms. To remove all of these issues from the realm (and the scrutiny) of the public square, and instead to simply lobby to have them recognized as religious claims, represents a certain failure of nerve—or a default to the public models of "millennialism" and "secularism," which leaves Catholics abandoning their tradition of "faith and reason," now in the American context of church-state discussions.

But there is also a sense that "government" is to be scorned in this scenario. Catholics are hardly naive about the failings of government; worldwide Catholicism has had every possible form of engagement with government over the last 2000 years. Today, together with its perch as a nonvoting member at the United Nations, the church has an extensive diplomatic corps and a wide network of relationships with many kinds of nongovernmental organizations. The "first freedom" movement, which seems to set religious freedom apart from other rights, also then privatizes it against its expression in public goods, public service, and publicly asserted rights and freedoms. Catholics, on the other hand, should support the freedom of the press and of assembly precisely because Catholicism asserts the compatibility of faith and reason—we seek the truth.

Gender, Sex, and Sexuality, Hidden Absolutes in the Assertion of Religious Freedom

Over three weeks in Vatican City, the 2018 Synod on Young People (on faith and vocational discernment) found the question of conscience emerging over and over in its small group discussions. In some ways, "conscience" came to stand for the many ways in which the experience of a young adult met the faith of the church amid the mediation of a quickly moving culture that locates "truth" and "authenticity" in expressive individualism. It was not surprising to find that reports from the Synod discussions tended to struggle with the balance between listening to the experience of young people, particularly when those experiences were at odds with church teaching, and emphasizing that a conscience formed by the church was the starting point for asserting its proper independence.[24] That particular struggle was almost inevitably about gender questions, whether the focus was sexual morality or identity (for example, the magisterium's discomfort with the designation "LGBT") or church norms about women (the fact that lay male religious, but not lay female religious, were selected as voting members of the synod was a flashpoint).

While our biological sex is given at birth—even if that "given" is indeterminate—"gender," the way in which we interpret (or even dispute) our sexed bodies, is forged at the intersection of received world and expressive subjectivity. Our experience of our sexed bodies is always already interpreted, an interpretation that *we have* because we always already have experiences in the world. In other words, we have no unmediated access to our sexed bodies, nor does our conscience proceed from an uninflected "point vierge."

Our conversational norms, including those that govern religion and gender, are forged in a similar social context. Thinking about charged topics such as abortion and same-sex marriage, Amelia Uelmen notes yet another dimension. These conversations take place not only in a context of actions and sanctions, they take place in a distinctly rhetorical context, in a fast-moving stream of ideas and claims, *of which the Church's voice is but one*. In this context, she notes, following John Haughey, that the rhetorical force of the language of "intrinsic evil" (language that appears in magisterial discussions of abortion and same-sex marriage) cuts through these discussions with a powerful absolutism. It calls believers to account for the ways in which their own reception of church teaching has been filtered or nuanced, and challenges the ways in which their own rhetoric has contributed to this evasion. Uelmen does recognize the need for scholarly discourse, for the back-and-forth of moral theologians as they parse careful distinctions.

> But from the perspective of pastors working to articulate a political and social framework, the concept of intrinsic evil holds a compelling power which may be, at least in part, the kind of energetic injection that Catholics need as they reflect on their role in political participation and public life. To use Haughey's metaphor, the concept of intrinsic evil helps to peel away the "stories" that "cover our actual moral condition in our communications with others" and "conceal our real condition even from ourselves."[25]

Thus, Uelmen applauds the language of *Forming Consciences for Faithful Citizenship* for its ability to bring the tension of this language into a pastorally focused discussion of Catholic voices in the public square. However, one could also ask if this use of language inevitably brings the shock of clarity envisioned by Haughey and Uelmen—or if this phrase simply imposes its *own* "story" that similarly "conceals." Is this rhetorical strategy, that "teaches" through the assertion of absolute truth, successful as a communication framework today?

This conundrum was certainly at issue in the competing conversations about conscience at the 2018 Synod. Some bishops stressed the role of a teaching church in the formation of conscience, others brought forward a listening church as a dialogical partner in this formation. All seemed to be aware, however, that public culture inflects the conversation on all sides. But what is revealed by this language when Haughey's "shock of clarity" applies only to questions of sex and gender?

In addition to the rhetorical context, there is also a social code that shapes our responses, one that emerges from a history of polarized discussions in the public square. Moral theologian Meghan Clark observes that in public conversation in the United States, law and justice tend to be conflated, *as if legality confers justice*. One example of this is the tendency to reduce undocumented immigrants to a single word, *illegals*, with the assumption that such a designation renders any consideration of the justice of a given situation moot, as if a concern for human dignity as a fundamental matter of justice was irrelevant in the face one whose total being is reduced to "illegal" in the face of "the law."[26] She reminds us that Martin Luther King Jr. not only broke the law in favor of justice, he also observed that the voices of white moderates often seemed to be "more devoted to 'order' than to justice."[27]

Indeed, in that scathing 1963 text "Letter from a Birmingham Jail," King's suspicion of "order" might also be seen as a rebuke of "decorum": King is seeking the shock of an interruption in the "decorum" of the white "order" that professes equality yet continues to practice the oppression and marginalization of black bodies. Here, too, the ghost of gender norms, interlaced with race and class, emerge more clearly in a consideration of the (assigned) role of women in the maintenance of "decorum." Contemporary African American women observe that white women in particular have been keenly invested in this pattern of "order-as-decorum." In her short story "The Welcome Table," Alice Walker needs only a few deft pages to sketch the story of an older African American woman, worn down by years of labor ("angular and lean…beaten by king cotton") who sets off on a Sunday morning to go to church. In a haze of age and encroaching senility, she walks into a church of white Christians and sits down, only to be tossed back into the street by the ushers. Walker's eye is on the white women of the church, and the way in which they need only a glance at their spouses to name what's at stake and what must be done.

> Those who knew saw the hesitant creeping up on them of the law, saw the beginning of the end of the sanctuary of Christian worship, saw the desecration of Holy Church, and saw an invasion of privacy, which they struggled to believe they still kept.[28]

For the members of that church, worship was a place where their sense of family, gender, and race could exist, unchallenged. In this sense of religion as a private sphere, of course, many things have gone unchallenged. In the recent words of one long-suffering woman who endured years of sexual abuse at the hands of a popular pastor without reporting it, "I didn't want to hurt the church."[29] Bridging that private space with public norms of accountability—for racism or sexism, for example—would, in this mindset, destroy what was most precious about it.

Therefore, in the current environment, Catholic voters need to ask questions as they are urged to vote in ways that will "preserve" "religious freedom." They should ask why some cases are championed as pertaining to religious freedom and some are not. They should know, as gender and public policy scholar Katherine Franke pointed out in a September 2018 essay in the *Washington Post*, that the Trump administration, led in these instances by Vice President Pence, has applied religious freedom protections in a highly partisan fashion, going far beyond the "government compelling interest" argument by simply targeting those with whom the administration does not agree. Thus, Franke observes, the religious convictions that move Unitarians to provide food and water for migrants crossing the Arizona desert, or Catholic religious women to protest a natural gas pipeline, are discounted.[30] Even if one supports the cases of religious freedom that the government supports—allowing entities not to have to provide contraception to employees or allow same-sex couples to adopt children—the concentration of "key issues" around sex and gender, as if these are the defining issues, should give Catholics pause.

In a recent address to the College Theology Society, theologian William Portier highlighted Pope Francis's use of the singular *America*, when addressing the U.S. Congress, to indicate the continuity among the peoples and countries of North and South America. Portier found this to be a necessary corrective to those who would suggest "a providential fit between Catholic natural law tradition and U.S. political institutions." Those in the United States make common cause on the basis of our commitment to the freedoms outlined in the First Amendment, Portier affirms, citing columnist E. J. Dionne's rejection, in April 2017, of the notion that our national bond is one of "blood and soil."[31] Yet "blood and soil," a phrase that animated German nationalism in the late-nineteenth and twentieth centuries, would echo on this side of the Atlantic just a few months later, as torches were raised in Charlottesville,

Virginia, the following August, in a recurrence of a nationalist racism that is always wedded to a perversion of traditional sexual norms. For this view, when racialized ties of blood are normative in a "masculinized," "nationalist" public square, the policing of "our women" in private will not be far behind.

In Conclusion

As Catholics consider their participation in public life, they should consider the actual object of calls for religious freedom. We know we don't see that freedom as a millennialist triumph that binds Christ to the progress of a specific country, nor do we see religious faith as something irrational, a precious hobby to be shielded from a fully secularized public square. We exercise our religious faith in dynamic conversation with a culture—indeed, in the history of the Christian faith, one cannot neatly separate the two. We more properly would draw on an approach that encourages dialogue between the common cause that animates "civil religionists" and the institutional integrity that "religious separationists" sought to preserve.[32]

Even with these, however, gender is the ghost haunting the idea of religious freedom, as this is exercised, for the most part, in the United States today. What is the story about sex and sexuality and gender that is most in need of privacy, of protection? Why is it that the policing of what it means to be female and male—particularly female—is seen as something that cannot be justified in the public square, and thus must be labelled as "private" "religious practice." When did the heart of Roman Catholicism get reduced to a private, sectarian attitude about sexual norms? By removing the story of sex and gender from public reason and public scrutiny, Catholics have forfeited their claim on the public square. That public square of civic virtue needs the rich tradition of faith and reason more than ever, risky as that project will be, as the human body becomes increasingly not only enhanced by, but a de facto product of technology. Fear of an open and free democracy, one that invites all to the table, should not keep us home, shielded by a false sense of freedom.

NOTES

1. Michael J. O'Loughlin, "New Data Suggest Clinton, Not Trump, Won Catholic Vote," *America*, April 6, 2017, https://www.americamagazine.org/politics-society/2017/04/06/new-data-suggest-clinton-not-trump-won-catholic-vote.

2. *Forming Consciences for Faithful Citizenship*, http://www.usccb.org/issues-and-action/faithful-citizenship/upload/forming-consciences-for-faithful-citizenship.pdf.

3. *Forming Consciences for Faithful Citizenship* 72.

4. Mark M. Gray, "Is Partisanship Trumping Faith," Nineteen Sixty-Four blog, June 19, 2018, http://nineteensixty-four.blogspot.com/2018/06/is-partisanship-trumping-faith.html.

5. Eric Sammons, "The Danger of the 'Common Good,'" Catholic Vote, October 3, 2018, https://www.catholicvote.org/the-danger-of-the-common-good/.

6. *Declaration on Religious Freedom* 6.

7. Archbishop Lori, "2016 Fortnight for Freedom Opening Homily," June 21, 2016, http://www.usccb.org/issues-and-action/religious-liberty/2016-fortnight-for-freedom-opening-homily-archbishop-lori.cfm.

8. Stephen F. Schneck, "President Kennedy and Archbishop Chaput: Religion and Faith in American Public Life," in *Voting and Holiness: Catholic Perspectives on Political Participation*, ed. Nicholas P. Cafardi (New York: Paulist Press, 2012), 232.

9. Schneck, "President Kennedy and Archbishop Chaput," 235.

10. *Declaration on Religious Freedom* 2. Gregory A. Kalscheur, "Conscience and Citizenship: The Primacy of Conscience for Catholics in Public Life," in Cafardi, *Voting and Holiness*, 107–25.

11. *Declaration on Religious Freedom* 5.

12. In 2015, "Sixty-seven percent (67%) of those currently married had cohabited before marriage with one or more partners [most likely, one of these was their current spouse]. Many of those currently unmarried or not cohabiting had cohabited before." Scott Stanley and Galena Rhoades, "Cohabitation Is Pervasive," Institute for Family Studies, June 20, 2018, https://ifstudies.org/blog/cohabitation-is-pervasive.

13. Luke A. Gatta, "Conscience in the Public Square: The Pivoting Positions of the USCCB and the ACLU around the Religious Freedom Restoration Act," *The Linacre Quarterly* 83 (2016): 447.

14. For example, the USCCB would hew to the language of Vatican II's *Declaration on Religious Freedom* in its claim that religious freedom means "that all men are to be immune from coercion on the part of individuals or of social groups and of any human power, in such wise that no one is to be forced to act in a manner contrary to his own beliefs, whether privately or publicly, whether alone or in association with others, within due limits."

15. Gatta, "Conscience in the Public Square," 448.

16. Gatta, "Conscience in the Public Square," 449.

17. Gatta, "Conscience in the Public Square," 450.

18. Cathleen Kaveny, "The Bishops and Religious Liberty," *Commonweal*, May 30, 2012, https://www.commonwealmagazine.org/bishops -religious-liberty.

19. Kaveny, "The Bishops and Religious Liberty."

20. "Remarks by Vice President Pence at Ministerial to Advance Religious Freedom," The White House, July 26, 2018, https://www.whitehouse .gov/briefings-statements/remarks-vice-president-pence-ministerial-advance -religious-freedom/.

21. The Editorial Board, Op-ed, "A Too-Narrow Vision of Religious Freedom," *New York Times*, August 18, 2018, https://www.nytimes.com/2018/ 08/18/opinion/sunday/trump-pence-religious-freedom-evangelicals.html.

22. "A Too-Narrow Vision of Religious Freedom."

23. "Religious Liberty," Catholic Vote, accessed November 27, 2019, https://catholicvote.org/discover/religious-liberty/.

24. Michael J. O'Loughlin, "Catholic Teaching on Conscience Is (Again) Topic of Discussion at Synod," *America*, October 16, 2018, https:// www.americamagazine.org/faith/2018/10/16/catholic-teaching-conscience -again-topic-discussion-synod.

25. Amelia J. Uelmen, "It's Hard Work: Reflections on Conscience and Citizenship in the Catholic Tradition," *Journal of Catholic Legal Studies* 47 (2017): 334–35. See also John C. Haughey, "*Veritatis Splendor* and Our Cover Stories," in Veritatis Splendor*: American Responses*, ed. Michael E. Allsopp and John J. O'Keefe (Lanham, MD: Rowan & Littlefield, 1995), 269–77.

26. Meghan J. Clark, "Why the Christian Call to Justice Supersedes the Legal Order," *U.S. Catholic* 83, no. 10 (October 2018): 10, https://www .uscatholic.org/articles/201809/why-christian-call-justice-supersedes-legal -order-31510.

27. Martin Luther King Jr., "Letter from a Birmingham Jail," April 16, 1963, https://www.africa.upenn.edu/Articles_Gen/Letter_Birmingham .html.

28. Alice Walker, "The Welcome Table," in *Listening for God: Contemporary Literature and the Life of Faith*, vol. 1, ed. Paula J. Carlson (Minneapolis: Augsburg Fortress, 1994), 110–11.

29. Laurie Goodstein, "He's a Superstar Pastor. She Worked for Him and Says He Groped Her Repeatedly," *New York Times*, August 5, 2018, https:// www.nytimes.com/2018/08/05/us/bill-hybels-willow-creek-pat-baranowski .html.

30. Katherine Franke, "Religious Freedom for Me, but Not for Thee," *Washington Post*, September 28, 2018, https://www.washingtonpost.com/ opinions/religious-freedom-for-me-but-not-for-thee/2018/09/28/297fffb4 -c340-11e8-8f06-009b39c3f6dd_story.html?utm_term=.2a5f3fe536d1.   Even more troubling is the recent case of Domineque Ray, whose request for an imam to be present at his execution was denied by the Supreme Court. USCCB, "U.S. Bishops' Chairmen Condemn Decision Preventing Muslim Man from Receiving Appropriate Spiritual Care at Execution," February 8, 2019, http://www.usccb.org/news/2019/19-034.cfm.

31. William L. Portier, "Reimagining the 'America' in American Catholicism," *Horizons* 44 (2017): 451, citing E. J. Dionne, "We Don't Call It Nationalists' Day," *Washington Post*, April 17, 2017. (Yet, at an October 22, 2018, rally in Houston, President Trump embraced the term. "'Really, we're not supposed to use that word,' he told supporters in a nod to the usual political sensibilities that he relishes disrupting. 'You know what I am? I'm a nationalist, O.K.? I'm a nationalist. Nationalist! Use that word! Use that word!'" Peter Baker, "'Use That Word!': Trump Embraces the 'Nationalist' Label," *New York Times*, October 23, 2018, https://www.nytimes.com/2018/10/23/us/politics/nationalist -president-trump.html).

32. Schneck, "President Kennedy and Archbishop Chaput," 232–35.

Questions for Further Reflection

1. The author says that neither major political party "maps onto the bishops' vision" in *Faithful Citizenship*. What does she mean by that?

2. In the 2016 elections, a large percentage of Catholic voters identified with neither political party. How large was this group and what were their concerns? How supportive were they of Church positions? Why do you suppose that such a large percentage of Catholics identified with neither political party?

3. What is the organization "Catholic Vote" and how have they represented or misrepresented the values of *Faithful Citizenship*? How

does the author think this group gets away with their distortion of *Faithful Citizenship*? Why would the bishops not call them to account for this?

4. What did the Second Vatican Council say about the right to religious freedom? On what notion is the idea that the state cannot compel or coerce religious belief based?

5. Has there been a stable concept of freedom of religion from the beginning of our republic? What were the founders' notions about the role of religion in public life? Which of those models drives the culture war debates of our times?

6. Explain what the author means by a clash between a "soft" millennialism and a rather "dogmatic" secularism? What does the author mean by these terms? To what results does she say this clash leads? How do these conflicting ideologies handle sexual issues?

7. How has the Catholic Church approached freedom of religion? How does it relate to conscience? How does it relate to the public square?

8. What historical circumstances led to the passage of the Religious Freedom Restoration Act (RFRA)? Which groups supported it? Why? What was the position of the U.S. bishops on RFRA? What about the ACLU? What has its position been? Why?

9. The author cites Kaveny for the proposition that while Catholics see a secular society infringing on its beliefs, the secular society sees a religious organization that wishes to discriminate. What does she mean by this? What societal/religious issues are involved here? What do these issues center around?

10. The author says that in the list of freedoms protected by the First Amendment, the understanding of freedom of religion has developed in ways that the understanding of the other First Amendment freedoms (speech, press, assembly, and petitioning the government for redress of grievances) have not. What has been distinct about the way the understanding of freedom of religion has developed? What argument did Pence make to advance this distinction? Why would "Catholic Vote" agree with Pence?

11. According to the author, why is this view of religion problematic for Catholics?

12. How did the question of conscience emerge at the 2018 Synod on Young People? What part did the experience of young people

play in this discussion? What happens when our experience is at odds with Church teachings? In what areas does this conflict seem most likely to occur? What do we look to in order to form our consciences: our own experience, Church teaching, or both?

13. In discussions on abortion and same-sex marriage, what is the effect of the rhetoric of "intrinsic evil"? Does it help to bring clarity or contention? What has been your own experience in discussing these issues and deciding where you stand on them? Do you think such issues are properly dealt with in the political realm?

14. The author, citing Meg Clark, says that in our discussions law and justice tend to get conflated, as if legality confers justice. What examples does the author give of this? Do you agree? Can you think of any other examples?

15. Why does the author cite the short story "The Welcome Table" by Alice Walker? What point is the author making with this story?

16. The author says that religious freedom protections can be applied in a highly partisan way. What examples does she give of this? Do you agree with these examples? Why or why not?

17. Why should Catholics be cautious of calls for religious freedom in the political arena? What harms can or have such claims led to?

6

How to Speak to Nones and All

Integrity about Religious Liberty

Bernard G. Prusak

Introduction

St. Peter's bark is leaking, if not yet foundering, and faith in democracy, too, appears to be in significant decline. How might Catholic bishops, educators, public intellectuals, and all other believers still in the pews—more specifically, those who hold that there is a distinctively Catholic witness and contribution to make to U.S. public life—respond? In the words of the chapter's title, how to speak to nones and all?

The Growth of Religious Disaffiliation and Democratic Decline

Here are some data points indicating the cultural context for this inquiry. According to a Pew Research Center survey published in 2015, slightly more than half of U.S. adults raised as Catholics have left the church at some point.[1] About one in five of those adults returned to the church, but two-thirds no longer consider themselves Catholic in any way, even so-called cultural Catholics.[2] Of those ex-Catholics, about one-fourth became conservative Evangelical Protestants (think of Vice President Mike Pence), and another quarter joined some other religion, but half became disaffiliated from religion altogether.[3] That is, they joined the growing number of "nones," currently nearing one quarter of U.S. adults, which is around the same number of U.S. Catholics in a population of 325 million.[4] Notwithstanding, the number of U.S. Catholics has held more or less steady over the last several decades, sustained by higher birth rates to Catholic women and all the more by immigration from predominantly Catholic countries.[5] As two researchers note, "Without the inflow of Latinos…, the American Catholic population would have experienced a catastrophic collapse."[6] Yet it has been found that, as Latinos and Latinas become more "Americanized," like everyone else they become more likely to leave the Catholic church, either joining another Christian tradition or disaffiliating from religion altogether.[7]

The trend toward disaffiliation is most pronounced among millennials, people who reached adulthood after 2000. All told, around a third of millennials identify as nones.[8] In a 2014 survey, 60 percent of millennials raised as Catholics reported never praying or attending church.[9] Equally telling, Georgetown University's Center for Applied Research in the Apostolate reports that church marriages have declined nearly 300 percent since 1970.[10] And while it has been found that teens raised in more conservative or self-styled orthodox Catholic households are somewhat more likely to practice into adulthood than are teens from more liberal Catholic households,[11] even enthusiasts for conservative Catholicism acknowledge that it has proved "a preservationist enterprise more than a dynamic one" inasmuch as it has "limited decline without producing impressive new growth."[12] What is more, it is worth noting that the association of religion with countercultural, reactionary politics appears to have been a significant factor in the growth of religious disaffiliation over the last thirty years.[13] People, especially young people, weakly attached to religion have increasingly become *other than* religious as prominent religious leaders have condemned and sought to turn back movements of personal liberation.[14] Surely the church's recurring sexual abuse scandal has not helped either.

Consistent with those findings, the image of the none in the news tends to be relatively young, college-educated, well-off, and politically progressive. These are, for example, the "spiritual but not religious" millennials who have engaged in dialogue with Catholic religious sisters in the initiative "Nuns & Nones."[15] According to 2016 statistics, however, more than 40 percent of the disaffiliated had a high school education or less,[16] and in 2014 a full third had incomes less than $30,000.[17] The "other nones," as they are called by the sociologist Nancy Ammerman, are more disengaged and more distrustful of social institutions.[18] By way of example, they are less likely to be married than high-education affiliates, high-education nones, and low-education affiliates. For what it is worth, they are also the least likely of all those groups to identify as Democrats. Instead, it appears they are the people who won Donald Trump the Republican nomination for the presidency and for whom President Trump's vision of "American carnage," in his inauguration address, squared with what they were seeing.[19]

Then there is declining faith in democracy to reckon with. Here again millennials stand out. According to data collected between 2010 and 2014, only 30 percent of millennials in the United States believed that it is "essential" to live in a democracy, as compared to more than 70 percent among people born before World War II.[20] A 2011 poll found that nearly a quarter of Americans between the ages of sixteen and twenty-four believed that democracy is a "bad" or "very bad" form of government.[21] Finally, whereas more than 40 percent of older Americans rejected the legitimacy of a military takeover should a democratically elected government prove incompetent, not even 20 percent of millennials agreed.[22] Coincidentally or not, this decline in faith in democracy has been joined in recent years by an attack on the unwritten rules of democracy, especially the need to exercise forbearance in the use of presidential power.[23] Against that background, it is no longer melodramatic to worry that even the United States might be slouching toward authoritarianism.

So let us consider again the question with which this chapter opened: How might Catholic bishops, educators, public intellectuals, and all other believers in the pews respond? How might they speak to Catholics, especially young Catholics, who are weakly attached to the church and presumably among the great numbers who are increasingly weakly attached to democracy?

Benedictine or Franciscan?

One recently prominent way to answer this question needs our attention before we go any further: the bishops and the rest should stop trying. That is the position of the political pundit Rod Dreher, who takes inspiration from a suggestion by Cardinal Joseph Ratzinger, before he became Pope Benedict XVI, that the future of Christianity in the West may be to "exist in small, seemingly insignificant groups that nonetheless live in an intensive struggle against evil and bring the good into the world."[24] Dreher adds that committed believers "will have to be somewhat cut off from mainstream society for the sake of holding onto the truth."[25] In his dramatic terms, in the current "culture of death," this "new Dark Age" of the West in which "we faithful orthodox Christians" find ourselves in "internal exile from a country we thought was our own," the only way to respond, if the faith is to "survive another generation or two," is to try "to build a Christian way of life that stands as an island of sanctity and stability amid the high tide of liquid modernity."[26] In sum:

> Rather than wasting energy and resources fighting unwinnable political battles, we should instead work on building communities, institutions, and networks of resistance that can outwit, outlast, and eventually overcome the occupation.[27]

There are at least two reasons to reject this response. First, as Bishop Robert McElroy of San Diego has remarked, "the unity of the Church must come from fidelity to the Gospel," not from an external threat.[28] And the gospel calls followers of Christ to go out to all the world to proclaim the good news of God's redemptive love.[29] Tending to the health of our communities and institutions, in the interest of transmitting faith from one generation to the next, certainly is crucial in this regard, but the end those communities and institutions serve goes beyond self-preservation, with the upshot that they must risk engaging with the dominant culture if they are to be true to themselves.[30] Second, the occupation, so to speak, consists of us. The Catholic Church is not a sect that could separate itself from the dominant culture.[31] Growing numbers of the 70 million-plus Catholics in the United States may be disaffiliating from the church, but a church that gave up on the baptized, practicing or not, would be giving up on its own theology and itself.[32] Moreover, withdrawing from the dominant culture in order to rebuild the church may or may not be Benedictine,[33] but it is clearly not Franciscan, at least as Pope Francis has shown that face of the church: reaching out to the "peripheries,"[34] ministering to the poor in body and spirit as well as the rich, or varying the image the tares as well as the wheat.

Pope Francis has indicated one direction for what bishops and the rest might say. "We cannot insist only on issues related to abortion, gay marriage, and contraception," the Pope famously remarked. "The church's pastoral ministry cannot be obsessed with the transmission of a disjointed multitude of doctrines to be imposed insistently."[35] In light of the well-documented disagreement of millennials with the bishops on homosexuality above all,[36] a reorientation of church teaching to lead with concern for all the destitute, abandoned, and underprivileged does appear well-advised.[37] But while it would be natural to focus first and foremost on *what* to say—and here we could argue, as many have, about the wisdom of the U.S. bishops' voter guide, *Forming Consciences for Faithful Citizenship*[38]—this chapter's concern is subtly different: as the title indicates, it is with *how* Catholic bishops, educators, and public intellectuals might speak to nones and all. In other words, this chapter is concerned with the question of style, as in the French expression, "*Le style, c'est l'homme même*": style is the man himself.

The Question of Style

It might be tempting to dismiss that expression as superficial.[39] After all, we should look beyond style, it might be countered, to the substance of a man or woman. Yet what a person is about is not so easily separable from how he or she goes about it. As the Jesuit historian John O'Malley has observed, "How I am—mean or kind, manipulative or straightforward—tells you the kind of human being I am."[40] Style is not merely ornamentation or dressing, say the pitch of a voice or the cut of a piece of clothing. Instead, considered more fully, the style of a speech, for example, can speak louder than its words. Style matters. This is a lesson that O'Malley and more recently the Catholic moral theologian and legal scholar (and contributor to this volume) Cathleen Kaveny have developed at length: O'Malley with attention to both Vatican II and what he calls the prophetic, academic, humanistic, and artistic cultures

of the West,[41] Kaveny with attention to the rhetoric of prophetic indictment, on the one hand, and the discourse of moral deliberation, on the
other.[42]

Style matters because it is communicative itself, for example of
respect or contempt, openness or close-mindedness. Imagine that you
have just introduced yourself to someone. What is communicated by
a vacant stare in response? On another level, the Holocaust survivor
Primo Levi recounts an interaction he had with a German chemist,
one Doktor Pannwitz, in Auschwitz. The Germans in charge of the
concentration camp had learned that Levi trained as a chemist in Italy;
he is brought to Pannwitz to prove his credentials, which if he does
means that he might be judged useful and allowed to survive. When
Levi is presented, the look Pannwitz gives him, Levi writes, "was not
between two men." It was, Levi goes on, "as if across the glass window
of an aquarium between two beings who live in different worlds."[43] We
can conclude: while certainly the medium is not always the whole of a
message, it is at least a message, and sometimes it is really all we need
to know. For one last example, the U.S. bishops' reported choice to produce videos to supplement *Faithful Citizenship* for the next presidential election cycle communicates that they care to meet people "where they are,"
so to speak, which it appears is increasingly watching videos on personal
devices rather than reading long essays.[44] The choice of medium conveys a message, but in this case it is hardly the whole of the message that
the bishops intend to communicate, and the choice of videos to speak to
people hardly exhausts the questions the bishops need to consider, including *how* the videos should go about trying to speak to people wherever
they are.

This chapter's title points to its question; the subtitle points to its
answer. One possible answer to the question of how to speak to nones
and all is what might be called a politics of integrity. By a politics of
integrity, understand a style of engagement in the public square. But
now we need to consider this question: What is it to carry oneself with
integrity? Otherwise put, what does modeling integrity look like?

On Integrity

In the political context, integrity is typically understood as "fidelity to those projects and principles which are constitutive of one's core

identity."[45] In other words, it is a matter of acting on one's own views, which presumably one believes to be the correct views, though the crucial consideration here is that they are one's own.[46] Thus understood, integrity bears a close resemblance to the ethic of expressive individualism, which is increasingly powerful in Western cultures.[47] Not surprisingly then, this is also the understanding of integrity that figures in the proliferating conscience wars within our culture wars: the many battles that have broken out in recent years pitting people committed to more traditional, conservative personal morality against people whose conduct they believe to be wrong, or in religious terms, sinful. By way of example, should a baker, florist, or photographer who objects to gay marriage have to service one anyway? Or should a gay couple who wants to be treated as equals to everyone else simply take no for an answer and seek services elsewhere? The central question in these battles may be put succinctly: Who should have to accommodate whom?

The identity view of integrity, as it is called, might seem to have little to recommend it to a tradition, like Catholicism, that holds that moral or evaluative truths do indeed exist and may be discovered by thinking objectively (carefully, critically, in dialogue with others) about the goods toward which we human beings are naturally drawn.[48] After all, what value should be accorded to acting on our *own* views whether those views are right or wrong? To make that question more pointed, does integrity have any value when a person's views appear just wrong?[49]

Yet the value of integrity, even so understood, should not be underestimated. As one philosopher has remarked, "Given the temptations we all face to backslide and act hypocritically, being faithful to one's core commitments is a rare and worthy thing." By contrast, "Acting inconsistently with one's professed values is always a moral failure, considered simply as such."[50] Accordingly, as a rule, a politics of integrity would acknowledge the value of a person's seeking to live out his or her views, whether we agree with those views or not, which is to say even when we disagree. In other words, as a rule, a politics of integrity would commend people for clearly articulating and standing by their views.[51] That is one (more) way that bishops and the rest might begin to speak to nones and all "where they are," even and perhaps especially when nones bring different, nontraditional points of view.

But it is only a beginning. Even if we agree that fidelity to core commitments is a rare and worthy thing, the identity view of integrity yields an incomplete picture of integrity as a moral excellence or virtue—that is, a way a person has of carrying herself in the world, which is where the question of style reenters our considerations. To be sure, a person of integrity stands by her views: she does not simply cave to pressure, as a person deficient in integrity does. To that extent, the identity view of integrity is correct: fidelity to core convictions is clearly a key part of what integrity is about. But it is just as clear that a person who refuses to entertain and take seriously reasons to revise her views is also deficient in integrity, though this person fails by going to the opposite extreme. She is not spineless, weak-willed, a backslider, or a hypocrite, but still she is in some sense lacking in honesty with herself.

To come at the same point from a different direction, if it is always a moral failure for a person to act inconsistently with her professed values, it is likewise a moral failure for a person to refuse to hear and weigh reasons to reevaluate those values.[52] A person who is so adamant about her views that she will not listen to people who think differently exhibits a vice, not the virtue of integrity. She exhibits what we might call a kind of spiritual stenosis. Her faithfulness to her views risks becoming idolatry, for she thinks more highly of herself than is warranted for a fallible, limited human being. By contrast, a person of integrity stands by her best judgment of what is really valuable or what ought to be done, but it is also part of integrity to recognize that, after all, our best judgment might be lacking, or at least open still to improvement.[53] Accordingly, standing by our best judgment means being open to hearing challenges to it.[54]

The upshot is that a politics of integrity would do more than acknowledge and honor the integrity of others. In seeking to model integrity fully, it would also make a point of listening to others and of taking seriously the challenges they present. It would eschew the defensive crouch and aggressiveness of the cultural warrior and seek to exemplify instead the humility befitting one deliberator among others. In so doing, it would model faith in democracy as well—in the capacity of we the people to come to terms with one another, which is to say find compromise that different parties can have good reason to affirm. Arguably, this is a style of politics that has lately gone missing in the United States.

Religious Liberty as Example

It is not difficult to imagine the retort at this point that such a politics is not only all too idealistic, but naive as well. Admittedly, with the recent (2018) change in the Supreme Court, it seems more than likely that our culture wars will intensify, as they did during the confirmation hearings of Justice Brett Kavanaugh. One consequence likely will be a yet greater exodus from the church; another likely will be the deepening of loss of faith in democracy, as the possibility of satisfactory compromise comes to appear ever more fantastic. Yet it would be a sin against the Spirit to give in to despair, as it would be a betrayal of the Prince of Peace to be seduced by the dream of winning the culture wars through the courts, as if the sexual revolution, women's liberation, and the movement toward equality for LGBT people could be overturned by judicial fiat.

It would be a yet deeper betrayal not to seek terms of peace when they can be had. So, this chapter will close by considering, in that light, how Catholics might practice a politics of integrity in the proliferating conscience wars briefly discussed above. The last decade's battles over the Affordable Care Act's so-called contraceptive mandate and over the legal obligations, or not, of bakers and florists and photographers to service gay weddings have all turned on what two legal scholars call "complicity-based conscience claims," which are "religious objections to being made complicit in the assertedly sinful conduct of others."[55] The United States Conference of Catholic Bishops filed briefs in support of such objections in each of the three major religious liberty cases that came before the U.S. Supreme Court over the last five-plus years: *Burwell v. Hobby Lobby* (2014), *Zubik v. Burwell* (2016), and *Masterpiece Cakeshop v. Colorado Civil Rights Commission* (2018). Say that the bishops were to make modeling integrity a priority. What difference might that make for the bishops' engagement in the public square on matters of religious liberty?

In all three briefs, the bishops cite a similar case that the Supreme Court decided nearly forty years ago, *Thomas v. Review Board of the Indiana Employment Security Division* (1981). Eddie Thomas was a Jehovah's Witness. He worked at a roll foundry making sheet steel, which is used to make in turn all sorts of things. The roll foundry closed, however, and Thomas's employer gave him a new job making tank turrets. For religious reasons, Thomas sought to be reassigned to work that was not directly for military purposes, only to learn that all his employer's remaining operations were in arms production. So he asked to be laid off. After his employer denied his request, he quit and applied for unemployment benefits in Indiana, his state of residence. But his application was denied, despite the recognition that he acted on his religious beliefs as a Jehovah's Witness, thus giving rise to the religious liberty case that eventually came before the Supreme Court.

In an 8–1 decision, the Court observed that Thomas "drew a line" between working in the roll foundry, which he found "sufficiently insulated from producing weapons of war," and working on tank turrets, which he believed made him complicit in the evil of war-making.[56] The Court went on to state that "it is not for us to say that the line he drew was an unreasonable one."[57] For "religious beliefs need not be acceptable, logical, consistent, or comprehensible in order to merit First Amendment protection."[58] Instead, the Court considered the question before it simply whether Thomas "terminated his work because of an honest conviction that such work was forbidden by his religion."[59]

Now there is an important confusion in the Court's decision. It is one thing sincerely to believe, on religious grounds, that war-making (or whatever else) is evil and that complicity in war-making (or whatever else) is likewise. Government, including the judiciary, has no business judging the reasonableness of such beliefs, or trying to arbitrate controversies among religious believers about how to interpret religious scriptures and traditions on such questions.[60] That much the majority decision in *Thomas* certainly has right.[61] But it is quite a different thing sincerely to believe that this or that particular action makes one complicit against one's religion. Here government surely must judge the reasonableness of the belief, unless it is prepared to countenance objections that might seem frivolous or even absurd.

Imagine that Eddie Thomas had not lost his job in the roll foundry, but instead quit after coming to believe that even making sheet steel made him complicit in evil, as some of that steel might go toward war-making, just as some tax dollars do. Would the Supreme Court have insisted that Thomas was entitled to draw that line, too, and that government just had to respect it without considering whether it was reasonable? What about the conscientious objector to war who refuses to pay taxes on the grounds that she sincerely believes doing so makes her complicit in evil against religious beliefs she also sincerely holds? Is the belief that paying taxes makes her complicit in war-making a religious belief beyond the scrutiny of the Court?—unlike, say, claims to have been treated negligently?[62] If so, should it be accommodated on grounds of free exercise of religion, or at least under the terms of the Religious Freedom Restoration Act (RFRA)?[63] Relying on Supreme Court precedent, the IRS currently rejects such arguments as frivolous.[64]

To clarify, the distinction that needs attention is between (1) sincerely believing on religious grounds that war-making (or whatever else) is evil and that complicity in war-making (or whatever else) is likewise and (2) sincerely believing that a particular action makes one complicit against one's religion.[65] Without question, the belief that war-making is evil may be a religious belief. There are more than a few Christian traditions, for example, that take Jesus's injunctions against violence to the letter.[66] The judiciary has no business considering the rightness or wrongness of that interpretation of the relevant biblical texts. It also may be a religious teaching that complicity in war-making is evil. The historical peace churches, like the Mennonites, again make for an example,[67] and again the judiciary has no business assessing this teaching. Further, religious authorities may teach that a particular action counts as complicity, and they may draw on a tradition of moral theology in order to make that claim, but it is a mistake to call such a claim itself religious and, on those grounds, to excuse it from the test of reasonableness.

The right understanding of the ethics of cooperation—that is, of when one is permitted to assist a principal agent in carrying out an act—is indeed important for religious authorities seeking to give believers guidance, and as it happens much of the terminology used in discussing the ethics of cooperation is derived from the Roman Catholic tradition. As the philosopher David Oderberg has observed, however, the theory of the ethics of cooperation developed in the Catholic tradition "has nothing particularly religious about it: it stands as a piece of moral philosophy," which is to say a work of human wisdom.[68] Moreover,

> applying principles of co-operation…to the facts of a particular case is a matter of *logic, prudence, and common sense*, not a matter of religious belief. When theologians, or religious authorities, apply the principles of co-operation to particular cases, they are neither explaining existing religious teaching, nor amplifying it. They are using logic, prudence, and common sense to derive particular conclusions about particular cases.[69]

It follows that the Supreme Court erred in treating Thomas's line-drawing as a religious belief beyond its scrutiny. In fact, the line Thomas drew between working in the roll foundry and working on tank turrets appears quite reasonable. He was aware that the sheet steel he made in the roll foundry could be used by others to make weapons of war, but he rightly understood his cooperation in what he believed to be the evil of war-making as remote, as his making sheet steel did not provide a probable instrument of wrongful use. Thus, it would have been unreasonable of him to hold that making sheet steel made him complicit in war-making. By contrast, making tank turrets is reasonably considered proximate to the making of war: it is reasonable to think that the cooperator's action does provide a probable instrument of what he believes to be wrongful use.[70] So the Court could have decided in favor of Thomas, as it did, but without treating his belief that a particular action was immoral and contrary to his religious beliefs as *itself a religious belief* that was not subject to the test of reasonableness.[71]

It might be objected: Why couldn't the belief that a particular action counts as immoral cooperation be religious, and what is meant by "religious" here anyway? In response, recall the story according to which Eddie Thomas did not lose his job in the roll foundry, but instead quit after coming to believe that even making sheet steel made him complicit in evil, as some of that steel might go toward war-making, just as some tax dollars do. Should we call such a belief "religious"? No doubt we could, given how elastic the term is, and perhaps our fictional Eddie Thomas would do so himself following legal advice, but what is gained through that choice is obfuscation. What is obfuscated is the fact that he is making a judgment about a particular case. Assessing the reasonableness of that judgment does not require assessing the reasonableness of his religious beliefs about the wrongness of war and the wrongness of complicity in war-making. Instead, the question is whether he has reasonable grounds to believe that a particular action, here making sheet steel, threatens to make him complicit against his religious beliefs. Are courts really to say to objectors: You alone are entitled to make that judgment, and under the terms of the First Amendment, or at least RFRA, government has no right to second-guess the judgment you make, but must seek ways to accommodate it, whether it is reasonable or not? The position hardly seems credible.

Against this background, integrity requires the bishops to cease claiming that "it should go without saying that it is the *particular religious objector's* view of complicity that is controlling,"[72] which is to say all that should matter to a court. That is correct as a characterization of the precedent set by *Thomas*, but the Court in *Thomas* was confused—as was the majority opinion in *Hobby Lobby* when it made use of *Thomas*,[73] and as was Justice Neil Gorsuch's concurring opinion in *Masterpiece*.[74]

There are at least three reasons why the bishops should be wary of perpetuating this confusion. First, it behooves Christians to put acknowledging truth before winning battles in our culture wars. People with worldly power might ask skeptically, "What is truth?"—after all, it does not always prevail in the court of law or in public opinion—but that of course is Pilate speaking, not Jesus.[75] The truth in question here is that a sincere belief that a particular action makes one complicit in what one believes, on religious grounds, to be evil is not itself a *religious* belief, but instead a judgment that is rightly subject to scrutiny, just as a claim to have been treated negligently is. Further, despite the bishops' claims to the contrary, a court would not be "substitut[ing] its own theology for that of a religious objector" by assessing the reasonableness of an objector's claim.[76] Theology is not needed to assess whether a claim is reasonable or not; logic, prudence, and common sense are, which courts excel in exercising. Admittedly, we need still an elaborated jurisprudence of cooperation, but there is no reason to think it could not be developed by courts as they go about the work of coming to terms with relevant cases.[77]

The second reason why the bishops should be wary is that, as noted in passing above, the Court's confusion about cooperation risks generating absurd results. The reason why the bishops should care about this risk is none other than the third reason why they should be wary of perpetuating the Court's confusion: namely, absurd results risk generating both resentment and eventually a backlash against the cause of religious liberty, which has already become suspect as cover for trying to undo cultural change.[78]

Unfortunately, *Zubik* makes for an apt example. Like *Hobby Lobby* two years prior, *Zubik* was focused on the Affordable Care Act's contraceptive mandate. More precisely, the case was concerned with whether the accommodations to the contraceptive mandate established by the Obama administration for religious nonprofit employers (as opposed to houses of worship) satisfied the terms of RFRA, or instead violated the petitioners' religious liberty. The petitioners, including Bishop David Zubik of Pittsburgh and, notoriously, the Little Sisters of the Poor, claimed that having to inform the federal government, their insurer, or their third-party administrator (TPA) that they were opting out of providing coverage for contraceptives would make them complicit in its provision, since the government, their insurer, or their TPA would then provide the coverage to which the petitioners objected. As Oderberg has remarked, however, "If explicitly opting out of some activity ipso facto made a person a cooperator in that activity, then the very idea of opting out would lose all meaning."[79] Now it is important to note that Oderberg is a defender of religious liberty over and against what he calls secular authoritarianism.[80] If friends of religious liberty find the petitioners' argument in *Zubik* absurd, imagine how it will play with people who are already put off by religion on account of its association with countercultural, reactionary politics.

Conclusion

How, then, should Catholic bishops, educators, public intellectuals, and all other believers respond? Visibly and deliberately listening to, taking seriously, engaging, and sometimes even granting opposing points of views might not lead the nones to return to religion, but millennials would have one less reason to leave it, and democracy, too, would have one less strike against it. In positive terms, by thus respecting millennials, Catholics might thereby earn respect in turn, which surely the church could use these days. Likewise, our democracy could use the vote of confidence that Catholics would show by seeking compromise rather than capitulation. Those seem like strong reasons indeed for Catholic bishops, educators, public intellectuals, and all other believers to try a new, less aggressive, more humble style of engagement in the public square.[81]

NOTES

1. Caryle Murphy, "Half of U.S. Adults Raised Catholic Have Left the Church at Some Point," Pew Research Center, September 15, 2015, http://www.pewresearch.org/fact-tank/2015/09/15/half-of-u-s-adults-raised-catholic-have-left-the-church-at-some-point/.

2. Murphy, "Half of U.S. Adults Raised Catholic." See further David Masci, "Who Are 'Cultural Catholics'?" Pew Research Center, September 3, 2015, http://www.pewresearch.org/fact-tank/2015/09/03/who-are-cultural-catholics/.

3. Michael Hout, "Saint Peter's Leaky Boat: Falling Intergenerational Persistence among U.S.-Born Catholics since 1974," *Sociology of Religion* 77, no. 1 (2016): 1–17, at 2.

4. See the Pew Research Center's Religious Landscape Study, accessed December 4, 2019, http://www.pewforum.org/religious-landscape-study.

5. Hout, "Saint Peter's Leaky Boat," 2.

6. Robert D. Putnam and David E. Campbell, *American Grace: How Religion Divides Us and Unites Us* (New York: Simon & Schuster, 2010), 299. See further 300: "Nearly seven in ten (67 percent) of young Catholics who attend church regularly are Latinos." And 301: "While the overall retention rate of Catholics is 63 percent, among Catholics there is a big gap between [so-called] Anglos and Latinos: 57 percent vs. 78 percent, respectively."

7. See Juhem Navarro-Rivera, Barry A. Kosmin, and Ariela Keysar, *Identificación Religiosa de los Latinos en los EEUU 1990–2008: Crecimiento, Diversidad y Transformación* (Hartford, CT: Trinity College, 2010).

8. See Pew Research Center, "'Nones' on the Rise," October 9, 2012, http://www.pewforum.org/2012/10/09/nones-on-the-rise/.

9. Hout, "Saint Peter's Leaky Boat," 9–10.

10. Center for Applied Research in the Apostolate, "Frequently Requested Church Statistics," accessed December 4, 2019, http://cara .georgetown.edu/frequently-requested-church-statistics/. The numbers are 426,309 in 1970 and 144,148 in 2017. Over the same period, weekly Mass attendance is down from 48 percent to 23 percent.

11. See Christian Smith et al., *Young Catholic America: Emerging Adults In, Out of, and Gone from the Church* (Oxford: Oxford University Press, 2014), 83–84.

12. Ross Douthat, *To Change the Church: Pope Francis and the Future of Catholicism* (New York: Simon & Schuster, 2018), 28. Notwithstanding, Douthat clings to the claim that there is "strong historical correlation between progressive theology and institutional decline" (191). Yet it is not only Saint Peter's bark that is leaking. Both white Mainline Protestants and more recently white Evangelicals have seen significant declines. White Mainline Protestants accounted for around 28 percent of the U.S. population in 1973. In 2016, that was down to 13 percent. White Evangelicals accounted for 23 percent in 1973, then as much as 28 percent in the mid-1990s. But in 2016 that number had fallen to 17 percent. See Putnam and Campbell, *American Grace*, 105, and Daniel Cox and Robert P. Jones, *America's Changing Religious Identity: Findings from the 2016 American Values Atlas* (Washington, DC: Public Religion Research Institute, 2017), 7, available at https://www.prri.org/wp-content/uploads/2017/09/PRRI -Religion-Report.pdf.

13. See Michael Hout and Claude S. Fischer, "Why More Americans Have No Religious Preference: Politics and Generations," *American Sociological Review* 67 (2002): 165–90, at 179. As Hout and Fischer write, it appears that

"the cause-effect relationship linking religion and politics" became *reciprocal* in the United States in the 1990s.

14. Hout and Fischer, "Why More Americans Have No Religious Preference," 178, characterizing the quarrel of unchurched believers as "not with God, but with people running organized religion." See further Charles Taylor, *A Secular Age* (Cambridge, MA: Harvard University Press, 2007), 502–3.

15. See https://www.nunsandnones.org. See further Michael Lipka and Claire Gecewicz, "More Americans Now Say They're Spiritual but Not Religious," Pew Research Center, September 6, 2017, http://www.pewresearch .org/fact-tank/2017/09/06/more-americans-now-say-theyre-spiritual-but -not-religious/.

16. See Cox and Jones, *America's Changing Religious Identity*, 29.

17. See the Pew Research Center's Religious Landscape Study, accessed December 4, 2019, http://www.pewforum.org/religious-landscape-study/ income-distribution/.

18. Nancy Ammerman, "The Many Meanings of Non-Affiliation," in *Empty Churches: Non-Affiliation in America*, ed. James L. Heft and Jan E. Stets (Oxford: Oxford University Press, forthcoming)

19. See Peter Beinert, "Breaking Faith," *The Atlantic*, April 2017, https://www.theatlantic.com/magazine/archive/2017/04/breaking-faith/ 517785/. Beinert works with data from the Public Religion Research Institute. President Trump's inaugural address is available at https://www.whitehouse .gov/briefings-statements/the-inaugural-address/.

20. Roberto Stefan Foa and Yascha Mounk, "The Signs of Deconsolidation," *Journal of Democracy* 28, no. 1 (2017): 5–15, at 5–6.

21. Foa and Mounk, "The Danger of Deconsolidation," *Journal of Democracy* 27, no. 3 (2016): 5–17, at 9.

22. Foa and Mounk, "The Danger of Deconsolidation," 12–13.

23. See Steven Levitsky and Daniel Ziblatt, *How Democracies Die* (New York: Crown, 2018), 195–203.

24. Joseph Ratzinger and Peter Seewald, *Salt of the Earth: The Church at the End of the Millennium*, trans. Adrian Walker (San Francisco: Ignatius Press, 1996), 16.

25. Rod Dreher, *The Benedict Option: A Strategy for Christians in a Post-Christian Nation* (New York: Sentinel, 2017), 4.

26. Dreher, *The Benedict Option*, 18 ("culture of death"), 47 ("new Dark Age"), 99 ("internal exile"), 18 ("another generation or two"), 54 ("island of sanctity and stability"). See 239–40 for further yearnings for "stability in a world of change."

27. Dreher, *The Benedict Option*, 12.

28. Robert McElroy, "Catholicism and the American Polity: Murray as Interlocutor," in *John Courtney Murray and the Growth of Tradition*, ed. J. Leon

Hooper and Todd David Whitmore (Kansas City: Sheed & Ward, 1996), 3–23, at 15.

29. See Mark 16:15 and Matthew 28:19.

30. Compare Cathleen Kaveny, *A Culture of Engagement: Law, Religion, and Morality* (Washington, DC: Georgetown University Press, 2016), 10: "The church, after all, is the body of Christ."

31. See Todd David Whitmore, "Immunity or Empowerment? John Courtney Murray and the Question of Religious Liberty," in *John Courtney Murray and the Growth of Tradition*, 149–74, at 160, whom I paraphrase here. It is interesting in this regard that Dreher moved from the Methodism of his youth (born 1967) to Roman Catholicism (1993) to Eastern Orthodoxy (2006). Orthodox Christians, Ethiopian as well as Eastern, make up about .5 percent of the U.S. population. See the Pew Research Center's report "Orthodox Christianity in the 21st Century," November 8, 2017, http://www.pewforum .org/2017/11/08/orthodox-christianity-in-the-21st-century/. As Whitmore notes, "Countercultural communities," such as Dreher desires, "have the best chance of staying intact when they remain a small minority of the population" (160).

32. By contrast, voluntary choice figures centrally in Dreher's vision of who is in and who is out; see *The Benedict Option*, 116–17.

33. The few Benedictines whom Dreher quotes sometimes give him material that does not quite fit with his polemic. See Dreher, *The Benedict Option*, 73, 94. See further the reflections of Gerald Schlabach, a Benedictine oblate, "The Virtue of Staying Put: What the 'Benedictine Option' Forgets about Benedictines," *Commonweal*, September 26, 2016, https://www .commonwealmagazine.org/virtue-staying-put, who observes that, having vowed to "living the rest of their lives in one place, within one community," Benedictines "cannot simply 'unfriend'" community members who do not share their views.

34. Pope Francis, *Evangelii gaudium* (2013), §20, https://w2.vatican .va/content/francesco/en/apost_exhortations/documents/papa-francesco _esortazione-ap_20131124_evangelii-gaudium.html.

35. Pope Francis and Antonio Spadaro, "A Big Heart Open to God," *America*, September 30, 2013, 15–38, at 26. Compare *Evangelii gaudium*. no. 35.

36. See, for example, Putnam and Campbell, *American Grace*, 129. See also the Pew Research Center's report "U.S. Catholics Open to Non-Traditional Families," September 2, 2015, http://www.pewforum.org/2015/ 09/02/u-s-catholics-open-to-non-traditional-families/.

37. Pope Francis, *Gaudete et exsultate* (2018), §101, https://w2.vatican .va/content/francesco/en/apost_exhortations/documents/papa-francesco _esortazione-ap_20180319_gaudete-et-exsultate.html. Compare Robert W. McElroy, "A Church for the Poor," *America*, October 21, 2013, 13–16.

38. United States Conference of Catholic Bishops, "Forming Consciences for Faithful Citizenship," http://www.usccb.org/issues-and-action/faithful-citizenship/forming-consciences-for-faithful-citizenship-title.cfm. "Faithful Citizenship" was published in 2007 and reissued in 2011 and 2015 with what the bishops called "limited revisions by way of update" (introductory note). See for criticisms, which unfortunately are relevant still given the bishops' plan to reissue the document again in 2019, the papers by Cathleen Kaveny and Vincent J. Miller in *Voting and Holiness: Catholic Perspectives on Political Participation*, ed. Nicholas P. Cafardi (New York: Paulist, 2012),126–34 (Kaveny) and 178–96 (Miller).

39. Compare Ludwig Wittgenstein, *Culture and Value*, bilingual ed., trans. Peter Winch (Chicago: University of Chicago Press, 1980), 78.

40. John W. O'Malley, *Four Cultures of the West* (Cambridge, MA: Harvard University Press, 2004), 31.

41. See O'Malley, *Four Cultures of the West* and *What Happened at Vatican II* (Cambridge, MA: Harvard University Press, 2008), 11–12 and 305–8.

42. See Kaveny, *Prophecy without Contempt: Religious Discourse in the Public Square* (Cambridge, MA: Harvard University Press, 2016).

43. Primo Levi, *Survival in Auschwitz*, trans. Stuart Woolf (New York: Collier, 1961), 96. See for discussion Cora Diamond, "Losing Your Concepts," *Ethics* 98 (1988): 255–77, at 264–65.

44. See Brian Roewe, "Bishops Decide to Supplement Rather Than Revise Faithful Citizenship Voter Guide," *National Catholic Reporter*, June 14, 2018, https://www.ncronline.org/news/politics/bishops-supplement-rather-revise-faithful-citizenship-voter-guide.

45. Cheshire Calhoun, "Standing for Something," *Journal of Philosophy* 92 (1995): 235–60, at 235. Compare Cécile Laborde, *Liberalism's Religion* (Cambridge, MA: Harvard University Press, 2017), 203.

46. Calhoun, "Standing for Something," 250.

47. See for discussion Charles Taylor, *Varieties of Religion Today: William James Revisited* (Cambridge, MA: Harvard University Press, 2002), 79–93.

48. See my *Catholic Moral Philosophy in Practice and Theory: An Introduction* (New York: Paulist, 2016), 188.

49. See John Corvino, "Reply to Anderson and Girgis," in John Corvino, Ryan T. Anderson, and Sherif Girgis, *Debating Religious Liberty and Discrimination* (Oxford: Oxford University Press, 2017), 207–34, at 211.

50. Gregory Bassham, email to the author, March 21, 2018.

51. The qualification "as a rule" seems well-advised lest it be thought necessary to express appreciation for "values" that are so abhorrent that they hardly warrant being called values.

52. I follow here Calhoun, "Standing for Something," 260: "Integrity calls us simultaneously to stand behind our convictions and to take seriously others' doubts about them."

53. Calhoun, "Standing for Something," 257.

54. It should be acknowledged that some challenges might be unintelligible: for example, a challenge to the belief (if that is the right term) that human beings are not for food. As Ludwig Wittgenstein remarked, "If a lion could speak, we could not understand it," which I take to suggest that there are some ways of conceiving of the world that are so alien to us that we can hardly entertain them without losing hold of our humanity. See Wittgenstein, *Philosophical Investigations*, bilingual ed., trans. Elizabeth Anscombe (Oxford: Basil Blackwell, 1958), pt. 2, §11, p. 223, and *Catholic Moral Philosophy in Practice and Theory*, 129–30.

55. Douglas Nejaime and Reva B. Siegel, "Conscience Wars: Complicity-Based Conscience Claims in Religion and Politics," *Yale Law Journal* 124 (2015): 2516–91, at 2519.

56. *Thomas v. Review Board of the Indiana Employment Security Division*, 450 U.S. 707, 715 (1981).

57. *Thomas*.

58. *Thomas*, 714.

59. *Thomas*, 715.

60. See *Thomas*: "Courts should not undertake to dissect religious beliefs because the believer admits that he is 'struggling' with his position....Courts are not arbiters of scriptural interpretation."

61. Compare *Employment Division v. Smith*, 494 U.S. 872, 887 (1990): "Repeatedly and in many different contexts, we have warned that courts must not presume to determine...the plausibility of a religious claim."

62. Compare David S. Oderberg, *Opting Out: Conscience and Cooperation in a Pluralistic Society* (London: Institute of Economic Affairs, 2018), 126.

63. Enacted in 1993 in response to the *Smith* decision, RFRA prescribes that "Government shall not substantially burden a person's exercise of religion even if the burden results from a rule of general applicability." Lest every citizen become a law unto him or herself—Justice Scalia's fear in *Smith* if every law had to jibe with citizens' religious practice and interests—Congress allowed for exceptions. Burdens resulting from rules of general applicability are legally permitted when the government can demonstrate that the burden "(1) is in furtherance of a compelling governmental interest; and (2) is the least restrictive means of furthering that compelling governmental interest." See 42 U.S. Code Chapter 21B, available online.

64. See the April 22, 2013, memorandum by the Office of Chief Counsel, Internal Revenue Service, on "Application of Section 6702 Penalty to Taxpayer Who Files a Return with War Complaint," available online.

65. Compare Oderberg, "Co-operation in the Age of *Hobby Lobby*: When Sincerity Is Not Enough," *Expositions: Interdisciplinary Studies in the Humanities* 11, no. 1 (2017): 15–30, at 21–22: "Whatever one thinks of the outcome in *Hobby Lobby*…, the point is that it was decided on the sole ground that the objectors *sincerely believed* they would be illicit co-operators. That is, the judgment was that [having to purchase insurance including coverage for allegedly abortifacient contraceptives] 'substantially burdened' the objectors' exercise of religion…*not* because they would be illicit co-operators in what they sincerely believed, according to religious teaching, to be an immoral act, but because they *sincerely believed* that, according to religious teaching, they would be guilty of such co-operation."

66. See Matthew 5:38–48.

67. See, for example, H. A. Penner, "Conscientious Objection to Military Taxation," *The Mennonite*, October 17, 2016, https://themennonite.org/opinion/conscientious-objection-military-taxation/.

68. Oderberg, *Opting Out*, 11. See also "Co-operation in the Age of *Hobby Lobby*," 27.

69. Oderberg, "Co-operation in the Age of *Hobby Lobby*," 19–20.

70. See, on proximate v. remote material cooperation, Oderberg, "The Ethics of Co-operation in Wrongdoing," in *Modern Moral Philosophy*, ed. Anthony O'Hear (Cambridge: Cambridge University Press, 2004), 203–27, at 224.

71. See again Oderberg, "Further Clarity on Cooperation and Morality," *Journal of Medical Ethics* 43 (2017): 192–200, at 196, whom I paraphrase here. Oderberg's recent extensive work on this topic was stimulated by the *Hobby Lobby* decision, in which Justice Samuel Alito cites "The Ethics of Co-operation in Wrongdoing," only to put aside the "difficult and important question of religion and moral philosophy" that the article concerns as beyond the purview of the Court. See *Burwell v. Hobby Lobby*, 573 U. S. ___ (2014), slip op. at 36–37.

72. Brief for the United States Conference of Catholic Bishops et al. as *Amicus Curiae*, 18, n. 16, *Masterpiece Cakeshop v. Colorado Civil Rights Commission*, 584 U.S. ___ (2018). Compare Brief for the United States Conference of Catholic Bishops et al. as *Amicus Curiae*, 10, 16, 17–18, *Burwell v. Hobby Lobby*, 573 U. S. ___ (2014), and Brief for the United States Conference of Catholic Bishops et al. as *Amicus Curiae*, 2–3, 30, *Zubik v. Burwell*, 578 U.S. ___ (2016). All three briefs can be found online.

73. See *Hobby Lobby*, slip op. at 36–37.

74. *Masterpiece Cakeshop v. Colorado Civil Rights Commission*, 584 U.S. ___ (2018), slip op. at 11 (Gorsuch, J., concurring): In *Thomas*, the Court "recognized that Mr. Thomas alone was entitled to define the nature of his religious commitments—and that those commitments, as defined by the faithful

adherent, not a bureaucrat or judge, are entitled to protection under the First Amendment."

75. See John 18:38.

76. Brief for the United States Conference of Catholic Bishops et al. as *Amicus Curiae*, 30, *Zubik v. Burwell*, 578 U.S. ___ (2016).

77. See, to begin with, chapters 4 and 5 of Oderberg's *Opting Out*, 40–85. As he writes, "the main theme of this book is that liberal societies need a developed statutory and case-law framework, built on sound legal and ethical theory, for freedom of conscience and religion to be given the sort of fundamental protection it deserves" (6).

78. For example, Nejaime and Siegel object that "conscience provisions allow advocates to rework a traditional norm that was once enforced through the criminal law into a norm that is now enforced through a web of exemptions in the civil law" and express concern that "accommodations that do not include mechanisms to offset significant third-party effects—such as those common in healthcare refusal laws—single out some citizens to bear the costs of others' religious convictions." See "Conscience Wars," 2556, 2585. Compare Kaveny, *A Culture of Engagement*, 67–68.

79. Oderberg, *Opting Out*, 65–66.

80. See, for example, *Opting Out*, 8.

81. The politics of abortion would make for another, more difficult example. See, to begin with, chapter 1 of my *Catholic Moral Philosophy in Practice and Theory*, "A Riskier Discourse: How Catholics Ought to Argue about Abortion," 21–40, and more recently Kaveny, "Could the Church Take a Risk? Thinking about Abortion after Ireland," *Commonweal*, June 11, 2018, https://www.commonwealmagazine.org/could-church-take-risk.

Questions for Further Reflection

1. Who exactly does the author mean by "the nones and all"?

2. The author says there appears to be a trend among millennials both to disaffiliate from organized religious groups and from organized political parties. Why do you think that is the case? What is the author's point of view on this?

3. What distinction does the author draw between a Benedictine and a Franciscan approach to young people who are only weakly attached

to the church or to democracy? Is either of these approaches workable? Is either preferable? Why?

4. The author quotes that "style is the man himself." What does he mean by this? What role does the author say that style plays in communication? Do you agree? Why or why not?

5. The author says that a politics of integrity is a possible way to address the nones and all. What does he mean by a politics of integrity? What does it mean to have integrity? How likely do you think such a politics of integrity will work in communicating with the nones and all?

6. What does the author say is the value of integrity in communicating with others? What is its value in politics? Are the two values the same? Explain.

7. How does integrity relate to listening to and hearing the contrary views of others? If I allow another's opinions to draw me away from my own values, am I acting with integrity? What is the role of dialogue in maintaining personal integrity?

8. The author thinks that an intensification of the culture wars will lead to a greater exodus from the church and a deeper loss of faith in democracy. What does he mean by this? Do you agree or not? Explain.

9. What was the "conscience war" engendered by the Affordable Care Act's provisions on contraception? Do you think that contraception is health care that should be covered by health insurance? What if your employer, through whom you get your health insurance, is an organization affiliated with the Catholic Church?

10. Once church-related employers objected to the Affordable Care Act's contraceptive mandate, the work-around that the government designed was that a church-related employer could simply notify the government that it was morally opposed to providing such contraception coverage, upon which notice, the insurer itself, at no cost to the church-related party, would provide the contraceptive coverage. The plaintiffs in *Zubik* and *The Little Sisters of the Poor* argued that even doing this (notifying the government that they would not provide the birth control coverage) made them violate their Catholic beliefs. How would you evaluate this argument? Can refusing to do something make you morally complicit in another party's doing it?

11. Do you think Mr. Thomas was reasonable in believing that, if he made tank turrets at his job, he would be violating the pacifist teachings of his religion? Would the same conclusion result if his job was only to make sheet metal that could be turned into tank turrets, or refrigerators, or automobiles? Who gets to decided what conduct does or does not make Mr. Thomas complicit in violating the teachings of his faith? Should this be Mr. Thomas's decision alone or does the larger society (the government, the courts) have a role in deciding how reasonable the connection is? If so, what would that role be?

12. What is the author's view about giving legal protection to Mr. Thomas's judgment on the relationship of his work assignment to what he considers sinful behavior prohibited by his faith? What distinction does the author draw here? Do you agree or disagree? Explain.

PART III

Life Issues

7

Shifting Abortion Politics

Charles Camosy

There must be a remedy even for such a crying evil as [abortion]. But where shall it be found, at least where begin, if not in the complete enfranchisement and elevation of women?

— Elizabeth Cady Stanton, feminist activist (1868)

Abortion is a moral right which should be left to the sole discretion of the woman involved.

— Ayn Rand, libertarian philosopher (1968)

I, for one, respect those who believe with all their hearts and conscience that there are no circumstances under which any abortion should ever be available....The choice guaranteed under our Constitution either does not ever have to be exercised or only in very rare circumstances.

— Hillary Clinton, presidential candidate (2005)

Introduction

I t is often said that the more things change, the more they stay the same. But that is simply not true of abortion politics and opinion in the United States. Though there has always been diversity of views, Americans have gone from generally thinking that most abortion is fundamentally evil (even in the viewpoint of serious feminists) to thinking that it is either a constitutional right or something in which government has no business being involved, to our current time, in which we are becoming increasingly uncomfortable with abortion. Alongside our shifting public opinion, we've had some downright bizarre political maneuvering. This has led Democrats and Republicans to take positions on abortion in line with something I call the (George) "Costanza strategy."[1] Abortion is one issue where they respond by *doing the opposite* of their natural political instincts and philosophies.

In this essay I will attempt to tell a shifting, complex, and strange story. I will begin by asking where we are now when it comes to our abortion practices in the United States. I will then, by tracing the political decisions that led us to the bizarre reality of the Costanza strategy, ask, How did we get here? Finally, I will show not only that Americans firmly reject our abortion practices and politics, but also will ask, Where are we going? And I hope to demonstrate that Americans will almost certainly reject these practices even more firmly in the years to come.

Our Current Abortion Practices

One poll-tested mantra for many "pro-choice" politicians is that abortion should be "safe, legal, and rare." But abortion is hardly rare in the United States. According to Planned Parenthood's research arm, "abortion remains a common experience for women in the U.S.; roughly one-third of women will have an abortion during their reproductive lifetime."[2] This equates to about 1.2 million abortions every year in the United States, which means that over 1 in 5 American pregnancies end in elective abortion.[3] Shockingly, that number is 40 percent in New York City. And in the Bronx, the home of the university I work for, the percentage of pregnancies that end in abortion approaches a stunning *50 percent*.[4]

President Obama, giving his now famous commencement address at the University of Notre Dame in 2009, asked us to acknowledge that "any" abortion is "heart-wrenching" and "not done casually."[5] This is surely the case for many women, especially when they are pressured and coerced by boyfriends, husbands, bosses, and parents. But given the numbers just cited above, Obama was obviously incorrect in making such a sweeping claim. Indeed, we have already seen that best-selling author Caitlin Moran thinks of her decision to have an abortion much like decisions about coloring her hair. A new book by Katha Pollitt, *PRO: Reclaiming Abortion Rights*, insists that not only is abortion anything but heart-wrenching, but it is part of normal reproductive medicine and a social good. The "1-in-3 Campaign" works hard to highlight the very high numbers of women having abortions so that it is seen as mere "access to basic medical care."[6] Comedian Sarah Silverman tweeted fake before-and-after photos of herself, joking that she got a "quickie" abortion in case *Roe v. Wade* was overturned.[7] Actress Emily Letts even filmed what she claimed to be her own abortion and put the video online to show "how positive it is."[8]

Obama's view also conflicts with Planned Parenthood's own statistics, which show that most abortions do not come out of the extreme situations for which most Americans think abortion is acceptable, that is, when serious life and health issues are involved or when a woman has become pregnant as a result of rape. Indeed, though women generally give multiple, complex reasons for having an abortion, 38 percent of those surveyed by Planned Parenthood claimed that "having a child would interfere with their education." Interestingly—and important for thinking about the coercive role many men play in abortion—more than half listed "being a single mother" or "having relationship problems" as a reason.[9]

Furthermore, of those who are diagnosed with Down syndrome as prenatal children, a shocking 90 percent are aborted.[10] (This despite the fact that people with Down syndrome are actually happier than those who are "normal.")[11] Even late-term abortion is increasingly used to abort fetuses with issues as minor as a cleft palate.[12] And as more people engage in very expensive rounds of in vitro fertilization, especially in order to have children later in life, abortion is becomingly increasingly important to make sure there is quality control over the product they are purchasing. In a recent *New York Times Magazine* article, a woman who requested that her pregnancy be "reduced" from twins to a single fetus said the following:

> Things would have been different if we were 15 years younger or if we hadn't had children already or if we were more financially secure....If I had conceived these twins naturally, I wouldn't have reduced this pregnancy, because you feel like if there's a natural order, then you don't want to disturb it. But we created this child in such an artificial manner—in a test tube, choosing an egg donor, having the embryo placed in me—and somehow, making a decision about how many to carry seemed to be just another choice. The pregnancy was all so consumerish to begin with, and this became yet another thing we could control.[13]

Quite understandably, a physician in the story asked, "In a society where women can terminate a single pregnancy for any reason—financial, social, emotional—if we have a way to reduce a twin pregnancy with very little risk, isn't it legitimate to offer that service to women with twins who want to reduce to a singleton?"

Some think of abortion as rare at least within the life experience of a woman, but more than 50 percent of Americans who have abortions have already had (at least) one abortion.[14] In addition, 61 percent of women who have abortions in the United States already have (at least) one child.[15] Some point out that the abortion rate would go down if we gave pregnant mothers the support and structures to raise their children and also to be full members of society. Structural injustice does indeed have something important to do with these very high numbers in the United States, and we could save the lives of many prenatal children if we resisted the structural injustices that women face. This must be a very high priority for anyone who identifies as "pro-life," and it will be an essential part of the Mother and Prenatal Child Protection Act. But as we will see, places like Sweden and the United Kingdom (despite having a large social welfare system for women and children) have abortion rates like that of the United States.[16]

It is also worth noting that the overwhelming majority of abortions in the United States take place early in pregnancy. It appears that only about 10 percent of abortions take place beyond the first twelve to thirteen weeks; but that still means that a whopping 120,000 abortions take place each year in the United States in the second and third tri-mesters.[17] In fact, tests that (attempt to) confirm that the fetus has Down syndrome are generally performed in the second trimester.[18] "Pro-lifers" have been arguing for decades that late-term abortion is the equivalent of killing newly born children, and in 2013 the country watched with horror and disgust as the Philadelphia abortion provider Kermit Gosnell was convicted of three counts of infanticide after botched abortions.[19] Since that time, though, as the *Washington Post*'s Melinda Henneberger has pointed out, these stories have not been covered by the national media, we have learned that Gosnell's story is hardly unique.[20] Similar stories have been covered by the local press in Houston, Dallas, New York, Florida, and Maryland.

When I engage someone who is "pro-choice" and explain my own basic position on abortion, I often get two questions: "What if the mother's life is in danger?" and "What if the woman has been raped?" Both are incredibly difficult and sensitive questions that must always be addressed with the utmost care and respect. But here is some per-spective to those questions: about 1 percent of all abortions take place in situations where the mother was raped,[21] and about 1 percent take place when the mother's life is threatened.[22] Let me be absolutely clear: these are agonizing and horrific circumstances, circumstances about which some public "pro-lifers" speak far too casually. However, respect for abortion rights in these cases is quite different from respect for abortion rights in the other cases just mentioned. Indeed, the overwhelming majority of abortions in the United States seem qualitatively different from the 2 percent represented by rape and the mother's endangered life.

How does our current political culture deal with the reality of abortion in the United States? Unsurprisingly, the two major parties try to use our culture's strong feelings about abortion to their own politi-cal advantage, and they do so via the Costanza strategy. The evidence appears to show that Republicans play on the concerns for prenatal children by claiming to stand for a big government that will regulate the intimately private and personal reproductive practices of women. And the evidence also appears to show that Democrats play on the con-cerns of many for women's rights by claiming to stand for privacy and freedom of the individual over and against the government's interest in protecting the vulnerable. How we got to a place where our political parties "do the opposite" on abortion is the focus of the next part of the chapter.

How Did We Get Here?

There was a time before the Costanza strategy. The first feminists—those who fought for the right of women to vote, for instance—were strongly skeptical of abortion, not least because they believed that men (and institutions run by men) coerced most abortions. The ground-breaking group Feminists for Life is one of the few organizations that recognizes and highlights this fact. Here are some quotes they have collected from their "Feminist Foremothers":[23]

SUSAN B. ANTHONY

Anthony referred to abortion as "child murder," and she further clarified,

> We want prevention, not merely punishment. We must reach the root of the evil. It is practiced by those whose inmost souls revolt from the dreadful deed.

> (*The Revolution* 4, no. 1 [July 8, 1869]: 4)

ELIZABETH CADY STANTON

Stanton wrote, regarding prostitution and the "murder of children, either before or after birth":

> For a quarter of a century sober, thinking women have warned this nation of these thick coming dangers, and pointed to the only remedy, the education and enfranchisement of woman....We believe the cause of all these abuses lies in the degradation of woman.

> (*The Revolution* 1, no. 5 [February 5, 1868]: 1)

There must be a remedy even for such a crying evil as this. But where shall it be found, at least where begin, if not in the complete enfranchisement and elevation of women?

(The Revolution 1, no. 10 [March 12, 1868]: 146–67)

EMMA GOLDMAN

The custom of procuring abortions has reached such appalling proportions in America as to be beyond belief....So great is the misery of the working classes that seventeen abortions are committed in every one hundred pregnancies."

(Mother Earth, 1911)

MATTIE BRINKERHOFF

When a man steals to satisfy hunger, we may safely conclude that there is something wrong in society—so when a woman destroys the life of her unborn child, it is evidence that either by education or circumstances she has been greatly wronged.

(The Revolution 1, no. 9 [September 2, 1869]: 138–39)

VICTORIA WOODHULL (THE FIRST FEMALE U.S. PRESIDENTIAL CANDIDATE)

The rights of children as individuals begin while yet they remain the fetus.

(The Revolution Woodhull's and Claflin's Weekly 2, no. 6 [December 24, 1870]: 4)

Every woman knows that if she were free, she would never bear an unwished-for child, nor think of murdering one before its birth.

(Wheeling [*West Virginia*] *Evening Standard,* Nov. 17, 1875)

These quotes, especially coming from pioneers and radicals whose lives were clearly dedicated to the rights and well-being of women, may sound odd to our contemporary ears. The story we are told today—especially in the privileged world of media, public policy, and academia—has changed. We are now told (often by male talking heads) that abortion rights are necessary for women in today's culture. What has changed since the days of Susan B. Anthony and Elizabeth Cady Stanton? How did such a dramatic shift take place? In answering these questions, I rely on the important work of the Democrat activist Kristen Day. Hers has been a voice crying in the wilderness on these matters, and it deserves a much broader audience.[24]

Before the Costanza Strategy

Day recalls the pivotal moment of the 1968 Democratic convention in Chicago. Democrats were a deeply divided party over the Vietnam War, but "immediate withdrawal" activists were well-organized, loud, and even violent. They did not hold most of the delegates, and they were enraged about the fact that their voices were not being heard. This explosive situation led to the now famous "Chicago riots" outside the convention hall. The Democratic Party was unable to unite itself around its nominee for president, Hubert Humphrey, who would go on to be defeated by Richard Nixon. In response to this defeat and in an attempt to have a more unified approach, party leaders reformed the nominating process to be more inclusive and broad so that everyone— even the activist groups—would feel that they were heard. Day argues that this resulted in aggressive and organized activists gaining more power over the platform and nominations. The broad base of the party was not as energized and aggressive, and the message was dominated by the activists.

At that time—obviously unlike today—being Democratic or Republican was not a predictor of how one would vote on abortion. In fact, when the state of New York passed the first sweeping abortion rights law, it was signed by none other than Republican governor Nelson Rockefeller. The law was repealed by the state legislature two years later, but it remained law when the repeal was vetoed by Gov. Rockefeller. In 1972, George McGovern was the Democratic candidate for president; he ran strongly and clearly against the Vietnam

War. He rejected an attempt to add an abortion rights plank to the party platform, calling abortion a "no win issue" and claiming that it should be left up to the states. McGovern had the chance to appoint two vice presidential candidates, and his choices were quite telling. The first was Thomas Eagleton of Missouri, a Catholic "pro-life" Democrat. When Eagleton stepped down, McGovern chose Sargent Shriver, another "pro-life" Democrat. Though "pro-choice" momentum was building in the party, and McGovern did receive some criticism for choosing "pro-life" running mates (along with serious concerns about Shriver's marriage to Eunice Kennedy, who was vehemently antiabortion), this sentiment had not yet taken over the party's power structures.

Meanwhile, though Republican governor Ronald Reagan was supporting and signing the bill that legalized abortion in California, Richard Nixon and other national Republican figures were attempting to convert Democratic Catholic voters into Republicans. For decades they had been an essential part of the liberal base, but now "pro-life" Catholic Democrats were sensing the shift in the party. Republicans took full advantage. According to Day, Nixon specifically courted Catholic leaders, such as the archbishop of New York, Terence Cardinal Cooke, with his position against abortion. Rather than simply leaving it to the states, as McGovern proposed, Nixon at least claimed to support equal protection of the law for all prenatal children.

The shift toward the Costanza strategy had begun.

The Turning Point

In 1973, *Roe v. Wade* made abortion broadly legal in all fifty states. Of the nine justices (all men), Justice Byron White (who was appointed by a Democratic president, John F. Kennedy) was one of only two dissenters and one of the most outspoken critics of the decision. Only one of the six justices who had been appointed by Republicans voted against Roe. Justice Harry Blackmun, appointed by Richard Nixon, wrote the majority opinion.[25] Day notes that this monumental decision gave the "pro-choice" camp serious momentum, and they worked even harder to add an abortion plank to the Democratic Party's platform. Indeed, they would attempt to exclude anyone who was "pro-life" from calling themselves liberal. In 1976, over the objections of their presidential nominee, Jimmy Carter, they successfully got abortion rights into the platform. Carter said he would have worded the plank differently because "abortions are wrong," and as president he planned programs to minimize them.

Republicans responded by pushing even harder in the other direction. Day relates how Republican leadership, and particularly that of Paul Weyrich and Henry Hyde, led the charge to unite with people like Jerry Falwell and the Moral Majority of the Christian right.[26] The abortion battle had been joined in earnest, and this was the crucial turning point. Day claims that Democrats, if they were to stay true to their principles, should have sided with Carter. They should have maintained that abortion was wrong and worked to give women the resources to resist the pressure (often applied by men) to get abortions. Instead, by going all in with the abortion-rights activists, they created an opportunity for Republicans to steal "pro-life" votes from the Democrats. In 1976 there were an astonishing 125 self-identified "pro-life" Democrats in Congress. Day recounts something that Democratic congressman Jim Oberstar used to say: people who opposed abortion didn't stop sending people to Congress, "they just stopped sending Democrats."

The Costanza strategy was now in full force, but it took some time for the party leopards to change their spots. This was clear when Republican Henry Hyde first offered his well-known amendment banning federal funding for abortion. President Gerald Ford, a Republican, initially leaned toward vetoing the bill; but when he heard that Jimmy Carter was going to support it, Ford claimed that he had the same position and would sign the bill. Despite this naked attempt to tie Carter to his party's stated position against the Hyde Amendment, it was Ford who would eventually go on to veto the bill. If this wasn't enough to show his true colors on abortion, Ford revealed himself as unabashedly "pro-choice" after his presidency when he decided to sit on the advisory committee of Republicans for Choice. As Kristen Day put it, "Neither candidate agreed with [his] prospective platform" when it came to abortion.[27]

Costanza Strategy Complete

The shift that had taken place within the Democratic Party could be personified in the person of Ted Kennedy. He had a strong "pro-life" voting record until the late 1970s, and once even said that abortion on demand was at odds with our basic civilizational values about respect for human life. He compared abortion with other kinds of population control and eugenics. But by the time he challenged Jimmy Carter for the Democratic Party's nomination in 1980, he had totally switched course and ended up pushing Carter to become more clearly in favor of abortion rights. Senator Joe Biden, future vice president of the United States, was also reliably "pro-life" until 1981. Democratic congressmen and presidential candidate Dick Gephardt had nearly a 100 percent "pro-life" voting record until the mid-1980s. Future vice president Al Gore, a Democrat, supported the Hyde Amendment and wrote constituents about his "deep personal conviction" that "abortion is wrong." Democratic activist Jesse Jackson, another former supporter of the Hyde Amendment, once said that "aborting a baby" affects the moral fabric of our nation. Even Democratic presidential candidate Dennis Kucinich very publicly claimed that he thought life begins at conception. Under pressure from the new party bosses, these and many others switched their positions. Day quotes the phrase coined by Kate Michelman, executive director of the National Abortion Rights and Action League (NARAL): "If you're out of touch with the pro-choice majority, you're out of office." Democrats now had their orthodoxy on abortion, and dissenters were not permitted.

In the other political camp, we have already discussed how Ronald Reagan signed the bill that made abortion legal in California. Remarkably, this same person would go on to take the presidency away from Jimmy Carter largely because he was somehow able to siphon off "pro-life" votes from what would come to be known as "Reagan Democrats." His choice for vice president, George H. W. Bush, had such a clear "pro-choice" record that Reagan took serious flak from "pro-lifers" for choosing Bush. By 1988, however, when it came time for Bush to make his own run at the presidency, he had changed his position on abortion to "pro-life." This even though his first nominee for the Supreme Court was Justice David Souter, a reliable supporter of abortion rights. Most recently, we saw Mitt Romney, the former pro-choice governor of Massachusetts, take only three years to shift his position and become "pro-life" for his own presidential campaigns.

Day notes that Bill Clinton once told Arkansas Right to Life that he "was opposed to abortion and government funding of abortions." But by his 1992 campaign for president, our current abortion orthodoxy in both parties was fully entrenched, and Clinton was forced to switch his views. One of the few high-profile heretics who resisted this shift was the energetically "pro-life" governor of Pennsylvania, Democrat Robert Casey. Before the 1992 convention, Casey was reelected governor of Pennsylvania by more than one million votes and carried sixty-six of sixty-seven counties in the state. His opponent was a pro-choice Republican. On every other issue Casey was solidly liberal: whether it was appointing more women to his cabinet than any other governor, championing nutrition programs for low-income families, and even trying to pass universal health care in his state. He was one of the most courageous people in his party to directly reject the Costanza strategy.

Someone like Casey, a successful and popular governor of a major state, should have been expected to speak at the 1992 Democratic convention. But he was denied this chance because of his views on abortion. To add insult to injury, five other "pro-choice" Republicans (including a key supporter of Casey's primary opponent) were invited to speak at the convention. Some said that Casey was denied a speaking slot because he didn't endorse Clinton for president, but plenty of others who did not endorse Clinton (including the governor of California, Jerry Brown) did speak at that convention. Casey was a politician who spent his life in support of the government's defense of the vulnerable over against the typical Republican trump-card ideas of individual privacy, freedom, and autonomy. But he was publicly humiliated because he refused to cave in to a constituency that bullied weaker Democrats into "doing the opposite" of what was at the heart of their political philosophy. Unfortunately for Casey—and despite his best efforts—the battle was already lost.

Abortion Views and Politics Today

Our current abortion politics are part of a larger political structure and conversation. And at first glance, this structure looks hopelessly polarized. After all, it has been widely reported that Congress is now more polarized than at any time since the Civil War. But that description of Congress, much like our abortion politics, doesn't reflect the complexity of what Americans believe. A recent Gallup poll, for instance, found the following breakdown in political affiliation in the United States:[28]

9 percent	Very Conservative
31 percent	Conservative
35 percent	Moderate
16 percent	Liberal
5 percent	Very Liberal
4 percent	No Opinion

This is hardly a polarized group of people: only 14 percent are in the "extremes." Furthermore, a 2014 NBC News/*Wall Street Journal* poll found that a majority of Americans now refuse to identify as either Democrats or Republicans.[29] Indeed, Gallup also recently found that a record 42 percent of the electorate explicitly thinks of themselves as "independent," refusing to put themselves in either the liberal or conservative camp.[30] Portending the future, fully half of millennials now identify themselves as independents.[31]

So the facts of what Americans believe about politics—unfiltered by the lazy binary "liberal/conservative" lens—is rather complicated. Most Americans are not extreme and cannot be put in a box: they will give you a "liberal" answer for one issue and then a "conservative" answer for another. The liberal/conservative binary just doesn't fit our complex political reality, and it will fit even less well going into the future. Indeed, I would argue that the coming demographic changes in the United States suggest that a fundamental change in our politics is right around the corner.

This is also true of our abortion politics. At first glance, especially viewed through the lens of the media, we seem hopelessly polarized: as if this is somehow a fight between those who (1) want to ban abortion altogether in the name of stopping genocide and (2) those who want to make all abortions legal in the name of women's equality. While some of the loudest voices in our public abortion debates hold these views, and while the medias tend to tell their stories this way in order to generate ratings, Americans have views on abortion that are even more complex than their political views in general. This should not be shocking, of course, given the bizarre way that our abortion political categories and "sides" came to be formed.

The poll numbers tell a very different story of what Americans believe.[32] According to a 2013 CNN poll, for instance, Americans thought abortion should be

25 percent	Always Legal
11 percent	Legal in Most Circumstances
42 percent	Legal in Few Circumstances
20 percent	Always Illegal

This reality, of course, does not fit into our lazy and imprecise "pro-life" vs. "pro-choice" sound-bite rhetoric. It is interesting that a 2013 NBC News poll found something similar, though they added some specifics to the question that will be very important for my argument:

26 percent	Always Legal
19 percent	Legal Most of the Time
42 percent	Illegal Except in Cases of Rape, Incest, and Mother's Life
10 percent	Illegal without Exception

A *New York Times*/CBS News poll, again, finds complexity. This was in response to questions about abortion availability:

42 percent	Abortion should be Generally Available
35 percent	Abortion should be Available under Stricter Limits
20 percent	Abortion should not be Permitted

One of the "stricter limits" that many Americans have in mind, for instance, is about when in a pregnancy abortion should be legal. A 2013 Gallup poll found the following:[33]

FIRST THREE MONTHS OF PREGNANCY

| 61 percent | Should be Legal |
| 31 percent | Should be Illegal |

SECOND THREE MONTHS OF PREGNANCY

| 27 percent | Should be Legal |
| 64 percent | Should be Illegal |

FINAL THREE MONTHS OF PREGNANCY

14 percent	Should be Legal
80 percent	Should be Illegal

Finally, there are situations in which Americans are clear that abortion should be legal. This according to a 2012 CNN poll:

"WHEN THE WOMAN'S LIFE IS IN DANGER"

88 percent	Legal
9 percent	Illegal

"WHEN THE WOMAN'S PHYSICAL HEALTH IS IN DANGER"

83 percent	Legal
12 percent	Illegal

"WHEN THE PREGNANCY WAS CAUSED BY RAPE OR INCEST"

83 percent	Legal
14 percent	Illegal

Hence, in summing up the views of Americans on abortion, we can safely draw at least two conclusions:

1. A very clear majority of Americans want to see abortion more restricted than it is now, especially in the "middle" weeks of pregnancy.
2. An overwhelming majority of Americans, including many who identify as "pro-life," want to see abortion legally available in the exceptional 2 percent of pregnancies (rape or incest and a threat to the life of the mother).

We now have even more evidence that the categories we use to describe our abortion politics are woefully inadequate. Most Americans are "pro-choice" in some situations, and most are "pro-life" in some situations. In answering the question "Do you support abortion?" most Americans will respond, "It depends on the situation." Indeed, we learned above that 70 percent of Americans say the term *pro-choice* describes them somewhat or very well, and nearly 65 percent simultaneously say the term *pro-life* describes them somewhat or very well. American abortion politics, at least in the general electorate, are complex and not polarized in the "us vs. them" way they are commonly portrayed. Though some find themselves on the extremes of the debate, most are in the complex middle.

The (Brief) Return of "Pro-Life" Democrats

Don't get me wrong, the Costanza strategy is still alive and well in Washington, DC. But we recently saw that, for a brief political moment, abortion politics could return to the complex—and more ideologically consistent—place they were before this strategy was used. After being soundly defeated by George W. Bush and the Republicans in 2004, Democratic Party leaders began to take a more inclusive approach and welcome "pro-life" Democrats into their fold. The result was that these "pro-life" Democrats had a significant effect on public policy, especially during the health-care reform debates. Bart Stupak, a former congressman from northern Michigan, offered an amendment designed to supplement the Hyde Amendment in prohibiting federal funding of abortion in the new health-care system. And despite outrage from "pro-choice" interest groups, the amendment passed with a coalition of "pro-life" Democrats and Republicans; indeed, a full one-quarter of the Democrat caucus voted for it.[34]

However, the Senate would respond by passing a version of health-care reform that did not include Stupak's amendment and gave no impression that they would ever include it. Stupak, along with twelve like-minded Democrats (whose votes were required for the House version to pass), tenaciously negotiated for their "pro-life" principles against the Senate version. After months of back-and-forth politics, Stupak and other "pro-life" Democrats managed to work out a compromise. Appropriately, the compromise was brokered with Senate leadership primarily by Gov. Casey's son, Sen. Robert Casey Jr. It contained a remarkable number of "pro-life" provisions:[35]

- Coverage for abortion is specifically excluded from the standard package of benefits that all insurers would be required by law to offer.
- Existing restrictions on the use of federal funds appropriated via the HHS appropriations bill (the Hyde Amendment) are maintained.
- The federal government, acting in its capacity as both a civilian and a military employer, continues to exclude abortion coverage from the policies it offers to its employees.
- The new exchanges of private health-care companies are required to offer at least one policy that does not cover abortion, something not available in the individual policy market in many places.
- States have the option of preventing insurers in their state from offering plans through the exchange that cover abortion.
- Federal premium subsidies cannot be used to purchase insurance coverage for abortion.
- While individuals purchasing coverage through the exchange have the option to use their own funds to purchase abortion coverage, they must make a separate premium payment to do so.
- Incorporation and passage of the Pregnant Women Support Act.[36]
- All of these elements are reaffirmed by the president of the United States in a high-profile executive order issued hours before the legislation's passage.

Several Republicans tried to claim that, in compromising with his opponents in negotiating the final deal, Bart Stupak and the "pro-life" Democrats had simply sold out their "pro-life" credentials. One even shouted out "baby killer!" as Stupak addressed the House a final time to assure passage of the bill. But much of the pro-choice lobby stood strongly against not only this kind of regulation of private insurance companies who participate in the health exchanges (because of the worry

135

that insurance companies would drop abortion coverage altogether), but also against the Hyde Amendment itself. Indeed, despite campaigning for president as a candidate who was against the Hyde Amendment, Obama signed an executive order that effectively gave it legal status such that it now no longer needs to be renewed with each budget.[37] This was a substantial victory for "pro-lifers."

However, the realignment in Washington was short-lived. The old guard "pro-life" movement found itself unable to imagine that it could work with Democrats, and movement leaders waged a multimillion-dollar political offensive, teaming with Republicans, to defeat "pro-life" Democrats in the midterm elections of 2010. This strategy worked: the caucus of "pro-life" Democrats was devastated, cut by more than 50 percent. Though Republicans had "their issue" back, this certainly did not mean that passing "pro-life" legislation was more likely. Indeed, given that they once again lost the inroads they had made with Democrats, "pro-lifers" lost the chance to repeat the bipartisan example of the health-care debates. Though there are moments outside the national scene that continue to buck the trend, the conventional wisdom appears to have returned to abortion politics.[38] At least for now, the two national parties have their issues right back where they want them.

What about *Roe*?

Some may find all of this interesting, but nevertheless will return to the bottom line: *Roe v. Wade* is the law of the land, and a clear majority of Americans support it.[39] According to a 2013 Quinnipiac poll, a very solid 63 percent agree with the decision. But to what, exactly, are these people agreeing? In a Pew Forum study done on the fortieth anniversary of *Roe v. Wade*, we learned that only 62 percent of Americans even know that this Supreme Court decision *is about abortion*.[40] And it is even more shocking that among those younger than thirty years old, this number falls to 44 percent! Furthermore, of those who know that *Roe* was about abortion, many don't know what the decision actually said or did. Many wrongly believe, for instance, that overturning *Roe* would mean making abortion illegal—instead of merely returning the issue to be decided by the states. To make matters worse, the questions asked in these polls themselves often misunderstand how *Roe* impacts abortion public policy.[41] So, what do the 63 percent who agree with the decision actually believe about abortion policy? The only honest answer is: we don't really know.

It is also worth mentioning that many people, even those who strongly support abortion rights, think that *Roe* was a bad decision and even wrongly decided. Linda Greenhouse, who covered the Supreme Court for the *New York Times* from 1978 to 2008, had the following to say about the decision:

> To read the actual opinion, as almost no one ever does, is to understand that the seven middle-aged to elderly men in the majority certainly didn't think they were making a statement about women's rights: women and their voices are nearly absent from the opinion. It's a case about the rights of doctors—fellow professionals, after all—who faced criminal prosecution in states across the country for acting in what they considered to be the best interests of their patients.[42]

To be clear, Greenhouse herself is a clear supporter of abortion rights. But she is dismayed that the opinion itself, which was decided by all men, has little to say about the rights and flourishing of women. She is joined by another important supporter of abortion and women's rights, Supreme Court Justice Ruth Bader Ginsburg. What follows is from the Associated Press story on her 2013 appearance at the University of Chicago Law School:

> U.S. Supreme Court Justice Ruth Bader Ginsburg says she supports a woman's right to choose to have an abortion, but feels her predecessors' landmark *Roe v. Wade* ruling 40 years ago was too sweeping and gave abortion opponents a symbol to target. Ever since the decision, she said, momentum has been on abortion opponents' side, fueling a state-by-state campaign that has placed more restrictions on abortion.
>
> "That was my concern, that the court had given opponents of access to abortion a target to aim at relentlessly," she told a crowd of students. "My criticism of *Roe* is that it seemed to have stopped the momentum that was on the side of change."
>
> The ruling is also a disappointment to a degree, Ginsburg said, because it was not argued in weighty terms of

advancing women's rights. Rather, the *Roe* opinion, written by Justice Harry Blackmun, centered on the right to privacy and asserted that it extended to a woman's decision on whether to end a pregnancy.[43]

Princeton's Peter Singer agrees with both Greenhouse and Ginsburg, even though, as I mentioned above, he is a supporter of the right to abortion and infanticide. Nevertheless, at the aforementioned Princeton conference aimed at finding common ground on abortion, Singer courageously countered the "pro-choice" activists present and argued that *Roe v. Wade* was a bad decision.[44] He argued that, instead of continuing to short-circuit the legislative process, the United States should have an actual national and legislative debate about abortion and have it come to some finality. Singer cites Europe and his native Australia as examples of places where this has happened, and the "pro-choice" position is basically settled without much opposition.

These three thinkers, along with many other folks who think that *Roe* is bad law, may get the chance to make the law better by having it returned to the states for a legislative process. As we will see at several points in this book, the legal standing and basis for *Roe* has shifted and changed so much over the decades that it is not clear what is holding the decision together. The court was divided 4–4 on abortion, with Justice Anthony Kennedy being the swing vote. With Kennedy's retirement and his replacement by Kavanaugh, that may have changed. But that is a question for our current court. Even more important than this, perhaps, is what the trends indicate for the future of American abortion politics.

Trends and Looking to the Future

Those who attempt to limit abortion in the United States are often described by their opponents as "moving backward." In the summer of 2013, for instance, the Texas legislature moved to ban abortion after twenty weeks and to require all abortion facilities to offer women easier access to hospitals should the abortion go wrong. Jamila Bey, writing in the *Washington Post*, spoke for many "pro-choice" people when she claimed that Texas was trying to "turn back the clock" on women's rights.[45] But those who view Europe as more progressive than the

United States on social issues like abortion might be surprised to learn that the Texas law is rather tame by comparison to European restrictions. Belgium, Denmark, France, Germany, Greece, Ireland, Italy, Holland, Spain, and Sweden, just to name a few, restrict abortion to well before twenty weeks. Many countries draw the line at twelve weeks, and many require that the procedure be done in a hospital.[46]

Spain may make their abortion laws even more restrictive—allowing them only in cases of rape or when the life or health of the mother is in danger.[47] How does the government justify this new legislation? The Spanish justice minister, Alberto Ruiz-Gallardon, claimed that the proposed law change is an attempt to push back against "structural gender violence against women." He said that "the mere fact of pregnancy" creates "pressure" that causes women to abort. "I think [about] the fear of losing my job or not getting a job as a result of pregnancy. I think women in these situations lack public support to freely choose an alternative to termination of pregnancy."[48]

U.S. Trends

Health care. Paid maternity leave. Commitment to international treaties and laws. Ecological concern. Especially for progressives, Europe stands for ideas and policies to which many hope the United States will also aspire. But with the Costanza strategy in effect, our political parties "do the opposite" here as well. Conservatives, who often criticize attempts to use Europe as a model for social issues, are pushing our abortion laws to be more like those in France and Sweden. Liberals, who often evoke Europe as a place of social progress, imagine such changes to be moving backward. But the reality is that we are slowly becoming more like Europe when it comes to abortion restrictions.[49] Despite the fact that there is no serious attempt to make abortion totally illegal, many dozens of bills have passed in recent years that significantly restrict abortion. Here are just a few:[50]

- Thirty-three states have passed informed consent laws (twenty-four include an ultrasound requirement);
- Thirty-one states have passed abortion clinic regulations;
- Thirty-eight states have passed parental notification/ involvement

- Thirty-eight states have wrongful-death laws that treat the unborn child as a person; eleven of these protect the fetus from fertilization *onward*. Thirty-seven states have fetal homicide laws, and twenty-five of these extend the protection from fertilization.
- Virtually every state today has prenatal-injury laws that compensate for prenatal injury at any time after conception.
- The pregnancy care centers allied with Care Net (a pro-life support network for women with difficult pregnancies), for example, grew from approximately 550 in 1999 to 1,130 in 2010; by contrast, the number of abortion clinics declined from 2,200 in 1991 to 689 in 2011.
- Abortion bans beyond the twentieth week of pregnancy are in place in twenty-one states.[51]

The trend shows no signs of slowing down. For instance, the year 2013 saw the second highest number of "pro-life" state laws passed in American history.[52] It is surpassed only by the year 2011, which holds the record.[53] There are many more in the pipeline.[54] One of the few attempts to change the law in the other direction was recently passed in the liberal state of New York.[55]

So let's be clear: There has been a broad and dramatic shift, especially in the last fifteen to twenty years, toward more abortion restrictions in the United States. And though almost no one suggests that abortion will be banned altogether, this trend of European-style restrictions will almost certainly continue for at least another generation.

The Future of Abortion Politics

Perhaps we should begin with the obvious. The laws just mentioned continue to be passed by legislatures because they have the support of the people. But our actual abortion practices, to which these laws are reacting, are totally out of step with what most Americans believe about abortion. Recall the following:

- 62 percent believe that abortion should be legal in "few" or "no" circumstances (CNN, 2013).

- 42 percent believe that abortion should be illegal except in cases of rape, incest, or a threat to the life of the mother; 10 percent believe that it should be illegal without exception (NBC, 2013).
- Abortion should be legal in
  - first trimester: 61 percent
  - second trimester: 27 percent
  - third trimester: 14 percent (Gallup, 2013)

Contrast this with abortion practices in the United States:

- 33 percent of women will have an abortion in their lifetime.
- 1.2 million abortions are performed every year.
- 20 percent of pregnancies end in abortion (40 percent in New York City).
- 90 percent of fetuses diagnosed with Down syndrome are aborted.
- 120,000 abortions are performed in the second and third trimesters.

Though our current political parties are using the Costanza strategy in order to raise money and turn out their base (because their stated views on abortion run so counter to their core political beliefs), little has been done by either national party to change abortion law. But it will not stay this way forever; eventually the will of the people about abortion will be reflected in our national public policy. This seems virtually undeniable, especially as we think about the coveted voters of the next generation: Hispanics, millennials, and women.

Hispanics are now the majority ethnicity in California; Texas will soon follow, along with much of the rest of the country. Though Hispanics disproportionately vote Democrat, they are certainly not reliable "pro-choice" voters. Far from it. As Dr. Victoria M. DeFrancesco Soto of NBC Latino mentioned during the heat of the 2012 elections, "On the issue of abortion Latinos are significantly more pro-life than non-Latinos."[56] For instance, Hispanics are 10 percent more likely than are whites to think that abortion should be made broadly illegal.[57] Dr. Soto also noted that Latino opposition to abortion changes little whether they identify as Democratic, Republican, or Independent. As Hispanics rightfully assume more positions in the power structures of the United States in the next generation or so, look for our abortion politics to change dramatically.

Yet the most obvious way that the electorate will shift over the coming ten to twenty years will come from the rise of the millennials. That young people are trending "pro-life" is well known, and it was the primary reason for the 2013 resignation of the NARAL's sixty-one-year-old president, Nancy Keenan.[58] This issue has been on the radar screen of "pro-choicers" at least since the appearance of a 2003 article in the *New York Times* entitled "Surprise, Mom, I'm Against Abortion."[59] Then trends were clear:

> A study of American college freshmen shows that support for abortion rights has been dropping since the early 1990s: 54 percent of 282,549 students polled at 437 schools last fall by the University of California at Los Angeles agreed that abortion should be legal. The figure was down from 67 percent a decade earlier. A New York Times/CBS News poll in January found that among people 18 to 29, the share who agree that abortion should be generally available to those who want it was 39 percent, down from 48 percent in 1993.

A 2003 Gallup poll also found that well over 70 percent of teenagers thought that abortion was "morally wrong."[60]

If the last two generations are anything to go by, people get more skeptical of abortion as they get older, and it is thus unsurprising that this trend has continued. In 2010, for instance, Gallup found that "support for making abortion illegal was growing fastest among young adults." They found this to be "a sharp change from the late 1970s, when seniors were substantially more likely than younger age groups to want abortion to be illegal."[61] For all millennials in 2012, only 37 percent consider abortion to be morally acceptable.[62] As I was writing this chapter, there was a debate brewing in Texas and in the U.S. House/ Senate about whether to ban abortion beyond twenty weeks gestation. In stories on these events, the *Washington Post* noted that, of people who were fifty years or older, 44 percent supported such a ban, while 52 percent of those eighteen to twenty-nine supported it.[63] Unsurprisingly, given that Catholics tend to be similar to the broader culture, this trend holds for young Catholics as well. A 2013 *New York Times* poll asked Catholics the following question: "Should the next pope be for or against legalized abortion?" In the age group forty-five to sixty-four, only 49 percent said "against," but among those eighteen to forty-four, that number rose to 58 percent.[64] Finally, "pro-choice" groups such as EMILY's List and NARAL are very publicly worried about something they call the "intensity gap."[65] Of young people who identify as "pro-life," 51 percent claim that abortion is an important issue. But for young people who identify as "pro-choice," that number plummets to 20 percent. As with Hispanics, the abortion discourse in the United States will change dramatically as millennials gain positions of power.

Finally, consider the all-important demographic of women. It is the commonly assumed wisdom that women are the group most opposed to "pro-life" policies; after all, aren't women the ones primarily affected negatively by restricting abortion rights? During the 2012 elections, some Democratic political operatives even suggested that these stances were part of a "war on women." But it is at least odd to claim that a particular policy stance is part of a war on women when more women than men support the policy. Returning to the *Times* poll that asked whether the new pope should be for or against legalized abortion: 60 percent of women said "against," compared to only 52 percent of men. Regarding the twenty-week ban, 50 percent of women were for it, compared with only 43 percent of men. In a 2013 Pew Forum study that asked whether having an abortion was morally acceptable, 49 percent of women said it was not, compared with 45 percent of men.[66] Once again, the conventional wisdom on abortion is called into question by the actual facts on the ground.

I want to finish this section by highlighting two things that deserve close watching. The first is the Costanza strategies of the political parties. With the Internet and social media virtually taking over political campaigns, it is unlikely that the party bosses will be able to hold on to power via political sleight of hand—and, at times, outright dishonesty. This shift has happened to a certain extent already in 2009 with the Stupak Health Care Reform and "pro-life" Democratic movement. We are already starting to see a shift in the abortion debate toward "libertarian vs. nonlibertarian" rather than "Democrat vs. Republican." Those who are opposed to abortion will realize that they need "pro-life" Democrats, while the "pro-choice" movement will continue to enlist Republicans in their cause. The Costanza strategy is unsustainable, especially in the Internet age, and will not last forever.

But the other factor to keep in mind doesn't require speculation. Many believe that the "pro-life" laws that the states are enacting are unconstitutional. In a May 2013 article for the *New Yorker* entitled "The Abortion Issue Returns," Jeffrey Toobin notes that a few of these have already been struck down by lower courts.[67] These judges most often claimed that such laws posed an "undue burden" on women, something prohibited by *Planned Parenthood v. Casey*, the major Supreme Court abortion case that came after *Roe v. Wade*. Toobin notes that the holdover from that 1992 decision was Anthony Kennedy. Will his replacement, Brett Kavanaugh, uphold a state law with a twenty-week (or earlier) ban? Mandatory ultrasounds? More abortion clinic regulations? Will Justice Kavanaugh think that they are "undue burdens"? What will it look like when these state laws come before the current Supreme Court? We don't know, but it deserves our very close attention.

Conclusion

Given current trends, the positions of key future demographics, and the legal challenges on the horizon, the question is not if the American national abortion policy will undergo a substantial change, but when. Though this may favor "pro-lifers," my view is not the result of special pleading or rose-colored glasses. Longtime "pro-choice" activist Frances Kissling of Catholics for Choice has been saying something similar for years. Accusing "pro-choice" activists of being out of touch with trends in the debate, she argued in a 2011 *Washington Post* op-ed that the rhetoric of "choice" and "freedom"—especially when combined with the view that abortion is just like any other medical procedure—is losing the argument in American culture.[68] Here she lays out the challenge rather directly:

> We can no longer pretend the fetus is invisible....We must end the fiction that an abortion at 26 weeks is no different from one at six weeks. These are not compromises or mere strategic concessions, they are a necessary evolution. The positions we have taken up to now are inadequate for the questions of the 21st century. We know more than we knew in 1973, and our positions should reflect that. The fetus is more visible than ever before, and the abortion-rights movement

needs to accept its existence and its value....Very few people would argue that there is no difference between the decision to abort at 6 weeks and the decision to do so when the fetus would be viable outside of the womb, which today is generally at 24 to 26 weeks.

Still, it is rare for mainstream movement leaders to say that publicly. Abortion is not merely a medical matter, and there is an unintended coarseness to claiming that it is. We need to firmly and clearly reject post-viability abortions except in extreme cases....Those kinds of regulations are not anti-woman or unduly invasive. They rightly protect all of our interests in women's health and fetal life. Even abortions in the second trimester, especially after 20 weeks, need to be considered differently from those that happen early in pregnancy.

When hardcore "pro-choice" activists like Frances Kissling suggest changes with which many "pro-life" activists are likely to agree, this is good reason to think that they will happen. When we refuse to let the extremists rule the debate, we can see that Americans have a large amount of overlap when it comes to what they believe about abortion. We truly are on the cusp of a new moment for public discussion of abortion in the United States.

My view is that the best arguments about these matters happen to be very consistent with what most Americans do believe and will continue to believe in even stronger numbers about abortion. I hope this essay has convinced you that the arguments we will explore are not the abstract claims of yet another ivory tower intellectual writing for the very few people in the world who can decipher what he is doing. Instead, because we are on the verge of a major cultural and legal shift on these matters, how the following arguments play out is of the utmost practical importance. The lives of millions and millions of prenatal children, as well as the fundamental freedoms of their mothers, hang in the balance.

NOTES

1. Many readers will be familiar with the popular TV show *Seinfeld*, which dominated American situation comedy ratings during the 1990s. In one of the most hilarious episodes in the series, George Costanza, one of the main

characters, decides to take on a new strategy and do the opposite of every instinct he's ever had. It works out quite well for him.

2. Kathryn Kost and Stanley Henshaw, "Trends in the Characteristics of Women Obtaining Abortions, 1974 to 2004," Guttmacher Institute (August 2008), http://www.guttmacher.org/pubs/2008/09/18/Report_Trends_Women_Obtaining_Abortions.pdf.

3. R. K. Jones and K. Kooistra, "Abortion Incidence and Access to Services in the United States 2008," *Perspectives on Sexual and Reproductive Health* 43, no. 1 (2011): 41–50, http://www.guttmacher.org/pubs/psrh/full/4304111.pdf.

4. "Vital Statistics," The New York City Department of Health and Mental Hygiene (2012), accessed June 24, 2013, http://www.nyc.gov/html/doh/html/data/vs-summary.shtml.

5. Barack Obama, "Address to Notre Dame's Class of 2009," (speech, Notre Dame, IN), *New York Times*, May 17, 2009, https://www.nytimes.com/2009/05/17/us/politics/17text-obama.html.

6. The 1 in 3 Campaign, "The 1 in 3 Campaign—OUR Abortions, OUR Stories, OUR Lives," accessed May 1, 2019, http://www.1in3campaign.org/about.

7. Olivia Fleming, "'Got a Quickie Aborsh': Comedienne Sarah Silverman Supports Pro-Choice Debate, Tweeting 'Before-and-After Abortion' Photos," *Daily Mail*, April 17, 2012, https://www.dailymail.co.uk/femail/article-2129490/Sarah-Silverman-posts-quicky-abortion-photo-Twitter-support-pro-choice-debate.html.

8. Heather Wood Rudulph, "Why I Filmed My Abortion," *Cosmopolitan*, May 5, 2014, http://www.cosmopolitan.com/advice/health/why-i-filmed-my-abortion.

9. Lawrence B. Finer et al., "Reasons U.S. Women Have Abortions: Quantitative and Qualitative Perspectives," *Perspectives on Sexual and Reproductive Health* 37, no. 3 (2005):110–18, http://www.guttmacher.org/pubs/journals/3711005.pdf.

10. Caroline Mansfield, Suellen Hopfer, and Theresa Marteau, "Termination Rates after Prenatal Diagnosis of Down Syndrome, Spina Bifida, Anencephaly, and Turner and Klinefelter Syndromes: A Systematic Literature Review," *Prenatal Diagnosis* 19, no. 9 (1999): 808–12, https://obgyn.onlinelibrary.wiley.com/doi/abs/10.1002/%28SICI%291097-0223%28199909%2919%3A9%3C808%3A%3AAID-PD637%3E3.0.CO%3B2-B.

11. Brian Skotko, Susan Levine, and Richard Goldstein, "Self-perceptions from People with Down Syndrome," *American Journal of Medical Genetics* 155, no. 10 (2011): 2360–69, http://onlinelibrary.wiley.com/doi/10.1002/ajmg.a.34235/full.

12. John Bingham, "MPs: Abortions Being Carried Out for Cleft Palates," *The Telegraph*, July 13, 2013, http://www.telegraph.co.uk/news/politics/10183668/MPs-Abortions-being-carried-out-for-cleft-palates.html.

13. Ruth Padawer, "The Two-Minus-One Pregnancy," *New York Times*, August 10, 2011, http://www.nytimes.com/2011/08/14/magazine/the-two-minus-one-pregnancy.html?ref=magazine.

14. "An Overview of Abortion in the United States," Guttmacher Institute (2014), accessed June 24, 2013, http://www.guttmacher.org/presentations/abort_slides.pdf.

15. Rachel K. Jones, Lawrence B. Finer, and Susheela Singh, "Characteristics of U.S. Abortion Patients, 2009," Guttmacher Institute (2010), accessed June 24, 2013, http://www.guttmacher.org/pubs/US-Abortion-Patients.pdf.

16. Though I will make no explicit arguments about contraception in this book, it is worth noting that both the United Kingdom and Sweden have sweeping and publicly supported use of contraception, and they still have a very high abortion rate.

17. "Fact Sheet: Induced Abortion in the United States," Guttmacher Institute (2014), accessed May 3, 2019, https://www.guttmacher.org/evidence-you-can-use/later-abortion.

18. Though a new blood test can be used to try to screen for Down syndrome in the first trimester, it would need to be confirmed by tests (usually by amniocentesis) in the second trimester.

19. Josh Voorhees, "Abortion Provider Kermit Gosnell Found Guilty on Three Counts of First-Degree Murder," *Slate*, May 13, 2013, https://slate.com/news-and-politics/2013/05/kermit-gosnell-jury-reaches-verdict-in-case-of-pa-abortion-doctor-accused-of-killing-babies.html.

20. Melinda Henneberger, "Are There More Abortion Doctors like Kermit Gosnell? And Do We Want to Know?" *Washington Post*, April 28, 2013, https://www.washingtonpost.com/blogs/she-the-people/wp/2013/04/28/are-there-more-abortion-doctors-like-kermit-gosnell-do-we-want-to-know/.

21. Finer et al., "Reasons U.S. Women Have Abortions."

22. Landrum Shettles and David Rorvik, *Rites of Life* (Grand Rapids, MI: Zondervan, 1983), 129.

23. "Herstory Worth Repeating," Feminists for Life, accessed June 28, 2013, http://www.feministsforlife.org/herstory/.

24. Kristen Day, *Democrats for Life: Pro-Life Politics and the Silenced Majority* (Green Forest, AR: New Leaf Press, 2006), 71–145.

25. Some now argue that Blackmun was convinced by other "pro-choice" colleagues (and their clerks) on the Court, and that he originally had a much more restrictive vision for *Roe*. See David Garrow, "How *Roe v. Wade* Was Written," *Washington and Lee Law Review* 71, no. 2 (Spring 2014): article

9, http://scholarlycommons.law.wlu.edu/cgi/viewcontent.cgi?article=4393& context=wlulr.

26. Though many in the movement are totally sincere today, there is some evidence that the religious right of the late 1970s self-consciously used abortion as an ad hoc way of creating a broader political coalition within the Republican Party. See Randall Balmer, *Thy Kingdom Come: An Evangelical's Lament* (New York: Basic Books, 2006), 16.

27. Day, *Democrats for Life*, 96.

28. Lydia Saad, "'Conservatives' Are Single-Largest Ideological Group," Gallup, June 15, 2009, https://news.gallup.com/poll/120857/Conservatives -Single-Largest-Ideological-Group.aspx.

29. Neil King Jr. and Allison Prang, "More Voters Turn on Obama," *Wall Street Journal*, October 30, 2013, https://www.wsj.com/articles/scorn -spreads-to-both-sides-1383172147.

30. K.N.C, "End of the Party?" *Economist*, January 8, 2014, http://www .economist.com/blogs/democracyinamerica/2014/01/american-politics.

31. Robert P. Jones, Daniel Cox, and Thomas Banchoff, "A Generation in Transition: Religion, Values, and Politics among College-age Millennials," *PRRI*, 2012, http://www.prri.org/research/millennial-values-survey-2012/.

32. "Abortion and Birth Control," CBS News Poll, accessed August 1, 2013, http://www.pollingreport.com/abortion.htm.

33. Lydia Saad, "Majority of Americans Still Support Roe v. Wade Decision," Gallup, January 22, 2013, http://www.gallup.com/poll/160058/ majority-americans-support-roe-wade-decision.aspx.

34. U.S. House of Representatives, "Final Vote Results for Roll Call 884," United States Congress (2009), http://clerk.house.gov/evs/2009/ roll884.xml. That such a large number of "pro-life" Democrats could vote for such a "pro-life" bill was the first sign that something was different this time around.

35. J. Peter Nixon, "A Pro-Life Victory?" *Commonweal* (March 22, 2010), https://www.commonwealmagazine.org/pro-life-victory.

36. See chap. 6 for a more detailed discussion of these provisions.

37. Jodi Jacobson, "Nelson Restrictions Most Likely Outcome of Recon-ciliation Process," Rewire.News, March 3, 2010, https://rewire.news/article/ 2010/03/03/nelson-restrictions-most-likely-outcome-reconciliation-process/; "White House Crafting Deal with Stupak on Executive Order," Rewire.News, March 21, 2010, https://rewire.news/article/2010/03/21/update-correction -white-house-crafting-deal-stupak-executive-order/.

38. In 2013, for instance, "pro-life" Democrats were essential in defeat-ing New York Gov. Andrew Cuomo's attempt to expand late-term abortion (Charles Camosy, "Late-Term Abortion Expansion Defeated in New York State...Thanks to Pro-Life Democrats," *Catholic Moral Theology*, June 22, 2013,

http://catholicmoraltheology.com/late-term-abortion-expansion-defeated-in
-new-york-state-thanks-to-pro-life-democrats/).

39. Some, including many legal scholars, may simply deny that *Roe* is
still the law of the land, especially given its successor cases, such as *Planned Parenthood v. Casey*, which have substantially modified the decision. I explore this in
some detail in later chapters.

40. Pew Research Religion and Public Life Project, "Roe v. Wade at 40:
Most Oppose Overturning Abortion Decision," January 16, 2013, http://www
.pewforum.org/2013/01/16/roe-v-wade-at-40/.

41. Raymond J. Ademak, "A Review: Public Opinion and Roe v. Wade:
Measurement Difficulties," *Public Opinion Quarterly* 58, no. 3 (1994): 409–18,
https://www.jstor.org/stable/2749730.

42. Linda Greenhouse, "Misconceptions About Roe v. Wade," *New York
Times*, January 23, 2013, https://opinionator.blogs.nytimes.com/2013/01/
23/misconceptions/.

43. Jason Keyser, "Ginsburg: Roe Gave Abortion Opponents a Target," *New York Daily News*, May 12, 2013, https://www.nydailynews.com/sdut
-ginsburg-roe-gave-abortion-opponents-a-target-2013may12-story.html.

44. Princeton UCHV, "Open Hearts, Open Minds, and Fair-Minded
Words: A Conference on Life and Choice in the Abortion Debate," October
15, 2010, https://jmp.princeton.edu/events/open-hearts-open-minds-and
-fair-minded-words-conference-life-and-choice-abortion-debate.

45. Jamila Bey, "Wendy Davis Beats the Clock, with an Assist from the
Gallery," *Washington Post*, June 26, 2013, http://www.washingtonpost.com/
blogs/she-the-people/wp/2013/06/26/wendy-davis-beats-the-clock-with-an
-assist-from-the-gallery/.

46. "Europe's Abortion Rules," BBC News, last modified February 12,
2007, accessed July 1, 2013, http://news.bbc.co.uk/2/hi/europe/6235557.stm.

47. Tobias Buck, "Spain's Mariano Rajoy in Fight to Reverse Liberalised Abortion Law," *Financial Times*, 2013, accessed May 3, 2019, https://
www.ft.com/content/376f6bf0-c477-11e2-bc94-00144feab7de.

48. "Gallardón: I Think of the Fear of Losing Their Jobs because of
Pregnancy," *El Pais Sociedad*, March 8, 2012, http://translate.google.com/
translate?act=url&depth=1&hl=en&ie=UTF8&prev=_t&rurl=translate
.google.com&sl=auto&tl=en&u=http://sociedad.elpais.com/sociedad/2012/
03/08/actualidad/1331177681_396483.html.

49. This fact is the fulfillment of the hope and argument first made
more than twenty-five years ago by Mary Ann Glendon in her *Abortion and
Divorce in Western Law: American Failures, European Challenges* (Cambridge, MA:
Harvard University Press, 1989).

50. Clarke D. Forsythe, "Progress after Casey," *National Review Online*, June 29, 2012, https://www.nationalreview.com/corner/progress-after-casey-clarke-d-forsythe/.

51. These are Alabama, Arkansas, Arizona, Georgia, Idaho, Indiana, Iowa, Kansas, Kentucky, Louisiana, Mississippi, Nebraska, North Carolina, North Dakota, Ohio, Oklahoma, South Carolina, South Dakota, Texas, West Virginia, and Wisconsin. Source: Rewire.News Legislative Tracker, "20-Week Bans," last updated April 15, 2019, accessed May 1, 2019, https://rewire.news/legislative-tracker/law-topic/20-week-bans/.

52. Paul Bedard, "70 New Anti-abortion Laws OK'd in 22 States, Second-Most Ever," *Washington Examiner*, January 2, 2014, http://washingtonexaminer.com/70-new-anti-abortion-laws-okd-in-22-states-second-most-ever/article/2541498.

53. Guttmacher Institute, "2012 Saw Second-Highest Number of Abortion Restrictions Ever," January 2, 2013, http://www.guttmacher.org/media/inthenews/2013/01/02/.

54. Linda Feldmann, "Eleven States Charging Hard against Abortion," *Christian Science Monitor*, June 14, 2013, https://www.csmonitor.com/USA/Politics/2013/0614/11-states-charging-hard-against-abortion/Arkansas-Legislature-overrides-governor-bans-abortion-after-12-weeks.

55. See https://www.nysenate.gov/legislation/bills/2019/s240.

56. Victoria M. DeFrancesco Soto, "Opinion: Can the Republicans Connect with Latinos on Abortion?" NBC Latino, August 24, 2012, http://nbclatino.com/2012/08/24/opinion-can-the-republicans-connect-with-latinos-on-abortion/.

57. Damla Ergun, "Majority Supports Legal Abortion, but Details Indicate Ambivalence," ABC News, July 25, 2013, https://abcnews.go.com/blogs/politics/2013/07/majority-supports-legal-abortion-but-details-indicate-ambivalence/.

58. Anna Simonton, "The Future of the Pro-Choice Movement," *The Nation*, February 6, 2013, http://www.thenation.com/article/172713/future-pro-choice.

59. Elizabeth Hayt, "Surprise, Mom: I'm Against Abortion," *New York Times*, March 30, 2003, https://www.nytimes.com/2003/03/30/style/surprise-mom-i-m-against-abortion.html?searchResultPosition=1.

60. Chris McComb, "Teens Lean Conservative on Abortion," Gallup, November 18, 2003, http://www.gallup.com/poll/9715/Teens-Lean-Conservative-Abortion.aspx.

61. Lydia Saad, "Generational Differences on Abortion Narrow," Gallup, March 12, 2010, http://www.gallup.com/poll/126581/generational-differences-abortion-narrow.aspx.

62. Robert P. Jones, Daniel Cox, and Thomas Banchoff, "A Generation in Transition: Religion, Values, and Politics among College-age Millennials," *PRRI*, April 19, 2012, http://www.prri.org/research/millennial-values-survey -2012/.

63. Sarah Kliff, "The Abortion Ban Texas Is Debating? It Already Exists in 12 Other States," *Washington Post*, July 1, 2013, http://www.washingtonpost .com/blogs/wonkblog/wp/2013/07/01/the-20-week-abortion-ban-texas-is -debating-already-exists-in-12-states/.

64. "Americans on the Catholic Church," *New York Times* and CBS News, March 6, 2013, https://archive.nytimes.com/www.nytimes.com/interactive/ 2013/03/06/us/catholics-america-poll.html.

65. Sarah Kliff, "Exclusive: NARAL President Nancy Keenan to Step Down," May 10, 2012, http://www.washingtonpost.com/blogs/wonkblog/ post/exclusive-naral-president-nancy-keenan-to-step-down/2012/05/ro/ gIQAn85PGU_blog.html.

66. Pew Research Religion and Public Life Project, "Roe v. Wade at 40: Most Oppose Overturning Abortion Decision," January 16. 2013, http://www .pewforum.org/2013/01/16/roe-v-wade-at-40/.

67. Jeffrey Toobin, "The Abortion Issue Returns," *New Yorker*, May 28, 2013, http://www.newyorker.com/online/blogs/comment/2013/05/ abortion-returns-to-the-supreme-court.html.

68. Frances Kissling, "Abortion Rights Are Under Attack, and Pro-Choice Advocates Are Caught in a Time Warp," *Washington Post*, February 18, 2011, http://www.washingtonpost.com/wp-dyn/content/article/2011/02/ 18/AR2011021802434.html.

Questions for Further Reflection

1. The author says that views on abortion have changed over the years. How?

2. In terms of the political response to abortion issues, the author says that the Republicans and Democrats use the "Costanza strategy." What does he mean by this? Do you agree? Why or why not?

3. What does the author say is incorrect about the statement that abortion is "safe, legal, and rare"?

4. At what stage in pregnancy do most abortions occur? What percent of abortions are due to rape or incest?

5. How does each political party attempt to use abortion for its own political advantage? What was the stance of each party on abortion before the Costanza strategy?

6. The author says that *Roe v. Wade* was not just a judicial turning point but also a political turning point on the abortion issue. How was it a judicial turning point? How was it a political turning point?

7. Does current thinking on abortion in the United States easily break down into liberal vs. conservative views? Or pro-life vs. pro-choice views? Why or why not?

8. What does the author mean when he talks about the return of the pro-life Democrats? In what context did this occur? What was the political fate of these pro-life Democrats?

9. What does the author say that Americans currently think about *Roe v. Wade*? Do you agree? Why or why not?

10. What trends does the author think the future holds for American views on abortion? On the regulation of abortion? How is abortion regulated now?

11. What does the author think is the future of abortion politics? Will the Costanza strategy prevail? Why or why not? What groups does he say are trending pro-life? Which are not? How will this affect our politics?

12. What will be the role of the U.S. Supreme Court in the future of abortion in the United States?

13. What should the role of the U.S. bishops be in abortion politics? What should the role of individual Catholics be?

14. What is the author's conclusion on the future of abortion in the United States? Do you agree or disagree? Why or why not?

15. How would you like to see abortion dealt with by our legal system? Would this influence the way that you vote?

8

Worker Justice as a Pro-Life Issue

Gerald J. Beyer

Worker justice is a pro-life issue. Violations of the dignity and rights of workers are literally a matter of life and death both domestically and abroad. According to the International Labor Organization (ILO), a worker dies from a work-related disease or accident every fifteen seconds.[1] The health and lives of millions of workers are imperiled by "an economy [that] kills," as Pope Francis has stated.[2] In this chapter, I argue that Catholic voters must consider whether or not a candidate will advance policies that protect or harm the "human right to life and limb" and livelihood of workers.[3] Moreover, I contend that being pro-life must entail advocating for all the rights of workers espoused by Catholic social teaching (CST). According to Pope Francis, a global economy that fails to provide "dignified work," which respects workers' rights, constitutes a "betrayal of the common good" and a threat to human dignity.[4] The structure of my argument follows CST's "see, judge, act" methodology. First, I describe the violence and threats to life workers endure globally and in the United States. Next, I evaluate the problems by applying CST on the rights of workers. Finally, I consider how voters might wrestle with worker justice as a pro-life issue at the ballot box.

153

Life, Death, and the Politics
of Dignified Work

Dignified work first and foremost protects the sanctity of life by ensuring the health and safety of all workers.[5] The ILO presently estimates more than 2.78 million people globally die annually from work-related accidents or diseases. In other words, more than 7,600 workers die every day from work-related causes.[6] Although fatal accidents in the workplace play a significant role, work-related diseases cause most of these deaths. For example, the ILO's 2013 report *The Prevention of Occupational Diseases* attributed 14 percent of all work-related deaths to accidents (321,000) and 86 percent to fatal diseases (2.02 million). Exposure to silica, asbestos, and mineral dusts put workers at risk for pneumoconioses. Illnesses such as chronic obstructive pulmonary disease, silico-tuberculosis, and silica- and asbestos-related cancers often lead to "permanent disability or premature death."[7]

Unsafe working conditions kill, but they also give rise to 310 million nonfatal workplace accidents and 160 million nonfatal work-related diseases annually.[8] These accidents and illnesses create tremendous financial, physical, and emotional burdens for workers, and impose a cost of roughly $2.8 trillion or 4 percent of global GDP.[9] Policy experts and trade unions have sought to address psychological harm and stress, an increasingly widespread problem for workers in a global economy that makes ever-greater demands on their minds, bodies, and time.[10] Work-related stress causes musculoskeletal and cardiovascular illness, as well as mental illnesses such as anxiety, depression, and suicidal ideation.[11]

In addition to exposing workers to potentially fatal occupational hazards and inhumane working conditions, the enemies of workers' rights also directly harm or kill laborers. Workers' efforts to form unions are often met with threats, beatings, arrests, and even death.[12] The number of countries where workers faced these types of violence rose from fifty-nine in 2017 to sixty-five in 2018. Trade unionists were killed in nine different countries, with nineteen murdered in Columbia alone. Governments in 65 percent of the world's nations forbid workers from forming or joining a union.[13] In addition, the ILO estimates almost 24.9 million people are modern slaves and endure forced labor, which obviously entails grave bodily and psychological harm.[14] Some estimates reach as high as two hundred million.[15] In developing countries, anywhere from

50 to 90 percent of jobs are in the informal economy. More than seven hundred million workers who toil in the informal sector earn below 1.25 USD daily and are not protected by any labor laws.[16] These workers' lives are thus threatened by extreme poverty, dangerous conditions, and exploitation without impunity. Workers in most countries are not protected from discrimination in the workplace on the basis of gender, ethnicity, religion, or disability.[17] Sexual harassment and "psychological forms of violence" in the workplace such as harassment, bullying, and mobbing are rampant.[18] In short, working around the globe is often severely debilitating and deadly. Many lives could be saved by implementing cost-effective measures that are already known and in use in some places. It is a matter of changing the "values and mindset of all stakeholders."[19]

This inhumane violence workers endure globally has gendered and racial dimensions. Modern capitalism was undergirded by racialized slavery and subjugation of women in homes, fields, and factories.[20] Today women and children are vastly overrepresented among workers in areas notorious for low pay and perilous, exploitative conditions: the informal sector, the service sector, textiles, caregiving, and domestic labor.[21] More than two hundred million children work globally, very often in dangerous conditions.[22] Women constitute more than 75 percent of garment workers.[23] In Latin America 90 percent of workers in export processing are women. In such industries employers often compel women to work eighty hours a week or more.[24] Women are often forced to take pregnancy tests before being hired. If they get pregnant, they are often either fired or forced to work in ways that cause severe risk to the unborn child. Women are six times more likely than men to lose a job for caring for sick children.[25] In other words, the environment that women work in does not respect life: their lives and the lives of their children are at risk.[26]

The racialization of labor intersects with the feminization of global employment. As one scholarly study concludes, "People of color, especially women of color, continue to do the hardest work for the lowest pay under the harshest working conditions."[27] In fact, the "ideal worker" in the global supply chain is a young "docile" woman from the Global South who has little choice but to accept poverty wages, terrible abuse, and hazardous work environments.[28] Multinational corporations successfully distract consumers from the plight of workers by "project[ing] corporate images that advance, sometimes even provocatively, a multicultural sensibility—as they amass huge profits from the exploitation of nonwhite labor."[29]

The United States

Because American voters comprise the primary audience for this book, it is important to highlight the labor situation in the United States. The United States compares favorably in some ways to parts of the global supply chain. For example, the United States has relatively strong antidiscrimination employment laws and overtime pay guarantees.[30] However, the *2018 ITUC Global Rights Index* lists the United States among those countries that have "systematic violations of workers' rights," along with countries like Vietnam, Haiti, Ethiopia, Paraguay, and Romania. The United States ranks below sixty-one other countries.[31] Workers in many low-wage industries are subject to wage theft, denial of breaks, retaliation for trying to form unions or complaining about working conditions, and other forms of abuse.[32] As Human Rights Watch contended, workers' freedom of association is "under sustained attack in the United States."[33] Workers in the United States serve as "guinea pigs" used to determine whether or not exposure to certain toxins poses a risk to the rest of society, as James Gross points out in *A Shameful Business*. Many Americans are generally ignorant of the widespread violations of the right to life and limb in this country, mistakenly believing that worker exploitation, sweatshops, and the like are only "Third World Problems."[34] In 2016, the United States Department of Labor reported 5,190 fatal workplace accidents, the most since 2008. Every day almost fifteen workers die as a result of a fatal accident at work.[35] When including workplace related illnesses, the death toll rises slightly above 100,000 per year according to the National Council for Occupational Health & Safety's report *Preventable Deaths 2016*.[36] More than 2,857,400 nonfatal workplace accidents or illnesses were recorded in 2016.[37] Many of these illnesses and deaths could be avoided if politicians took enforcement of the 1970 Occupational Safety and Health Act seriously rather than catering to corporate antiregulation lobbyists.[38]

Logging, fishing, and transportation continue to have among the highest numbers and rates of fatalities.[39] Many other industries flagrantly mistreat and expose workers to dangerous chemicals and conditions in the United States. I have written about the widespread prevalence of chronic strain disorders, sexual harassment, and other forms of exploitation of hotel workers in the United States.[40] Here I want to highlight the poultry industry and agricultural sector.

Nonfatal injury and illness rates in the poultry industry are five times greater than the U.S. average.[41] It has a higher rate of injury than logging, coal mining, and oil and gas extraction.[42] Workers are forced to work at breakneck speed with sharp, dangerous instruments in close quarters. As a result, more than half of cutters and deboners report having been injured on the job. Many injuries go unreported, due to threats and/or fear of retaliation by employers.[43] Poultry workers are regularly exposed to ammonia, chlorine, other toxins, and carcinogens. They also have much higher rates of depression and anxiety, which experts attribute to the physically and mentally debilitating working conditions.[44] The poultry industry recruits "some of the world's most vulnerable immigrants" from places such as Guatemala. Many fear protesting their wretched situation due to their immigration status.[45] At the same time, the industry enjoys increasingly greater profits as chicken consumption has tripled since 1978.[46]

Contrary to the mythical, romantic portrayals of American agrarian life, farming is one of the most dangerous workplaces in the United States. Farmworkers' fatality rate is five times greater than among all workers.[47] In 2013, the fatality rate among crop production workers (22.9 deaths per 100,000 workers) surpassed industries such as mining (15.1 deaths per 100,000 workers) or construction (9.7 deaths per 100,000 workers).[48] As many as 81 percent of farmworkers are immigrants, mostly hailing from Mexico.[49] Experts caution that data pertaining to the morbidity and mortality of migrant farmworkers is "skewed down due to fear of reporting health problems, poor enforcement of labor and health policies in agriculture and the fact that many Latin American migrants return to their home countries as they age or become disabled."[50] Nonetheless, it is clear that they have higher rates of many illnesses, including malnutrition, blood disorders, anemia, numerous cancers, abnormal liver and kidney function, encephalitis, leptospirosis, salmonellosis, and others. Prevalence of tuberculosis is six times higher than in general. Farmworkers have greater risk of miscarriage and giving birth to children with birth defects. Furthermore, the majority of migrant farmworkers and their families live below the poverty line, without health insurance and in squalid conditions.[51] An estimated twenty thousand farmworkers are poisoned by pesticides annually, with the real incidence likely much higher.[52] The Coalition of Immokalee Workers has uncovered over 1,200 cases of human slavery among the fields of the Southeastern United States in the last few decades.[53] Some estimate that as many as fifteen thousand forced laborers are trafficked into the United States annually, with 10 percent of them in forced agricultural labor.[54]

In the United States many people work but still live in poverty. According to the latest (2016) government data, more than forty million people live below the federal poverty line. More than 7.6 million people rank among the working poor. That same year, 4.1 million families lived in poverty even though at least one member worked.[55] About a quarter of all poor people aged eighteen to sixty-five work at least fifty weeks per year.[56] Oxfam American contends that "tens of millions" are employed in low wage work (earning less than $20,000 year) in the United States, which has the highest proportion of such jobs among all wealthy countries.[57] Women are also more likely to be among the working poor, while blacks and Hispanics are roughly twice as likely as whites and Asians.[58] "In 2017, 8.6 percent of white workers were paid poverty wages....In contrast, 19.2 percent—nearly one in five—Hispanic workers were paid poverty wages, and 14.3 percent—roughly one in seven—black workers were paid poverty wages."[59] Even advanced degrees no longer prevent Americans from joining the "hyper-educated poor." In more than 28 percent of families receiving food stamps, the head of the household had some higher education. The number of people with advanced degrees obtaining various forms of federal aid has tripled in recent times.[60]

The working poor face dramatic, often life-threatening situations, such as forgoing health care for themselves and their children, working two or three jobs, or leaving their children in their homelands while sending back remittances in order to survive.[61] "Being poor in the United States is so hazardous to your health…that the average life expectancy of the lowest-income classes in America is now equal to that in Sudan or Pakistan."[62] One study concluded that as many as 5,550 lives could have been saved between 2008 and 2012 by raising the minimum wage to fifteen dollars in New York City.[63] However, millions of workers are still paid poverty wages, even if the Fight for Fifteen movement has made some progress on this front.[64] As a recent EPI report states, "for the large majority of workers over the last four decades, wages were essentially flat or falling, apart from a few short bursts of growth."[65] Meanwhile CEO pay exceeds the minimum wage worker's pay 774 to 1.[66]

Supporting workers' rights (to a living wage, for example) could also save the lives of young children and help them stay healthy. Recent research shows a correlation between increasing minimum wages and decreasing the alarmingly high infant mortality rate in the United States (ranked fifty-first in the world, below Belarus, Cuba, and Bosnia and Herzegovina, for example).[67] Increasing the minimum wage in every state by just one dollar above the federal level could decrease low birth weight births by 1 to 2 percent and decrease postneonatal mortality by 4 percent annually.[68] Children also suffer and die due to the fact that the United States is the only rich country in the world without paid parental leave. Most OECD countries guarantee a full six months paid maternity leave, while sixty-six countries ensure fourteen weeks of paid paternity leave. According to the World Policy Center, there is clear evidence that laws mandating paid parental leaves, sick leave, family medical leave, and breastfeeding breaks significantly lower infant and child morbidity and mortality.[69] Unlike the United States, countries supporting these policies understand what a genuine pro-family politics requires.

U.S. politics and laws have historically favored corporate profits over workers' rights.[70] However, American workers today are facing increasing threats. Prior to the 2016 election, I argued that Donald Trump's record on labor issues augured a grim future for American workers.[71] Unfortunately, the evidence supports this prediction. The Obama Administration implemented numerous occupational health and safety enhancements.[72] The Trump administration dismantled as many as fourteen of them in the early months of his presidency.[73] For example, the administration eliminated the Fair Pay and Workplace Safety Rule, which the Obama administration had instituted to strengthen oversight of federally contracted companies to improve their compliance with occupational safety laws and penalize them for wage theft.[74] Millions of U.S. workers experience wage theft, which often jeopardizes their livelihood.[75] The Trump administration delayed implementing an Obama era regulation designed to limit workers' exposure to silica for over a year and a half, a delay likely fatal to workers. As many as 2.3 million workers annually are exposed to silica dust, which kills an estimated six hundred workers a year.[76] The administration also postponed, then enfeebled, beryllium regulations. Beryllium dust causes lung cancer and other illnesses.[77]

Under Trump, the EPA has seemingly cowered to industry by stalling discussion of a report that establishes a link between leukemia and exposure to unsafe levels of formaldehyde in certain industries.[78] Experts from within the EPA itself and other organizations have decried the EPA's new regulations pertaining to asbestos, stating that it permits currently banned uses.[79] Asbestos is a known carcinogen that kills an estimated fifteen thousand Americans per year.[80] The ILO called for a ban of asbestos in 2006 and lists it as the primary cause of work-related lung cancer.[81] The Trump administration has weakened mining safety regulations. It has astonishingly eliminated regulations on offshore oil rigs that the Obama administration implemented in order to prevent another Deepwater Horizon disaster, which killed eleven people and spilled millions of barrels of oil into the Gulf of Mexico. Under Trump the USDA has abolished line speed limits in hog processing plants and increased the limits at poultry processing plants from 140 to 175 birds per minute.[82] OSHA is seeking to diminish reporting requirements of injuries and deaths for companies with more than 250 workers. In the words of Peg Seminario, director of occupational safety and health for the AFL-CIO, Trump's deregulation agenda has eviscerated "core worker protections and union rights" and has been "totally anti-worker."[83]

The ascendance of Neil Gorsuch and Brett Kavanaugh to the Supreme Court also does not bode well for worker safety and labor rights, given their stark antilabor history. Gorsuch authored the opinion in *Epic Systems v. Lewis*, which undercuts the ability of workers to sue collectively to recover stolen wages.[84] His vote in the *Janus v. AFSCME* case tipped the scale in favor of antilabor groups who backed Janus and to whom Gorsuch apparently has ties.[85] The decision will severely drain unions of the financial resources needed to represent workers and will cause them to dwindle even more.[86] Kavanaugh has consistently ruled in favor of corporations and against workers in workplace safety, employment discrimination, and collective bargaining cases throughout his career.[87] His now infamous *Seaworld* opinion caused labor advocates to contend he sees overregulation as a bigger threat than allowing workers to be maimed or killed.[88] Kavanaugh also argued that undocumented workers have no rights and cannot join unions.[89]

In addition to appointing antilabor judges, Trump has decreased the regulatory power of the NLRB by eliminating some NLRB regional offices or cutting their budgets, installing two pro-business attorneys to the NLRB, and curtailing its ability to protect workers' rights.[90] While Bernie Sanders proposed the Stop Bad Employers by Zeroing Out Subsidies Act (Stop BEZOS Act) encouraging Amazon to raise its minimum pay to fifteen dollars an hour, Trump and his party oppose raising the federal minimum wage.[91] Despite Trump's bluster, the average American worker earned *less* after the first eighteen months of his presidency.[92] He has fallen well short of his promises to create new jobs.[93] He has proposed a "budget-neutral approach to parental leave" that would require parents to draw from their retirement benefits. The plan would cause low-wage workers and those with bigger families to delay retirement more than the wealthy.[94]

CST on Workers' Rights and the Sacredness of Workers' Lives

In the light of Catholic social teaching, the global and U.S. economies egregiously violate the dignity and rights of workers, which CST has vigorously defended for centuries.[95] St. John Paul II, who said his time in forced labor during World War II enabled him to "learn the Gospel anew," contended the gospel must be applied to the world of work.[96] In his encyclical on human labor, *Laborem exercens*, he spelled out how and why. Like his predecessors, John Paul argued workers have rights in accordance with natural law. However, the gospel also conveys that God became human, toiled as a carpenter, and thereby revealed that the dignity of all work resides in the human person doing the work, not the work itself. We must also recognize Christ remains present in every worker.[97] Thus, every worker has inviolable rights, regardless of the type of labor. Among those rights are the following: the right to work; the right to a just wage (at a minimum, a living wage that enables one worker to support a family); the right to affordable health care; to rest (at least one day per week and a yearly vacation); to retirement pensions; unemployment insurance; workers' compensation; paid maternity leave; and safe working conditions. Workers also have the rights to unionize, to collective bargaining, to participation in workplace decisions, and to strike when other means of protecting their rights fail.[98] John Paul II added that women have the right to "equal pay for equal work, protection for working mothers, fairness in career advancements, and equality of spouses with regard to family rights."[99] According to John Paul II, these rights are needed to "ensure the life and health of workers and their families."[100] All of society, including employers and the state, must protect these rights by adopting "careful controls and adequate legislative measures to block shameful forms of exploitation, especially to the disadvantage of the most vulnerable workers, of immigrants and of those on the margins of society."[101] Strong unions are also necessary to promote worker justice and redress the imbalance of power between labor and management.[102]

As the empirical realities discussed earlier reveal, promoting workers' rights is a necessary component of building a "culture of life," to use St. John Paul II's language.[103] Pope Francis has reinforced the notion that Catholics must promote what Cardinal Bernardin and others have called the consistent ethic of life.[104] Francis insists in *Gaudium exultate* that although Catholic teaching against abortion remains unwavering, "equally sacred, however, are the lives of the poor, those already born, the destitute, the abandoned and the underprivileged, the vulnerable infirm and elderly exposed to covert euthanasia, the victims of human trafficking, new forms of slavery, and every form of rejection."[105] Francis also articulates a consistent ethic of life approach in *Evangelii gaudium* 213–15:

> Among the vulnerable for whom the Church wishes to care with particular love and concern are unborn children, the most defenseless and innocent among us....This defense of unborn life is closely linked to the defense of each and every other human right. It involves the conviction that a human being is always sacred and inviolable, in any situation and at every stage of development....There are other weak and defenseless beings who are frequently at the mercy of economic interests or indiscriminate exploitation.

Evangelii gaudium specifies that the commandment "thou shall not kill" forbids acceptance of an "economy of exclusion and inequality" that "kills." This economy uses human beings then discards them, rather than according them the inviolable dignity they deserve (§53). It is not difficult to see how this applies to workers in the global economy. In fact, Francis has made the connection explicit on numerous occasions. For example, in his address to workers in Sardinia, he condemned a global economy that idolizes profits rather than provide "dignified work" for all. An economy that fails to provide such work eliminates "social hope" and is a form of "hidden euthanasia" according to Francis. Francis also argued that dignified work must be seen as part of the broader framework of what CST calls integral ecology: "Work must be combined with the preservation of creation, so that this may be responsibly safeguarded for future generations. Creation is not a good to be exploited but a gift to look after."[106]

The USCCB has echoed this consistent ethic of life in *Faithful Citizenship*: "The right to life implies and is linked to other human rights—to the basic goods that every human person needs to live and thrive. All the life issues are connected, for erosion of respect for the life of any individual or group in society necessarily diminishes respect for all life. The moral imperative to respond to the needs of our neighbors—basic needs such as food, shelter, health care, education, and meaningful work—is universally binding on our consciences and may be legitimately fulfilled by a variety of means."[107] Following *Gaudium et spes*, the document lists "deliberately subjecting workers or the poor to subhuman living conditions" among other intrinsic evils and supports "social and economic policies" that promote all the rights of workers affirmed by modern Catholic social teaching.[108] Coupled with the USCCB's strong advocacy for workers' rights in numerous documents and their annual Labor Day Statements, it should be clear that concern for the right to life and limb, along with all other workers' rights, should weigh heavily on the consciences of voters. These issues cannot be dismissed as "optional concerns" or matters of "prudential judgment," as opposed to intrinsic evils like abortion and euthanasia as some Catholic commentators have suggested.[109]

Preaching on James 5, Pope Francis has claimed employers who exploit workers are "leeches" that commit "mortal sin" and should not call themselves Christian.[110] As *Gaudium et spes* (§27) stated, subjecting workers to "disgraceful working conditions" and treating them "as mere instruments of profit" is intrinsically evil.[111] In other words, exploiting or abusing workers directly constitutes formal cooperation in evil, which is never justifiable and is likely to cause scandal in the church. Buying goods made in sweatshops or investing in companies that violate workers' rights also ensnares us in evil, but may be permissible if we attempt to mitigate the harm and other conditions are met.[112] Likewise, voting for politicians who do not support workers' rights also constitutes cooperation in evil. If a Catholic voter casts a ballot with the *intention* of further eroding workers' rights by voting for a candidate whose policies will harm workers, the voter commits formal cooperation in evil.[113] This may seem unlikely. However, many Catholics today do not support workers' rights, often because they subscribe to a radical libertarian (neoliberal), free-market ideology.[114] Catholic teaching rejects this ideology, and blames its adherents' choices for the plight of the poor and the various forms of violence that workers routinely experience. As Pope Francis stated, "Youth unemployment, informality, and the lack of labor rights are not inevitable; they are the result of a previous social option, of an economic system that puts profit above man [*sic*]."[115]

Even though Catholic voters have a *prima facie* duty not to vote for a candidate who does not respect the right to life, limb, and livelihood of workers and their families, they may do so for other "truly grave moral reasons" while rejecting the candidate's anti-worker stance.[116] Catholics often face painful choices when voting because candidates and their parties rarely embrace the consistent ethic of life approach of CST. According to the USCCB, in such situations Catholics should carefully discern which candidate is "less likely to advance" policies that promote "an intrinsically evil act" and "more likely to pursue other authentic human goods." Thus, after careful study of the fullness of Catholic social teaching and a candidate's track record and policy proposals, Catholics must make difficult decisions in their conscience about for whom to vote, or to "take the extraordinary step of not voting."[117]

Regardless of how one ultimately votes, a Catholic must seriously contemplate how a candidate will foster or violate the rights of workers both in the United States and globally. Catholics should also stand in solidarity with all workers by encouraging elected officials to support pro-labor policies and practices. While U.S. elected officials have the most immediate effect on workers' rights domestically, they also have influence on working conditions abroad via bilateral and multilateral trade agreements and U.S. hegemony in organizations like the WTO and IMF.[118] Unfortunately, both the IMF and the American Chamber of Commerce have lobbied governments to weaken labor standards.[119] NAFTA originally included a "side agreement" pertaining to the rights of workers (the North American Agreement on Labor Cooperation). However, only one unsuccessful labor violations case was filed after unions demanded action for two years.[120] The 2018 trade agreement between Mexico, Canada, and the United States contains stronger labor standards (against forced labor and violence against workers, for example) but critics worry that enforcement still relies on apathetic governments to file labor standards complaints, not workers or unions themselves.[121] Catholicism's call to global solidarity demands that Catholics do not solely consider the welfare of American workers.[122] As consumers, individuals and institutions can purchase ethically made goods and support the work of NGOs like the Workers' Rights Consortium and United Students against Sweatshops.[123] Such organizations have campaigned successfully to coax companies into better protecting workers' rights.[124] Nonetheless, voters should also encourage U.S. officials to enforce the labor provisions of trade agreements to protect workers' rights everywhere; engage the WTO on this issue; and ratify and uphold the International Covenant on Economic, Social and Cultural Rights, which includes labor rights, and all ILO labor standards.[125]

In closing, let me suggest several questions that voters should ask themselves, which correspond to issues treated in this chapter.

- Does the candidate's record and platform provide evidence that she/he will promote more stringent occupational safety regulations and will enforce them (by, for example, funding OSHA better and creating stiffer penalties against violators)?
- Does the candidate support raising the federal minimum wage? If so, to what degree and will it be indexed to inflation after being raised?
- Does the candidate accept St. John XXIII's contention that "disproportionately high" wages are unjust, particularly when many workers earn below a living wage?[126]
- Does the candidate demonstrate genuine interest in decent health care for all and parental and other leave policies that will foster the health and longevity of workers and their children?
- Will the candidate enact and defend policies that reflect Pope Francis's contention that "there is no good society without a good union"?[127]
- Will the candidate choose judges and NLRB officials whose history demonstrates that they will fairly adjudicate claims between workers and management,

and generally support the rights of workers rather than excessively emphasizing corporate and investor profits?

- Does the candidate support robust labor standards that will protect the health, safety, and livelihoods of all workers, both domestic and global, in international trade agreements and potentially in WTO rules?
- Does the candidate reject the ideology of market fundamentalism, which espouses radical libertarian economics and a distorted notion of freedom that gives primacy to corporate and investor profit over the dignity and rights of workers?
- Does the candidate commit to full dignified jobs and just wages for all, while recognizing the need to see workers' rights within the larger framework of integral ecology (by promoting green jobs, for example)?

This list does not exhaust the concerns related to workers' rights. However, negative answers to these questions would reveal a lack of commitment to the rights to life, limb, and livelihood of workers and their families. Thus, voting for such a candidate should weigh heavily on the conscience of Catholics, who should themselves unequivocally reject violations of the rights of workers. As St. John Paul II contended, defending the rights of workers is a matter of fidelity to Jesus Christ, who "devoted most of the years of his life on earth to *manual work*."[128]

NOTES

1. International Labor Organization (hereafter ILO), "ILO Calls for Urgent Global Action to Fight Occupational Diseases," April 26, 2013, https://www.ilo.org/global/about-the-ilo/newsroom/news/WCMS _211627/lang--en/index.htm.

2. *Evangelii gaudium* 53.

3. I borrow the term "right to life and limb" from James A. Gross, *A Shameful Business: The Case for Human Rights in the American Workplace* (Ithaca: ILR Press/Cornell University Press, 2010), 104–26. See also Emily A. Speiler, "Risks and Rights: The Case for Occupational Safety and Health as a Core Worker Right," in *Workers' Rights as Human Rights*, ed. James A. Gross (Ithaca: Cornell University Press, 2003), 94.

4. Pope Francis, *Pastoral Visit to Cagliari: Meeting with Workers*, September 13, 2013, https://w2.vatican.va/content/francesco/en/speeches/2013/september/documents/papa-francesco_20130922_lavoratori-cagliari.html.

5. Gross, *A Shameful Business*, 104.

6. ILO, "Safety and Health at Work," accessed December 10, 2019, https://www.ilo.org/global/topics/safety-and-health-at-work/lang--en/index.html.

7. ILO, "The Prevention of Occupational Diseases," March 25, 2013, 4–5, https://www.ilo.org/safework/info/WCMS_208226/lang--en/index.htm.

8. ILO, "ILO Calls for Urgent Global Action." See also ILO, "The Prevention of Occupational Diseases," 4–5.

9. ILO, "ILO Calls for Urgent Global Action." See also ILO, "The Prevention of Occupational Diseases," 4–5.

10. See Valentina Forastieri, "Prevention of Psychosocial Risks and Work-Related Stress," *International Journal of Labour Research* 8, no. 1–2 (2016): 12–13.

11. Forastieri, "Prevention of Psychosocial Risks," 15. See also ILO, "The Prevention of Occupational Diseases," 6.

12. Stephanie Luce, *Labor Movements: Global Perspectives* (Chichester, UK: Polity, 2011), 61–62; Gross, *A Shameful Business*, 78–80.

13. International Trade Union Confederation, *2018 ITUC Global Rights Index*, accessed December 10, 2019, https://www.ituc-csi.org/IMG/pdf/ituc-global-rights-index-2010-en-final-2.pdf.

14. ILO, "Forced Labor, Modern Slavery and Human Trafficking," accessed December 10, 2019, https://www.ilo.org/global/topics/forced-labour/lang--en/index.htm.

15. On slavery in the global economy, see Vincent A. Gallagher, *The True Cost of Low Prices: The Violence of Globalization* (Maryknoll, NY: Orbis Books, 2006), 69–74.

16. Christine Firer Hinze, *Glass Ceilings and Dirt Floors: Women, Work, and the Global Economy* (Mahwah, NJ: Paulist Press, 2015), 81.

17. World Policy Analysis Center, "Does the Constitution Guarantee Protection from Gender Discrimination at Work?," accessed December 10, 2019, http://worldpolicycenter.org/policies/does-the-constitution-guarantee-protection-from-discrimination-at-work/does-the-constitution-guarantee-protection-from-gender-discrimination-at-work.

18. Jane Pillinger, "Psychosocial Risks and Violence in the World of Work: A Trade Union Perspective," *International Journal of Labour Research* 8, no. 1–2 (2016): 36–39.

19. See Jukka Takala et al., "Global Estimates of the Burden of Injury and Illness at Work in 2012," *Journal of Occupational and Environmental Hygiene* 11, no. 5 (2014): 336.

20. See Sven Beckert and Seth Rockman, *Slavery's Capitalism: A New History of American Economic Development, Early American Studies* (Philadelphia: University of Pennsylvania Press, 2016); Hinze, *Glass Ceilings and Dirt Floors*.

21. Hinze, *Glass Ceilings and Dirt Floors*, 77–81; Pillinger, "Psychosocial Risks and Violence in the World of Work," 47.

22. See World Policy Analysis Center, "Child Labor," accessed December 10, 2019, http://worldpolicycenter.org/topics/child-labor/policies.

23. Sarah Adler-Milstein and John M. Kline, *Sewing Hope: How One Factory Challenges the Apparel Industry's Sweatshops*, 1st ed. (Oakland: University of California Press, 2017), 15. See also Workers Rights Consortium, "Gender-Based Violence and Discrimination," accessed December 10, 2019, https://www.workersrights.org/issues/gender-based-violence-and-discrimination/.

24. Gallagher, *The True Cost of Low Prices*, 85. See also Adler-Milstein and Kline, *Sewing Hope*, 15–16.

25. Jody Heymann, *Forgotten Families: Ending the Growing Crisis Confronting Children and Working Parents in the Global Economy* (Oxford: Oxford University Press, 2006), 126. See Adler-Milstein and Kline, *Sewing Hope*, 31.

26. For more detail than I can provide here, see Heymann, *Forgotten Families*.

27. Edna Bonacich, "The Racialization of Global Labor," *American Behavioral Scientist* 52, no. 3 (2008): 345.

28. Bonacich, "The Racialization of Global Labor," 350; Hinze, *Glass Ceilings and Dirt Floors*, 78; Adler-Milstein and Kline, *Sewing Hope*, 15.

29. Adolph L. Reed, *Class Notes: Posing as Politics and Other Thoughts on the American Scene* (New York: New Press, 2000). See also Gerald J. Beyer, "Nike's Token Equality: New Campaign Masks the Truth about Workers' Rights," *Religion Dispatches*, March 21, 2017, http://religiondispatches.org/the-moral-and-religious-case-against-nikes-latest-advertising-moves.

30. Jody Heymann, Alison Earle, and Jeffrey Hayes, *The Work, Family, and Equity Index: How Does the United States Measure Up?* (Boston: Institute for Health and Social Policy, 2007), https://www.worldpolicycenter.org/sites/default/files/Work%20Family%20and%20Equity%20Index-How%20does%20the%20US%20measure%20up-Jan%202007.pdf. See also World Policy Center, "Adult Labor and Working Conditions," accessed December 10, 2019, https://www.worldpolicycenter.org/topics/adult-labor-and-working-conditions/policies.

31. The best countries, with only "sporadic violations of workers' rights" are, for example: Austria, Denmark, Uruguay, Slovakia, Ireland, Iceland, Italy,

and Sweden. See International Trade Union Confederation, *2018 ITUC Global Rights Index.*

32. Annette Bernhardt, Ruth Milkman, and Nik Theodore, "Broken Laws, Unprotected Workers: Violations of Employment and Labor Laws in America," *A Report of the National Employment Law Project*, September 21, 2009, 2–6, https://www.nelp.org/publication/broken-laws-unprotected-workers-violations-of-employment-and-labor-laws-in-americas-cities/.

33. See Gross, *A Shameful Business*, 79–80.

34. Gross, *A Shameful Business*, 105–6.

35. United States Department of Labor Occupational Safety and Health Administration, "Commonly Used Statistics," accessed December 10, 2019, https://www.osha.gov/oshstats/commonstats.html; Bureau of Labor Statistics, "Census of Fatal Occupational Injuries Summary, 2016," December 19, 2017, https://www.bls.gov/news.release/cfoi.nr0.htm.

36. National Council for Occupational Safety and Health, *Preventable Deaths 2016*, accessed December 10, 2019, https://www.coshnetwork.org/sites/default/files/preventable-deaths-2016.pdf. See also Takala et al., "Global Estimates of the Burden of Injury and Illness at Work in 2012." Speiler and Gross have decried the "shameful" lack of reliable and comprehensive accounting, which underestimates workplace injuries and illnesses in the United States. Speiler, "Risks and Rights," 79; Gross, *A Shameful Business*, 105.

37. Bureau of Labor Statistics, "Injuries, Illnesses, and Fatalities," accessed December 11, 2019, https://www.bls.gov/iif/.

38. Gross, *A Shameful Business*, 109–19.

39. Samuel Stebbins, Evan Comen, and Charles Stockdale, "Workplace Fatalities: 25 Most Dangerous Jobs in America," *New York Times*, January 9, 2018, https://www.usatoday.com/story/money/careers/2018/01/09/workplace-fatalities-25-most-dangerous-jobs-america/1002500001/. Statistics for each industry are available at https://www.bls.gov/news.release/cfoi.nr0.htm.

40. Gerald J. Beyer, "Workers' Rights and Socially Responsible Investment in the Catholic Tradition: A Case Study," *Journal of Catholic Social Thought* 10, no. 1 (2013).

41. Oxfam America, *Lives on the Line: The Human Cost of Cheap Chicken* (Boston: Oxfam America Inc., 2015), 22, https://www.oxfamamerica.org/static/media/files/Lives_on_the_Line_Full_Report_Final.pdf.

42. Huiqi Xu, Maureen Strode, Andrew Withers, "Poultry Processing Workers Still Face High Numbers of Injuries," *Midwest Center for Investigative Reporting*, June 28, 2018, http://investigatemidwest.org/2018/06/28/poultry-processing-workers-still-face-high-number-of-injuries.

43. Strode et al., "Poultry Processing Workers Still Face High Numbers of Injuries."

44. Oxfam America, *Lives on the Line*, 26.

45. Michael Grabell, "Exploitation and Abuse at the Chicken Plant," *The New Yorker*, May 1, 2017, https://www.newyorker.com/magazine/2017/05/08/exploitation-and-abuse-at-the-chicken-plant.

46. Oxfam America, *Lives on the Line*, 11.

47. Seth M. Holmes, *Fresh Fruit, Broken Bodies: Migrant Farmworkers in the United States* (Berkeley: University of California Press, 2013), 101.

48. National Council for Occupational Safety and Health, *Preventable Deaths*, 16. The report draws on Jeffrey Meitrodt, "Tragic Harvest," *Minneapolis Star Tribune*, Oct. 4, 5, 6, 7, 2015. In 2016, the fatal accident rates of some other industries passed farming. See Bureau of Labor Statistics, "Table 3: Fatal Occupational Injuries Counts and Rates for Selected Occupations, 2015–16," last modified December 18, 2018, https://www.bls.gov/news.release/cfoi.t03.htm.

49. Holmes, *Fresh Fruit, Broken Bodies*, 99.

50. Holmes, *Fresh Fruit, Broken Bodies*, 100.

51. Holmes, *Fresh Fruit, Broken Bodies*, 101–3.

52. Farmworker Justice, "Exposed and Ignored: How Pesticides Are Endangering Our Nation's Farm Workers" (2013), 6, https://www.farmworkerjustice.org/sites/default/files/aExposed%20and%20Ignored%20by%20Farmworker%20Justice%20singles%20compressed.pdf.

53. Coalition of Immokalee Workers, "Anti-Slavery Program," accessed December 11, 2019, http://ciw-online.org/slavery/.

54. Bon Appetit Management Company Foundation, "Inventory of Farmworker Issues and Protections in the United Sates" (March 2011), 30–31, https://www.ufw.org/pdf/farmworkerinventory_0401_2011.pdf.

55. Bureau of Labor Statistics, "A Profile of the Working Poor, 2016," Report 1074 (July 2018), https://www.bls.gov/opub/reports/working-poor/2016/home.htm.

56. Center for Poverty Research, "Who Are the Working Poor in America?," accessed December 11, 2019, https://poverty.ucdavis.edu/faq/who-are-working-poor-america.

57. Oxfam America, *Working Poor in America* (Boston: Oxfam America Inc., 2014), https://www.oxfamamerica.org/static/media/files/Working-Poor-in-America-report-Oxfam-America.pdf.

58. David Cooper, "Workers of Color Are Far More Likely to Be Paid Poverty Level Wages Than White Workers," *Economic Policy Institute*, June 21, 2018, https://www.epi.org/blog/workers-of-color-are-far-more-likely-to-be-paid-poverty-level-wages-than-white-workers/.

59. Cooper, "Workers of Color."

60. Alissa Quart, *Squeezed: Why Our Families Can't Afford America* (New York: Ecco, 2018), 35.

61. See Quart, *Squeezed*.

62. Peter Reuell, "For Life Expectancy, Money Matters," *The Harvard Gazette*, April 11, 2016, https://news.harvard.edu/gazette/story/2016/04/for-life-expectancy-money-matters/. The article draws on Raj Chetty et al., "The Association between Income and Life Expectancy in the United States, 2001–2014: Association between Income and Life Expectancy in the United States," *JAMA* 315, no. 16 (2016). See also Javier M. Rodriguez, "Health Disparities, Politics, and the Maintenance of the Status Quo: A New Theory of Inequality," *Social Science & Medicine* 200 (2018).

63. Tsu-Yu Tsao et al., "Estimating Potential Reductions in Premature Mortality in New York City from Raising the Minimum Wage to $15," *American Journal of Public Health* 106, no. 6 (2016).

64. Oxfam America, *Working Poor in America*.

65. Josh Bivens, Elise Gould, and John Schmitt, "America's Slow-Motion Wage Crisis: Four Decades of Slow and Unequal Growth," *Economic Policy Institute*, September 13, 2018, 4, https://www.epi.org/files/pdf/153535.pdf.

66. Oxfam America, *Working Poor in America*.

67. Laura Bliss, "Higher Minimum Wages Are Good for Newborn Health," *City Lab*, June 28, 2016, https://www.citylab.com/equity/2016/06/15-minimum-wage-health-newborn/488891/; Maggie Thomas, "Saving Lives by Raising Wages," *Public Health Post*, October 29, 2016, https://www.publichealthpost.org/research/saving-lives-raising-wages/; The National Bureau of Economic Research, "Why Is Infant Mortality Higher in the US than in Europe?," Bulletin on Aging and Health Home No. 1 (2015), http://www.nber.org/aginghealth/2015no1/w20525.html; Global infant mortality rankings from https://www.cia.gov/library/publications/the-world-factbook/rankorder/2091rank.html.

68. Kelli A. Komro et al., "The Effect of an Increased Minimum Wage on Infant Mortality and Birth Weight," *American Journal of Public Health* 106, no. 8 (2016): 1514–15.

69. Alison Earle et al. *The Work, Family, and Equity Index*. Detailed reports are available at https://www.worldpolicycenter.org/events-and-launches/fmla-turns-25-time-for-paid-leave.

70. See the comprehensive discussion in Gross, *A Shameful Business*.

71. Gerald J. Beyer, "Donald Trump and the Rights and Dignity of Workers," *National Catholic Reporter*, May 13, 2016, https://www.ncronline.org/blogs/ncr-today/donald-trump-and-rights-and-dignity-workers.

72. See Laborer's Health and Safety Fund of North America, "What Has the Obama Administration Done on Occupational Health and Safety?" LHSFNA 9, no. 5 (October 2012), https://www.lhsfna.org/index.cfm/lifelines/october-2012/what-has-the-obama-administration-done-on-occupational-safety-and-health.

73. Kay Bechtold, "Panel Raises Concerns about OSHA, NIOSH under Trump," accessed December 11, 2019, https://www2.aiha.org/publications-and-resources/TheSynergist/AIHANews/Pages/Panel-Raises-Concerns-about-OSHA,-NIOSH-Under-Trump.aspx.

74. Dave Jamieson, "Trump Repeals Regulation Protecting Workers from Wage Theft," *Huffington Post*, March 27, 2017, http://www.huffingtonpost.com/entry/trump-repeals-regulation-wage-theft_us_58d9408ee4b03692bea814c9.

75. David Cooper and Teresa Kroeger, "Employers Steal Billions from Workers' Paychecks Each Year," Economic Policy Institute, May 10, 2017, https://www.epi.org/publication/employers-steal-billions-from-workers-paychecks-each-year/; Philip Mattera, "Grand Theft Paycheck: The Large Corporations Shortchanging their Workers' Wages," Good Jobs First.org (June 2018), https://www.goodjobsfirst.org/sites/default/files/docs/pdfs/wagetheft_report_revised.pdf; Wage Theft, "Why Millions of Working People Are Not Getting Paid and What We Can Do about It," accessed December 11, 2019, http://www.wagetheft.org/.

76. Dave Jamieson, "The Human Cost of Trump's Rollback on Regulations," *Huffington Post*, April 16, 2017, https://www.huffingtonpost.com/entry/trump-rollback-regulations-cost_us_58f1375be4b0bb9638e3f72c; Alan Ferguson, "Court of Appeals Rejects Industry Challenge to Silica Rule, Requests OSHA to Consider Medical Removal Projections," *Safety + Health*, January 28, 2018, https://www.safetyandhealthmagazine.com/articles/16557-court-of-appeals-rejects-industry-challenge-to-silica-rule-requests-osha-to-consider-medical-removal-protections.

77. Kim Slowey, "OSHA Extends Deadlines for Some Aspects of Beryllium Standard outside of Construction," *Construction Dive*, August 13, 2018, https://www.constructiondive.com/news/osha-enforces-new-beryllium-standard/523336/. See also Deborah Berkowitz, "NELP Comments on Proposed OSHA Beryllium Rule," NELP, September 13, 2017, https://www.nelp.org/publication/nelp-comments-on-proposed-osha-beryllium-rule.

78. Amanda Grennell, "Does Formaldehyde Cause Leukemia? A Delayed EPA Report May Hold the Answer," *PBS Newshour*, August 29, 2018, https://www.pbs.org/newshour/science/does-formaldehyde-cause-leukemia-a-delayed-epa-report-may-hold-the-answer.

79. Ian Haydon, "EPA's New Asbestos Rule: Philadelphia Doctors Cite the Doctors," *Philly.com*, August 10, 2018, http://www2.philly.com/philly/health/epa-asbestos-trump-mesothelioma-cancer-philadelphia-20180810.html; Lisa Friedman, "EPA Staff Objected to Agency's New Rules on Asbestos Use, Internet Emails Show," *New York Times*, August 10, 2018, https://www.nytimes.com/2018/08/10/climate/epa-asbestos-rule.html; Alex Formuzis, "Russian Asbestos Giant Praises Trump Administration Actions to

Keep Deadly Carcinogen Legal," *EWG*, July 11, 2018, https://www.ewg.org/release/russian-asbestos-giant-praises-trump-administration-actions-keep-deadly-carcinogen-legal#.W7ahRmhKhmq.

80. See Sonya Lunder, "Asbestos Kills 12,000–15,000 People per Year in the U.S.," Asbestos Nation, accessed December 11, 2019, http://www.asbestosnation.org/facts/asbestos-kills-12000-15000-people-per-year-in-the-u-s/.

81. Sugio Furuya et al., "Global Asbestos Disaster," *International Journal of Environmental Research and Public Health* 15, no. 5 (2018): 2.

82. See "Trump USDA to Allow Faster Poultry Line Speeds, Ignoring Danger to Workers and Consumers," NELP, October 4, 2018, https://www.nelp.org/news-releases/trump-usda-allow-faster-poultry-line-speeds-ignoring-danger-workers-consumers/; and Eleanor Goldberg and Dave Jamieson, "USDA Spares Poultry Workers Faster Line Speeds, but Hog Workers May Not Get So Lucky," *Huffington Post*, January 31, 2018, https://www.huffingtonpost.com/entry/usda-spares-poultry-workers_us_5a7226b1e4b03699143ef3b4.

83. Ian Kullgren, "Trump Rolls Back Worker Safety Rules," *Politico*, September 3, 2018, https://www.politico.com/story/2018/09/03/trumps-worker-safety-regulations-protections-unions-806008. See also "Putting Workers First? The Year in Review," NELP, December 14, 2017, https://www.nelp.org/publication/putting-workers-first-2017-in-review/.

84. Mark Joseph Stern, "Neil Gorsuch Just Demolished Labor Rights," *Slate*, May 21, 2018, https://slate.com/news-and-politics/2018/05/neil-gorsuch-demolished-labor-rights-in-epic-systems-v-lewis.html.

85. Elizabeth Warren, "The Supreme Court Has an Ethics Problem," *Politico*, November 01, 2017, https://www.politico.com/magazine/story/2017/11/01/supreme-court-ethics-problem-elizabeth-warren-opinion-215772. See also Mark Joseph Stern, "Gorsuch Casts Decisive Vote as Supreme Court Crushes Public Sector Unions," *Slate*, June 27, 2018, https://slate.com/news-and-politics/2018/06/janus-v-afscme-supreme-court-crushes-public-sector-unions-thanks-to-neil-gorsuchs-decisive-vote-and-samuel-alito.html.

86. Joseph A. McCartin, "Labor's Existential Crisis," *Commonweal*, July 23, 2018, https://www.commonwealmagazine.org/labors-existential-crisis.

87. See Robert Weismann, *An Analysis of Judge Kavanaugh's Opinions in Split-Decision Cases*, Public Citizen, August 29, 2018, https://www.citizen.org/sites/default/files/kavanaugh-split-decisions-report.pdf; Alliance for Justice, "SCOTUS Nominee: Brett Kavanaugh," accessed December 11, 2019, https://www.afj.org/scotus-nominee-brett-kavanaugh; Nathan Robinson, "Why Everyone Should Oppose Brett Cavanaugh's Nomination," *Current Affairs*, August 6, 2018, https://www.currentaffairs.org/2018/08/why-everyone-should-oppose-brett-kavanaughs-confirmation.

88. See Steven Greenhouse, "Seaworld's and Kavanuagh's Missing Empathy Gene," *The American Prospect*, September 21, 2018, http://prospect .org/article/seaworld-and-kavanaughs-missing-empathy-gene.

89. See Robert Weismann, *An Analysis of Judge Kavanaugh's Opinions in Split-Decision Cases*; Nathan Robinson, "Why Everyone Should Oppose Brett Cavanaugh's Nomination."

90. See Ian Kullgren, "Trump Rolls Back Worker Safety Rules"; Dave Jamieson, "Trump's Labor Law Enforcer Freezes Worker-Friendly Reforms Made Under Obama," *Huffington Post*, December 3, 2017, https://www .huffingtonpost.com/entry/trump-nlrb-labor-board-counsel-union reforms _us_5a2440bce4b0a02abe91e2d3; and Erik Gunn, "So Long, Labor Rights: The NLRB, under Trump, Is Facing Unprecedented Attack" (The Progressive, Inc, 2018).

91. Arthur Delaney and Dave Jamieson, "Amazon Called for Raising the Minimum Wage. Republicans Say It's Fine as It Is, Thanks," *Huffington Post*, October 5, 2018, https://www.huffingtonpost.com/entry/amazon-called -for-raising-the-minimum-wage-republicans-say-its-fine-as-it-is-thanks_us _5bb79cfae4b01470d05147fe; *The Economist*, "Amazon's $15 Minimum Wage Is Welcome," October 4, 2018, https://www.economist.com/united-states/ 2018/10/04/amazons-15-minimum-wage-is-welcome.

92. Robert J. Schapiro, "Don't Be Fooled: Working Americans Are Worse Off under Trump," *The Washington Post*, September 30, 2018, https://www .washingtonpost.com/opinions/dont-be-fooled-working-americans-are-worse -off-under-trump/2018/09/30/f789f198-be82-11e8-be70-52bd11fe18af _story.html?utm_term=.7412c1957251.

93. Isaac Arnsdorf and Lena Groeger, "What Happened to All the Jobs Trump Promised?" *Pro Publica*, January 29, 2018, https://projects.propublica .org/graphics/trump-job-promises; Joseph Geevarghese, "Trump Is Failing to Bring Back American Jobs," *The Hill*, accessed December 11, 2019, https:// thehill.com/opinion/white-house/404629-trump-is-failing-to-bring-back -american-jobs.

94. Elizabeth Bruenig, "Trump's Paid Family Leave Plan Would Punish Those Who Choose to Have Kids," *Washington Post*, February 7, 2018, https:// www.washingtonpost.com/opinions/trumps-paid-family-leave-plan-would -punish-those-who-choose-to-have-kids/2018/02/07/dc612c0c-0b85-11e8 -95a5-c396801049ef_story.html?utm_term=.fa8728768ee4.

95. On this history, see, for example, Joe Holland, *Modern Catholic Social Teaching: The Popes Confront the Industrial Age, 1740–1958* (New York: Paulist Press, 2003).

96. Author's translation of the Polish text: http://www.mogila.cystersi .pl/index.php?option=com_content&view=article&id=133:homilia-jana -pawla-ii&catid=48:jan-pawe-ii-w-mogile&Itemid=150.

97. John Paul II, *Laborem exercens* 6. See also John Paul II, *Redemptor hominis* 1, 8, 10, 13.

98. See John Paul II, *Laborem exercens* 19; and Pontifical Council for Justice and Peace, *Compendium of the Social Doctrine of the Church* (2005), nos. 287–304.

99. John Paul II, "Letter of John Paul II to Women" (1995), no. 4, https://w2.vatican.va/content/john-paul-ii/en/letters/1995/documents/hf _jp-ii_let_29061995_women.html.

100. John Paul II, *Laborem exercens* 19.

101. John Paul II, *Centesimus annus* 15; see also no. 40.

102. John Paul II, *Laborem exercens* 8, 11, 14, 20. See also Leo XIII, *Rerum novarum* 47–49; John Paul II, John Paul II, *Centesimus annus* 15; Benedict XVI, *Caritas in veritate* 25.

103. See John Paul II, *Evangelium vitae* 3, 21, 78–101.

104. David Gibson, "Pope Francis Breathes New Life into Bernardin's Contested Legacy," *National Catholic Reporter*, October 26, 2013, https://www .ncronline.org/news/people/pope-francis-breathes-new-life-bernardins -contested-legacy. See also John Coleman, "Pope Francis and the Consistent Ethic of Life," in *Pope Francis and the Future of Catholicism in the United States*, ed. Erin Brigham, David E. DeCosse, and Michael Duffy (San Francisco: University of San Francisco Press, 2016); and Joseph Bernardin and Thomas A. Nairn, *The Seamless Garment: Writings on the Consistent Ethic of Life* (Maryknoll, NY: Orbis Books, 2008).

105. Francis, *Gaudium exultate* 101.

106. Pope Francis, *Pastoral Visit to Cagliari: Meeting with Workers*, September 22, 2013, https://w2.vatican.va/content/francesco/en/speeches/2013/ september/documents/papa-francesco_20130922_lavoratori-cagliari.html. On integral ecology, see Francis, *Laudato si'* 124–63.

107. United States Conference of Catholic Bishops, *Faithful Citizenship* (2015), no. 25, http://www.usccb.org/issues-and-action/faithful-citizenship/ forming-consciences-for-faithful-citizenship-title.cfm.

108. *Faithful Citizenship* 23, 73.

109. See *Faithful Citizenship* 29–30; and Robert W. McElroy, "Pope Francis Makes Addressing Poverty Essential," *America*, October 8, 2013, https://www .americamagazine.org/church-poor. See also *Faithful Citizenship* 29–30.

110. Pope Francis, "Modern-Day Leeches," May 19, 2016, https://w2.vatican .va/content/francesco/en/cotidie/2016/documents/papa-francesco-cotidie _20160519_modern-day-leeches.html; and Salvatore Cernuzio, "It Is a Mortal Sin to Exploit Workers and Scam on Their Salaries," *La Stampa*, May 24, 2018, http://www.lastampa.it/2018/05/24/vaticaninsider/it-is-a-mortal-sin-to -exploit-workers-and-scam-on-their-salaries-9n1spJcbEqbgPZOCyZmtMO/ pagina.html.

111. See also John Paul II, *Evangelium vitae* 3.

112. I elaborate this argument fully in Gerald J. Beyer, "Advocating Worker Justice: A Catholic Ethicist's Toolkit," *Journal of Religious Ethics* 45, no. 2 (2017).

113. See *Faithful Citizenship* 34.

114. See Joe Holland, *100 Years of Catholic Social Teaching Defending Workers and Their Unions: Summaries and Commentaries for Five Landmark Papal Encyclicals* (Washington, DC: Pacem in Terris Press, 2012), 1–2; Kristen Hannum, "Labor Pains: What Wisconsin Tells Us about Catholics and Unions," *U.S. Catholic* 76, no. 8 (2011).

115. Pope Francis, "Address to World Meeting of Popular Movements," *Zenit*, October 29, 2014, https://zenit.org/articles/pope-s-address-to-popular-movements/. See also Francis, *Evangelii gaudium* 55; Francis, *Pastoral Visit to Cagliari*; John Paul II, *Centesimus annus* 34–35; 40–42. For a similar critique of the global economy from a labor economist, see Luce, *Labor Movements*, 121.

116. See *Faithful Citizenship* 35.

117. *Faithful Citizenship* 36–37.

118. On the WTO framework and labor standards, see "Labour Standards: Consensus, Coherence and Controversy, World Trade Organization, accessed December 11, 2019, https://www.wto.org/english/thewto_e/whatis_e/tif_e/bey5_e.htm.

119. International Trade Union Confederation, *2018 Global Index*, 42–43.

120. Stan G. Duncan, *The Greatest Story Oversold: Understanding Economic Globalization* (Maryknoll, NY: Orbis Books, 2010), 104–18; Dani Rodrik, "Can Trade Agreements Be a Friend to Labor?," Project Syndicate, September 14, 2018, https://www.project-syndicate.org/commentary/trade-agreement-labor-provisions-small-practical-effect-by-dani-rodrik-2018-09.

121. Rodrik, "Can Trade Agreements Be a Friend to Labor?"; and Kimberly Ann Elliott, "Trump's NAFTA Rebrand Looks More Like the TPP, Minus the Partnership," World Politics Review, October 9, 2018, https://www.worldpoliticsreview.com/articles/26291/trump-s-nafta-rebrand-looks-more-like-the-tpp-minus-the-partnership.

122. On global solidarity, see *Faithful Citizenship*. 90; John Paul II, *Redemptor hominis* 16; and John Paul II, *Sollicitudo rei socialis* 39; *Gaudium et spes* 24–32.

123. See Beyer, "Advocating Worker Justice."

124. See, for example, https://www.workersrights.org/bangladesh-accord/ and http://usas.org/.

125. On the last point, see Gross, *A Shameful Business*, 206–07.

126. John XXIII, *Mater et magistra* 70.

127. Pope Francis, "Audience with Delegates from the Confederation of Trade Unions in Italy (Confederazione Italiana Sindacati Lavoratori, CISL),"

June 28, 2017, http://press.vatican.va/content/salastampa/en/bollettino/
pubblico/2017/06/28/170628a.html.

128. John Paul II, *Laborem exercens* 6.

Questions for Further Reflection

1. The author says that workers' rights are a pro-life issue. How does he support that statement?

2. What does the author say are the physical costs of unsafe working conditions? What are the economic costs?

3. The author says that those who oppose workers' rights harm or kill workers. How does he justify that assertion? Do you agree or disagree with his conclusion? Explain. Pope Francis has said that the modern economy is one that kills. Is the author saying the same thing as the pope or is he saying something different? How?

4. What does the author mean when he says that anti-worker violence has gender and racial dimensions? What facts does he cite to substantiate this conclusion? Do you agree? On what facts do you base your conclusion?

5. The United States ranks rather low on the Global Rights Index of workers' rights. What accounts for this ranking? Does this trouble you, or do you see it as a simple fact of the economic life of our nation? Explain.

6. How many workers in the United States die each year from either workplace accidents or work-related illnesses? How many nonfatal workplace injuries/accidents are there each year in the United States? Which industries are the most dangerous? Do you believe that our politics can or should change this situation? Why or why not?

7. The author writes of Americans who work regular jobs but who still live in poverty. How does the author define this group and how

many people are in it? Is this a homogenous group or does it vary by race, sex, and ethnicity?

8. The author says that the working poor often cannot afford health care. Do you see this as a pro-life issue? What remedy would you propose for it? Should anyone die in the United States because they are too poor to afford health care? Does the larger society have any obligation to these persons? Do you have any personal obligations to them?

9. What is the practical effect of a government removing or watering down existing rules for workplace safety? Do you see this as a pro-life issue? Why or why not?

10. What is the effect of antilabor judges on workers' rights? Why would a judge, especially a Catholic judge, be antilabor?

11. What does the church teach about workers' rights and the sacredness of workers' lives? Can you cite papal teaching to support your answer?

12. What is the church's teaching on the "consistent ethic of life"? Who does this consistent ethic of life cover?

13. Pope Francis has strongly criticized our throwaway society. What does the pope mean by a throwaway society? How would this criterion apply to workers' rights?

14. What do the U.S. bishops say about workers' rights in *Faithful Citizenship*? Do the bishops think that this is a pro-life issue? What document from the Second Vatican Council do the bishops rely on? What does that document say on this topic?

15. Should Catholics vote for candidates for public office who oppose workers' rights? Is this an absolute pro-life issue that demands that Catholics act to protect life, or is there a moral balancing test here? Explain.

16. Are the author's suggestions on the questions that a Catholic voter should ask him/herself regarding workers' rights helpful to you? Which questions would you omit or downplay? Which questions would you add? Why? How would you personally answer the author's questions?

9

Ending War Is a Priority for Pope Francis

How about U.S. Voters?

Lisa Sowle Cahill

Pope Francis's 2017 World Day of Peace Message was titled "Nonviolence: A Style of Politics for Peace."[1] In fact papal condemnations of violence have dominated the magisterial profile on war and peace since the Second Vatican Council, if not before. But U.S. voters lack commitment on this issue. In 2018, fifteen years after the beginning of the Iraq war, U.S. soldiers were still in Iraq, and U.S. military forces were engaged in campaigns across at least seven countries in the Middle East, Central Asia, and Africa.[2] On the one hand, many citizens want disengagement from conflicts abroad, because U.S. military investment competes for resources with domestic priorities. A bipartisan advocacy group found in 2018 "a national voter population that is largely skeptical of the practicality or benefits of military intervention overseas, including both the physical involvement of the US military and also extending to military aid in the form of funds or equipment as well."[3] Yet, on the other hand, according to a 2016 Gallup poll, Americans also favor U.S. military action as an effective strategy in the U.S. "war on terror."[4] U.S. voters seem to judge armed force and killing mainly in terms of what does or does not benefit them, not in terms of the broader common good. Among Republican voters in 2018, the top issue was "national security."[5] A majority of Americans approve the use of drones (unmanned missile strikes) against perceived extremists, for example in Pakistan, Yemen, and Somalia, even though imprecise targeting has resulted in thousands of mass casualty civilian deaths.[6] In fact, according to a 2017 Stanford University poll, "A majority of Americans prioritize protecting U.S. troops and achieving American war aims, even when doing so would result in the use of nuclear weapons and the deaths of millions of civilians in another country."[7] Yet the gospel challenges the morality of killing even soldiers or aggressors; and to the extent that Christian tradition has validated war, it has done so under strictly limiting conditions, including noncombatant immunity.

Catholic Teaching on Peace and War

Nonviolence, forgiveness, and reconciliation are ideals in the Gospels. In biblical texts often cited, Jesus exhorts disciples to "love your enemies," "turn the other [cheek]," and "pray for those who persecute you" (Matt 5:38–48). If God's reign is already beginning to transform history through the ministry of Jesus, then human beings should follow his example, transforming relations in both church and society. Yet peacemaking efforts are not always successful, exposing ourselves and others to the risks of injustice, injury, and death. Moreover, Jesus's command to "love your neighbor" (Mark 12:31) seems to require not nonresistance to evil, but action to protect the vulnerable, even if armed force is necessary to do so. Catholic social teaching has thus struggled for centuries with the problem of how to respond to violence and other injustices, given the gospel commands to love God, neighbor, and even enemies. This is an especially great challenge given that the Catholic tradition sees political participation as a moral and social responsibility, and sees government, stable social institutions, and the rule of law as necessary to just political life, both nationally and internationally. The most important values in a Catholic approach to politics are the dignity of the person, the common good, and peace with justice for all. But the realities of history and politics are such that protecting these very goods sometimes seems to demand armed military or peacekeepers.

For this reason, Christianity has developed a theory of the so-called just war, grounded primarily in the thought of Augustine and Aquinas. While they recognized the Evangelical ideals of love and nonviolence, they believed that Christian identity and political responsibility could be compatible if force were used within defined limits and were subordinated to the goals of peace and justice. Of course, in practice, no war is ever fully "just." Whatever the justice of the cause, it is a fact historically that every war results in major loss of life, including civilian life; leads to atrocities and violations of human rights; damages combat veterans with physical, psychological, and spiritual injuries; and devastates social infrastructure and the material environment in ways that make recovery difficult if not impossible. For these reasons, the 2015 edition of the U.S. bishops' *Faithful Citizenship* warns,

> War is never a reflection of what ought to be, but a sign that something more true to human dignity has failed. The Catholic tradition recognizes the legitimacy of just war teaching when defending the innocent in the face of grave evil, but we must never lose sight of the cost of war and the harm to human life. Nations should protect the dignity of the human person and the right to life by finding more effective ways to prevent conflicts, to resolve them by peaceful means, and to promote reconstruction and reconciliation in the wake of conflicts.[8]

The mid-twentieth-century Catholic moralist and political thinker John Courtney Murray defined the purpose of just war theory as "to condemn war as evil, to limit the evil it entails, and to humanize its conduct as far as possible." Yet he also acknowledged that the paradox involved in trying to fit violence into the order of justice "is heightened when this effort takes place at the interior of the Christian religion of love."[9]

Given these morally problematic aspects and consequences of war, how do we judge when a war is just? How do we determine what it means to carry out a war justly? Too often, public justifications of war focus on "national interests" alone and limit consideration of means in war to pragmatic and utilitarian judgments of what will accomplish goals or bring victory, regardless of effects on civilian lives and societies. But the just war tradition deriving from Augustine and Aquinas yields two categories of just war criteria, *jus ad bellum* (justice in going to war) and *jus in bello* (justice in the conduct of war). These criteria offer a broader moral perspective and establish that calculations of self-interest and military advantage are not only insufficient but immoral if not constrained by criteria of justice. Different versions of the criteria of just war have evolved over time, but they typically include, regarding *ad bellum*, just cause, right intention, last resort, legitimate authority, proportion, and reasonable hope of success. The key *in bello* criterion is "discrimination" or noncombatant immunity. To these, recent thinkers have added a new category, *jus post bellum* (justice after war).[10]

The Christian tradition of just war thinking begins with the fourth-century Catholic bishop Augustine, who built on the ideas of his teacher, Ambrose. Augustine lived in North Africa, at that time part of the Roman Empire. Before his time, Christians had been a minority sect in the empire, and while tolerated for the most part, had no legal religious rights and sometimes suffered persecution. This changed in Augustine's time, when the Christian emperors Constantine and his successor Theodosius gave Christianity legal status and protection. This meant that Christians had a new interest in protecting the empire from Germanic invasions from the North, and in supporting imperial measures to maintain social order and stability. While earlier Christian teachers condemned killing in war, and military service insofar as it involved killing, Augustine justified the participation of Christians in government and military for the purpose of seeking and keeping the peace.

Though he never arrived at a systematic analysis of war, three criteria of justice in war can be taken from his writings: right intention, legitimate authority, and just cause (seeking the peace). These three criteria are the backbone of the later just war tradition. Distinctive of Augustine is his core idea that all Christian life, including war, must be governed by the virtue of love: love of God as the highest good (*summum bonum*), and of all else in relation to God. Therefore, he defends war as "loving punishment" of the ones killed.[11] Positively, this puts love at the center of all Christian action. Negatively, it not only suggests that killing itself can be a loving act, but also that punishment is sufficient cause for war, whatever its usefulness to the common good and to furthering peaceable relations after the conflict. Augustine's modern interpreters tend to see protection of the innocent as the way to understand war as a loving action and emphasize restoration of peaceful social existence as the primary cause for war.

Thomas Aquinas is a thirteenth-century Dominican scholar who was born in Italy and taught at the University of Paris. He built on Augustine's three criteria of a just war but shifted some of their meanings. Like Augustine, Aquinas saw the three criteria of justice in going to war as legitimate authority, right intention, and just cause. For Aquinas, just cause is defined as protection of the common good or "common weal." The legitimate authority is the one who has responsibility for the common weal; right intention is focused on sustaining or restoring it. Aquinas does not try to validate war on the basis of love, but instead makes justice and the common good more central. Aquinas confronts the counterargument that war contradicts the Sermon on the Mount, "do not resist an evildoer" (Matt 5:39). While conceding that such teachings "should always be borne in readiness of mind," Aquinas thinks it necessary sometimes for a Christian warrior to "act otherwise for the common good, or the good of those with whom he is fighting" (fellow soldiers on the same side).[12]

Aquinas did give some consideration to the justice of means in war: it is wrong to violate covenants, but acceptable to set ambushes, since both sides expect them. Yet the morality of the conduct of war did not become a major concern of just war theorists until after World Wars I and II. The practice of area bombing (bombing cities and civilian areas), especially the use by the United States of nuclear bombs against civilian populations in two Japanese cities, led to a moral consensus among just war theorists that killing civilians is always wrong, no matter what aim of war is supposedly to be gained by it.

The 1992 *Catechism of the Catholic Church*[13] first gave just war theory explicit church backing (§§2302–17), though it stresses the obligation to avoid war and stipulates that even defensive war must meet very strict conditions, including a serious prospect of meeting success without provoking even greater evils. Generally speaking, Catholic just war theorists today reflect the growing reserve of church teachers about the justification of war. Many explicitly qualify their position as "stringent" or "restrictive" just war theory. Just war criteria in such approaches are used to critique and reject most proposed uses of armed force, and to subject all military interventions to ongoing scrutiny. In fact, argues Gerard Powers, even a "restrictive, or strict, interpretation of just war…is incomprehensible apart from a peacebuilding ethic."[14] If a commitment to peacebuilding is not more fundamental and primary than justifications of war, then the criteria of right intention and last resort cannot be met.

Along the same lines, a recent development within just war theory is the category of *jus post bellum*, whose criteria make it a moral requirement for those who embark on and wage war to consider how their policies and actions will affect the justice of conditions after war. Catholic theologians Mark Allman and Tobias Winright maintain that, on biblical and theological grounds, every conflict should be concluded under circumstances that are compatible with long-term peace.[15] *Jus post bellum* criteria include consequences for social goods such as public utilities, education, health care, economic productivity, and environmental pollution; as well as for the achievement of just peace accords excluding "victor's justice"; and the establishment of the rule of law, a transitional government, an effective police force, and democratic elections favoring self-government.

Recent Catholic Teaching on Just War

Next, we shall turn to some episcopal teaching documents that may be more familiar to Catholic voters in the United States than papal encyclicals and other papal statements on war and peace, as well as more directly relevant to U.S. political trends and election challenges. The following section will return to the larger picture of magisterial teaching, showing that the recent sweep of the tradition, culminating with Pope Francis, is more condemnatory of war, and more insistent on effective nonviolent solutions, than most in the United States realize. A final section will consider the relevance of these developments to U.S. voters and some strategies to bring public attitudes more in line with Catholic social teaching.

The U.S. Bishops' 1983 Pastoral Letter *The Challenge of Peace: God's Promise and Our Response* was written toward the end of the Cold War, six years before the fall of the Berlin Wall.[16] The document garnered a significant amount of press attention at the time, and helped shape public discourse about an important problem: the contest between the two "superpowers," the United States and the Soviet Union, then poised to destroy each other (or their allies) with massive arsenals of nuclear weaponry and a policy of "mutual assured destruction." *The Challenge of Peace* rather uneasily joined a biblical call to the peace of God's kingdom, with the use of just war theory to validate what it termed "a strictly conditioned moral acceptance of nuclear deterrence" (§186). This acceptance was contingent on a real commitment to arms reduction and practical steps to nuclear abolition. The bishops absolutely ruled out the actual use of a nuclear weapon and nuclear war (§§138–88).

The ten-year anniversary document, *The Harvest of Justice Is Sown in Peace*, was authored after the 1990–91 Gulf War, and alludes to the threats of terrorism and nuclear proliferation.[17] It calls for greater restraint on "just war" validations of military action, yet affirms self-defense and humanitarian intervention in ethnic violence and genocide. Its more important focus, however, is positive and proactive peacemaking, including economic and social development, as the way to make progress toward a world without violence.

In *Forming Consciences for Faithful Citizenship*, the U.S. Catholic bishops' advisory message to voters, about a page is devoted to war and peace. The discussion opens with the assertion that we must be committed to avoiding war and building peace, and with the concern that citizens may become disengaged from U.S. involvement in conflicts abroad as a political issue because of their sheer number. The bishops endorse military action as a last resort to defend the innocent, but completely reject torture, "preventive war," and any use of indiscriminate weapons, including nuclear weapons. Voters should be committed to "progressive nuclear deterrence," reducing the global arms trade, resolving humanitarian and refugee crises, and reallocating military funding to serve the needs of the poor (§§68–69).

But to the extent that the U.S. public does prioritize these issues, they give them a domestic spin toward internal welfare and interests. According to a *Huffington Post* poll, gun control and immigration within the United States were among the top three priorities for voters approaching the 2018 midterm elections, but "foreign policy" was a priority for only 6 percent.[18] Another poll found that Republicans put "national security" at the top of the list, while Americans overall put it second.[19] These rankings focus the "war and peace" lens on fears of and dangers to U.S. citizens; suggest that Americans want more not less armed force directed at perceived threats to the homeland; and cut against the broader goals of reducing reliance on military solutions, reallocating military resources, addressing root causes of violence globally, and crafting humanitarian policies toward refugees. As will become clear, these trends are also at odds with the momentum of papal social teaching.

Papal Teaching since Vatican II[20]

Both the Second Vatican Council document *Gaudium et spes* (1965) and John XXIII's *Pacem in terris* (1963) were written at the height of the Cold War, and in light of the superpowers' nuclear competition. Both documents question the continuing usefulness of received just war criteria, proposing that "it is contrary to reason to hold that war is now a suitable way to restore rights which have been violated" (*Pacem in terris* 127; see also *Gaudium et spes* 79–80). *Gaudium et spes* still legitimates defensive wars, and John XXIII does not condemn them. Yet both envision modern war in terms of unimaginable destruction and depict the arms race as an ongoing source of global injustice to the poor. War and preparation for war are given an increasingly negative moral evaluation (*Pacem in terris* 112–13; *Gaudium et spes* 80–81).

The central theme and heart of these two documents are gospel-inspired and nonviolent peace, along with international relations built on trust, not threats of war. Pope John joins the Christian faithful with all who are "of good will," praying that Christ will banish "whatever might endanger peace" and "transform all men into witnesses of truth, justice and brotherly love" (§171). *Gaudium et spes* depicts gospel non-violence similarly. Praising all who "renounce the use of violence in the vindication of their right," it summons Christians "to 'practice the truth in love' (Eph 4:15) and to join with all true peacemakers in pleading for peace and bringing it about" (§78). The Council for the first time recognizes a right of individual conscientious objection to bearing arms (§78).

Paul VI, John Paul II, Benedict, and Francis all advance the trajectory of peacemaking. Catholic tradition has justified war historically, and the *Catechism of the Catholic Church*, the *Compendium of the Social Doctrine of the Church*,[21] and various national bishops' conferences continue to do so. The popes continue to recognize the right to defense and the duty to protect the innocent, but they do not further validate or elaborate the idea of just war or its criteria. The standards of peace, nonviolence, and peacebuilding dominate treatments of international conflict today. For example, the *Compendium* associates peace with justice, respect for the dignity of all persons, and civil life ordered to the common good. The failure of peace is war; and alternative solutions to international conflicts are urgently necessary (§§494–98). New developments include the following: language that more strongly contrasts war and nonviolent peace, often with phrasing that indicates that violence is never justified; the therefore paradoxical introduction by John Paul of a duty of humanitarian intervention (not excluding armed force); a refusal to defend any specific war or military intervention as just; a strengthened connection between practical work for justice ("development"), nonviolence, and peace; naming of environmental reasons to avoid war; calls for broad social conversion; and outreach to interreligious as well as intercultural and international partners.

For Paul VI, "reconciliation is the way to Peace" (1975 World Day of Peace Message). In words repeated almost verbatim by subsequent popes, he exhorts, "No more war, war never again! Peace, it is peace which must guide the destinies of people and of all mankind" (1965 Address to the United Nations General Assembly). Not only does Paul VI hope (with *Gaudium et spes*) that war will eventually be prohibited by international law (1975 World Day of Peace Message), he states in no uncertain terms that "the Church cannot accept violence, especially the force of arms" (*Evangelii nuntiandi* 37). Following Gandhi, Pope Paul urges all to make nonviolence a national and international policy (1976 World Day of Peace Message). Yet Paul VI does seem to accept the legitimacy of armed revolution to resist serious violations of human dignity and the common good (*Populorum progressio* 31). This pope's greatest contribution is his insistence that the only true way to peace is to fight injustice, and to actualize human rights, economic justice, and stable, participatory social and political institutions. "If you want peace work for justice" (1972 World Day of Peace Message; citing the 1971 Synod of Bishops' *Justitia in mundo* 6). And most famously, "the new name for peace is development"—not to be equated with neoliberalism or unrestrained market capitalism (*Populorum progressio* 87).

John Paul II announces just as clearly that "Violence is evil," "a lie," and "the enemy of justice" (Homily at Drogheda, Ireland, September 29, 1979, 18–20). Like his predecessors, John Paul believes violence leads to cycles of injustice, and he deplores the scale of modern war. Adding to Paul VI's emphasis on justice and development, his own call for solidarity as an active commitment to the common good of all, John Paul titles his 1987 World Day of Peace Message "Development and Solidarity: Two Keys to Peace." But the 1990s were to see humanitarian disasters in the former Yugoslavia, Rwanda, and Somalia met with international apathy or ineffectiveness. Hence this pope validates the new concept of "humanitarian intervention" (2002 World Day of Peace Message 11). As he asserted regarding Bosnia, when "populations are succumbing to the attacks of an unjust aggressor, States no longer have a 'right to indifference.'" It seems clear that "their duty is to disarm this aggressor, if all other means have proved ineffective" (Address to the Diplomatic Corps, January 16, 1993).

Along the same lines, and responding again to recent events, John Paul allows for a nation's right of defense against terrorism (2002 World Day of Peace Message 5), even while holding up forgiveness and interreligious cooperation as better paths to peace. Yet when confronted in advance with specific military interventions such as the Gulf War and a U.S. invasion of Iraq, John Paul rejects war as "darkness" (Easter Sunday Message, April 1, 1991)[22] and "a defeat for humanity" (Address to the Diplomatic Corps, January 13, 2003). Rejecting the idea that war is ever inevitable, he urges dialogue and diplomacy in accord with international law.

Benedict XVI resurfaces the basic question whether a just war can even exist today, confirms the war against Iraq was unjust, and notes that modern weapons invariably harm noncombatants.[23] "Violence never comes from God" (TV Interview, Good Friday, April 22, 2011). Specifically embracing gospel nonviolence, Benedict calls "love your enemies" its "magna carta." Nonviolence is for Christians not merely a type of behavior, much less obedience to a heteronomous norm. It is "a person's way of being, the attitude of one who is convinced of God's love and power, who is not afraid to confront evil with the weapons of love and truth alone" (Angelus Address, February 18, 2007; see also TV Interview, Good Friday, April 22, 2011). "Violence is contrary to the Kingdom of God" (Angelus Address, March 11, 2012). On a visit to Cameroon, Benedict declared that all genuine religion rejects any type of violence ("The Saving Message of the Gospel Needs to be Proclaimed," March 17, 2009).

Nevertheless, like John Paul before him, Benedict endorses humanitarian intervention under the rubric "responsibility to protect." "Recognition of the unity of the human family, and attention to the innate dignity of every man and woman, today find renewed emphasis in the principle of the responsibility to protect" (Address to the General Assembly of the United Nations, New York, April 18, 2008). Benedict places humanitarian intervention or the responsibility to protect in international contexts such as UN intervention, or intervention by an international coalition, in which the presumable and implied means is armed force. Neither he nor John Paul II explicitly rejects this possibility. Yet, seeming skeptical about whether violence can actually end violence, Benedict adds in *Caritas in veritate* that the responsibility to protect must be implemented "in innovative ways" (§7).

Benedict follows both Paul VI and John Paul II in seeing economic and political "development" as necessary solutions to social problems, and the best way to prevent and remedy injustices. He repeatedly confirms this aspect of Catholic social teaching in his World Day of Peace Messages (2009, 2010, 2011), and makes it the centerpiece of *Caritas in veritate*, an encyclical written to commemorate *Populorum progressio*.

It will come as no surprise that Pope Francis reaffirms these same themes, often in the same phrases. He summons international parties in conflict to move toward peace through dialogue, reconciliation, negotiation, and compromise. He insists on nonproliferation and disarmament, especially of nuclear arms. Praying for peace in Egypt, Francis is clear on the unacceptability of war: "The true force of the Christian is the force of truth and love, which means rejecting all violence. Faith and violence are incompatible!" The way of Jesus is the way of peace, solidarity, reconciliation, "living for God and for others." The strength of the Christian is "the force of meekness, the force of love" (Angelus Address, August 19, 2013). When, like John Paul and Benedict, Francis is confronted by a possible military intervention, specifically in Syria by U.S. and French "superpower," he is insistent that "war brings on war! Violence brings on violence." (Angelus Address, August 31, 2013).

He expands on these themes by looking to the example of Christ:

My Christian faith urges me to look to the Cross....*Violence is not answered with violence*, death is not answered with the language of death. In the silence of the Cross, the uproar of weapons ceases and the language of reconciliation, forgiveness, dialogue, and peace is spoken. This evening, I ask the Lord that we Christians, and our brothers and sisters of other religions, and every man and woman of good will, cry out forcefully: *violence and war are never the way to peace!*...War always marks the failure of peace, it is always a defeat for humanity. Let the words of Pope Paul VI resound again: "No more one against the other, no more, never!...War never again, never again war!" "Peace expresses itself only in peace, a peace which is not separate from the demands of justice but which is fostered by personal sacrifice, clemency, mercy and love." Forgiveness, dialogue, reconciliation—these are the words of peace, in beloved Syria, in the Middle East, in all the world! ("Vigil of Prayer for Peace" [in Syria], September 7, 2013).

After the publication of *Laudato si'*, connecting war and ecological destruction (§56), Pope Francis urged the United Nations in New York to support sustainable development while protecting the environment. He uncovered the hypocrisy of talking about peace while manufacturing arms; and rebuked international leaders for failing to find peaceful solutions to global conflicts, especially in the Middle East (Address to the General Assembly of the United Nations, September 25, 2015).

Some ambiguity in Pope Francis's position on violent force surfaces regarding the dilemma of how to defeat international terrorist organizations. In August 2014, the pope remarked informally to reporters that dialogue even with the so-called Islamic State (IS or ISIS) should not be considered a "lost cause." Moreover, while defense against aggression is morally just, he seems to think it should take nonviolent forms. "I can only say that it is licit to stop the unjust aggressor. I underscore the verb 'stop'; I don't say bomb, make war—stop him. The means by which he may be stopped should be evaluated."[24]

Pope Francis has amplified calls from every one of his predecessors since Pius XII for nuclear disarmament. This call was loud and clear in John XXIII's *Pacem in terris*, written during the Cold War. His message that, even if proponents of nuclear deterrence claimed that this policy is averting nuclear war, not only is deterrence a dangerous game, but it is also an injustice being done to the poor through the enormous consumption of resources needed for the build-up and refinement of nuclear systems.[25] In the early years of the administration of U.S. President Donald J. Trump, the North Korean "supreme leader" Kim Jong-un and the president were alternating hostile threats with gestures of diplomacy. Pope Francis reacted with a firm denunciation of nuclear weapons and new iterations of the nuclear arms race. In 2017, at a Vatican conference (sponsored by the Dicastery for Promoting Integral Human Development) of Nobel laureates, government and United Nations officials, theologians, and peace activists,[26] Francis "firmly condemned" not only the use of nuclear weapons, but also the threat of their use, and their mere possession.[27] This went beyond prior papal statements on deterrence, effectively repudiating the "strictly conditioned acceptance" of deterrence endorsed in *The Challenge of Peace.*

From Popes to People

The message against military violence and in favor of nonviolent approaches to resolving international conflicts has consistently been issued from the Vatican for over fifty years. But that message has yet to be heard by most U.S. Catholic theologians, bishops, or the faithful, many of whom either assume that just war theory sits at the center of the church's war and peace teaching, or who adhere to political views that are shaped more by attitudes prevalent in their own culture. In 1993, *The Harvest of Justice* asserted,

> National leaders bear a moral obligation to see that nonviolent alternatives are seriously considered for dealing with conflicts. New styles of preventive diplomacy and conflict resolution ought to be explored, tried, improved and supported. As a nation we should promote research, education and training in nonviolent means of resisting evil. Nonviolent strategies need greater attention in international affairs.[28]

But in the United States, at least, this message has not registered with most Catholics. "Nonviolence" is associated with pacifism and Roman Catholicism is not a pacifist church, many would say. Gospel ideals are admirable, even heroic, but also unworkable in the real political environment, even a bit naive. Translating nonviolence into "preventive diplomacy and conflict resolution" is marginal to the way most of our elected representatives approach foreign policy. Influencing them to think and do otherwise is outside the reach of ordinary voters, who are absorbed by immediate issues that affect them personally, such as jobs, education, immigration policies, and health care.

Under Pope Francis, the Vatican has been making renewed efforts to take the message of nonviolence to an expanded audience internationally. One aim of the effort is to communicate that nonviolent political strategies have been and can be more effective than is generally assumed. Another is to enlist practical commitment by reaching out across a broader spectrum of society, so that teaching statements and

191

documents do not remain mere pieces of paper and website links. In April 2016, the Pontifical Council for Justice and Peace and Pax Christi International (shortly thereafter subsumed under the new Dicastery for Promoting Integral Human Development) cosponsored a conference in Rome on "Nonviolence and Just Peace."[29] Nine members of the council were present at the meeting, including its head, Cardinal Peter Turkson of Ghana. The aim of the conference was to displace just war theory from its historically central place in Catholic thinking about war, by advocating a just peace framework for transforming conflicts by non-violent means.

In his message to conference attendees, Pope Francis called for the revitalization of tools of active nonviolence and the transformation of violence through peacemaking initiatives. Yet he also cited *Gaudium et spes* to the effect that governments have a right to legitimate defense.[30] At the theoretical level, the just peace framework would subject conflict resolution to criteria such as human security and the common good, positive peace not merely the absence of violence, restorative justice, rule of law, and participatory decision-making both horizontally and vertically. At the practical level, just peace would involve conflict-transforming practices such as direct nonviolent action, diplomatic initiatives, inter-religious political organization in civil society, unarmed civilian peace-keeping, public rituals of repentance, and initiatives of reconciliation.

The conference itself was highly dialogical, involving short presentations and many discussion opportunities, both by the entire assembly of about eighty, and in smaller groups sorted by language or region. Not all participants were pacifists, and some were advocates of just war theory. Yet all were highly favorable to nonviolent means of resolving conflicts, to Catholic activism for peace, and to theologies supporting peacebuilding. They agreed that the first mandate of the church and theology is not to debate uses of force *in extremis*, but to create the conditions that make force unnecessary.

One of the most striking aspects of the Rome conference was that it drew on a global representation of Catholics (along with a few Protestants and Orthodox). A high proportion of these participants were from areas that had experienced or were then experiencing widespread violent conflict and social devastation—as in Gulu in Northern Uganda, Iraq, South Sudan, Colombia, Mexico, Croatia, the Philippines, Sri Lanka, and Palestine. Several participants expressed vehement objection to the very concept of a "just war," saying that it only aids and abets the perpetration of more violence, giving those who have the might to cause violence the tools to rationalize it as just. Many of these participants shared stories and personal experiences of situations in which courageous, faith-based action had successfully mitigated violence and mediated peace agreements.

The concluding document of the conference urged that priority be given to the Catholic commitment to nonviolence, to the promotion of just peace theory, and—much more controversially—to the elimination and prohibition of any Catholic validation of just war theory whatsoever, whether in pastoral documents, scholarship, or teaching. This includes humanitarian intervention. Conference participants were not asked to sign the final statement (implying endorsement of all specific contents), but to vote on whether it should go forward as a consensus document. The support was virtually unanimous.

The situation of most participants was far different from that of North American Catholic social ethicists and other academics, who see just war theory as potentially restraining, limiting, and even condemning war, and who are developing categories such as *jus post bellum* and *jus ante bellum* precisely to fulfill these functions. People living in war-torn zones have ample existential confirmation that theoretical rubrics such as these simply do not work as intended, especially when insurgents, warring ethnic groups, and repressive governments do not share the commitments behind them, Catholics in the United States have reason to be skeptical too about how important just war criteria really are to our national leadership, particularly in light of recent nuclear threats and our continuing immoral policy of nuclear deterrence, but also in light of long and costly engagements in the Middle East and elsewhere that have brought high costs in terms of human lives lost, increasingly dysfunctional states, motivation for terrorist networks, and displacement of local populations.

In the United States, however, post-conference media attention and theological discussion focused disproportionately on the merits (or lack thereof) of just war theory,[31] to the detriment of promoting active, widespread, grassroots-to-global peacebuilding as a mark and calling of the global Catholic Church. Following on the appeal of the Rome conference to Pope Francis for an encyclical on nonviolence and just peace, the pope issued a 2017 World Day of Peace Message titled "Nonviolence: A Style of Politics for Peace."[32] In it, Pope Francis laments the fact that having passed through the last century's two World Wars, and endured nuclear proliferation and "deterrence," humanity is now in the grip of a "world war fought piecemeal." "Where does this lead? Can violence achieve any goal of lasting value? Or does it merely lead to retaliation and a cycle of deadly conflicts that benefit only a few 'war-lords'?" (§2). Citing his predecessors on the importance and possibility of nonviolence, he insists that it does not amount to "surrender, lack of involvement and passivity." Nonviolent peacebuilding strategies have worked in many countries and situations in the past, bringing more success in establishing "a just and lasting peace" than armed violence, even when it meets just war criteria (§4). Pope Francis therefore calls on "political and religious leaders, the heads of international institutions, and business and media executives," as well as ordinary citizens everywhere, to take up the task of constructive, creative, and successful peacebuilding (§6).

Without necessarily repudiating just war theory and humanitarian intervention (as the popes to date have not), much more attention can and should be given to the many accounts of successful peacebuilding strategies provided at the conference,[33] by the Catholic Peacebuilding Network and other faith-based organizations, and by the United States Institute of Peace and the United Nations.[34] A presenter at the Rome conference was Maria Stephan, a social scientist and director of the Program on Nonviolent Action at the United States Institute of Peace, who has worked for the State Department, for example, in Afghanistan.[35] Stephan and coauthor Erika Chenoweth argue that nonviolent resistance is twice as successful as armed revolt, producing resolutions that are much less likely to devolve into renewed violence.[36] Even loosely coordinated citizen activism can produce a "movement mindset" across a broad spectrum of society, using such strategies as protests, boycotts, civil disobedience, and other forms of nonviolent noncooperation, which separate regimes from their main sources of power and enable the emergence of competing forms of social organization and leadership. Stephan argues that, even in the face of a volatile situation like Syria, much could be accomplished if outsiders funded and supported movements for nonviolent resistance, rather than turning immediately to debates about military options.[37]

In October 2017, a follow-up conference to the Rome event was held at the University of San Diego, attended by bishops (including Cardinal Turkson), theologians, military officers, and faculty of the U.S. military academies.[38] In her keynote address, Stephan argues that nonviolent civil resistance "is a functional alternative to violence" with short- and long-term positive results. She does not claim that nonviolent strategies always work, or that armed humanitarian intervention can never save lives. However, in the United States at present there is no political will to support investment in major humanitarian causes, and they often fail to secure peace and stability in the long run. Moreover, U.S. military leaders have been and can be strong advocates in Washington for nonmilitary solutions such as diplomacy and development. They also realize that rights-violating security forces make poor partners for the establishment of human security and the rule of law.[39] Turning to the role of the Catholic Church internationally and at home, she makes recommendations including research and outreach at Catholic universities, the integration of just peace and conflict transformation into religious education, homilies and sermons, communication between church leaders and government officials (which has been effective in conflict torn societies such as Colombia), and diplomacy and initiatives by the Vatican Secretary of State and the Holy See's representatives to the UN in New York and Geneva.

The Power of U.S. Voters

The devastating injustices and social consequences of violence, including domestic violence, hate crimes, the death penalty, gun violence, and police shootings of unarmed black men and boys, challenge U.S. voters in many ways. These all deserve to be electoral priorities. And terrorism and nuclear weapons naturally get our attention when they are aimed at us. But we also have a responsibility for wars and other types of societal conflict (ethnic-religious violence, civil wars, drug wars, conflicts over natural resources, actions of and within repressive or failed states) that occur beyond our borders, especially if our nation and its leaders play a part in creating or maintaining them. American voters may give up on the global ravages of war and conflict as priorities because the problems are too big, voters feel powerless to make a difference, or the problems may just seem too far away to matter as much as threats and injustices occurring here at home.

However, our church leaders, especially today Pope Francis, not only have a larger vision, they also have confidence that "the people" can build momentum that will influence leaders in a new direction. In

"Nonviolence: A Style of Politics for Peace," Pope Francis asks everyone to cultivate nonviolence in their own decisions, relationships, and
actions, in all the ways they deal with one another on a daily basis (§1).
No one who lives in the United States today can fail to miss the polarization, divisive language, and accusations that pervade the Internet,
television, and even personal interactions. Voters often seem captive to
an "us vs. them" mentality that works its way up into electoral politics
and elected representatives from mayors, state legislatures, and gover-
nors, to Congress, to the presidency.[40]

But this means that voters have the power to turn public discourse
in another direction too. Pope Francis pleads with us to let "respect and
sincere dialogue" begin in our families, and reach to neighborhoods,
churches, coworkers, and political parties, including people from eth-
nicities, races, and religions different from our own (§5). His message to
voters is captured in a statement worth quoting at length:

> It is a challenge to build up society, communities and busi-
> nesses by acting as peacemakers. It is to show mercy by refus-
> ing to discard people, harm the environment, or seek to win
> at any cost. To do so requires "the willingness to face conflict
> head on, to resolve it and to make it a link in the chain of
> a new process." To act in this way means to choose solidar-
> ity as a way of making history and building friendship in
> society. Active nonviolence is a way of showing that unity is
> truly more powerful and more fruitful than conflict. Every-
> thing in the world is inter-connected. Certainly differences
> can cause frictions. But let us face them constructively and
> non-violently, so that "tensions and oppositions can achieve
> a diversified and life-giving unity," preserving "what is valid
> and useful on both sides." (§7)

Prophetic denunciations and protests of U.S. military policy and
spending can call attention to an issue and rally the base of those who
already agree with the cause, inspiring them to do more and to work for
their goals. Protesters hope and even assume that collective action can
pressure those in power to fulfill their political roles in ways that benefit
the human good of all. But it is also necessary to build bridges across
social divisions, to reach out to those who see things differently from us,

giving them the benefit of the doubt at least until some honest interactions have occurred. This requires creativity and persistence.

To a great degree, the global military presence of the United States is dependent on elected officials at the highest levels: the president and Congress. What that presence looks like concretely also depends on how our military and civilian leaders are trained to see their roles and those of the people serving under them. Elected representatives do not always reflect "the will of the people" in a perfect or unmitigated way. But expectations from their constituents are important. Diplomatic and military personnel also reflect their cultures in various ways. Voters should remember this not only at the ballot box, but in political discourse leading up to that final opportunity for choice. Candidates will be nominated and voters will vote based on larger cultural dynamics, worldviews, and attitudes. In the United States these dynamics, views, and attitudes have become very polarized and un-self-critical. They reflect a climate of fear and competition, and do not foster the Catholic standards of respect for the dignity of all, and a universal (not merely local or even national) vision of the common good. Prophets who identify these pernicious trends are needed, but just as necessary, if not more so, are bridgebuilders who reach across the cultural divides.

Thoughtful political dialogues in line with Catholic social tradition are essential to responsible Catholic political participation. A confrontational approach to political differences is not usually the most effective way to enlarge the horizons of others. Creating a culture of dialogue and responsible voting takes work, time, and patience. Often it is better to build trust on the common ground of shared interests and goals, growing mutual confidence before raising problems such as militarism, U.S. policies that risk civilian lives, and the dangers of nuclear buildup. Pax Christi meetings and parish justice and peace committees tend to draw out the "true believers." But coming together around local political causes not divided along red-blue lines, improvements in public or Catholic education, parish social initiatives, sponsoring an immigrant family, or bringing meals to the elderly can generate a sense of "we're in this together." Ending divisions, polarizations, vitriol, and exclusionary politics at home is key to creating a political culture in which violence no longer appears as an attractive strategy to serve "American interests" abroad. To return to Pope Francis's 2017 World Day of Peace Message, to be a peacebuilder "means to choose solidarity as a way of making history and building friendship in society. Active nonviolence is a way of showing that unity is truly more powerful and more fruitful than conflict" (§7).

NOTES

1. Pope Francis, World Day of Peace Message, January 1, 2017, https://w2.vatican.va/content/francesco/en/messages/peace/documents/papa-francesco_20161208_messaggio-l-giornata-mondiale-pace-2017.html.

2. Joshua Keating, "Fifteen Years After the Start of the Iraq War, the U.S. Is at War in at Least Seven Countries," *Slate*, March 19, 2009, https://slate.com/news-and-politics/2018/03/fifteen-years-after-the-start-of-the-iraq-war-the-u-s-is-at-war-in-at-least-seven-countries.html.

3. James Carden, "A New Poll Shows the Public Is Overwhelmingly Opposed to Endless US Military Interventions," *The Nation*, January 9, 2018, https://www.thenation.com/article/new-poll-shows-public-overwhelmingly-opposed-to-endless-us-military-interventions/.

4. Frank Newport, "American Public Opinion, Terrorism and Guns," *Gallup* blog, June 13, 2016, https://news.gallup.com/opinion/polling-matters/192695/american-public-opinion-terrorism-guns.aspx.

5. Tara Golshan, "Most American Voters Prioritize the Economy. Republicans Are Voting on National Security," May 3, 2018, *Vox*, https://www.vox.com/2018/5/3/17314664/2018-midterm-polls-policy-priority-voters.

6. Thomas Gibbons-Neff, "Civilian Deaths under US-led Air Strikes Hit Record High under Donald Trump," *The Independent*, March 25, 2017, https://www.independent.co.uk/news/world/americas/us-politics/donald-trump-civilian-deaths-syria-iraq-middle-east-a7649486.html. On the ethics of drone strikes, see Kenneth R. Himes, *Drones and the Ethics of Targeted Killing* (Lanham, MD: Rowman & Littlefield, 2015).

7. See Clifton B. Parker, "Public Opinion Unlikely to Curb a U.S. President's Use of Nuclear Weapons in War, Stanford Scholar Finds," *Stanford News*, August 8, 2017, https://news.stanford.edu/2017/08/08/americans-weigh-nuclear-war/. See also similar results from a University of Maryland poll, "American Public Attitudes toward North Korea's Nuclear and Missile Programs," presented at the Brookings Institution, January 8, 2018, https://www.brookings.edu/wp-content/uploads/2017/12/us-japan_northkoreasurveyquestions.pdf.

8. United States Conference of Catholic Bishops, *Forming Consciences for Faithful Citizenship: A Call to Political Responsibility from the Catholic Bishops of the United States with Introductory Note*, November 2015, http://www.usccb.org/issues-and-action/faithful-citizenship/.

9. John Courtney Murray, "Remarks on the Moral Problem of War," *Theological Studies* 20 (1959): 57.

10. For a more detailed discussion of the sources that follow, see "Just War and the Gospel," in Tobias Winright and Laurie Johnston, eds., *Can War Be Just in the Twenty-First Century? Ethicists Engage the Tradition* (Maryknoll, NY: Orbis, 2015), 1–13.

11. Augustine, "Commentary on the Lord's Sermon on the Mount," XX.63, in *The Fathers of the Church*, vol. 11, *Saint Augustine: Commentary on the Lord's Sermon on the Mount*, ed. Roy J. Deferrari (New York: Fathers of the Church, Inc., 1951), 90. See also Augustine, "Letter 138, to Marcellinus," in *Saint Augustine: Letters*, vol. 3, trans. Wilfred Parsons (Washington, DC: Catholic University of America Press, 1953), 44.

12. The key source of Aquinas's views is his major work: Thomas Aquinas, *Summa Theologiae*, II–II. Q 40.

13. *Catechism of the Catholic Church*, accessed August 9, 2018, http://www.vatican.va/archive/ENG0015/_INDEX.HTM.

14. Gerard F. Powers, "From an Ethics of War to an Ethics of Peacebuilding," in Heinz-Gerhard Justenhoven and William Barbieri Jr., eds., *From Modern Just War to Modern Peace Ethics* (Berlin and Boston: De Gruyter, 2012), 275–312.

15. Mark J. Allman and Tobias L. Winright, *After the Smoke Clears: The Just War Tradition and Post War Justice* (Maryknoll, NY: Orbis, 2010); and Allman and Winright, "Growing Edges of Just War Theory: *Jus ante bellum, jus post bellum*, and Imperfect Justice," in *Journal of the Society of Christian Ethics* 32, no. 2 (2012): 173–91.

16. National Conference of Catholic Bishops, *The Challenge of Peace: God's Promise and Our Response*, May 3, 1983, http://www.usccb.org/upload/challenge-peace-gods-promise-our-response-1983.pdf.

17. National Conference of Catholic Bishops, *The Harvest of Justice is Sown in Peace*, November 17, 1993, http://www.usccb.org/beliefs-and-teachings/what-we-believe/catholic-social-teaching/the-harvest-of-justice-is-sown-in-peace.cfm.

18. See Ariel Edwards-Levy, "Voters Say Health Care Is a Top Issue in the 2018 Election—A Good Sign for Democrats," *Huffington Post*, April 6, 2018, https://www.huffingtonpost.com/entry/voters-say-health-care-is-their-top-issue-in-the-2018-election-thats-a-good-sign-for-democrats_us_5ac642e2e4b09d0a119103c4.

19. Golshan, "Most American Voters Prioritize the Economy."

20. All Council documents and papal encyclicals, World Day of Peace messages, addresses, and other formal statements may be accessed at the Vatican website, www.vatican.va; or by entering the title into an Internet search engine.

21. *The Compendium of the Social Doctrine of the Church*, April 2005, http://www.vatican.va/roman_curia/pontifical_councils/justpeace/documents/rc_pc_justpeace_doc_20060526_compendio-dott-soc_en.html.

22. Clyde Haberman, "Pope Denounces Gulf War as 'Darkness,'" *New York Times*, April 1, 1991, https://www.nytimes.com/1991/04/01/world/pope-denounces-the-gulf-war-as-darkness.html. This speech is apparently not available on the Vatican website.

23. "Cardinal Ratzinger on the Abridged Version of Catechism," *Zenit*, May 2, 2003, https://zenit.org/articles/cardinal-ratzinger-on-the-abridged-version-of-catechism/.

24. Kathryn Jean Lopez, "Pope Francis on Iraq," *National Review*, August 18, 2014, http://www.nationalreview.com/corner/385672/pope-francis-iraq-kathryn-jean-lopez.

25. John XXIII, *Pacem in terris* 112: "Justice, then, right reason and consideration for human dignity and life urgently demand that the arms race should cease; that the stockpiles which exist in various countries should be reduced equally and simultaneously by the parties concerned; that nuclear weapons should be banned; and finally that all come to an agreement on a fitting program of disarmament, employing mutual and effective controls."

26. Cindy Wooden, "Consistently Anti-nuke: Pope Continues Papal Pleas for Disarmament," *Catholic News Service*, October 31, 2017, http://www.catholicnews.com/services/englishnews/2017/consistently-antinuke-pope-continues-papal-pleas-for-disarmament.cfm. This article reviews statements of previous popes against nuclear weapons.

27. Pope Francis, "Prospects for a World Free of Nuclear Weapons and for Integral Disarmament," November 10, 2017, https://w2.vatican.va/content/francesco/en/speeches/2017/november/documents/papa-francesco_20171110_convegno-disarmointegrale.html. This statement constitutes a condemnation of the position accepting the morality of deterrence in the U.S. bishops' 1983 Pastoral Letter, *The Challenge of Peace*. This moral condemnation, which in my view is not only principled but persuasive, returns us to the question posed by Reinhold Niebuhr: What is a politically feasible alternative? What should be and can be a path to that alternative? For a debate on the merits of the pope's statement, see Michael C. Desch and Gerard F. Powers, "No More Nukes: An Exchange," *Commonweal*, February 9, 2018, https://www.commonwealmagazine.org/no-more-nukes.

28. *Harvest of Justice*, part I.B.1.

29. After the conference a follow-up organization, the Catholic Nonviolence Initiative, was created under the leadership of Pax Christi. Its website includes conference background materials, conference participants and videos, and follow-up activities, as well as a link to a book based on conference papers,

Marie Dennis, *Choosing Peace: The Catholic Church Responds to Gospel Nonviolence* (Maryknoll, NY: Orbis, 2018).

30. This message is included in *Choosing Peace*, 1–5.

31. For a sample of the early debate, see Mark J. Allman and Tobias Winright, "Protect Thy Neighbor: Why Just War Tradition Is Still Indispensable," *Commonweal*, June 2, 2016, https://www.commonwealmagazine.org/protect-thy-neighbor; and Lisa Sowle Cahill: "A Church for Peace? Why Just War Theory Isn't Enough," *Commonweal*, July 11, 2011, https://www.commonwealmagazine.org/church-peace.

32. This is available on the Vatican website at https://w2.vatican.va/content/francesco/en/messages/peace/documents/papa-francesco_20161208_messaggio-l-giornata-mondiale-pace-2017.html (accessed August 10, 2018), on that of the Catholic Nonviolence Initiative, and in *Choosing Peace*, 221–29.

33. *Choosing Peace* provides many examples, most taken from the concrete experience of participants in the Rome conference.

34. For an overview, see Susan Hayward, *Religion and Peacebuilding*, United States Institute of Peace Special Report, August 3, 2012, https://www.usip.org/publications/2012/08/religion-and-peacebuilding.

35. See Maria J. Stephan, "Active Nonviolence: An Effective Political Tool," in *Choosing Peace*, 147–57.

36. Erika Chenoweth and Maria J. Stephan, *Why Civil Resistance Works: The Strategic Logic of Nonviolent Conflict* (New York: Columbia University Press, 2011).

37. Maria J. Stephan, "Why Support for Syria's Nonviolent Fighters Is Key to Ending the War," Waging Nonviolence: People-Powered News and Analysis, April 21, 2017, https://wagingnonviolence.org/feature/support-nonviolent-fighters-syria/.

38. For more information, a list of participants, and links to papers and videos, see "The Catholic Church Moves towards Nonviolence? Just Peace Just War in Dialogue," USD Conference, October 6–7, 2017, https://www.sandiego.edu/cctc/events/past-events/just-peace-just-war.php.

39. In her paper, Stephan recommends Admiral Dennis Blair, *Military Engagement: Influencing Armed Forces Worldwide to Support Democratic Transitions* (Washington, DC: Brookings Institution Press, 2013).

40. See Eduardo Porter, "Whites' Unease Shadows the Politics of a More Diverse America," *New York Times*, May 22, 2018, https://www.nytimes.com/2018/05/22/business/economy/trump-election-ethnic-diverse-whites.html; Amina Dunn, "Trump's Approval Ratings so Far Are Unusually Stable—and Deeply Partisan," August 1, 2018, Pew Research Center, http://www.pewresearch.org/fact-tank/2018/08/01/trumps-approval-ratings-so-far-are-unusually-stable-and-deeply-partisan/; and Diana C. Mutz, "Status Threat,

Not Economic Hardship, Explains the 2016 Presidential Vote," *Proceedings of the National Academy of Sciences*, April 23, 2018, http://www.pnas.org/content/early/2018/04/18/1718155115.

Questions for Further Reflection

1. How has Catholic social teaching struggled to deal with the problem of how to respond to violence and other injustices? Why?

2. What is the Catholic theory of a "just war"? How did this theory develop? Is any war ever fully just? How do we judge whether a war is just? What are the criteria? Can a just war be waged with unjust methods? What do the bishops say in *Faithful Citizenship* about this?

3. What does the *Catechism of the Catholic Church* say about just war? What Pastoral Letters did the American bishops write about just wars? Do they accept the possibility of a just war? Do they put any limits on this theory?

4. What did the Second Vatican Council and subsequent popes teach about just wars? Is this the same as the traditional teaching on this subject? How does the need to combat terrorism fit into the just war theory?

5. How have the recent popes dealt with the U.S. wars in the Middle East? Did they perceive them as just wars? If not, can American Catholics continue to participate in or support these wars?

6. How does the duty to protect the innocent and helpless affect a just war analysis? Can this apply to recent events in the Middle East and Afghanistan?

7. How well have the papal teachings on war and peace been received by the American faithful? When was the last time you heard a sermon on military violence? On abortion? American flags are prominently displayed on many church altars, usually beside a papal flag. Should they be? Should we sing patriotic hymns at Mass?

8. Can nonviolence ever work in an international context? Can a nation ever "turn the other cheek"? Do the leaders of a nation have

an obligation to protect their people against external aggression by the use of force? What kind of force? Nuclear? Conventional?

9. Do you think that Catholicism is a pacifist faith? What is a valid Catholic alternative to just war theory? Is it pacifism or something in between? How would a "just peace" framework function today? Is there a difference between pacifism and nonviolence? Are Catholics allowed to be either/neither?

10. Can you think of any reasons to oppose a just war theory? Does Catholicism help to validate a just war theory? If so, how? Is there a downside to such a validation?

11. Is there a problem trying to apply these theoretical rubrics to real-life situations of war? What would those be?

12. Do you think that just war criteria are important to Catholics in the United States? Do these criteria influence the way Catholics vote? Should they?

13. Is it proper to oppose the just war theory to the peace-building theory? Are they categorical opposites?

14. What does Pope Francis say about nonviolence in his 2017 World Day of Peace message? Does he repudiate a just war theory in that message?

15. Can nonviolence ever be as effective as the use of force? If so, in which situations? If not, why not?

16. Why does the United States seem to have so little interest in major investments in humanitarian causes across the world? Is this something that American Catholics should campaign for in our politics? Or should national interests come first?

17. What has the U.S. military's role been in advocating nonmilitary solutions? Why do you think that has been the case?

18. In which ways do the devastating injustice and social consequences of violence challenge Catholic voters? Is there a religious answer, rooted in our faith, to these problems?

19. What does the author say is the role of church leaders in combatting violence? What is the role of Catholic voters?

10

Conscience and the Military

Tobias Winright

Peace, Sanctuary, Liturgy, and Conscience

"Peace be with you!" Upon reading those four words, another four words in response should have immediately come to mind: "And with your spirit." When I speak at Catholic parishes and other Christian churches on the topic of theology, ethics, and war and peace, I usually open with this familiar greeting, and every time most, if not all, attendees respond this way. They do so even if the presentation is not in a church building. When in the sanctuary or in a nearby classroom at the church, though, there is less hesitation; it seems almost second nature to utter these words that are regularly spoken during worship. This peaceful greeting and the gesture of passing the peace are, I believe, more significant than often assumed.

That word *sanctuary* is noteworthy, too. It refers to a place of refuge and safety. In other words, it is a space in which violent conflict is supposed to be absent. But it is meant to be even more, as the ritual of the passing of the peace during worship time suggests. That is, the sanctuary is not only a space where we are supposed to be *free from* violence,

204

but *free for* making and building peace—a peace that, as the Second Vatican Council in its Pastoral Constitution on the Church in the Modern World (*Gaudium et spes*) put it, "is not merely the absence of war" but, rather, "based on justice and love."[1] Coincidentally, the word *sanctuary* appears also in the Pastoral Constitution in association with conscience, where it is called our "most secret core and sanctuary," in which we encounter God and discern God's voice concerning the law of love for God and our neighbor.[2] And that conscience, the Council emphasized, must remain operative even when it comes to "the subject of war."[3]

Conscience is more than the intellect, more than a mental exercise. Yet, as Kathryn Lilla Cox notes, "Sometimes Roman Catholics and/or their bishops associate a well-formed conscience with intellectually assenting to a magisterial or episcopal teaching."[4] She adds, though, that conscience also involves the heart, "the totality of the human person," including, in addition to intellectual reasoning, his or her emotions, feelings, attitudes, dispositions, and affections. Accordingly, in addition to *information*, conscience requires *formation*. One of the key ways that conscience is formed and shaped for Christians is through the liturgy and their participation in worship, which includes not only instruction through the reading and hearing of Scripture, as well as from the homily, but also rituals, gestures, art, music, and more.[5]

I begin this chapter on "Conscience and the Military" with attention to these connections between peace, sanctuary, liturgy, and conscience because what we say and do in the sanctuary during worship should be informing and forming the sanctuary of our conscience, including on life and death issues, whether these be our participation in the military or our voting for political candidates who will deal with foreign policy, taxes, and military spending. Although I have already quoted from official Catholic documents on the subject, I think that Kenneth R. Himes, OFM, makes an accurate observation when he writes, "The vast majority of Catholics do not read magisterial statements....It is not the intellectual appeal of theological documents which moves people at the level of the daily life of the church. For Roman Catholics it is the Sunday Eucharist that continues to be the important ecclesial experience."[6]

This is our starting point. Regardless of whether one is a pacifist who believes all war is immoral and that only nonviolent methods may be morally used, or whether one is a just war adherent who believes that war might be morally justifiable and that military force may be morally used, for all Catholics the question of conscience and the military should be a serious issue because peace is our fundamental orientation and goal. Thus, as Joseph J. Fahey points out, "A grave burden rests, then, on each person to form his or her conscience about war."[7] But we cannot do so alone or from scratch. We need others. That is why the U.S. Catholic bishops published their benchmark 1983 Pastoral Letter, *The Challenge of Peace*: "to help Catholics form their consciences and to contribute to the public policy debate about the morality of war."[8] Again, the bishops emphasized, in relation to modern war, "the requirement for proper formation of conscience."[9] That's a strong word, *requirement*. The formation of conscience on this moral issue is not simply optional, that is, if someone happens to have time or interest, but instead, obligatory.

Such formation, though, already should be regularly happening. I believe that such formation begins for Catholics and other Christians during worship, even in the small, seemingly insignificant gestures we perform during the liturgy, such as the passing of the peace. Indeed, the U.S. bishops "encourage every Catholic to make the sign of peace at Mass an authentic sign of our reconciliation with God and with one another. This sign of peace is also a visible expression of our commitment to work for peace as a Christian community."[10] Although it may seem completely removed from, or at odds with, such "real world" matters, the gesture of passing the peace should orient and direct how we Catholics reflect on conscience and the military.

Of course, not only the passing of the peace, but the entire "Mass in particular is a unique means of seeking God's help to create the conditions essential for true peace in ourselves and in the world."[11] Here the bishops mention also the communion rite, the Lord's Prayer, and the petitions for peace during the general intercessions at Mass (as the *Catechism* notes, "The Church prays: 'From famine, pestilence, and war, O Lord, deliver us'").[12] Just think about all that we say, sing, pray, hear, and do during worship.[13] Indeed, the Mass itself *is* a moral activity: we reply, "It is right and just" to give thanks (*eucharisto* is Greek for "thanksgiving") to the Lord our God. From the *Gloria*—where we sing, "Glory to God in the highest, and peace to God's people on earth"—to the communion rite—where the priest prays, "Lord Jesus Christ, you said to your apostles: I leave you peace, my peace I give you. Look not on our sins, but on the faith of your Church, and grant us the peace and unity of your kingdom"—peace is emphasized. The same is the case with the Lord's Prayer, when the priest adds, "Deliver us, Lord, from every evil, and grant us peace in our day," and then says, "The peace of the Lord be with you always," to which the congregation responds, "And with your spirit."[14] Before receiving communion, the assembly sings the *Agnus Dei*, praying that the Lamb of God, who takes away the sins of the world, will "grant us peace." Finally, at the conclusion of the Mass, the priest or deacon blesses us, "The Mass is ended, go in peace." Even the other options for the priest or deacon include reference to peace: "Go in the peace of Christ" or "Go in peace to love and serve the Lord." To which we respond, "Thanks be to God!" In sum, the liturgy underscores the U.S. Catholic bishops' teaching that there should be an initial presumption in favor of peace and against violence and war.[15] Thus, the bishops declare, "Peacemaking is not an optional commitment. It is a requirement of our faith."[16] Again, this is our starting point and our basic orientation, mandatory as well.

A Personal Note

Before proceeding further, however, and lest readers assume that what follows will be an ivory tower defense of some sentimental pacifism, let me add a personal note about why I often teach and write about this question, even though as a theological ethicist I also teach and write about other moral issues. For me, questions about conscience and the military are not merely theoretical or academic. I was raised in a blue-collar family—farmers and factory workers—and when I became a teenager, my mother did something different by becoming a police officer. Growing up, I considered several possible careers and callings: priest, politician, lawyer, soldier. Raised a Catholic, I attended a small, rural parochial school, and I admired saints like Francis of Assisi. I loved singing, "Let there be peace on earth, and let it begin with me." At the same time, however, I loved playing "army" with my toy soldiers and with my neighbors and our toy guns. I remember, too, when my grandmother, Grandma Hug, once told me, while I was playing with my plastic soldiers on the kitchen floor, "War is bad."

As a first-generation college student, I worked full-time for the local metropolitan sheriff's department where my mother worked. I was also in Army R.O.T.C. and even trained a bit at Fort Benning in Georgia, because I considered a military career. I ended up not pursuing the latter, though, because my conscience felt uncomfortable about the possibility of being involved in an unjust war (the horrors of Vietnam impacted me even though it happened when I was a small child) or being ordered by a commanding officer to do something unlawful (I was aware of the Nuremberg Trials following World War II when Nazis attempted to use "I was only obeying orders" as an excuse for their atrocities). I also wrestled with the use of force in my law enforcement work. Not only did I occasionally witness unjust use of force (i.e., excessive force and police brutality) by fellow officers, I also saw the violence that people commit against each other and against those pledged to serve and protect them. I, myself, used force on others, and I, too, have scars from the violence of others. Of course, while my own experiences pale in comparison to many others', especially those (including several of my students) who have served in combat in recent wars, all this seemed far removed from the peace of Christ I experienced during worship in the sanctuary. Nor was my conscience at peace. Although I believed that armed force may be morally justified and used, I also felt a sense of discomfort about it.

At the time, one of my professors, a Roman Catholic political theorist who believed that ethics should play an important role in foreign policy, introduced me to just war theory, to Vatican II's *Gaudium et spes*, and to the U.S. bishops' *The Challenge of Peace*.[17] This framework of moral reasoning with its principles governing the just use of force came to inform my conscience concerning both my work in law enforcement and my discernment about the military. At the same time, after seeing the 1982 movie *Gandhi*, I read and wrestled with his writings and life; indeed, his principled and pragmatic nonviolence inspired and challenged me. I therefore also began to read works by theological ethicists in defense of Christian pacifism.[18] To be sure, I became so immersed in these questions about violence and peace that, upon graduation with my B.A., I went to graduate school to study theology and ethics. After that, I became a professor and, even then, for a few years at first, I was also a reserve police officer, teaching ethics for a city police department while also patrolling part-time for it. It is with this background that I have attempted for over three decades now to take seriously the issue of conscience and the military.

Faith and the World

One of the main obstacles I encounter, however, when I give presentations on the topic of conscience and the military is that many

Catholics continue to compartmentalize or bifurcate their faith from their lives and their livelihoods, or what they experience during the Mass from what they do in the world. Yet, as the Second Vatican Council taught in the Constitution on the Sacred Liturgy, the eucharistic liturgy is the font and summit of the Christian life.[19] Likewise, the Pastoral Constitution on the Church in the Modern World held that those Christians are in error "who think that religion consists in acts of worship alone…and who imagine they can plunge themselves into earthly affairs in such a way as to imply that these are altogether divorced from the religious life."[20] Because of this chasm, it is tempting to have a "blank check" mentality regarding war and peace issues, giving "blind obedience" to political authorities and commanding officers who, it is assumed, must do "whatever is necessary." Not surprisingly, as moral theologian Patrick T. McCormick has lamented, the actual "default position" of the "vast majority of American Catholics and Christians" is that they evidently "approach the moral analysis of every call to arms with a strong presumption in favor of war."[21] Likewise, moral theologian Laurie Johnston refers to how "American Catholics overall tend to be very willing—even too willing—to trust their government authorities absolutely," and she adds that some of her own students have said, "Yes, I'm a Catholic—but I'm an American first."[22] Patriotism here has morphed into nationalism, making Catholics and their fellow citizens less likely to question their country's decisions on military actions. This is one of the reasons why I think, with all due respect, the U.S. Conference of Catholic Bishops' document *Forming Consciences for Faithful Citizenship* instead should have been titled something more like *Forming Faithful Catholic Consciences for Moral Citizenship*.

Why? In contrast to such erroneous separation and compartmentalization of faith and life, of ethics and politics, and what we do during worship and do in the world—all of which actually inverses that to which we are actually "faithful"—the *Catechism*, drawing on *Gaudium et spes*, instructs, "The Church and human reason both assert the permanent validity of the *moral law during armed conflict.* The mere fact that war has regrettably broken out does not mean that everything becomes licit between the warring parties."[23] Might does not make right and winning should only be done rightly. The conscience that is informed and formed by the liturgy and its emphasis on peace and peacemaking must be followed even when making decisions (whether to join the military, to vote for a certain candidate or tax, to follow an order during combat, to support or protest a foreign policy, and so on) having to do with the military. Catholics are expected to follow their conscience's discernment of the moral law and its requirements in these matters. For this reason, the Catholic Church recognizes both conscientious objection and selective conscientious objection. That is, while all Catholics are obligated to be peacemakers (Matt 5:9, "Blessed are the peacemakers, for they will be called children of God."), the bishops acknowledge that it is "the *how* of defending peace which offers moral options."[24] The Catholic Church allows for both nonviolence (traditionally called *pacifism*) and legitimate defense using armed force (traditionally called *just war*) as ways of being peacemakers. Either approach requires, and in turn must be expressive of, a rightly informed and formed moral conscience.

Conscientious Objection and Christian Nonviolence

Regarding general conscientious objection, the *Catechism* teaches, "Public authorities should make equitable provision for those who for reasons of conscience refuse to bear arms; these are nonetheless obliged to serve the human community in some other way."[25] That phrase "for reasons of conscience" refers to deeply held religious and theological beliefs about Jesus's life and teachings. The *Catechism*, quoting *Gaudium et spes*, also says that these nonviolent Catholics "bear witness to evangelical charity."[26] In other words, they embody and practice the love that Jesus Christ taught and practiced, including for the enemy (Matt 5:44). In their interpretation, such love entails the refusal to bear arms. Indeed, the U.S. bishops declare, "We believe work to develop nonviolent means of fending off aggression and resolving conflict *best reflect* the call of Jesus both to love and to justice."[27] An early proponent of such a nonviolent approach to peacemaking was Tertullian (c. 144–c. 240 CE) who, regarding Jesus's arrest in the Garden of Gethsemane, wrote, "The Lord in disarming Peter henceforth disarms every soldier."[28] Significantly, many early Christian martyrs, such as St. Maximilian (died 295 CE) and St. Marcellus (died 298 CE), were executed by the Roman authorities for their refusal to serve in the military.[29]

According to the U.S. bishops, nonviolent Christians "have from the earliest days of the church committed themselves to *a non-violent lifestyle.*"[30] The bishops' reference to "lifestyle" conveys how such pacifism is *not* to be equated with *passivity*, for those who subscribe to this approach, as was stipulated above in the *Catechism*, "are nonetheless obliged to serve the human community in some other way" and to "safeguard human rights"—that is, they should seek to address conflict and to build peace using only nonviolent means and methods. And, as indicated by the above references to Tertullian and the martyrs, pacifism and nonviolence were the norm for most Christians during the first three centuries of the history of the church.

One prominent early Christian teacher, Origen (c. 185–254 CE), based Christians' refusal to fight in the Roman military not only on the New Testament's portrayal of Jesus, who "nowhere teaches that it is right for His own disciples to offer violence to any one, however wicked," but also on the liturgical grounds that Christians "fight" for a peaceful and just order by "forming a special army—an army of piety—by offering our prayers to God."[31] Origen also observed that just as the Romans permit their priests, who offer sacrifices to their gods, to "keep their hands free from blood" by not requiring them to fight in the military, so too should all Christians (not only the priests) be allowed to worship their God without being required to be a part of the military and getting blood on their hands.[32] Another early Christian writer, St. John Chrysostom (c. 347–407 CE), even more explicitly pointed out the way that bloodshed is inconsistent with Christian worship and, in particular, with the Eucharist:

> The Lord has fed us with his own sacred flesh….What excuse shall we have, if eating of the lamb we become wolves? If, led like sheep into pasture, we behave as though we were ravening lions? This mystery [of the Eucharist] requires that we should be innocent not only of violence, but of all enmity, however slight, for it is the mystery of peace.[33]

This viewpoint was also evident in the disciplinary and catechetical rules of the church from the third century until around the fifth century. The *Canons of Hippolytus*, for example, stipulated,

> Of the magistrate and the soldier, let them not kill anyone, even if they receive the order to do so….Anyone who has an authority and does not do the justice of the gospel, let him

be cut off and not pray with the bishop. Let…a believer…if he desire to be a soldier, either cease from his intention or, if not, let him be rejected.[34]

In addition to abhorrence of the shedding of blood, the early Christians worried about the problem of idolatry and the military. Indeed, rituals were required of Roman officers, which soldiers had to attend and thereby give their indirect support of, including sacrifices to, and worship of, the Roman emperor, Caesar. Relatedly, many military units often had their own cult, wherein a particular god was worshiped in return for that god's favor and assistance. Because for Christians "Jesus is Lord," they refused to join the Roman military with its idolatrous practices. Notice that their refusal to commit idolatry hinged on the question of whom to *worship*. In other words, discernment of ultimate loyalty (i.e., to what does one give absolute worth or value, or to whom is one really faithful?) was essential. Both martyrs Maximilian and Marcellus expressed their grave concerns about idolatry even more explicitly than about bloodshed. They refused to pledge their absolute allegiance to the emperor. One might say that, for them, it was more important to follow their conscience and be faithful Catholics than faithful citizens, if these two commitments ever were to conflict.

Although beginning in the fourth century this nonviolent approach to peacemaking became overshadowed by the just war approach, it did not become extinct. Indeed, it survived among religious orders, such as the Franciscans, and other reform groups over subsequent centuries. Moreover, as reflected in its approval by the Second Vatican Council and subsequent magisterial documents, including the U.S. bishops' 1983 Pastoral Letter, in the past century pacifism and nonviolence have gained wider attention and more adherents. Inspired by effective nonviolent movements, such as those led by Gandhi and Martin Luther King Jr., much work is being done today on peace studies and conflict mediation, resolution, and transformation. In their 1994 statement appearing in the wake of successful nonviolent revolutions in the Philippines and in Eastern Europe, the U.S. Catholic bishops observed that "recent history suggests that in some circumstances [nonviolence] can be an effective public undertaking as well."[35] That is, nonviolence as a method can be more effective than war, less costly in blood and treasure than war,[36] and can even lead to reconciliation. It also seeks to address the root causes of conflict, thereby preventing it in the first place. Many

Catholic and other Christian scholars, clergy, and activists, including those who do not subscribe to pacifism, have in recent years devoted themselves to developing and implementing "just peacemaking" practices and a "just peace" approach to peacebuilding, including in regions south of the equator.[37]

More recently, in their "Appeal to the Catholic Church to Re-Commit to the Centrality of Gospel Nonviolence," issued in April 2016, some eighty Catholic activists and scholars, whose gathering at the Vatican was cosponsored by Pax Christi International and the Pontifical Council for Justice and Peace, implored the church to revive and reestablish "Gospel nonviolence" as its approach for dealing with conflict, and they urged Pope Francis to write an encyclical on nonviolence and just peace in order to show official, magisterial support for their proposal.[38] Both pacifists and non-pacifists have expressed support for this renewed focus on nonviolence.

Boston College's Lisa Sowle Cahill writes that a "newer approach sometimes called 'peacebuilding'" is gaining traction, giving "almost exclusive priority to the positive and nonviolent cultivation of peace."[39] That "almost" is noteworthy, for it acknowledges that disagreement continues as to whether peacebuilding entails absolute nonviolence, or pacifism. Some supporters of the "Appeal to the Catholic Church to Re-Commit to the Centrality of Gospel Nonviolence" who are pacifists appear to want the church to concentrate instead *solely* on gospel nonviolence. Nevertheless, Catholics today who are seeking to inform their conscience regarding issues involving the military should agree that nonviolence and peacebuilding ought to be more of a priority. Support for more research and development of effective nonviolent methods, tools, and practices, as well as more emphasis on diplomacy, should be noncontroversial for Catholics. As the U.S. bishops suggest in *Forming Consciences for Faithful Citizenship*, "Nations should protect the dignity of the human person and the right to life by finding more effective ways to prevent conflicts, to resolve them by peaceful means, and to promote reconstruction and reconciliation in the wake of conflicts."[40]

Just War and a Life of Peace

In addition to general conscientious objection, pacifism, and nonviolence, the U.S. Catholic bishops express support for selective conscientious objection, which refers to a person's "objection to participation in a particular war, either because of the ends being pursued or the means being used."[41] Both of these reasons for objecting presuppose the framework of moral reasoning traditionally known as just war theory. The "ends being pursued" alludes to the *jus ad bellum* (i.e., *why* and *when* embarking on war is morally justified) category of principles, specifically the principles of just cause and right intent. The "means being used" refers to the *jus in bello* (i.e., *just conduct* during war) category of principles, including discriminate and proportionate force. Nonetheless, the church insists that Christians, even enlisted soldiers, may refuse to participate in a given war or follow certain orders if he or she views them as immoral. The just war mode of reasoning about armed force presumes that morality ought to continue to apply even concerning war. As noted earlier, the *Catechism* states, "The Church and human reason both assert the permanent validity of the *moral law during armed conflict*."[42] That refers to *jus in bello* considerations, but it also applies *prior* to armed conflict, with *jus ad bellum* considerations: "The strict conditions for legitimate defense by military force require rigorous consideration. The gravity of such a decision makes it subject to rigorous conditions of moral legitimacy."[43] The word *rigorous* is twice used because of, as the nonviolent witness of pacifists reminds us, "the gravity of the physical and moral risks of recourse to violence, with all its destruction and death."[44]

Admittedly, as was observed earlier by Patrick McCormick, too many Catholics and other Christians have failed to be rigorous enough when it comes to the morality of war. Indeed, this is part of the reason why the appeal issued in 2016 by Catholic scholars and activists exhorted the Catholic Church to "no longer use or teach 'just war theory.'" They asserted, "We believe that there is no 'just war,'" because it has been "used to endorse rather than prevent or limit war," and it "undermines the moral imperative to develop tools and capacities for nonviolent transformation of conflict."[45] I suspect, however, that most Catholics and others have not been well-informed about just war principles, even though these are available in pastoral statements such as *The Challenge of Peace* and, also, in the *Catechism*.[46] As Daniel M. Bell Jr. has observed, even though "just war" is often invoked, "few Christians know about the kinds of judgments and disciplines upon which the tradition is built. Few can name the criteria, much less unpack how they might be faithfully applied."[47] I am not assigning blame here, and I admit that the church at all levels, including the bishops, clergy, theologians, laity, and the like, must do a better job in educating about all of this.

In other words, to form Christian consciences about the morality of war, there is, Bell writes, "much to do between wars, not only teaching the criteria but also nurturing the virtues commensurate with the tradition—justice, temperance, patience, courage and so forth—through preaching and teaching, liturgy and works of mercy."[48] And this point brings us back to where we began in this chapter. Through their regular participation in the Mass and its peacemaking gestures and rituals, Catholics should be at least disposed to and oriented toward peace and its attendant virtues. Above all, they should possess a proper intent, which several theologians have claimed is the primary principle of Catholic just war theory, running through all of the others. That is, the *jus ad bellum* criterion of *right intent* entails seeking to establish a *just peace*, a goal that is shared by nonviolent Catholics.[49] This goes back to St. Augustine (354–430 CE), who is regarded as one of the "fathers" of the Christian just war tradition.

Augustine held that the aim of a just war—its right intent—should be to restore a just peace. In his letter to Boniface, a Roman general in Africa who, after his wife's death, desired to retire and become a monk, Augustine wrote,

> Peace should be the object of your desire. War should be waged only as a necessity and waged only that through it God may deliver men from that necessity and preserve them in peace. For peace is not to be sought in order to kindle war, but war is to be waged in order to obtain peace. Therefore even in the course of war you should cherish the spirit of a peacemaker.[50]

Here Augustine addresses both *jus ad bellum* (when war "should be waged") and *jus in bello* ("in the course of war") concerns, each of which are to be tethered to peace and peacemaking.

Moreover, Augustine added that "we do not ask for vengeance on our enemies on this earth. Our sufferings ought not constrict our spirits so narrowly that we forget the commandments given to us….We love our enemies and we pray for them. That is why we desire their reform and not their deaths."[51] In this way Augustine did not think that just war contradicted Jesus's injunction to love one's enemies. Just war aims

215

to turn the enemy from their wicked ways and to help them to rejoin the community of peace and justice. Augustine wrote, "Therefore, even in waging war, cherish the spirit of a peacemaker, that, by conquering those whom you attack, you may lead them back to the advantages of peace."[52] A mournful mood should accompany, also, those who fight or support a just war. Augustine warned that the "real evils in war are love of violence, revengeful cruelty, fierce and implacable enmity, wild resistance, and the lust of power,"[53] all of which would be at odds with establishing a just peace.

Although since the time of Augustine the just war tradition admittedly has been abused over the centuries, it has also helped to reduce violence. And, when it hasn't, it at least provides a basis from which to critique unjustified war and unjust conduct within war. Without it, there would be no rules of engagement. Instead, might would make right. The intentional killing of civilians would be no different from the killing of combatants. Of course, pacifists may regard both forms of killing to be equivalent to murder; however, most Catholics and others see a difference, even though the deaths of combatants too are not to be celebrated but, rather, mourned.[54] Still, most Catholics and others should approach just war with more scrutiny and restraint. That we haven't always done so is not a reason, in my view, for no longer teaching or using just war theory; instead, we need to teach it better and use it with more integrity—that is, more consciously and conscientiously, informed and formed by the liturgy.

This would mean taking each of the just war criteria robustly and rigorously. In addition to the *jus ad bellum* criterion of right intent, we would expect strict adherence to the criteria of just cause, legitimate authority, probability of success, last resort, and proportionality. Indeed, these have served as the basis for Catholic critiques of preventive war (is it really a last resort in response to a grave and imminent threat?), of wars launched without a clear idea of what counts as success (war against an ideology such as terrorism rather than against an actual enemy), and of military actions that likely will cause greater evils than good (military intervention that probably will lead to even greater civilian deaths than are already happening). Likewise, we would expect the *jus in bello* criteria of discrimination (noncombatant immunity) and proportionality (on a micro scale, the amount of force employed) to be taken just as seriously. These are the basis for Catholic criticisms of indiscriminate weapons of mass destruction, such as cluster munitions, land mines, chemical and biological weapons, and nuclear weapons. They also come into play regarding the use of drones and other new technologies.[55] In recent years, theological ethicists and others have begun to develop just war reasoning for *jus post bellum*, which includes criteria and practices aimed at establishing a just and lasting peace in the wake of a war, thereby hopefully reducing the likelihood of war reigniting.[56] In addition, in his encyclical *Laudato si'*, Pope Francis links concerns about violence and war with environmental degradation and devastation: "War always does grave harm to the environment and to the cultural riches of peoples, risks which are magnified when nuclear power and biological weapons are borne in mind," and he calls on political leaders to "pay greater attention to foreseeing new conflicts and addressing the causes which can lead to them."[57] Here we see an updated and extended application of the just war criteria of proportionality and discrimination to encompass nonhuman creation.

Catholic moral theologian Brian V. Johnstone has recommended that we reincorporate just war theory within "the wider teleological [i.e., end goal] vision, such that the ethic itself must be integrated into a life of peace and friendship with God, and with one another, of which the causal power is the divine energy, the Spirit of Jesus risen…[which] is to be embodied in the community of the faithful, and extended to the whole human community by the *opus* or work of peace."[58] In my view, such an approach appears more consonant with the liturgical starting point of this present chapter.

Before closing, it should be noted that since the Second Vatican Council, magisterial documents, such as the *Catechism of the Catholic Church*, the *Compendium of Catholic Social Doctrine*, and statements by Popes John Paul II, Benedict XVI, and Francis have tended not to use the phrase "just war" but instead the expression "just defense" or "legitimate defense" of the innocent through the use of armed force.[59] Nonviolent methods, too, have been encompassed within the umbrella of "legitimate defense." Hence, Drew Christiansen, SJ, has suggested that official Catholic teaching on war today is "a composite of nonviolent and just war elements."[60] This seems accurate to me, even if many of those who issued the appeal calling on the church to no longer teach or use just war believe otherwise. Among those participants, though, was Lisa Sowle Cahill, and I think her recent effort to move us toward "peacebuilding" is helpful and important, so that "debates about whether violence is forbidden or permitted in extreme situations are not central," and primary emphasis is given to exploring and promoting alternatives "that are constructive, bridge-building, and politically effective."[61]

Conclusion

To conclude, as James F. Keenan, SJ, has written, "Liturgy is where we understand ourselves as the people we are called to become," and we "identify ourselves" by the sign of the cross that we make at the beginning and end of the Mass—a gesture that "frames not only the liturgy but our lives."[62] Of course, such formation does not transpire automatically or always, which is why the bishops of the Second Vatican Council, in the "Constitution on the Sacred Liturgy," wrote, "The Church earnestly desires that all the faithful be led to that FULL, CONSCIOUS, and ACTIVE participation in liturgical celebrations called for by the very nature of the liturgy."[63] Educating Catholic Christians about what we say and do during worship should help us to be more intentional about and receptive to the grace of God that transforms us to be a peaceable people.

NOTES

1. Second Vatican Council, Pastoral Constitution on the Church in the Modern World (*Gaudium et spes*) 77–78, http://www.vatican.va/archive/hist_councils/ii_vatican_council/documents/vat-ii_const_19651207_gaudium-et-spes_en.html. See also the *Catechism of the Catholic Church* 2304, http://www.vatican.va/archive/ccc_css/archive/catechism/p3s2c2a5.htm.

2. Pastoral Constitution on the Church in the Modern World 16.

3. Pastoral Constitution on the Church in the Modern World 79.

4. Kathryn Lilla Cox, *Water Shaping Stone: Faith, Relationships, and Conscience Formation* (Collegeville, MN: Liturgical Press, 2015), 87.

5. Cox, *Water Shaping Stone*, 88.

6. Kenneth R. Himes, "Eucharist and Justice: Assessing the Legacy of Virgil Michel," *Worship* 62 (May 1988): 214.

7. Joseph J. Fahey, *War and the Christian Conscience: Where Do You Stand?* (Maryknoll, NY: Orbis Books, 2005), 24. Another introductory, accessible book on the subject that I recommend is Mark J. Allman, *Who Would Jesus Kill? War, Peace, and the Christian Tradition* (Winona, MN: Anselm Academic, 2008).

8. National Conference of Catholic Bishops (NCCB), *The Challenge of Peace: God's Promise and Our Response* (Washington, DC: United States Catholic

Conference, 1983), §16, http://www.usccb.org/upload/challenge-peace-gods
-promise-our-response-1983.pdf.

9. NCCB, *The Challenge of Peace*, §231.

10. NCCB, *The Challenge of Peace*, §295. St. Pope John Paul II advocated
"gestures of peace" that foster peace in people's hearts, in their lives in the community, and in the world, and Pope Francis affirms "any small gesture which
sows peace and friendship," "simple daily gestures which break with the logic
of violence, exploitation and selfishness," and "small gestures of mutual care"
that are "also civic and political." See Pope John Paul II, "*Pacem in Terris*: A Permanent Commitment" (Message for the World Day of Peace, 2003), http://
w2.vatican.va/content/john-paul-ii/en/messages/peace/documents/hf_jp
-ii_mes_20021217_xxxvi-world-day-for-peace.html; Pope Francis, *Laudato si'*
("On Care for Our Common Home") 230–31, http://w2.vatican.va/content/
francesco/en/encyclicals/documents/papa-francesco_20150524_enciclica
-laudato-si.html.

11. *The Challenge of Peace*, §295. Similarly, at the end of its chapter on war
and peace, the *Compendium of the Social Doctrine of the Church* says, "In particular,
the Eucharistic celebration, 'the source and summit of the Christian life,' is a
limitless wellspring for all authentic Christian commitment to peace." Pontifical Council for Justice and Peace, *Compendium of the Social Doctrine of the Church*
(Washington, DC: United States Conference of Catholic Bishops, 2004), §519.
Moreover, the next-to-last footnote (n. 1102), which is by far the longest of the
footnotes in that chapter, highlights the emphasis on peace that runs throughout the Mass.

12. *Catechism of the Catholic Church* 2327.

13. For more on the Mass, including its order and components, see
http://catholic-resources.org/ChurchDocs/Mass.htm. See also http://www
.usccb.org/prayer-and-worship/the-mass/, where there are also some documents available on "Liturgy and Life" and "Sacraments and Social Mission:
Living the Gospel, Being Disciples."

14. These words and the sign of peace go back to the New Testament.
The apostle Paul instructed Christians, "Greet one another with a holy kiss"
(Rom 16:16; 1 Cor 16:20; 2 Cor 13:12). Indeed, at that time and place (the
ancient Mediterranean world), people greeted one another with a kiss (they
still do in parts of Europe and the Middle East) rather than a handshake, and
this was a sign of peace. Paul therefore encouraged Christians to exchange this
sign of peace, just as the risen Jesus Christ repeatedly greeted his disciples with
"Peace be with you" (Luke 24:36; John 20:19; 20:21; 20:26).

15. *The Challenge of Peace*, §§70, 80, 83, and 120.

16. *The Challenge of Peace*, §333.

17. I wrote about Regis Factor's impact on my life in "Way beyond 'the
Way,' but It Paved the Way: On C. S. Lewis's *The Abolition of Man*," in *Take and*

Read, ed. Dianne Bergant and Mike Daley (Berkeley, CA: The Apocryphile Press, 2017), 19–23.

18. Some of the first books I read on Christian pacifism were by United Methodist theological ethicist Stanley Hauerwas, who taught at the University of Notre Dame before he moved to Duke University, including his *Against the Nations: War and Survival in a Liberal Society* (Notre Dame, IN: University of Notre Dame Press, 1985) and *Should War Be Eliminated? Philosophical and Theological Investigations* (Milwaukee, WI: Marquette University Press, 1984).

19. Second Vatican Council, The Constitution on the Sacred Liturgy (*Sacrosanctum concilium*) 10, http://www.vatican.va/archive/hist_councils/ii_vatican_council/documents/vat-ii_const_19631204_sacrosanctum-concilium_en.html.

20. Pastoral Constitution on the Church in the Modern World 43.

21. Patrick T. McCormick, "Violence: Religion, Terror, War," *Theological Studies* 67, no. 1 (March 2006): 159.

22. Laurie Johnston, "The Catholic Conversation since 9/11: A Moral Challenge," in *The Impact of 9/11 on Religion and Philosophy: The Day that Changed Everything?* ed. Matthew J. Morgan (New York: Palgrave Macmillan, 2009), 114.

23. *Catechism of the Catholic Church* 2312 (italics in original), quoting *Gaudium et spes* 79.

24. *The Challenge of Peace*, §73.

25. *Catechism of the Catholic Church* 2311.

26. *Catechism of the Catholic Church* 2306, quoting *Gaudium et spes* 78.

27. *The Challenge of Peace*, §78; emphasis added.

28. Tertullian, "Christians and Military Service," in *War and Christian Ethics*, 2nd ed., ed. Arthur F. Holmes (Grand Rapids, MI: Baker Academic, 2005), 44.

29. See "The Acts of Maximilian" and "The Acts of Marcellus," in *Christian Peace and Nonviolence: A Documentary History*, ed. Michael G. Long (Maryknoll, NY: Orbis Books, 2011), 31–32. See also Tobias Winright, "Roman Catholicism, Pacifism In," in *The Encyclopedia of Religion and War*, ed. Gabriel Palmer-Fernandez (New York: Berkshire/Routledge, 2004), 379–84.

30. *The Challenge of Peace*, §111; emphasis added.

31. Origen, "On Government Service," in *War and Christian Ethics: Classic Readings on the Morality of War*, 2nd ed., ed. Arthur F. Holmes (Grand Rapids, MI: Baker Book House, 1975), 48–49.

32. Quoted in Eileen Egan, *Peace Be with You: Justified Warfare or the Way of Nonviolence* (Maryknoll, NY: Orbis Books, 1999), 28.

33. St. John Chrysostom, *Homilies*, in *Short Breviary*, ed. Monks of St. John's (Collegeville, MN: St. John's Abbey Press, 1975), 220–21, sermon 33. St. Thomas Aquinas (1225–74 CE) also noted that what is celebrated at the Eucharist is at odds with bloodshed in war, although this observation led him

to exempt only priests and bishops, who preside over the Eucharist, from participating in the military. See Thomas Aquinas, *Summa Theologica*, trans. Fathers of the English Dominican Province (Westminster, MD: Christian Classics/Benziger Brothers, Inc., 1948), II–II, Q. 40, art. 2.

34. Quoted in Fahey, *War and the Christian Conscience*, 44.

35. National Conference of Catholic Bishops, *The Harvest of Justice Is Sown in Peace* (Washington, DC: United States Catholic Conference, 1994), 5.

36. Matthew A. Tapie, James W. McCarty III, and Justin Bronson Barringer, eds., *The Business of War: Theological and Ethical Reflections on the Military-Industrial Complex* (Eugene, OR: Cascade, 2020).

37. For example, Glen Stassen, ed., *Just Peacemaking: The New Paradigm for the Ethics of Peace and War*, rev. ed. (Cleveland, OH: Pilgrim Press, 2008). Also, see Robert J. Schreiter, R. Scott Appleby, and Gerard F. Powers, eds., *Peacebuilding: Catholic Theology, Ethics, and Praxis* (Maryknoll, NY: Orbis Books, 2010); Schreiter's chapter on "The Catholic Social Imaginary and Peacebuilding: Ritual, Sacrament, and Spirituality" links liturgy and peacebuilding. On similar efforts toward "just peace," see Tobias Winright, "Your 'Just Peace' Reading List," *National Catholic Reporter* (December 21, 2016), https://www.ncronline.org/books/2017/08/your-just-peace-reading-list.

38. The two-page "Appeal to the Catholic Church to Re-Commit to the Centrality of Gospel Nonviolence" is available at Pax Christi USA's website, accessed December 17, 2019, https://paxchristiusa.org/2016/04/15/statement-an-appeal-to-the-catholic-church-to-recommit-to-the-centrality-of-gospel-nonviolence/.

39. Lisa Sowle Cahill, *Blessed Are the Peacemakers: Pacifism, Just War, and Peacebuilding* (Minneapolis: Fortress Press, 2019), 1.

40. United States Conference of Catholic Bishops, *Forming Consciences for Faithful Citizenship* (Washington, DC: United States Conference of Catholic Bishops, 2015), §68, http://ccc.usccb.org/flipbooks/faithful-citizenship/files/assets/basic-html/page-1.html.

41. *The Challenge of Peace*, §233. Current U.S. law does not allow for selective conscientious objection.

42. *Catechism of the Catholic Church* 2312.

43. *Catechism of the Catholic Church* 2309.

44. *Catechism of the Catholic Church* 2306, quoting from *Gaudium et spes* 78.

45. For my responses to the Appeal, see Mark J. Allman and Tobias Winright, "Protect Thy Neighbor: Why the Just-War Tradition Is Still Indispensable," *Commonweal* 143, no. 11 (June 17, 2016): 7–9; Tobias Winright, "Why I Shall Continue to Use and Teach Just War Theory," *Expositions: Interdisciplinary Studies in the Humanities* 12, no. 1 (2018): 142–61, available at https://expositions.journals.villanova.edu/article/view/2325/2230; and Tobias Winright, "Just

War and Imagination Are Not Mutually Exclusive," *Horizons* 45, no. 1 (June 2018): 114–19.

46. *The Challenge of Peace*, §§84–110, *Catechism of the Catholic Church* 2309.

47. Daniel M. Bell Jr., "In War and in Peace: Implications of Just War Theory," *Christian Century* 122, no. 18 (September 6, 2005): 26. See also his book *Just War as Christian Discipleship: Recentering the Tradition in the Church rather than the State* (Grand Rapids, MI: Brazos Press, 2009).

48. Bell, "In War and in Peace," 33. See also Daniel M. Bell Jr., "Can a War against Terror Be Just? Or, What Is Just War Good For?" *Crosscurrents* 56, no. 1 (Spring 2006): 34–45.

49. See Joseph E. Capizzi, *Politics, Justice, and War: Christian Governance and the Ethics of Warfare* (Oxford: Oxford University Press, 2015).

50. Augustine, Letter 189, trans. J. G. Cunningham, in *The Nicene and Post-Nicene Fathers* (1st series), 1; reproduced in Holmes, *War and Christian Ethics*, 62–63.

51. Augustine, *Augustine: Political Writings*, ed. E. M. Atkins and R. J. Dodaro (New York: Cambridge University Press, 2001), 135.

52. Augustine, Letter 189, in Holmes, *War and Christian Ethics*, 63.

53. Augustine, *Reply to Faustus the Manichean*, bk. 22, chap. 74, trans. R. Stothert, in *The Nicene and Post-Nicene Fathers* (1st series), 4:69–76; reproduced in Holmes, *War and Christian Ethics*, 64.

54. G. E. M. Anscombe, "War and Murder," in *Nuclear Weapons and Christian Conscience*, ed. Walter Stein (London: The Merlin Press, 1961), 45–62.

55. Kenneth R. Himes, *Drones and the Ethics of Targeted Killing* (Lanham, MD: Rowman & Littlefield, 2015).

56. Mark J. Allman and Tobias L. Winright, *After the Smoke Clears: The Just War Tradition and Post War Justice* (Maryknoll, NY: Orbis Books, 2010); Mark J. Allman and Tobias L. Winright, "Growing Edges of Just War Theory: *Jus ante bellum, jus post bellum*, and Imperfect Justice," *Journal of the Society of Christian Ethics* 32, no. 2 (Fall/Winter 2012): 173–91.

57. Pope Francis, *Laudato si'* 57. See Tobias Winright, "Peace on Earth, Peace with Earth: *Laudato si'* and Integral Peacebuilding," in *All Creation Is Connected: Voices in Response to Pope Francis's Encyclical on Ecology*, ed. Daniel R. DiLeo (Winona, MN: Anselm Academic, 2018), 195–211.

58. Brian V. Johnstone, "The War on Terrorism: A Just War?" *Studia Moralia* 40, no. 1 (June 2002): 51.

59. Drew Christiansen, "Whither the 'Just War'?" *America* 188, no. 10 (March 24, 2003): 7–11; Drew Christiansen, "After Sept. 11: Catholic Teaching on Peace and War," *Origins* 32, no. 3 (May 30, 2002): 33, 35–40.

60. Christiansen, "Whither the 'Just War'?" 8.

61. Cahill, *Blessed Are the Peacemakers*, 1.

62. James F. Keenan, *The Works of Mercy: The Heart of Catholicism* (Lanham, MD: Rowman & Littlefield, 2005), 92–93. In short, there should be "an intimate connection between how the church prays, what it believes, and how it acts"—*lex orandi, lex credendi, lex agenda*; see Dennis J. Billy and James Keating, *The Way of Mystery: The Eucharist and Moral Living* (New York: Paulist Press, 2006), 41.

63. Second Vatican Council, "Constitution on the Sacred Liturgy" 14; emphasis in original.

Questions for Further Reflection

1. The author gives a rather complex definition to the word *sanctuary*. What does he mean by this concept? What would your definition of *sanctuary* be?

2. The author does the same with the term *conscience*. What does he mean by this concept? What would your definition of *conscience* be? How does the author relate the term *conscience* to *sanctuary*?

3. How does the author say conscience is formed? Do you agree? Which ways do you use to form your conscience? What role do church teachings play in your formation of conscience? What role do the opinions of your friends play in your formation of conscience?

4. The author quotes the U.S. bishops' statement that "Mass in particular is a unique means of seeking God's help to create the conditions essential for peace in the world." What do the bishops mean by this according to the author? How does participation in the liturgy of the Mass aid conscience formation on questions of war and peace? Has the Mass had this effect on you?

5. What effect did the author's recounting of his personal history have on your evaluation of his perspective? Did it make you more or less likely to discount his opinions? Why?

6. The author says that Catholics compartmentalize or bifurcate their faith from their lives. What does he mean by this? Do you ever feel yourself doing this? What good is a faith that is not lived? Does your

faith affect the way you feel about politics, about the way you vote? Why or why not?

7. What effect does this "bifurcation" have on the way American Catholics approach the moral analysis of America's wars? Do you know where in the world today American forces are engaged in combat, even in support roles? Do you know to which nations America sells weapons and how they are used? Do you feel it is your moral duty to know these things? Do you feel it is your moral duty to know which politicians support these things? Why or why not?

8. What does the church teach about conscientious objection? What moral obligations does such objection bring with it?

9. What is the history of the church's teaching on nonviolence? What did Jesus say about nonviolence? What did the church fathers teach about nonviolence? What was the problem with service in the Roman army and idolatry? Could you draw an analogy between that ancient military problem and any military problems today that might require an abdication of conscience?

10. What does the author mean by "just peacemaking"? What is the difference between "just peacemaking" and pacifism?

11. What does the concept of "peacemaking" entail? What does *Faithful Citizenship* say about this? When you vote, do you think about voting for candidates who are peacemakers? Why or why not?

12. What is the difference between *jus ad bellum* and *jus in bello*? Is there such a thing as a moral approach to how war is conducted?

13. What is the Catholic teaching on "just war"? Why do some Catholic scholars think that the church should no longer teach a just war theory? What does the author say have been the benefits of the just war theory?

14. What is "right intent" in just war theory? What did St. Augustine teach about this?

15. What has been the recent change in Catholic terminology regarding just wars? What does this change in terminology signify?

PART IV

Character Issues

11

The Rise of Populism

A Theo-Ethical Critique

Christina Astorga

President Trump has been catapulted to power and is maintained in power by the phenomenon of populism. This essay explores this phenomenon and locates how Trump fits into its landscape. I will begin by using the data of political science to study Trump as a populist. As a theological ethicist I will then bring to bear on his populism a theo-ethical critique based on an analysis of Jesus's cleansing of the temple. In this critique, I present Jesus as the norm of a true populist and discuss how a leader who claims to be a populist either rises to this norm or deviates from it.

In my essay, the concept of populism is based on the central argument of Benjamin Moffit in his book *The Global Rise of Populism*. There he writes, "We need to move from seeing populism as a particular thing or entity toward viewing it as a political style that is performed, embodied, and enacted across a variety of political and cultural contexts."[1] He asserts that this shift of viewing populism is in keeping with the time when media makes politics ubiquitous in many disparate manifestations and contexts. Except from drawing examples from the Trump presidency to elucidate the populist nature of his governance, this essay does not present an in-depth political analysis, since it is not meant to be a work of political science. The significance of this study will, I hope, be its contribution from a theo-ethical perspective to the ongoing discourse of the Trump presidency. Weal or woe, the impact of his presidency affects us all, and with this essay I wish to provide a particular perspective to the ongoing discussion. This essay is divided into three main parts. The first part presents the features of the phenomenon of populism using Moffit's perspective; the second part studies how Trump is a populist in the light of these features; and the third part presents Jesus as the true standard of a populist based on an analysis of his cleansing of the temple.

The Phenomenon of Populism

Populism is a complex phenomenon that has been a subject of contentious debate in the field of political science. It has become one of the main political buzz words of the early twenty-first century. A search of the term yields over five million hits on Google, of which over four thousand refer to recent news stories. The loose usage of the term *populism* has always been a bone of contention in academic studies. Several academics have argued that its loose usage and a lack of consensus as to its definition render the concept of populism meaningless and useless for academic studies. I argue otherwise. A term that is used so often and so broadly has a relevance for academic disciplines to study.

However plural populism has been cognitively conceptualized and defined, we live in fact in populist times. Over the past two decades, particularly in the last decade or so, the world has seen the rise of populists: Europe, in the rise in Silvio Berlusconi and Marine Le Pen; the United States, in the Tea Party, a populist grassroots movement that made its mark in history when it caused the 2013 government shutdown. Figures like Sarah Palin, Ted Cruz, and Donald Trump gave a face to American populism. Thaksin Shinawatra, Joseph "Erap" Estrada, Pauline Hanson, Winston Peters, and Rodrigo Duterte are architects of Pacific populism. Africa is no stranger to the rise of populism, for it has witnessed the populist presidencies of Yoweri Musevini, Michael Sata, and Jacob Zuma.[2] What was once a marginal reality, relegated to another era or to only certain parts of the world, is now a mainstay of contemporary politics across the globe.

Populism matters. It is an important concept for understanding the contemporary political landscape. A brief essay could not consider how populism has developed as a concept throughout its entire history. But populism at its core, however it is approached, signifies a divide between the "people" and the "elite" or between "us" and those "others." Cas Mudde puts forward a minimal definition of *populism* "as a thin-centered ideology that considers society to be ultimately separated into two homogenous and antagonistic groups, the 'pure people' versus the 'corrupt elite' and which argues that politics should be an expression of the *volente general* (general will) of the people."[3] The crucial distinction in populism is between the people and the elite and the distinction is moral, making it a form of moral politics, involving a Manichean worldview.

In this global environment, we can no longer speak of direct and unmediated populism from the leader to the people. While that is not altogether gone, it is not how contemporary populism commonly navigates its terrain. A new breed of savvy populist leaders knows how to utilize media technologies to their advantage. The increased use of mediated populism through the Internet and the social networking has made its impact ubiquitous. Benjamin Moffit in his aforementioned book, *The Global Rise of Populism*, postulates a new framework for conceptualizing populism as a political style. Several other authors have also used the term *political style* in the populist literature, but only in relation to rhetoric, communicative strategies, or discourse. Moffit moves beyond these references and emphasizes the performative, aesthetic, and relational aspects of contemporary populism. While political style may seem superficial or inessential, nothing could be farther from the truth, for it relates to the power of an appeal *to* people, which, however ambiguous, should never be underestimated.[4] Political style sees the "leader as *the performer*, 'the people' as the *audience*, and crisis and media as *the stage* on which populism plays out."[5]

What are the features of populism as a political style? Moffit proposes three features based on his study of thirty contemporary populists. First, an appeal to the people versus the elite; second, the use of bad manners; and third, the perception of crisis, breakdown, or threat.[6] The people are the central audience of the populists and the subjects of their performance. Presenting the people as the true holders of sovereignty and invoking them as the mainstream and the heartland of politics, the populist demonstrates his or her affinity with them. He or she drives a wedge between them and the elite or other related signifiers such as the establishment or the system. Others may also be targeted, such as asylum seekers, immigrant workers, or particular minority groups as enemies of the people, but they are viewed as linked to the elite, who are blamed for the policies that have resulted in the influx of these others into the country who have then become threats to the livelihood and jobs of the people. The populist presents himself or herself as the people's champion, they who have been "let down," "ripped off," "fleeced," rendered powerless, or badly governed.[7]

A function of this appeal to the people is the populists' identification with the people's ordinary or common life. Presenting themselves as different from experts and technocrats, they champion the people's common sense. An example of this is the language of Preston Mannings of the Reform Party of Canada, whose charter declared, "We believe in the common sense of the common people,"[8] and in Sarah Palin's self-description as "just your average hockey mom." The use of slang, swearing, political incorrectness, as opposed to the use of rational, formal, and technical language marks the populist's political style. This distinction of language is evident, for example, between the formal style of Al Gore and the populist style of Palin. Gore's style is that of the establishment: serious, earnest, intelligent, rational, substantive, with gravitas; Palin's are those of the "outsider": directness, playfulness, anecdotal, lacking substance, with disregard for hierarchy.

What constitutes bad manners may differ from one cultural context to another. Such manners, however expressed, connect the populist to the people as real, unpretentious, and down to earth, apart from and uncaring for the opinion of the elites. Bad manners may consist of the use of speech, body language, gestures, or ways of dressing, all of which are part of the populist style.[9]

Populism gets its impetus from the perception of crisis, breakdown, or threat that calls for urgent and decisive action. The crisis can arise from a perceived imminent breakdown of the government or it can be related to an economic collapse, military threats, immigration problems, or social problems. Populists capitalize on the crisis situation and promise short-term and swift action. For instance, the Philippine president's promise to eradicate the drug problem in the Philippines in three months created a myth of political machismo that appealed to many unthinking Filipinos. Simplifying the terms and terrain of political debate, populists offer solutions that defy the complex machinery of governance. Anything that addresses the crisis through the long route of consultations, debate, and policy changes is ignored because it does not serve the populist appeal. This is politics that has become instrumentalized and utilitarian.[10]

Populism as political style in its three features is criticized for its lack of substance. Paul Taggart has referred to populism's "empty heart,"[11] Yves Mény and Yves Surel have called it an "empty shell,"[12] and others have called it a "thin" or "thin-centered" ideology. It is a populism that can appear across various contexts and ideological spectrums, from right to left. Focusing on performers, audiences, stages, and performative repertoires, it plays out in the theatre of politics.

Trump as a Populist

Using Moffit's three features of populism as a political style, namely an appeal to the people versus the elite, the use of bad manners, and a perception of crisis, breakdown or threat, an analysis of the Trump political style follows. These features are related to him to show how populism as a way of political style is shaped by him in the context of American politics.

The book *The Great Revolt*, authored by Salena Zito and Brad Todd, delves deep into the minds and hearts of the voters that make up the new populist conservative coalition that brought Trump and the Republican majorities into office in 2016.[13] Referring to this same constituency, political scientist Charles Murray, in his landmark 2012 book, *Coming Apart*, noted the growing disconnect between the cultural norm makers in the country and the millions of everyday Americans. His book paints the lives of upper-middle-class families who have never lived outside of the upper-middle-class bubble. His premise is that these people, who yield much power in culture, commerce, and government, and who have much influence on the course of the nation, are making judgments about what is good for other people based on their highly atypical lives. Murray noted that the epicenters of these upper-middle-class families, whom he calls the "narrow elite," people with national influence, are the "Big Four" centers of cultural impact: New York, Los Angeles, San Francisco, and Washington, DC—"the places that drive entertainment, technological innovations, government, global finance, and the mass media."[14]

The emerging populist-conservative coalition represented the resistance to the mores and power of these Big Four clusters, where the hyper-educated and metropolitan class resided. "The driving construct of otherness, manifest by Trump voters in both the Republican primaries and the general election, is at its core driven by perception of respect."[15] As Cindy Hutkins, a store owner in Baldwin, Michigan, says, "We spent all of our lives doing things; we pay our taxes; we give back to our communities; we volunteer at our churches, coached or served on the PTA at our kids' schools. And we voted for President Obama but still we are ridiculed. Still we are called racists. There is no respect for anyone who is just average and trying to do the right things."[16] Amy Giles-Maurer, in the same vein of thought, explains, "Our culture in Hollywood or in the media gives off the distinct air of disregard to people who live in the middle of the country. As if we have no value or do not contribute to the betterment of society. It's frustrating. It really makes you want to stand and yell, 'We count,' except of course, we don't. At least not in their eyes."[17] Michael Martin of Erie, Pennsylvania, pursuing the same line of thought, says, "All hard work has value. All people eventually contribute to the fabric of the country. But live in a small or medium-size town and you would think we were dragging the country down. What we do here matters. We aren't a country just made up of large metropolitan areas—our politics and our culture up until now has dictated that we are less than in the scale of importance and value."[18] Trump's campaign went straight to the heart of the grievances of those who live outside the zip codes of the Big Four, and presented him as their ally against the so-called elite. In his victory speech after a key early primary in Nevada, Trump famously said, "I love the poorly educated," a remark that drew swift rebuke from mainstream media.[19]

But do his actions, particularly in his policies, match his words? While he ran on the promise of lifting up the economically disadvantaged, his tax cuts focused predominantly on the rich. The idea that the tax cuts were going to trickle down to the middle class and give raises to workers ended up being a mirage. According to Americans for Tax Fairness, a political advocacy group devoted to tax reform, "businesses received nine times more in cuts than what they passed on to their workers." It was also found that "companies spent 37 times as much on stock buy backs than they did on bonuses and increased wages for workers."[20] President Trump didn't replace Obamacare with "something terrific" as he promised. For a long time that "something terrific" was an unknown entity. Now we have finally learned his grand plan for health care for the country. It is, as Catherine Rampell, puts it, "Don't get sick. Ever." That was what she said was the message of the Administration's new rule expanding the availability of insurance plans. The rule deals with "short term" health plans, but which, however, under new regulations, will be allowed to last up to 364 days and be renewed for up to 36 months. So, it is not short term after all. Plus, these new plans are not subject to any of the protections required by the Affordable Care Act.[21] "Short-term plans can turn away people with preexisting conditions, including asthma and acne. They can charge older or sicker people with prohibitively expensive premiums. Or they can enroll such people at what looks like a bargain-basement rate and then refuse to pay for any care related to preexisting illnesses—including illnesses that enrollees didn't even know they had when they enrolled, such as cancer or heart disease. Some plans have dropped consumers as soon as they got an expensive diagnosis, sticking them with hundreds of dollars in unexpected medical bills."[22]

Trump's battle cry was "drain the swamp," but has that even been attempted? A group of nearly two hundred Democratic senators and representatives sued President Trump over alleged violations of the Foreign Emoluments Clause of the Constitution. Under this clause, federal officials, including the president, are not allowed to accept any foreign "present, emolument, office, or title" without permission from Congress. The plaintiffs alleged that Trump "has a financial interest in vast business holdings around the world that engage in dealings with foreign governments and receive benefits from those governments." Since Trump has denied them their constitutional duty to give or withhold their consent, they allege that he has compromised their roles as members of Congress.[23]

That Trump champions the cause of the socially and economically disadvantaged is also questionable. For example, on the campaign trail, he promised repeatedly that he would not cut Medicare benefits. But his proposed 2019 budget included $266 billion in cuts to Medicare, which provides health insurance to fifty-eight million Americans sixty-five years of age and older and to people with disabilities. There is also a freeze on most funding under the Older Americans Act, which provides for social and nutrition services for seniors including Meals on Wheels. The Senior Community Service Employment Program, which provides job training to low-income job seekers ages fifty-five and older would also be eliminated.[24] Nancy Altman, president of Social Security Works, writes, "It is noteworthy that Republicans just passed, for almost the same price tag, a huge tax giveaway to their donors. So that's the Republican plan: save money by gutting programs for the elderly and transfer it to the billionaire class."[25] Trump quietly signed an executive order directing federal agencies to strengthen the work requirements for various welfare programs. This could eventually affect recipients of Medicaid, food stamps, housing assistance, and cash welfare. Advocates for the poor noted that many recipients of government assistance are working but their jobs yield too little income to cover all their basic necessities.[26] While Trump cuts welfare, the safety net of the poorest and most vulnerable in society, he boasts of funding the biggest and strongest military in the world. In the equation of life and death, the poor and the most vulnerable appear to be the lowest priority.

Kelly Brown Douglas asks, "How did it happen? How has a man whose campaign was filled with racist, xenophobic, and misogynistic vitriol and who mounted a racialized 'birther' campaign against the nation's first African American president, while promising 'Law and Order'/Wall Building protectionist politics—how has this man been elected president in a country that proclaims, 'life, liberty, and the pursuit of happiness' for all?"[27]

To be fair, there are those who would argue that Trump's election had little if anything to do with sexism, religious bigotry, or even racism. They claim that he won because he addressed the economic anxieties of those in the "Rust Belt" demographic, the white working-class voters who rose in revolt against the elite. While this may be true, the fears, anxieties, and woes that he stokes seem woven into a narrative that was racist in intent and spirit.[28] He tacitly endorses the worst of American values—the consummate attractions of money, sex, and power—which are alluring to many Americans.[29] This is not to mention his passing acquaintance with the truth. The *Washington Post*'s Fact Checker Blog has been tracking Trump's misstatements, untruths, and lies. As of January 2020, he was over sixteen thousand. For example, he has claimed that the administration "did an unappreciated great job" dealing with Hurricane Maria when it struck Puerto Rico in 2017. That contradicts official reports of an estimated death toll at between 2,658 and 3,290, and with full power not restored for eleven months after the hurricane.[30] Before the UN assembly of world leaders, he claimed that he has accomplished more than any other president in history at the same point in their presidencies, only to elicit the laughing derision of his diplomatic audience.

That he divines his own truth, as what Kelly Conway calls alternative facts, is simply a normalization of lying as a way of life, both personal and public.[31] His supporters, however, have remained steadfast, as pragmatism trumps morality. Or they simply believe him when he blames the media as spreading "fake news" about him. What is important above all for them is that he pursues their people versus the elite agenda. He comes across as a person with no external and objective moral reference. His transactional ethics are premised on whatever works. It is no wonder that he has earned the unbridled condemnation of the former CIA Director John Brennan, who said, in a tweet, "When the full extent of your venality, moral turpitude, and political corruption becomes known, you will take your rightful place as a disgraced demagogue in the dustbin of history."[32]

Populism gets its impetus from the perception of crisis, breakdown, or threat, and at the same time, aims to induce crisis through dramatization and performance. "Make America Great Again" was Trump's campaign slogan. What this seems to mean to its proponents is to make America white again. It taps into America's defining narrative of exceptionalism, which is very much tied to the culture of whiteness. For Trump, making America great again means "bombing the Islamic State, strengthening the military, controlling the borders, building a wall between the United States and Mexico, deporting undocumented persons, banning Muslim immigrants, limiting refugees, renegotiating trade agreements, and imposing tariffs on Chinese and Mexican goods."[33]

During the campaign, candidate Trump spoke of other countries taking advantage of the United States. "We have lost the respect of the entire world," he protested. He set the alarm against America losing its global command, which it must regain, appealing to white males who seek white hegemony and domination. They are behind Trump's immigration policies that are directed against those "others" whom they regard as threats to their way of life.

Trump pits being a nationalist against being a globalist, as if one should cancel out the other in an either/or equation. It is apparent from his nationalist and populist rhetoric that his "America First" policy tends toward isolationism. He has made controversial decisions to renege on key international commitments of the United States. For example, he withdrew the United States from the Paris Agreement, a commitment by countries across the world to curb climate change and global warming. However, he said that the United States will renegotiate to reenter the accord but on his own terms. Hoping to bring jobs back to the United States, under his "America First" policy, he reversed U.S. involvement with the TPP (Trans-Pacific-Partnership), which was aimed at tying the economies of twelve countries. He pulled out of the United Nation's culture and education body, UNESCO, which he accused of having an "anti-Israel bias." The landmark nuclear accord with Iran, which was negotiated by the Obama administration together with Germany, France, and Britain, lifted most of the economic sanctions against Iran, in exchange for which Iran agreed to restrict its nuclear program, disabling it from producing a nuclear bomb, and subjecting itself to rigorous inspections. Trump nullified the commitment of the United States to this accord and he restored the harsh sanctions in the most consequential foreign policy action of his presidency. And finally, he withdrew from the United Nations Human Rights Council, accusing it of being hypocritical and self-serving. He took all these actions unilaterally, breaking alliances that previous U.S. presidents of both parties had maintained over the decades.

Paul Waldman writes that "no one should be fooled about what Trump is doing. His ideology and goals have not changed. He's still vilifying immigrants to charge up his angry base. He still wants not just to stop illegal immigration but to cut back on legal immigration as well. And his impulses are as cruel as ever. Right now he and his advisers, particularly those such as Stephen Miller, who have long sought to make America whiter, are not retreating. They're devising ways to make immigration policy as brutal as they can get away with."[34] This is the same man who opened his bid for office in 2015 by saying that Mexicans are rapists, who targeted Muslims in his travel ban, who announced that he was cancelling the Deferred Action for Childhood Arrivals (DACA) program, leaving thousands of young people vulnerable to deportation, who ripped families apart, putting children in cages while deporting their parents—actions that are heartless and brutal, if not racist and xenophobic.[35] This is the same man who would do all of this to the vulnerable and powerless, but could not unequivocally condemn the hatred, intolerance, and violence of the white supremacists at Charlottesville.[36] This is the same man who borrows despotic language to refer to the free press, who praises authoritarian leaders like Putin and Duterte, and who has put democratic institutions (for example, the press, FBI, Justice Department) under assault.[37] In his book *Trump in the White House: Tragedy and Farce,* John Bellamy Foster writes,

Not only a new administration, but a new ideology has now taken up residence at the White House: neofascism. It resembles in certain ways the classical fascism of Italy and Germany in the 1920s and '30s, but with historically distinct features specific to the political economy and culture of the United States....Neofascist discourse and political practice are now evident every day in virulent attacks on the racially oppressed, immigrants, women, LBGTQ people, environmentalists, and workers. These have been accompanied by a sustained campaign to bring the judiciary, governmental employees, the military and intelligence agencies, and the press in line with this new ideology and political reality.[38]

Trump is a populist as described by the terms of populism. He fits into its landscape in the light of the three features of Moffit's view of populism: an appeal to the people versus the elite, the use of bad manners, and the perception of crisis, breakdown, and threat. But is this what populism should aspire to? Is this brand of populism the problem or is it only symptomatic of a much bigger problem?

Theo-Ethical Critique

JESUS AS A POPULIST

Populism invokes the "power to the people," which carries echoes of previous struggles for emancipation. The emotional appeal of "power to the people" is employed by populists to create a solidarity among those excluded and marginalized against the elite with the rallying cry of "enough" to injustices and oppression. Populism, however, can be deceiving, for it can be used by a leader for self-aggrandizement or self-perpetuation in power. The story of the cleansing of the temple shows how Jesus, who is the true populist, exercised his power solely for the sake of the people, especially for the poor and marginalized.

The story of the temple-cleansing exposes the injustice done to the Gentile converts to Judaism. Entering the temple, Jesus is met by people selling cattle, sheep, and doves, while the money changers were seated at their tables. Such a scene is expected as pilgrims celebrate the Passover at the temple. What caused Jesus's wrath was what was happening in the area of worship. The trading and commerce occurred in the out-ermost court—the Court of the Gentiles. With the commotion created by the sellers and money changers and the space being used for keeping the animals for worship, the Gentiles were deprived of the only space they were allowed at the temple for their worship. Instead of being able to pray or meditate in peace, they were distracted by the marketplace noise. As it is, they were already marginalized, and to deprive them of their only worship space violated their dignity and their rights.[39] The space provided for them to worship was instead used by the powers of the temple to house animals, stalls, feed supplies, and the other essen-tials necessary for maintaining animals for temple sacrifice. "Exactly where one man should have a chance to serve only his Maker and to become human, money-making sanctioned by religion proves the 'real' god and claims man's loyalty."[40] With a whip of cords, Jesus drove out the sheep, cattle, and the money changers. But he told the sellers to take their doves out of the place, for they were the only sacrifice animal that the poor could afford to buy. Had Jesus knocked over the cages in anger with the birds flying out, the poor would have to borrow money to buy other offerings, cattle and sheep, which only the rich could afford.[41]

It was not just the injustice against the Gentiles regarding their right to their space of worship that caused the wrath of Jesus. He con-demned the entire temple system that oppressed and exploited the poor, who were made to pay an annual temple tax. However, they were not allowed to use the everyday Roman coins for this because of the pagan images on them. They had to have the currency converted by the money changers to Jewish shekels for an exorbitant fee. Not just the money changers but also the priests of the temple fed on the poor. Greedy and rapacious, they used religion as a cover for their exploita-tion of the poor. The cleansing of the temple was the cleansing of the den of thieves who stole from the poor to enrich themselves in their positions of power.[42]

The cleansing of the temple is located at the beginning of the Gospel of John instead of at the end during Holy Week, as it is in the Synoptic Gospels. According to Craig Koester, "Jesus' action in the Jeru-salem Temple is the companion piece to the miracle at Cana,"[43] that opens chapter 2 in John's Gospel and begins John's account of Jesus's three-year ministry. "After a sign of abundance, Jesus now performs a sign reminiscent of the acts of Israel's prophets, in which the authority of the dominant religious authorities is questioned."[44] For John, these two events frame the meaning of Jesus's mission and ministry. "The Cana scene's faint references to Jesus' death and resurrection ('On the third day'; 'my hour'; 'revealed his glory')[45] and the temple scene which follows it portrays tension, conflict, judgment."[46]

The Cana scene and the temple scene in the Gospel of John are filled with the same spirit as Luke 4:18–19, where, at the outset of his ministry, Jesus read from the scroll of Isaiah as he set his heart on the ministry for the poor and downtrodden:

> The Spirit of the Lord is upon me,
> because he has anointed me
>   to bring good news to the poor.
> He has sent me to proclaim release to the captives
> And recovery of sight to the blind,
>   to let the oppressed go free,
> to proclaim the year of the Lord's favor.

Elizabeth Schussler-Fiorenza writes, "Jesus was not crucified because of his theological teachings but because of their potentially subversive character and the political threat to the imperial colonial system."[47] It is the very religiosity of Jesus, the very faith at the foundation of his life, that profoundly engaged him in the political and public issues of his day. There was no separation. The religiosity and faith that drew him intimately in prayer with God is the very same religiosity and faith that put him in the arena of the public and political issues of his day. This is liberation Christology at its edge in Jesus, as the liberator against all forms of injustice and exploitation. Jesus, thus, as the kenosis of God, is the self-disclosure of God, who fully entered into the human condition, became one among us, and embracing the poverty of the poor as his own, acts as a saving and liberating God.

Jesus is the true populist, whose prophetic work for people brought him into conflict with the power systems and institutions of his time. To pose a threat to the established power could be fatal. Those who dared challenge such enormity of power put themselves at the edge of life and death. Jesus put himself at the edge for his people. He faced death as the final act of a life so fully lived for them. He is the true populist.

At the core of the populism of Jesus is his genuine love for the people, especially the poor and the marginalized, his compassion for them and his solidarity with their lot. Putting his entire life on the line for them, he embraces their pain and suffering as his own, their fight for justice and liberation as his mission. At the core of the populism of Trump is Trump. He went right into the heart of the economic woes of the people and capitalized on them, to catapult himself to power. But when he assumed power, the policies that he espoused were not those that would promise a better life for the people, but rather would exacerbate the inequity between those who have plenty like himself, and those who have so little. It is perhaps unfair to compare anyone to the Lord. That standard will never be met. But that does not mean that we should not try, that we should not judge others and ourselves by his standard. But based on authentic populism, true concern for the least among us, if Jesus is the genuine populist, Trump is the travesty.

NOTES

1. Benjamin Moffit, *The Global Rise of Populism: Performance, Political Style, and Representation* (Stanford, CA: Stanford University Press, 2016), 3.

2. Moffit, *The Global Rise of Populism*, 1.

3. Cas Mudde, "Populist Radical Right: A Pathological Normalcy," *West European Politics* 33, no. 6 (2010): 1167–86, at 23.

4. Moffit, *The Global Rise of Populism*, 4–5.

5. Moffit, *The Global Rise of Populism*, 5.

6. See Moffit, *The Global Rise of Populism*, 43–45.

7. Moffit, *The Global Rise of Populism*, 43–44.

8. Moffit, *The Global Rise of Populism*, 44.

9. Moffit, *The Global Rise of Populism*, 44.

10. Moffit, *The Global Rise of Populism*, 45.

11. Paul Taggart, *Populism* (Buckingham, UK: Open University Press, 2000), 4.

12. Yves Mény and Yves Surel, "The Constitutive Ambiguity of Populism," in *Democracies and the Populist Challenge*, ed. Yves Mény and Yves Surel (Basingstoke, UK: Palgrave Macmillan, 2002), 1–21, at 4.

13. Salena Zito and Brad Todd, *The Great Revolt* (New York: Crown Forum, 2018).

14. Charles Murray, *Coming Apart: The State of White America, 1960–2010* (New York: Crown Forum, 2012), 100.

15. Zito and Todd, *The Great Revolt*, 236–37.

16. Zito and Todd, *The Great Revolt*, 237.

17. Cited in Zito and Todd, *The Great Revolt*, 237.

18. Cited in Zito and Todd, *The Great Revolt*, 237.

19. Zito and Todd, *The Great Revolt*, 234.

20. Nicole Goodkind, "Trump's Tax Cuts Didn't Benefit U.S. Workers, Made Rich Companies Richer, Analysis Finds," *Newsweek*, April 10, 2018, https://www.newsweek.com/republican-tax-cuts-trump-wage-increases-879800. See also Heather Long, "Trump's Tax 'Reform' Looks Like Tax Cuts for the Rich," *Washington Post*, September 25, 2017, https://www.washingtonpost.com/news/wonk/wp/2017/09/25/trumps-tax-reform-looks-like-tax-cuts-for-the-rich/; and Editorial Board, "You Know Who the Tax Cuts Helped? Rich People," New York Times, August 12, 2018, https://www.nytimes.com/interactive/2018/08/12/opinion/editorials/trump-tax-cuts.html.

21. Catherine Rampell, "We've Finally Learned Trump's Grand Plan for Fixing Health Care," *Washington Post*, August 2, 2018, https://www.washingtonpost.com/opinions/trump-to-american-voters-stay-healthy-or-drop-dead/2018/08/02/e526d9e0-968b-11e8-810c-5fa705927d54_story.html.

22. Rampell, "We've Finally Learned Trump's Grand Plan." See also Paul Demko and Adam Cancryn, "Trump's Losing Fight against Obamacare," *Politico*, August 1, 2018, https://www.politico.com/story/2018/08/01/trump-obamacare-health-insurance-719300.

23. Tate Brown, "Federal Judge Rules Congressional Democrats May Pursue Trump Emoluments Lawsuit," *Jurist*, August 1, 2018, https://www.jurist.org/news/2018/10/federal-judge-rules-congressional-democrats-may-pursue-trump-emoluments-lawsuit/. Although this case was eventually dismissed, another emoluments case in the Second Circuit is still pending.

24. Michele Singletary, "Attention, Seniors: Trump's Budget Is Coming for Your Medicare Benefits," *Washington Post*, February 19, 2018, https://www.washingtonpost.com/news/get-there/wp/2018/02/19/attention-seniors-trumps-budget-is-coming-for-your-medicare-benefits/.

25. Cited in Singletary, "Attention, Seniors." See also Linda Qiu, "Trump Falsely Claims He's Saving Medicare and Social Security, Which He Says Democrats Are 'Killing,'" *New York Times*, September 7, 2018, https://www.nytimes.com/2018/09/07/us/politics/fact-check-trump-medicare-social-security-.html; Tami Luhby, "4 Ways the Trump Administration Wants to Change Medicare," *CNN*, August 22, 2018, https://www.cnn.com/2018/08/22/politics/medicare-trump/index.html.

26. Scott Horsley, "President Trump Turns Attention to Welfare Programs," *NPR*, April 10, 2018, https://www.npr.org/2018/04/10/601332980/president-trump-turns-attention-to-welfare-programs. See also Bryce Covert, "The Not-So-Subtle-Racism of Trump-Era 'Welfare Reform,'" *New York Times*, May 23, 2018, https://www.nytimes.com/2018/05/23/opinion/trump-welfare-reform-racism.html?action=click&module=RelatedLinks&pgtype=Article.

27. Kelly Brown Douglas, "Donald Trump and the 'Exceptionalist' Truth about America," in *Faith and Resistance in the Age of Trump*, ed. Miguel A. De La Torre (Maryknoll, NY: Orbis Books, 2017), 10.

28. Douglass, "Donald Trump and the 'Exceptionalist' Truth," 10.

29. Jim Wallis, "White Christian Complicity in Trump's Victory and Responsibility Now for Faith, Resistance, and Healing," in De La Torre, *Faith, Resistance in the Age of Trump*, 156.

30. Glen Kessler, Salvador Rizzo, and Meg Kelly, "President Trump Has Made More Than 5000 False or Misleading Claims," *Washington Post*, April 29, 2019, https://www.washingtonpost.com/politics/2019/04/29/president-trump-has-made-more-than-false-or-misleading-claims/.

31. Stephen Collinson, "Trump Divines His Own Truth without Consequences," *CNN*, May 7, 2018, https://www.cnn.com/2018/05/07/politics/donald-trump-presidency/index.html.

32. Sean Russman, "Ex-CIA Chief John Brennan to Trump: 'America Will Triumph over You,'" *USA Today*, March 17, 2018, https://www.usatoday.com/story/news/politics/onpolitics/2018/03/17/ex-cia-chief-john-brennan-says-trump-displaced-demago/434948002/.

33. Kwok Pui-Lan, "Trump and Changing Geopolitics in Asia-Pacific," in De La Torre, *Faith and Resistance in the Age of Trump*, 83.

34. Paul Waldman, "Don't Be Fooled: Trump's Immigration Policy Is Still Incredibly Cruel," *Washington Post*, June 21, 2018, https://www.washingtonpost.com/blogs/plum-line/wp/2018/06/21/dont-be-fooled-trumps-immigration-policy-is-still-incredibly-cruel/?utm_term=.5d927fadcde5.

35. Waldman, "Don't Be Fooled."

36. Chris Cillizza, "Donald Trump's Incredibly Unpresidential Statement on Charlottesville," *CNN*, August 13, 2017, https://www.cnn.com/2017/08/12/politics/trump-charlottesville-statement/index.html.

37. "Senator Flake Compares Trump's Rhetoric to Stalin," *CNN*, video, January 17, 2018, https://www.cnn.com/videos/politics/2018/01/17/jeff-flake-senate-floor-stalin-comparison-sot.cnn.

38. John Bellamy Foster, *Trump in the White House: Tragedy and Farce* (New York: Monthly Review Press, 2017), 19–20.

39. Christopher Rowland points out in his essay "The Temple in the New Testament" that "the 'cleansing' of the Temple may…have been less a protest against the Temple than a summons to reform," in *Temple and Worship in Biblical Israel*, ed. John Day (New York: T&T Clark, 2007), 470. The reform that Rowland is referring to is that of social reform of the inequity between the Gentiles and Jews, and all who are seeking to worship the one true God.

40. Frederick Herzog, *Liberation Theology: Liberation in the Light of the Fourth Gospel* (New York: Seabury Press, 1972), 58.

41. Gerald L Borchert, *John 1–11*, New American Commentary 25A (Nashville: Broadman & Holman Publishers, 1996–2002), 163.

42. Richard Horsley explains, "The demand for tribute to Rome and taxes to Herod in addition to tithes and offerings to the Temple and priesthood dramatically escalated the economic pressures on peasant producers, whose livelihood was perennially marginal at best." "Jesus and Empire," in *In the Shadow of Empire*, ed. Richard A. Horsley (Louisville, KY: Westminster John Knox Press, 2008), 80. Elsa Tamez writes, "Oppressors are thieves and murderers, but their ultimate purpose is not to kill or impoverish the oppressed, as these are but secondary consequences. Their primary objective is to increase their wealth at whatever cost." *Bible of the Oppressed* (Maryknoll, NY: Orbis Books, 1982), 41.

43. Craig R. Koester, *Symbolism in the Fourth Gospel: Meaning, Mystery, Community* (Minneapolis: Augsburg Fortress, 2003), 86.

44. Gail R. O'Day and Susan E. Hylen, *John* (Louisville, KY: Westminster John Knox Press, 2006), 37.

45. Thomas L. Brodie, *The Gospel According to John: A Literary and Theological Commentary* (New York: Oxford University Press, 1993), 177.

46. Brodie, *The Gospel According to John*, 177.

47. Elizabeth Schüssler Fiorenza, *Jesus: Miriam's Child, Sophia's Prophet: Critical Issues in Feminist Christology* (New York: Continuum, 1994), 93.

Questions for Further Reflection

1. What definitions of populism does the author offer? What do you think is the best definition of populism?

2. What is Moffit's definition of populism? What are the features of populism as a political style?

3. How does a populist present himself/herself as the champion of the people? What divisive tactics does this championship require? Why would this type of populism appeal to people? Why is language a part of this appeal? Why are manners a part of this appeal?

4. The author says that populism requires the perception of crisis, breakdown, or threat. Why? Do you agree or disagree? Explain.

What perceived crises, breakdowns, or threats might affect national elections in the United States?

5. The author says that populism as a political style is criticized for its lack of substance. What does she mean by this?

6. What are the Big Four clusters and what part do they play in the emerging populist-conservative divide?

7. Why does the author think that current economic policies have not lifted up the poor? Give some examples. Why does the author think that the swamp has not been drained? Give some examples. Why does the author think that the cause of the socially and economically disadvantaged has not been advanced? Give some examples. Do you agree or disagree with the author's analysis of these issues? Explain.

8. How does the author back up her point that the president is using crisis, breakdown, or threat to advance his form of populism? What examples does she give? Do you agree or disagree with her analysis? Explain.

9. How is immigration policy a part of the populist agenda?

10. What point does the author make about the structure of the temple in Jerusalem and Jesus's action in cleansing it? How was this a populist action?

11. What importance does the author give to the fact that in the Gospel of John the cleansing of the temple comes early in Jesus's ministry, as opposed to its placement during Holy Week, the end of his ministry, in Matthew, Mark, and Luke? How does she relate this to other themes in John's Gospel?

12. The author says that while the cleansing of the temple accounts differ a bit in the four Gospels, they still make the same point. What point is that? How is this point important to the author's analysis?

13. The author says that the cleansing of the temple proclaims who Jesus is. What does she mean by this? And how does this make him a populist?

14. Is it realistic to expect political leaders to have the same values as religious leaders? Why or why not?

12

Voting as a Moral Act

Candidates, Issues, and Election Guides[1]

M. Cathleen Kaveny

The Act of Voting

What do we *do* when we vote in an American political election? Most fundamentally, we exercise our responsibility as citizens in a representative democracy, in a polity in which we are both sovereigns and subjects. We select those individuals who will exercise political authority on our behalf, in accordance with the limits on role and term length specified in the community's foundational documents (for example, the federal and state constitutions). We participate in the choice of those persons to whose judgment we will defer during their appointed time in office.

Why should we vote? Political scientists have devoted a great deal of attention to this question, because the odds are overwhelming that no individual vote will make any appreciable difference, particularly in national elections.[2] Because they do not think they will change the outcome, many people decline to participate in the process.[3] While understandable, a decision to opt out is, in my view, deeply mistaken; more

245

specifically, it reduces the purpose of the practice of elections to crude, consequentialist terms.

It is true, of course, that the primary function of an election is *selective*; one member of a field of candidates is chosen by the electorate to lead the community by serving in a particular office. There are, however, other purposes with which one can cast a vote. For example, voting can also be *expressive*. By their votes, citizens can "send a message" about their general attitude on the course of the government to those who assume or remain in power. This message may result in policy change; in fact, we frequently see how such messages may yield midterm course corrections. Significantly, however, voting is also *contributive*. Given the structure of the government, (adult) citizens share joint responsibility for selecting our own leaders. The contributive function of voting cannot be neatly captured in consequentialist terms, because it is participation in the electoral process that matters, not merely the result.

The practice of *holding* elections is also a social, collaborative project. We cast our votes as individuals. The direct political import of those votes, however, is forged in a context that is doubly social; it is determined by who else is running for office, and who else is voting in that election. The indirect political import of voting is also socially determined. If large numbers of people refuse to vote or large, identifiable groups of people (for example, minorities and women) are prevented or discouraged from voting, the viability and stability of the electoral system is threatened. Each of us may go into the voting booth alone, but voting is anything but a solitary act.

On a practical level, what do we *do* when we vote? As I noted above, most fundamentally and straightforwardly, we *select* a candidate to assume or retain public office and to serve the relevant political community by assuming a distinct array of political duties. Selecting a candidate for public office is an exercise of practical reason, which itself incorporates judgment about a candidate's probable exercise of practical reason over the sphere of his responsibilities while in office. Voting, therefore, involves a combination of judgment (about the merits of the candidate) and prediction (about the nature of the challenges that the individual holding the office will face during the upcoming term). In assessing candidates for a particular office, four considerations are paramount:

1. *Competence*—Does the candidate have the intellectual capacity, the experience, the temperament, and judgment to do the job?
2. *Character*—Does the candidate have a good set of moral values, and the integrity to pursue them in situations of temptation and fear?
3. *Collaboration*—Can the candidate work well with other people, both political allies and opponents?
4. *Connections*—What are the moral and practical ramifications of the candidate's political and financial connections for the way he or she will carry out the job? Politicians do not act alone; they take their place within networks of political power, including party affiliations, lobbyists, and big corporate and individual donors.

The point of electing candidates to an office, after all, is to empower and to enable them to accomplish a set of tasks, both specified and unspecified, in service of the common good. In evaluating candidates, the foregoing considerations point to various factors involved in being an "empowered and enabled" political servant. These factors are not fungible. Moreover, there is a certain minimum level of achievement that is indispensable with respect to each level; saintly demeanor does not make up for lack of experience or intelligence; strategic brilliance does not compensate for antisocial behavior.

Moreover, precisely because politics is not a solitary activity, the same criteria for holding political power ought to be applied with respect to the key party leaders with which a particular candidate is affiliated. In some cases, in fact, it is the voter's view of the party leadership that ought to be decisive. Depending upon the situation in a particular political community, "voting the party" rather than a particular candidate may be a strategy that is morally justified. If party politics are strong, then voters in a general election often find themselves choosing between already assembled political teams with competing governing strategies and priorities.

The opposite of empowering and enabling, of course, is thwarting and hindering. In some cases, perhaps too many cases, a voter may exercise the selective function of the ballot in a negative rather than a positive way. Voting is a crude instrument for setting a community's social and political direction; sometimes the best one can do is to prevent a deadly crash here and now, in the hope of setting a better course down the road. There are instances in which a responsible voter will describe what he or she is doing as casting a clear vote *against* one candidate or party rather than voting *for* that candidate or party's opponent. Sometimes, of course, the situation facing a voter is far more ambiguous. Suppose none of the candidates score particularly well on the four criteria identified above; the best one can do is to pick the candidate whom one believes, overall, to be the *least worst* leader. In this situation, sometimes too common, voters are not selecting leaders for their virtues but for their relative lack of key vices.

The *expressive* function of voting is extremely important from a practical perspective but logically secondary to the selective function. It comes into play when voters want to send a message to those seeking to hold office, or to influence those in office. A vote can function as a crude form of communication, to those newly elected to office and to incumbents who will stand for election in the future. In our political era, of course, the meaning of a vote is debated, fleshed out, and perhaps altered by the auxiliary forces of the political system, including incessant polling and political commentary.

The *contributive* function of voting is fulfilled by participation in the process of choosing the community's political leadership. It also, generally, requires that each citizen educate him- or herself on the state of the community, the candidates available to lead it, and the various political programs offered as overarching plans of government.

The Relationship of Issues and Candidates

In the foregoing paragraphs, I have argued that citizens vote primarily for candidates—individuals running for particular offices, who are to be assessed in the context of their political collaborators—not for "issues." But many voting guides, including the ones distributed by the U.S. Catholic bishops over the years, are actually "issue" guides. What, then, is the relationship between candidates and issues? The answer to this question depends upon the answer to a prior question: what, exactly, is an "issue"?

The term is general, even imprecise. In common usage, it gestures vaguely toward a topic or a question that is currently the subject of discussion or controversy. In our current political discussion, the term can refer to a complex problem with many causes, both natural and social (hunger, global warming, illegal immigration); it can refer to the working of an entire sector of social life (the economy); it can refer to a morally objectionable practice, whether legal or illegal (abortion, drug use); it can refer to a particular legislative proposal (authorizing gay marriage, banning capital punishment); it can refer to a deliberate policy or decision by a governing body (sending troops to the Middle East, authorizing "enhanced interrogation"); and it can refer to a fundamental value that operates through many spheres of life, public and private, political and social (free exercise of religion).

Given the imprecision surrounding the meaning of the term *issue*, how do we begin to pin down a candidate's relationship to the issues, or one issue in particular? We frequently say that a candidate has a "stance" on an issue. What does that mean? At a minimum, it means that he or she has (1) a judgment that a particular situation poses a problem for the common good; (2) a view about what has caused that situation; and (3) a proposal for doing something to remedy the problem.

Each of these factors can incorporate both moral and factual considerations, sometimes in extremely complicated ways. One may think that global warming does not pose a problem because one is unconvinced by the scientific data proffered to support the theory, or because one believes that the end of the world is imminent as God prepares to punish humanity for our sins. One may think that abortion in a particular society is a problem because one judges that it counts as the intentional killing of human beings, or because it hinders the nationalist ambitions of a "superior" race (for example, the view of some Nazis). In assessing a candidate's stance on the "issues," then, voters need to consider all three factors identified in the preceding paragraph. Many times they are interrelated; very frequently, one's view of the reason a particular situation harms the common good will affect one's view of its cause; and that view, in turn, will significantly determine the proposal to remedy it.

Why ought a candidate's stance on key issues be important? First, because it reveals important aspects of a candidate's suitability for office, including information important to assessing the candidate's character, competence, collaboration, and connections. Obviously, something about a candidate's character may be revealed by his or her stance on an issue. At the same time, we must tread cautiously in moving from a candidate's position on an issue to a wholesale judgment of moral probity or aptitude for leadership, particularly in mixed questions of fact and value. We need to ask ourselves whether the factual judgment embedded in a moral position is "reasonable, but wrong." Moreover, in assessing a candidate's stance, it is also important not to take everything he or she says at face value. Politicians are not always truthful about their positions or honest about the depth of commitment with which they hold them. The candidate's moral character, however, is not the sole factor illuminated by a stance on key issues. Competence, connections, and collaborative possibilities are revealed as well. The candidate's diagnosis of the problem and proposed solutions shed light on intellectual and practical competence, as well as ability to marshal collective resources and to work together with political allies and opponents to address a given set of problems.

Assessing the relationship between a candidate for office and a given issue begins, but does not end, with considering a candidate's stance on key issues in the abstract. An election is not a seminar; voters ought not to evaluate candidates' stances on the issues solely from a purely academic vantage point but in direct relationship to their ability to affect them. *Perspective* in assessing candidates' stands on issues is important in determining how to cast one's ballot. Voters, after all, rightly care about the issues not merely because they reveal something about the character and qualifications of the candidate. They also care because it matters, in a fundamental way, what *is done* about them.

Consequently, evaluating a candidate's stance on issues must not be done from on high but from an action-oriented and pragmatic perspective. First, issues should loom larger to the extent that they are within the purview of the office to which the candidate aspires. From an action-oriented, pragmatic perspective, the views of a potential school board member on peace in the Middle East are not particularly salient, although the issue itself is crucial.[4] Second, voters ought to pay particular attention to the final component identified above regarding a candidate's stance on an issue: his or her concrete proposal for addressing it, and thereby remedying the threat it poses to the common good. In some cases, a voter rightly supports candidates who adopt the soundest policy, even if they do so for less-than-sound reasons.

Issues and Priorities

Looking at the relationship between issues and candidates from an action-oriented, pragmatic perspective is instructive about how we should think about issues more generally. Recall that the several meanings of the word *issue* hold together both a situation and its outcome; a problem *at* issue, so to speak, begs for a resolution *to* issue from the relevant debate and discussion. Evaluating and prioritizing issues in the context of elections, then, more generally requires us to assess the threat each problem poses for the common good—and to also consider the possibility and necessity of ameliorating those problems through governmental intervention.

Because political issues tend to press us to formulate an action plan, they are susceptible to being ranked in different ways that are at least partially incommensurable. On the one hand, some issues are *important*, even *fundamental*; they go to the basic structure, values, and political arrangements of the country. Who counts as an equally protectable person? Who gets to vote in elections? What are basic due process requirements that must be followed by law enforcement officials? On the other hand, some issues are *urgent*: the problem they pose must be addressed now, or the immediate well-being of the nation, its stability, and the welfare of the people are seriously threatened. Natural or man-made disasters, such as a catastrophic earthquake or a meltdown at a nuclear plant, or a widespread famine, fall into this category.

Much of the difficulty in ranking issues stems from the fact that the fundamental and the urgent may compete for time, attention, and limited resources. Upon reflection, this competition is not surprising; action items in the two categories compete in similar fashion in nearly every area of human activity, from work responsibilities to child-rearing. Time management experts and strategists tell us that as agents, most people face the danger of mis-categorizing too many tasks as urgent, and thereby consistently putting off consideration of more fundamental issues.[5] At the same time, however, there *is* such a thing as an urgent problem. Maintaining the foundation of a house is important, indeed fundamental to the well-being of the entire building. At the same time, if the roof is leaking or lightning has set it afire, those problems must be addressed first.

By virtue of their urgency, some issues cannot be assessed and addressed in predictable ways. Sometimes, urgent issues arise—or mature to a crisis point—unexpectedly. Holders of higher office may be remembered by their responses to issues that were wholly or largely unanticipated at the time they were elected. No one expected George W. Bush's presidency to be defined by his response to terrorism; the attacks on the Twin Towers in 2001 reconfigured the entire nation's priorities. Responsibly electing national leaders always involves some assessment of their ability to address new and unexpected challenges and situations.

Finally, the action-eliciting, resolution-oriented nature of political issues generates an additional criterion according to which they must be evaluated: amenability to improvement. In prioritizing issues, therefore, it is important to consider both the possibility and the likelihood of solving (or significantly ameliorating) the problem associated with the issue by the morally acceptable means at hand.

One might object that one can redefine an issue to pick out a subset of the problem that *is* addressable in this manner. We do not, after all, consider sin as such a political issue but we do treat one subset of sins—serious violations of the rights of others—as a political matter, in our tort and criminal law. This objection, which has a great deal of merit, suggests two responses. First, particularly in the context of elections, citizens ought to take care to define political issues in ways that are tied closely to the identification of a politically cognizable problem, a diagnosis of its cause, and proposed solution. This circumscribed definition of an issue is not necessary for all purposes, or even for all political purposes. The venerable American tradition of the jeremiad, a stylized speech by a politician or a preacher decrying the failings of the people and calling for repentance, demonstrates that there is a time and a place for general allusions to the social and moral problems of the country. Nonetheless, at the time of a national election, issues should be described in circumscribed terms that are geared to appropriate political intervention. So, for example, a crucial political issue might be defined "violent crime" or "cybercrime," not the vices of injustice, excessive anger, greed, and dishonesty more generally.

Second, this last example makes clear that problems are overlapping. These vices may not be narrowly definable as political issues, but they point to problems to be addressed by different realms of civil society, including families, churches, synagogues, and mosques. State and federal law may not be able to target these vices directly, but they can make indirect progress by enabling and encouraging the appropriate bodies to do so. Furthermore, through its pedagogical role, state and federal lawmaking can make it clear that violent crimes and cybercrimes are problematic not merely because they violate justice, but also because they are the fruits and exemplification of morally disturbing patterns of activity.

Rethinking *Faithful Citizenship*

The foregoing analysis of candidates and issues, I think, allows us to gain some critical perspective on the voting guide issued by the United States Conference of Catholic Bishops. *Forming Consciences for Faithful Citizenship* and earlier guides are largely framed as issue guides, not voting guides. In my view, this is a missed opportunity. Think, for example, of how the Catholic debate about the choice between Hilary Clinton and Donald Trump might have been elevated if the bishops had helped focus attention on what it means to vote for a candidate rather than an issue.

The bishops' tax-exempt status prevents them from endorsing or opposing particular candidates; it does not, however, prevent them from reflecting on general qualifications of a candidate, in terms of his or her competence, collaborative abilities, connections—and character. What are the *virtues* of a good public servant? Western political philosophy includes a number of reflections on this question—some profound, and some troubling.[6] Recent Catholic moral theology has witnessed a resurgence of interest in the role of virtue in the moral life; it would make sense to extend the analysis to the virtues necessary for political leadership, particularly in a pluralistic liberal democracy such as our own. In my view, exposition of the necessary virtues would also highlight the capacities necessary to promote the primary virtues of autonomy and solidarity, as I have argued elsewhere.[7]

What should the bishops say about how, morally, citizens ought to cast their votes? Proper moral analysis of the act of voting must consider not only the three functions of the act of voting but also the structure of the act itself. To put it bluntly, apart from referenda items, voters are asked to select among people, not positions. So, in casting their ballots, voters must make a direct choice between or among candidates running for a given office, not between or among issues.

In my view, this fundamental feature of casting a ballot should serve as a touchstone for recalibrating our reflections on the moral implications of the act of voting. Election guides, for example, would do well to place more emphasis on assessing the fitness of candidates for office in a contextual, comparative way. In general, voters ought to assess a candidate's general competence in terms of the requirements for the office that is sought. That evaluation should include scrutiny of both the candidate's moral character—paying particular attention to the virtues and vices most likely to be involved in the elected post—and the candidate's social and political networks. With whom will they work? To whom will they be loyal? These are key questions. Many election guides, however, do not concentrate on describing virtues and vices of candidates; they emphasize instead the issues they perceive to be (or hope to be) relevant to the voters. The election guides issued over the years by the United States Conference of Catholic Bishops are no exception to this generalization.

How, then, ought citizens to think morally and practically about the issues relevant to casting one's ballot for a particular candidate in a particular election? I have suggested that the term *issue* is too vague to be helpful for practical decision-making because too often the word simultaneously encompasses a diagnosis of a problem, an account of its cause, and a proposed solution. Evaluating a candidate's stand on the issues, accordingly, requires careful attention to each of these three factors. A further complication is that political issues and the underlying problems they highlight claim our attention in different ways. As I argued above, some issues are *important*, even fundamental, because they go to the basic structure of the political community. Others are *urgent*, because the mandate to protect the well-being of the community demands that they be addressed here and now. Issues, then, are not abstract propositions about the community; they are action items in that they are the problems that can be addressed by the tools available to political officeholders. Consequently, voters ought not to evaluate the relative significance of issues in the abstract but should instead consider the specific context of whether and to what degree the problems identified by the issues can be ameliorated by the particular candidate seeking a particular office.

What about abortion? It is, after all, the issue that prompted the U.S. bishops to issue a voting guide in the first place in 1976, and it has consistently occupied pride of place in subsequent guides. To begin addressing this question, some context is necessary. The most straightforward way of undoing *Roe v. Wade* (1973) is to pass a constitutional amendment declaring that the Constitution does not include a right to privacy that encompasses a woman's decision to terminate her pregnancy. But the difficulty of passing such an amendment has led large segments of the pro-life movement, including the U.S. bishops' conference, to concentrate on achieving that same goal indirectly, by electing a series of presidents who will over time remake the Supreme Court with justices able and willing to overturn *Roe*.

This is not a moral decision. It is a matter of political strategy. Yet it has numerous moral implications. More specifically, supporting a constitutional amendment directly targeted at undoing *Roe* conflicts with few, if any, of a voter's duties to promote the common good. While any change to the fundamental law of the country is potentially destabilizing, the prospect of such a narrowly targeted amendment merits serious consideration by anyone (1) who believes that equally protectable human life begins at any time before birth; (2) who thinks *Roe* itself is a bad decision; or (3) who judges more generally that controversial questions ought to be decided by the elected officials in the legislatures, not by the courts.

But in my mind, the pro-life movement's indirect strategy of making abortion a litmus-test issue for voters, with the expectation that they will elect officials who will somehow overturn *Roe*, does raise red flags. The duty of a voter is to promote the common good, by selecting the best candidate for a political office considering the range of factors I have outlined in this chapter. Given that most officeholders have multifaceted responsibilities, voters cannot consider only one issue—even a fundamental issue—in casting their ballots. Presidential elections are no exception.

Forming Consciences for Faithful Citizenship rightly says that Catholics are not to be single-issue voters.[8] It does not, however, elaborate on why that is the case. In this essay, I have attempted to make a case for that statement, centering my analysis on the nature and purpose of the act of voting. Voting is a role-related moral obligation, incumbent upon qualified citizens who are both sovereigns and subjects in our representative democracy. The moral obligation of citizens in their roles as voters to promote the common good necessarily requires consideration of several competing responsibilities.

More specifically, citizen-voters rightly consider their other role-related obligations in casting their votes. It is not selfish to help build a society in which individuals can fulfill their moral and religious responsibilities to others. Moreover, no one disputes that these responsibilities of voters are, like those of officeholders, multifaceted. For example, parents have a duty to provide for their children; therefore, it is morally correct for a mother or father to work at a job that will materially provide for their sons and daughters, rather than donating all their time to a pro-life lobbying group. Analogously, in threatening economic circumstances, it can be equally morally correct for parents to vote for candidates most likely to protect the jobs by which they provide for their children, even if those candidates are pro-choice. To take another example, surely it is morally permissible to direct some of one's surplus funds toward the victims of a catastrophic disaster rather than donating everything to the local crisis pregnancy center. But as our government has the basic obligation to provide for victims of national disasters, it follows that voters are morally obliged to consider which governmental candidates will best fix the broken disaster-response system. In some certain elections, that consideration may be decisive.

Moreover, even the question of Supreme Court candidates has moral implications. An appointment to the highest court in the land is a lifetime appointment. It is important to remember that a Supreme Court justice will cast a vote not only on abortion, but also on many other matters pertaining to the common good. In my judgment, the "originalist" jurisprudence that animated Justice Antonin Scalia and many judges and legal scholars to oppose *Roe* is not only flawed philosophically. It has also resulted in many other decisions that vitiate the common good, including decisions undermining universal health care, and promoting business interests over economic justice and political integrity. How does one balance the prospect of overturning *Roe* against other harms to the common good? How is that balance altered by the fact that overturning *Roe* will simply return the question to the states, many of which will legalize abortion on their own authority?

There are no easy or automatic answers to such questions. They require discernment. Voters, with their multifaceted obligations, cannot blinder themselves and focus single-mindedly on one issue in the abstract, even if the issue is abortion. Voters must select among candidates, not among issues—and they are morally required to do so in light of the concrete challenges and possibilities for the common good posed by a specific election at a specific time.

NOTES

1. This essay is a revised version of chapter 8 ("Voting and Faithful Citizenship") from my book, *Law's Virtues: Fostering Autonomy and Solidarity in American Society* (Washington, DC: Georgetown University Press, 2012). Reprinted with permission. www.press.georgetown.edu.

2. See, for example, André Blais, *To Vote or Not to Vote: The Merits and Limits of Rational Choice Theory* (Pittsburgh: University of Pittsburgh Press, 2000); and Jocelyn A. J. Evans, *Voters and Voting: An Introduction* (London: Sage Publications, 2004).

3. See, for example, Gustavo López and Antonio Flores, Pew Research Center, "Dislike of Candidates or Campaign Issues Was Most Common Reason for Not Voting in 2016," June 1, 2017, http://www.pewresearch.org/fact-tank/2017/06/01/dislike-of-candidates-or-campaign-issues-was-most-common-reason-for-not-voting-in-2016/. See also Pew Research Center, "Who Votes, Who Doesn't, and Why: Regular Voters, Intermittent Voters, and Those Who Don't," October 18, 2006, http://people-press.org/2006/10/18/who-votes-who-doesnt-and-why/.

4. Even here, of course, matters are complicated. With some exceptions (for example, celebrity candidates), most politicians build a career in a deliberate, step-by-step fashion. Some attention must be given to nurturing young candidates with sound views, even if those views are not immediately relevant to their entry-level positions in politics.

5. See, for example, Peter Turla, "How to Make Wise Choices when You Set Priorities," Timeman.com, accessed December 19, 2019, http://www.timeman.com/Articles/timemanagementtipsforprioritysetting.shtml and Hillary Chura, "Entrepreneurs Take Time to Organize Their Time," *New York Times*, Aug. 10, 2006, C7.

6. See, for example, Aristotle's *Politics*, Aquinas's *Commentary on Aristotle's Politics*, and his treatise on the virtues in II–II of the *Summa Theologica*, Machiavelli's *The Prince*, and Hobbes's *Leviathan* (1660).

7. Cathleen Kaveny, *Law's Virtues* (Washington, DC: Georgetown University Press, 2012).

8. "As Catholics we are not single-issue voters." FC-2012, §42.

Questions for Further Reflection

1. The author says that voting has a selective, an expressive, and a contributive function. What does she mean by that? Explain each different function. Is one function more important than another? If so, why?

2. What does the author say is the importance of the collaborative aspect or function of voting?

3. Voting involves assessing candidates for public office. According to the author, what considerations go into that assessment? Is any one of these more important than the others? Why?

4. What is the point of electing candidates to office according to such an assessment? How would you define the common good? Can my common good be different from your common good?

5. The author also says that voting can be for purposes of thwarting or hindering. Why would that be a reason for someone to vote? Can you think of an example? Have you ever voted to thwart or hinder a candidate or a cause? Explain.

6. The author says that sometimes people want to send a message with their votes. How does she say this works? What function of voting is this? Do you agree? Do you think this type of voting works? How can we be sure what the message you are sending is by voting against someone?

7. What does the author mean by voting issue guides? Have you ever seen such guides for Catholic voters? What did they say? What issues did they focus on? Were these issues an adequate depiction of what in your faith is important to you? Were they an adequate depiction of the Catholic faith overall?

8. How can we judge a candidate's stance on an issue? Are there any criteria for this? What examples of contemporary voting issues does the author give? Can you think of any others?

9. Why is a candidate's stance on a given issue important? What standard should voters use to determine what a candidate's stance truly is?

10. Is it fair to judge a candidate's own personal morals/values based on the political stands that the candidate takes on certain issues? Why or why not? How would you judge a candidate's personal morals? Are a candidate's personal morals important to how you vote?

11. What does it mean to say that voters should judge a candidate's stand on an issue directly in proportion to the candidate's ability to affect that issue?

12. Is every issue in an election as important as every other issue? What are some issues in recent elections that have motivated you to vote a certain way? Why? Were some issues more important to you than others? How do we and how should we prioritize issues? Are you aware that the American bishops' document *Forming Consciences for Faithful Citizenship* prioritizes issues? Do you know what those issues are?

13. The author says that it may be difficult to prioritize voting issues. Why does she think this is so? On what personal basis/values do you prioritize the issues that draw you to vote?

14. Are all issues susceptible to political solutions? If not, how do such issues get solved?

15. How does the author think that the American bishops' document *Forming Consciences for Faithful Citizenship* should be reoriented? What are her arguments to support this reorientation? Do you agree or disagree with the author? Explain.

16. The author says that making the "abortion issue" a litmus test for voting raises red flags. What does she mean by this? Should Catholics be single issue voters? What do the bishops in *Faithful Citizenship* say about this? What does the author think about this? What do you think? Why?

13

Reclaiming Catholic Identity in the Trump Era

John Gehring

Introduction

Donald Trump's election wasn't only an indictment of a coarsening culture drowning in celebrity worship, or a stark reminder that many voters have lost so much faith in the establishment political system that a real estate mogul turned reality television star seemed a viable candidate for the most powerful office in the world. Both of those maladies deserve treatment if our democracy is to recover from its current feverish sickness. No less urgent is the challenge Trump's improbable victory presented to the role of faith in public life. In particular, Catholic leaders, institutions, and commentators who aspire to help shape the consciences of faithful citizens must grapple with what role they unwittingly may have played over the years in paving the way for President Trump's ascent.

The Trump Campaign and the Catholic Response

Trump began his presidential campaign with the old demagogue's playbook of fear and division tucked under his arm. In a speech announcing his candidacy, Trump demonized Mexican immigrants as "rapists," warned of "tremendous crime," and quickly promised to build a "big, beautiful wall" between the United States and Mexico. The wall became totemic—taking on near-mythical status—and reflected his pitch to the electorate: You're under threat. Waves of dark-skinned criminals are coming. Only I can save you. The sales pitch was particularly calibrated to middle-aged and older white Americans anxious about demographic changes that are making the country distinctly less white and less Christian. Robert Jones, the CEO of Public Religion Research Institute and author of *The End of White Christian America*, has appropriately dubbed these Americans "nostalgia voters." Trump's racialized warnings about crime and immigration were nothing new for the candidate. In an attempt to delegitimize Barack Obama, he spent years peddling "birther" conspiracy theories that the nation's first black president wasn't born in the United States. His race baiting and scapegoating go back decades earlier to 1989, when five black and Latino teens were convicted of rape in Central Park. Two weeks after the youths were arrested, Trump took out advertisements in all four major New York daily newspapers that read—"Bring Back the Death Penalty. Bring Back Our Police!" In an interview on CNN that year, Trump told Larry King that "maybe hate is what we need if we're gonna get something done." The teens were wrongfully convicted and later exonerated.

During the presidential campaign, as Trump's anti-immigrant appeals continued to escalate, Cardinal Timothy Dolan of New York lamented in a *New York Daily News* op-ed that "nativism is alive, well—and apparently popular!" In an interview with the Associated Press, Santa Fe Archbishop John Wester described the rhetoric in the campaign as "deplorable" for "scapegoating people like the immigrant, the refugee and the poor." Two prominent conservative Catholics, Robert George of Princeton University and John Paul II biographer

George Weigel (both of whom have been reliable public supporters of Republican candidates in the past) wrote an open letter in the *National Review* urging Catholics and "all men and women of goodwill" to reject Trump. Calling him "manifestly unfit to be president," they described Trump's "appeals to racial and ethnic fears and prejudice" as "offensive to any genuinely Catholic sensibility." On a set of issues with particular appeal to more conservative voters, Weigel and George wrote that "there is nothing in his campaign or his previous record that gives us grounds for confidence that he genuinely shares our commitments to the right to life, to religious freedom and the rights of conscience." After Trump's victory, a few days before inauguration, Cardinal Joe Tobin of Newark tweeted that "a fearful nation talks about building walls and is vulnerable to con men. We must challenge the fear before we are led into darkness."

White Catholic voters appeared not to be listening to bishops or other Catholic leaders warning about the incompatibility of Trumpism and traditional Catholic social doctrine. While Trump's success with white Evangelicals dominated the media headlines, 56 percent of white Catholics voted for him, a decisive factor in states such as Wisconsin, where Trump became the first Republican presidential candidate to win since Ronald Reagan carried the state in 1984. Despite Trump's history of race-baiting and demagoguery, some Catholic leaders held out hope that the presidency would change him. In his final days as U.S. Ambassador to the Holy See, Ken Hackett, the former president of Catholic Relief Services, told the Catholic News Agency (CNA), that he expected Trump to be influenced by the "reality of governing" and expressed optimism that "good will prevail."

Trump's Policies in Office

To say that sunny prediction didn't come to fruition is an understatement. Trump has emboldened racists, infamously saying there were "very fine people on both sides" of a violent white supremacist rally in Charlottesville, Virginia, that left a young woman dead. His administration instituted a cruel policy of separating undocumented immigrant families at the border that was swiftly denounced by Catholic bishops and nearly every religious denomination in the country. Trump also ended Temporary Protected Status (TPS), a program with bipartisan support over the years, for more than 200,000 nationals of El Salvador in the United States, many of whom were displaced by earthquakes and fled violent conditions in their home country. In the fall of 2018, Secretary of State Mike Pompeo announced that the United States would cap its intake of refugees at thirty thousand for the year during the worst migration crisis since World War II. Bishop Joe Vasquez of Austin, Texas, chair of the United States Conference of Catholic Bishops' Committee on Migration, called it a "deeply disturbing" decision that "contradicts who we are as a nation." Consolidation of power no matter the cost to human dignity seems to be Trump's most identifiable core conviction. Asked by Lesley Stahl of *60 Minutes* why he publicly mocked Christine Blasey Ford, who claims that Supreme Court Justice Brett Kavanaugh sexually assaulted her when they were both teenagers, Trump responded curtly, "It doesn't matter. We won."

Single-Issue Politics and the Failure to Form Consciences

Church leaders can't avoid asking hard questions about what the rise of an authoritarian demagogue who governs by insult and fear says about the failure of forming consciences. Specifically, there should be sober conversation about how a decades-long retreat from a consistent ethic-of-life engagement with politics both diminishes the pro-life cause and has electoral consequences that are hostile to a Catholic vision for the common good. Trump's promise to antiabortion voters that he would appoint Supreme Court justices who would overturn *Roe v. Wade* persuaded many conservative Catholics to vote for him. Long before that promise from a thrice-divorced, erstwhile pro-choicer who was caught on tape boasting about grabbing women's genitalia, the Catholic narrative in public life had already solidified around abortion as the most fundamental issue for Catholic voters. When Ronald Reagan's 1984 reelection campaign began, John O'Connor had recently been appointed New York's archbishop. When a pro-choice Catholic, Geraldine Ferraro, became the party's vice-presidential candidate, O'Connor eagerly jumped into the fray. "I do not see how a Catholic in good conscience can vote for an individual expressing himself or herself as favoring abortion," the archbishop said during a televised news conference. After Reagan told the

Pennsylvania Pro-Life Federation that the "time has come for Congress to act and pass a human life amendment," O'Connor quipped to the crowd: "I didn't tell you to vote for Ronald Reagan, did I?" Another archbishop appointed that year by Pope John Paul II also turned up the heat. Cardinal Bernard Law of Boston, who two decades later would resign in disgrace after media revelations of widespread clergy sexual abuse, called abortion "the critical issue in this campaign." At a press conference at his stately residence, Law released a statement signed by seventeen other Catholic bishops from Maine, Vermont, New Hampshire, and Massachusetts. The bishops acknowledged that "nuclear holocaust is a future possibility," but added "the holocaust of abortion is a present reality." Law insisted the church wasn't endorsing anyone. "This statement is directed at all candidates and all voters," he said, before adding coyly, "I think Geraldine Ferraro is a candidate." The cycle repeated itself in 2000 when Sen. John Kerry, a Catholic, ran for president. A vocal minority of outspoken bishops, including former Philadelphia Archbishop Charles Chaput, insinuated they would deny Kerry communion for his pro-choice views. When a newly elected Barack Obama was invited to give the commencement address at the University of Notre Dame in 2009, the backlash from more than two dozen bishops came swift and strong. Archbishop John Nienstedt of St. Paul and Minneapolis (who later resigned after the archdiocese became embroiled in clergy sexual abuse scandals), described the invitation as a "tragedy" and called the president, whose advocacy in Chicago churches was partly funded by the U.S. bishops' Catholic Campaign for Human Development, an "anti-Catholic politician." Philadelphia Archbishop Chaput said the invitation amounted to "prostituting our Catholic identity." The era of consistent ethic-of-life Catholicism, as expressed most clearly by the late Cardinal Joseph Bernardin of Chicago, had been replaced by a fundamentalist, single-issue approach to politics that wounded the church's credibility in public life, already ailing from the clergy abuse crisis. Writing in *America* magazine, the Archbishop Emeritus John Quinn of San Francisco summarized the impact of this shortsighted approach in a 2009 essay:

> For most of our history, the American bishops have assiduously sought to avoid being identified with either political party and have made a conscious effort to be seen as transcending party considerations in the formulation of their

teachings. The condemnation of President Obama and the wider policy shift that represents signal to many thoughtful persons that the bishops have now come down firmly on the Republican side in American politics. The bishops are believed to communicate that for all the promise the Obama administration has on issues of health care, immigration reform, global poverty and war and peace, the leadership of the church in the United States has strategically tilted in favor of an ongoing alliance with the Republican Party....There is no disagreement within this [U.S. bishops'] conference about the moral evil of abortion, its assault upon the dignity of the human person, or the moral imperative of enacting laws that prohibit abortion in American society. But there is deep and troubled disagreement among us on the issue of how we as bishops should witness concerning this most searing and volatile issue in American public life. And this disagreement has now become a serious and increasing impediment to our ability to teach effectively in our own community and in the wider American society.

For all the appropriately urgent statements now coming from the U.S. Conference of Catholic Bishops' denouncing Trump administration policies, there should be a discussion about the role Catholic leaders played in creating a context in which Catholic voters could feel justified in voting for a misogynistic, nativist, megalomaniac all in the name of advancing the pro-life cause.

Did the Bishops Help to Elect Trump?

White Catholics who voted for Trump (Latino and black Catholics rejected him overwhelmingly) because of his promise to appoint Supreme Court justices who would end constitutional protections for abortion were willing to ignore or justify his campaign of demagoguery and dehumanization because they viewed opposing abortion as the defining marker of Catholic identity. This is the unambiguous message Catholic voters heard for years by conservative bishops who portrayed Barack Obama as an enemy of the church; by the Knights of Columbus who funded the church's religious liberty campaigns; by groups like

265

Catholic Answers who circulated formulaic voting guides that reduced the fullness of Catholic social teaching to a few hot button issues that largely aligned with the Republican Party. In this distorted context, prudential judgement—an essential theological principle of discernment—too often became a convenient "get-out-of-jail-free" card for Catholic lawmakers to rationalize breaking with the church on issues such as immigration, economic justice, the death penalty and climate change. When the goal of overturning *Roe v. Wade* overshadows other central life issues to such a disproportionate degree that Catholic voters have lost the ability to recognize that creating a culture of life isn't served by a single-issue theology, this isn't only a political problem, but a major catechetical challenge. In other words, Catholic institutions—Catholic media, churches, and universities—have failed to transmit the depth and breadth of church teaching when Trump's xenophobic, "America First" Christian nationalism is viewed as morally acceptable, or at least a deal worth taking for a Supreme Court ruling that would send abortion policy back to the states.

Fr. Frank Pavone, director of Priests for Life, exemplified this transactional attitude. After describing Trump's personal behavior as "repulsive," Pavone told Catholic News Agency in an interview before the election that he would vote for Trump and encourage others to also. "What an incredible reparation Mr. Trump is making now for any past faults, by the very fact that he is running as the Republican nominee for president, and is ready to nominate the right kind of judges and sign the right kinds of legislation, which will steer our nation away from so many morally corrupt public policies," Pavone said.

It is encouraging to see that some bishops are growing more aware of the damage done by pro-life advocates who seem willing to sell out the integrity of Catholic teaching for political advantage. Bishop Anthony Taylor of Little Rock, Arkansas, refused to attend a local March for Life in 2018 after organizers chose a death-penalty supporter as the keynote speaker. Arkansas's Republican attorney general, Leslie Rutledge, "has good anti-abortion credentials but otherwise is decidedly not an appropriate pro-life speaker," the bishop wrote in a letter to his diocese, because she has "worked tirelessly to secure the execution of four criminals who pose no further threat to society." The organization leading the march, Arkansas Right to Life, refused the bishop's request to find a new speaker. "As you know, the church teaches a consistent ethic of life in which human life and human dignity must be protected from the first moment of conception to natural death and every stage in between," the bishop emphasized in his letter. "This means, among other things, that all lives have inherent God-given dignity. Even people who have been sentenced to death possess this dignity, which is why capital punishment must be acknowledged."

Pope Francis's Approach and His Critics

Pope Francis, who recently developed church teaching on the death penalty by declaring it "inadmissible" in all cases, is helping to resuscitate seamless-garment Catholicism. In one of his first interviews after becoming pope, Francis cautioned that "the moral edifice of the church is likely to fall like a house of cards" if the church is "obsessed with the transmission of a disjointed multitude of doctrines." We cannot, the pope said, "insist only on issues related to abortion, gay marriage and the use of contraceptive methods." Francis is using the power of his global pulpit to advocate for a culture of life that recognizes protecting life in the womb must be connected to addressing "an economy of exclusion and inequality" that kills, and with ecological threats that increasingly displace vulnerable people. "Everything is connected," Francis writes in *Laudato si'*, an encyclical that both drew from the teachings of earlier popes and also elevated environmental justice as a central life issue.

The pope's determination to rescue Catholic identity from a narrowly defined agenda has energized a new generation of bishops. Bishop Robert McElroy of San Diego has argued persuasively that the church's engagement with politics needs to change. "Both the substance and methodology of Pope Francis's teachings on the rights of the poor have enormous implications for the culture and politics of the United States and for the church in this country," Bishop McElroy has written. "These teachings demand a transformation of the existing Catholic political conversation." This is still not the prevailing perspective in an American episcopacy largely shaped by the lengthy papacy of John Paul II and the eight-year tenure of his former doctrine chief Pope Emeritus Benedict XVI. The bishops' conference is shifting in the Francis era, but lay staff and episcopal leaders who seem skittish of the pope's call for "a new balance" in how the church articulates moral teachings still control the levers of influence. A letter sent to Pope Francis from the former director of the doctrine committee at the bishops' conference is instructive in understanding the resistance the pope faces as he prioritizes a pastoral theology of accompaniment and discernment. Father Thomas Weinandy, a member of the Vatican's International Theological Commission, accused the pope of fostering "chronic confusion" in his teachings, "demeaning" the importance of doctrine, and causing faithful Catholics to "lose confidence in their Supreme Shepherd." The priest's biggest complaint is with Pope Francis's document on family life, *Amoris laetitia*, which has sparked blowback from some conservative Catholic leaders for its reflections on divorced and remarried Catholics. While the pope did not make wholesale changes to church teaching that prohibits divorced and remarried Catholics from receiving communion until they get an annulment, he encouraged clergy to discern situations on a case-by-case basis. "To teach with such an intentional lack of clarity inevitably risks sinning against the Holy Spirit, the Spirit of truth," Father Weinandy wrote with startling audacity. After years of leading with a political strategy disproportionately focused on abortion and same-sex marriage, the emergence of a theological resistance movement inside the church aimed at Pope Francis, and wide-scale clergy sexual abuse cases back in the headlines, Catholic bishops face a crisis of credibility when it comes to influencing the consciences of Catholic voters.

A Poor Church for the Poor

Authority and teaching influence can't simply be assumed, especially when it comes to young Catholics and millennials. Bishops and other clergy must earn their credibility in a diverse and distracted public square where institutions from government to churches are viewed with increasing skepticism. The hierarchy in the United States also faces a particular challenge to build a "poor church for the poor" because a wealthy church situated at the axis of global capitalism includes influential Catholics who make an idol of free-market ideologies and often put corporate power before labor rights. A 2018 conference hosted by the business school at the Catholic University of America in Washington underscores that reality. The wife of billionaire industrialist Charles Koch, former Republican presidential candidate Carly Fiorina, and prominent free-market champion Arthur Brooks of the American

Enterprise Institute headlined the $2,000-a-ticket "Principled Entre-preneurship and Dignity of Work" meeting. The conference was only the latest in a series of elite gatherings coordinated by the university's business school in partnership with the Napa Institute, a network that attracts Catholic philanthropists on the right, business leaders, conserva-tive bishops, and some Republican Catholic politicians. The cozy rela-tionship between Catholic University—a Vatican-chartered institution with bishops on the board—and the nation's most influential funders of the conservative political movement underscores the influence of wealth and power in the American church. The university's business school has received more than $14 million from the Charles Koch Foundation over the past five years, a curious wellspring of resources given that the Kochs' vast conservative political networks and front-groups promote libertarian policy goals that stand in stark contrast to traditional Catho-lic social teaching on labor, the role of government, and the environ-ment. The university's business school is named after Timothy Busch, an Orange County, California, attorney who owns several luxury resorts and Trinitas Cellars, which sells an eighty-dollar bottle of Cabernet named after Pope Francis (Cabernet FRANCis). The megadonor to various Catholic causes gave the university $15 million, its largest ever donation, in 2016. Busch, who is also cofounder and chairman of the board at the Napa Institute, holds political views that are firmly in sync with the Koch brothers, whom he has praised as influencing his business philosophy. Busch, honored in 2016 by the Pontifical North American College, the U.S. bishops' seminary in Rome, has called the minimum wage an "anti-market regulation that leads to unemployment." Along with the Napa Institute, he hosted a $1,250-a-ticket meeting at the Trump International Hotel in Washington advertised as a "an exclusive gathering of 'Catholic leaders, clergy, and important DC insiders.'" At the 2017 event, there wasn't any mention of the Kochs' well-funded attacks on public sector unions or Republican efforts to pass "right-to-work" legislation that the U.S. bishops' conference strongly opposes. Instead, Busch and other Catholics assembled at the gathering, which attracted former Republican Senator Rick Santorum and Supreme Court Justice Samuel Alito, consistently praised President Trump as the most "pro-life" president in history. The meeting also mixed tra-ditional Catholic religious practices with moments that were inappro-priately nationalistic. The event opened with a "Patriotic Rosary for the Consecration of our Nation" that included readings from George

Washington and John Adams. Another reading in the rosary booklet came from Confederate General Robert E. Lee and appealed to God "in the defense of our homes and our liberties, thanking Him for His past blessings, and imploring their continuance upon our cause and our people." It was stunningly insensitive at best to mix up Lee and the Southern cause with the Holy Rosary, especially at a time when President Trump has emboldened the "alt-right," and white nationalists are basking in the glow of renewed attention and proximity to power. The news that Trump's former chief strategist Steve Bannon—a Catholic who espouses anti-immigrant policies and advises right-wing politicians across Europe—is collaborating with Cardinal Raymond Burke to create a curriculum at the *Dignitatis Humanae* Institute outside of Rome underscores the danger of Christian nationalism finding a home inside the church.

Conclusion

The myriad challenges Catholic leaders must confront both inside the church and in the public square require a willingness to discern new paths that might bring opportunity and renewal from the depths of crisis. A church rooted in the *via crucis* is a church that knows pain and failure and, transformed by God's grace, leads us out of the darkness. This opportunity for rebirth and reform will only happen if those in the hierarchy still clinging to clerical privilege renounce spiritual worldliness, look to the peripheries, and listen as much as instruct. Perhaps in that humbled place church leaders will find wisdom from below and begin to discover a voice that can lead and inspire a new generation of Catholics.

Questions for Further Reflection

1. What does the author mean by the phrase "nostalgia voters"? Who is he referring to? What could some of the nostalgic values of these voters be?

2. When a politician says, "Maybe hate is what we need if we're gonna get something done," what is your response? Can a Christian ever endorse such an approach to politics? Why or why not?

3. Do you think an appeal to racial and ethnic fears and prejudice is offensive to any genuinely Catholic sensibility? Can a Catholic ever vote for a politician who makes such appeals? What if that politician is running against a candidate who is stridently in favor of abortion rights?

4. Can a Catholic conscientiously vote for a candidate who stokes racial and ethnic divisions in the hope that he/she will change once in office? Would that hope be a sufficient moral justification to ignore the candidate's hate-mongering? What, if anything, could justify a Catholic voting for such a candidate?

5. The United States has set a cap of admitting thirty thousand refugees a year to our country. Does the United States have a moral obligation to accept refugees from strife-ridden parts of the world? Does your answer change if the United States is responsible for the strife that created the refugees to begin with? What are a nation's obligations to those around the world seeking a place of refuge? What are a Catholic voter's obligations to such people?

6. Does the rise of an authoritarian demagogue, who boasted about brutalizing women, who apparently, but narrowly, won the white Catholic vote in the United States mean that our bishops have failed to properly form the consciences of their people? Is that even the bishops' job? What about the bishops who tacitly endorsed such a candidate because he was antiabortion? Do they have any moral culpability in the suffering wreaked upon refugees, families at the border, or minority groups once this person is in office? Why or why not?

7. Were you aware of the statements of Cardinal O'Connor and Cardinal Law in favor of the 1984 reelection of President Reagan because he was antiabortion? Do you think it's the hierarchy's job to make such public judgments? When you hear a bishop or a cardinal giving such a political endorsement, what is its effect on you? Does it make you more or less likely to vote for the hierarchically endorsed candidate? Why?

8. What do you think of the tactics of Catholic bishops who announce publicly that they would deny communion to a Catholic politician who fails to support the church's position on abortion? Do we vote for Catholic politicians so that they can put the various positions of the church into law?

9. Do you agree with Archbishop Emeritus John Quinn's assessment that the bishops got something wrong in their condemnation of President Obama? What does Archbishop Quinn think that they got wrong? What effect does Archbishop Quinn think this will have on the bishops' ability to teach? Do you agree or disagree? Why?

10. What is the author referring to when he speaks of "prudential judgment"? Is this a term that you are familiar with? What does it mean? How does the author think that prudential judgment works when Catholics are making political choices?

11. What does the author mean by "damage done by pro-life advocates who seem willing to sell out the integrity of Catholic teaching for political advantage"? What sort of damage is this? What effect does the author think it will have on the bishops' overall teaching ability?

12. How does the teaching of Pope Francis change the perspective of single-issue political engagement by Catholics? Has the pope's perspective affected the American bishops' political statements in any way? What are the arguments of those opposed to the pope's perspective? Do you find these arguments credible? Why or why not? Has the pope's perspective affected the way you see political issues in any way? If so, how?

13. Do you think that focusing on single issue politics affects the bishops' credibility? What happens to the church in the United States if our bishops lack credibility? Besides single-issue politics, do you think our bishops have done anything else to weaken the teaching voice of the church in the United States? In your opinion, are these issues connected in any way?

14. What does the author say has been the effect of wealthy right-wing Catholics on the American church? Should people be able to buy influence in our church with their money? Do you think that money can change the church's teachings or will it only affect what emphasis is given to some teachings versus others? Can you think of any examples to back up your answer? Why would a bishop listen to a

rich person over a poor person? Do you think that American bishops ever have extended conversations with poor persons? Do you think that American bishops ever have extended conversations with wealthy persons? Explain your reasons.

15. Can the bishops, in good conscience and good faith, ally themselves with the political agenda of wealthy donors to the church? Should there be such a thing as a "patriotic rosary"?

PART V

How Our Bishops Teach

14

An Informed Laity

Understanding the Church's Political and Legal Advocacy

Angela C. Carmella

Introduction

Thoughtful lay Catholics who seek guidance on how faith shapes an understanding of the common good and, in turn, how civic acts like voting can be consistent with their faith and conscience have numerous resources to consider. They might consult *Forming Consciences for Faithful Citizenship* (2015), published by the United States Conference of Catholic Bishops, which provides a moral framework, complete with categories and priorities, for approaching a wide array of public policy issues during election season. Additionally, they might consider information posted on the USCCB website regarding political action or religious liberty, as well as statements of a particular bishop made in connection with various political, economic, and social issues.

In order to reflect critically on these and similar resources, lay Catholics must first understand the ways in which the church itself has been a political and a legal actor in the public sphere, as well as the impacts of that activism. This is essential for contextualizing the statements on civic responsibility. At the moment, immigration reform is a high priority for church leaders.[1] But for decades, bishops, individually and collectively, have thrust the institutional church into active public advocacy in legislatures and courts on a few key issues: opposing abortion and same-sex marriage and demanding autonomy for Catholic entities to maintain moral standards and at the same time to avoid liability from sex abuse suits. This "life-marriage-religious liberty" activism[2] has had real consequences for political discourse. Surely, some of it has kept ethical issues concerning the sanctity of life at play in the health-care context.[3] But as moral theologian David Hollenbach, SJ, and ethicist Thomas Shannon have noted, this advocacy has fed the political polarization that impedes efforts to address urgent matters of the common good.[4] Further, as others have noted, it has contributed to the mistaken notion that religion in the political realm aligns exclusively with conservative causes[5] and that law is capable of making society "moral."[6] Moreover, the advocacy has compromised the church's public witness on the full range of moral-political matters essential to a just society. The prominence of some moral matters—highly visible disputes over contraception, for instance—creates an inaccurate impression of church priorities, with a younger generation unaware of the church's efforts on poverty, racism, and workers' rights.[7] Finally, the advocacy creates tension between harsh public adversarial positions and merciful and compassionate pastoral ministry.[8]

Indeed, the church's intense public activism on a narrow set of issues leaves lay Catholics ill-equipped to bring their faith to other issues central to the common good. And guidance on voting only reinforces the imbalance. While *Faithful Citizenship* describes a broad range of moral concerns, spanning the liberal-conservative divide as Catholic moral and social teachings must, it nevertheless instructs voters that pro-choice or pro-gay marriage candidates are presumptively unqualified unless there are "truly grave moral reasons" to vote otherwise (*Faithful Citizenship* 35, hereinafter *FC*). How, then, to engage and wrestle with issues of poverty, health care, workers' rights, immigration reform, national security, racial tensions, and the environment? How to address other pressing assaults on human dignity and the common good—the corrosive nature of political discourse; the disruptive aspects of technology and social media; distortions caused by monied groups in politics and litigation; pervasive racism and tribalism; the proliferation of weapons; violence against women; the widening gap between rich and poor; the crisis of mental illness and addiction; decaying public infrastructure;

failed energy policies; and the now-common natural disasters related to climate change? Catholics are thus susceptible to the agendas set by the political parties or other "thought influencers," even though, as the bishops have noted, citizens "should be guided more by our moral convictions than by our attachment to a political party or interest group" (*FC* 14).

The church's unrelenting sex abuse scandals further reinforce the need to reflect independently and broadly beyond *Faithful Citizenship* and similar resources. Because of this "moral catastrophe,"[9] the bishops' prophetic authority in the political realm has weakened. Yet lay Catholics continue to have civic responsibilities and are capable of drawing on the church's rich and broad intellectual tradition of justice and the common good in order to directly engage the political and policy issues of the day.

Political and Legal Advocacy Opposing Abortion and Same-Sex Marriage

The church has spoken out on many moral issues of social, cultural, political, and economic import. A delegation of bishops visited the border in the summer of 2018 to witness to family unity when families were being separated and children detained in cages. Indeed, a glimpse of the USCCB's website reveals numerous policy statements and letters to political leaders on a wide variety of issues that span the current political divide—issues that mirror the church's many ministries. Like other religious institutions in the United States, the USCCB and other Catholic entities frequently weigh in on moral issues; the First Amendment's Free Speech and Free Exercise Clauses protect this. Indeed, the church's own teachings urge this type of engagement. The *Declaration on Religious Freedom*, issued in 1965 during the Second Vatican Council, calls for precisely such involvement:

> Religious bodies have the right not to be hindered in their public teaching and witness to their faith, whether by the spoken or by the written word....In addition, it comes within the meaning of religious freedom that religious bodies should not be prohibited from freely undertaking to show *the special*

279

value of their doctrine in what concerns the organization of society and the inspiration of the whole of human activity."[10]

Despite the impressive breadth and sophistication of the bishops' concerns, the church's moral-political agenda since the 1970s has centered on efforts to oppose abortion and, for the last twenty years, to oppose the recognition of same-sex unions, both defined as intrinsic evils.[11] The bishops have been involved in efforts to restrict abortion and same-sex marriage through a variety of direct and indirect forms of political and law-related activity.[12]

With this advocacy, the church has placed itself squarely within a coalition of conservative religious organizations, especially those sponsored by Evangelical Protestants, in the "culture wars." It has also focused primarily on *legal* reform. Surely, interfaith cooperation on common causes is not new, but the overtly partisan approach of the Evangelicals sets an adversarial tone. And while the Catholic desire runs deep for harmony among the eternal law, moral law, and civil law, church teaching has long recognized the limits of law and the criteria for the legitimacy of law: that it be enforceable and effective, promote justice and reflect prudence, and benefit the common good.[13] In this connection, civil law is not capable of abolishing all that is immoral in society. Simply criminalizing abortion and sodomy will not end abortions or same-sex relations. Further, overturning Supreme Court decisions that allow abortion and same-sex marriage will only return the question to the states. Yet, despite these obvious limitations, church leaders have persistently sought legal solutions to moral issues.

LOBBYING TO END OR PREVENT LEGALIZED ABORTION AND SAME-SEX MARRIAGE

State laws against contraceptives and abortions began to erode in the 1960s. With the Supreme Court striking the prohibition on the use and sale of contraceptives in 1965,[14] the church did not fight to reverse this. Church leadership heeded the advice of theologian and public philosopher John Courtney Murray, SJ, the primary architect of the *Declaration on Religious Freedom*. In 1966, he concluded that contraception was not a legitimate topic for public regulation: civil law should not "prescribe everything that is morally right and…forbid everything that is morally wrong."[15] Instead, civil law protects public morality while private morality is "left to the personal conscience," as a matter of religious freedom in a pluralistic society.[16] Murray wrote,

> It may be argued that contraception raises an issue of public morality because it has public consequences—an effect on the birth rate, on family morality, on the rise of hedonism, etc. On the other hand, it does not seem that these public consequences can be controlled by law. It further seems that the effort at legal control results in other social evils— contempt for the law (already widespread), religious strife within the community, etc.[17]

Then Murray, the champion of religious liberty for Catholics in a pluralistic society, concluded that "the authority of the Church declares the moral law—that contraception is contrary to the moral law. But the authority of the Church does not decide what the civil law should be. This decision rests with the civil community, its jurists and legislators."[18]

Abortion was a different matter, as it involves an unborn child. The bishops actively opposed state efforts to liberalize abortion laws.[19] Then, after the Supreme Court's 1973 decision in *Roe v. Wade*,[20] the USCCB and Catholic conferences at the state level mobilized to overturn it.[21] USCCB supported the ultimately unsuccessful "Human Life Amendment" to the federal Constitution, and filed amicus briefs, on its own or with other religious organizations, in every abortion case at the Supreme Court since *Roe*.[22] Along with other pro-life organizations, they have supported state and federal restrictions on abortions ever since. While courts have overturned many of those efforts, they have upheld others, such as waiting periods, counseling requirements, and restrictions based on fetal age.[23] Further, the Hyde Amendment has banned federal Medicaid coverage of abortion for forty years. This stance is so intense that the bishops have refused even to support laws consistent with church teaching because of a remote possibility that those laws would be used to promote abortions. The USCCB did not support passage of the Religious Freedom Restoration Act of 1993 (RFRA), which protects religious claimants from certain types of burdensome regulations, because the text of the legislation did not explicitly prevent religious claims to an abortion right. Similarly, the bishops—the most prominent voices calling for universal health care for decades—did not support the Affordable Care Act because they were concerned that abortion funding might follow, despite President Obama's 2010 Executive Order to the contrary. It is not surprising that NARAL Pro-Choice America called the USCCB and the National Right to Life Committee its two main opponents.[24]

The church's message on abortion vis-à-vis Catholic politicians and Catholic voters weighs heavily toward pro-life activism. In the past, some bishops denied the Eucharist to pro-choice politicians and urged the laity to favor pro-life candidates. *Faithful Citizenship* reflects a somewhat more moderated view, noting that Catholics "may reasonably decide to vote for [a pro-choice] candidate for other morally grave reasons. Voting in this way would be permissible only for truly grave moral reasons, not to advance narrow interests or partisan preferences or to ignore a fundamentally moral evil" (*FC* 35). Nonetheless, "a voter may legitimately disqualify a [pro-choice] candidate from receiving support" (*FC* 42) even if that candidate, if elected, will have little or no actual effect on abortion-specific laws.[25]

The bishops have also been involved in political and legal advocacy at the federal and state level in support of traditional marriage and in opposition to the civil recognition of domestic unions and same-sex marriage. They contended that government has a legitimate interest in relationships that produce children, in having those children raised by a mother and father, and in preventing the erosion of the traditional family and the attendant societal decay. Despite the passage of the federal Defense of Marriage Act (DOMA) in 1996, change was rapid. Within twenty years, the Supreme Court found sodomy laws and DOMA unconstitutional and, with the decision in *Obergefell v. Hodges*, determined that same-sex couples have a fundamental right to marry.[26] While the USCCB had supported DOMA (as well as the "Marriage Amendment" to the federal constitution) and had filed amicus briefs in favor of traditional marriage,[27] the Catholic-Evangelical coalition was unable to prevent same-sex marriage from achieving legal status.

Efforts at the state level were responsible for this erosion of traditional marriage.[28] First came the recognition of domestic partnerships. Then states began to recognize same-sex marriage after 2000. By 2015, eighteen states had legalized it. State Catholic conferences opposed these efforts and supported repeal of laws where same-sex marriage had been recognized. Further, they supported efforts in about thirty states to amend state constitutions to define traditional marriage. Many of these succeeded, but federal district courts found them unconstitutional. The Catholic-Mormon coalition supporting California's Proposition 8 (defining traditional marriage) involved the church in a bitter political and legal fight.

As with abortion, *Faithful Citizenship* categorizes a policy of "redefining marriage to deny its essential meaning" as an intrinsic evil. And as with abortion, a Catholic is told she may vote for a candidate who supports same-sex marriage "for other morally grave reasons" (*FC* 35). Again, as with abortion, a voter may "legitimately disqualify [such] a candidate from receiving support" (*FC* 42), even though that candidate, if elected, may have little authority to affect same-sex marriage.

LOBBYING AND LITIGATING FOR EXEMPTIONS

At the moment, the bishops' pro-life and pro-family vision of the common good has not prevailed in law. Religious groups that fail to persuade legislatures and courts of their vision often avail themselves of another type of advocacy: demanding exemptions to ensure that they themselves are not complicit in the evils that they oppose. Exemptions are either legislatively granted or court mandated, if they are recognized at all. On matters of abortion and same-sex marriage, the church thus claims protection for all its related entities—schools, hospitals, social service agencies, and the like—to operate without complicity in the evils of the dominant culture.

Shortly after *Roe*, Congress in 1974 passed the first "conscience clause" to protect health-care professionals and entities that refused to provide abortions and sterilizations.[29] The exemption came in response to a court-ordered sterilization at a Catholic hospital. Over the years, the bishops have successfully advocated for federal conscience protection, which ensures the moral autonomy necessary for Catholic hospitals and physician training programs to comply with the church's *Ethical and Religious Directives* on health care.[30] Forty-four states have also enacted conscience clauses to allow abortion refusals, usually providing that the objector will not suffer any penalty, discrimination, or liability due to the refusal.[31] Some states also include sterilization refusals; a few include contraception.

Conscience exemptions become important in the post-*Obergefell* world where there is new attention to LGBT discrimination and recognition of same-sex marriage. The USCCB amicus brief in *Obergefell* voiced concerns over the potential stigma of bigotry and the possibility of having to affirm same-sex marriage "as a condition of…receiving government contracts, participating in public programs, or being eligible for tax exemption."[32] This concern was not purely academic: Catholic Charities adoption agencies in some states have had to surrender licenses because they refused to place children with same-sex couples; even the Solicitor General caused great alarm among churches when he acknowledged during oral argument "that tax exemptions of some religious institutions would be in question if they opposed same-sex marriage."[33] *Obergefell* itself was unclear about how traditionalists would be protected; it noted only that churches must be free to teach their faith. But the recent decision in *Masterpiece Cakeshop*, in which a baker who refused on religious grounds to make a cake for a same-sex wedding, held government action unconstitutional if it exhibits hostility toward traditional beliefs about marriage.[34]

To ensure far-reaching protection, the USCCB supports the federal First Amendment Defense Act (FADA), which has been introduced in Congress.[35] It provides that no person (including for-profit and nonprofit entities) will suffer penalties for acting in accordance with the traditional beliefs regarding marriage. If passed, Catholic entities could not be denied federal benefits, funding, or licensing, and would be protected in their tax-exempt status. Catholic agencies would be free to refuse any services bishops deemed cooperation with evil, such as marital and family counseling or housing assistance. But the more realistic strategy has been to seek legislative exemptions on one item at a time, as in the adoption arena. Nine states now exempt agencies like Catholic Charities from discrimination laws when they refuse to place children with same-sex couples.[36]

Ratcheting Up the Call for Religious Liberty: More on Autonomy and Conscientious Objection

The church has used the First Amendment and related statutes to call for exemptions well beyond the topics of abortion and same-sex marriage. Beginning in the 1990s, bishops fought to protect the autonomy of their internal operations and the church's financial assets from increasing numbers of tort suits brought over the failed super-vision of abusive priests.[37] Bishops, as heads of dioceses, invoked the First Amendment to defend against claims of negligent supervision. That defense, which argued against state scrutiny of internal church decisions, succeeded in some places. In time, however, courts in most states have rejected any such notion of autonomy or immunity and have allowed cases to proceed against church institutions. As a direct and indirect result, about $3 billion have been paid to victims and twenty dioceses and orders have filed for bankruptcy or otherwise set aside funds for victims.[38] Under the specter of increased scrutiny from state governments, the USCCB in 2002 passed the *Charter for the Protection of Children and Young People* and commissioned an independent study, which noted the widespread nature of the problem. Indeed, even now the parameters of the crisis continue to widen. Catholic conferences at the state level continue to lobby against so-called windows legislation—laws that lift the statutes of limitation on sex abuse claims, spending millions of dollars on this effort.[39] They have been successful in some states, but the tide may turn against them, given the recent wave of revelations of the Pennsylvania grand jury and of unprecedented revelations of semi-narian victims. The bishops, together with the global church leadership, now understand the scope and depth of the crisis and are beginning to respond. Of course, had the church's initial claims to constitutional immunity from tort action been widely successful, it is unlikely that comprehensive reform efforts would have been contemplated.

In the same period, the church also vigorously challenged state requirements to provide contraceptive insurance coverage to employ-ees, which had been mandated by women's health equity laws passed in the late 1990s. New York and California exempted churches and their close affiliates but did not exempt religiously affiliated educational, health care, and social service entities. Catholic Charities agencies of the Albany and Sacramento dioceses argued unsuccessfully that the First Amendment required the states to expand the religious employer exemption to include these types of religious nonprofits.[40] The loss meant that they provided the coverage under protest.[41]

It is against this background of failed constitutional claims that the church sounded its 2012 rallying cry for religious liberty. In 2011, the federal Department of Health and Human Services (HHS), led by Kathleen Sibelius—who had been denied communion while governor of Kansas because of her pro-choice stance—issued draft regulations for implementation of the Affordable Care Act. One provision required employers to provide insurance coverage for contraceptive and sterilization services at no cost to the employee; four of the twenty contraceptives on the list were considered to have abortifacient potential.[42] The regulation provided a narrow religious employer exemption for churches and their close affiliates; like the New York and California state law counterparts, this exemption did not include religious nonprofits like universities, hospitals, and social service agencies.[43]

Catholic and Evangelical Protestant outrage was immediate and sustained. After considerable public comment through administrative law channels, the Obama Administration offered the religious nonprofits an "accommodation."[44] This compromise did not extend the exemption to universities, hospitals, or service agencies. Instead, under the accommodation, any entity objecting to providing the coverage was required to notify the government, which then shifted the obligation to the insurers or third-party administrators. Employees would still receive the coverage, just not from the objecting entity. Bishops found this unacceptable. Rather than view it as "remote or indirect material cooperation,"[45] which would have allowed Catholic entities to participate, church plaintiffs insisted that the accommodation still required them to play an "integral role in the regulatory scheme" of providing the coverage.[46] They objected to "facilitating" the contraceptive coverage by providing a notice and by maintaining an insurance contract with the insurer that would provide it.[47] In this way compliance with the accommodation would have "ramifications [that] are eternal."[48]

In response to this regulation, the USCCB created the Ad Hoc Committee for Religious Liberty. It proclaimed that the HHS contraception mandate was an attack on religious liberty, conscripting Catholic individuals and institutions into the service of advancing secularism and denying them the right to conscientiously object to the cooperation with evil. The Committee acted with great speed, issuing *Our First, Most Cherished Liberty: A Statement on Religious Liberty*, in April 2012.[49] Citing Martin Luther King Jr.'s *Letter from Birmingham Jail*, the bishops called the contraception mandate an unjust law, which is "no law at all. It cannot be obeyed." The document listed other assaults on religious liberty, including the closure of adoption agencies that refused to place children with same-sex couples; the loss of a government contract because the Obama administration insisted the contractors provide contraception to victims of human trafficking; and state immigration laws passed in

2011 that characterized some types of pastoral care as the harboring of undocumented immigrants. Viewing such laws as assaults on the extensive public ministries of the church and ostracism of religious voices from contributing to the common good, the Committee wrote, "Restrictions on religious liberty are an attack on civil society and the American genius for voluntary associations."

In the document, the bishops urged one another to be "the 'conscience of the state,' to use Rev. King's words." They propose a "special 'fortnight for freedom,' in which bishops…arrange special events to highlight the importance of defending our first freedom" and invited all to join "in an urgent prayer for religious liberty." *Commonweal*'s editors, who thought the statement "vastly exaggerates the extent to which American freedoms of all sorts and of religious freedom in particular are threatened," worried that "the tenor of the bishops' statement runs the risk of making this into a partisan issue during a presidential election in which the leaders of one party have made outlandish claims about a war on religion or a war against the Catholic church."[50]

Litigation exploded, with about one hundred cases filed, many of which involved Catholic family-owned businesses (challenging the mandate) and Catholic entities (challenging the accommodation).[51] The USCCB actively supported the plaintiffs' quest for a full exemption under RFRA with robust *amicus* participation, not without some irony, given the fact that the bishops had withheld support of RFRA decades earlier due to concerns that women would use it to gain the right to an abortion.[52] Businesses prevailed in *Burwell v. Hobby Lobby Stores, Inc.*[53] The nonprofit victory was less clear given that the merits of the claims were not reached.[54] But the contraception "mandate" is now optional under the Trump administration. The full-court press challenge to the HHS rule had proved an enormous victory for the church. One hundred cases further solidified that "religious liberty" meant protection of conservative causes, a mantle taken up by President Trump, who has actively pursued (through executive orders and administrative rulings/exemptions) a broad pro-life protection of conscience. Indeed, the Trump administration supports a more comprehensive enforcement of federal conscience protection, a more robust involvement of faith-based organizations, and exemptions from compliance with antidiscrimination protections based on sexual orientation.[55]

In 2017, the USCCB converted the Ad Hoc Committee on Religious Liberty to permanent status. Bishops were concerned not only with the continuing need for exemptions in the face of pressures relating to abortion and LGBT matters,[56] but also with a more general decay in respect for religious liberty. The USCCB website now features a "Call to Prayer" for members that echoes precisely its political and legal advocacy: life, marriage, and religious liberty.[57] It is instructive to note that law professor Douglas Laycock, champion of religious freedom for his entire career, most articulate defender of the church autonomy doctrine, and primary drafter of RFRA, has attributed this loss of respect for religious liberty to the culture wars: "Persistent Catholic opposition to the French Revolution permanently turned France to a very narrow view of religious liberty; persistent religious opposition to the Sexual Revolution [by conservative churches] may be having similar consequences here."[58] Throughout the culture wars, groups on both sides have tried to prevent the liberty of the other side. He has urged a cease-fire, advising pro-choice and pro-gay rights groups to focus on securing their own rights and advising religious groups to focus on protecting their own liberty.

Lay Catholics as Citizens: Considering the Limits of Law and the Common Good

John Courtney Murray, SJ, stressed that the religious protections of the First Amendment were intended to be "not articles of faith but articles of peace."[59] He wrote, they "have no religious content. They answer none of the eternal human questions....Therefore they are not invested with the sanctity that attaches to dogma, but only with the rationality that attaches to law."[60] The Religion Clauses were born of "social necessity"—to ensure a social environment in which people of different faiths "might live together in peace."[61] Murray knew that to achieve peace within America's pluralism, governance would have to rest on the diverse views of citizens and religious groups.

Catholic teaching holds that civil law, while critical for life in common, has its limits. In general, it must be enforceable and effective; it must promote justice and reflect prudence; and it must benefit the common good.[62] As described earlier in the contraception context, Murray knew the limits of civil law, especially with respect to establishing a moral society. "Catholic moral tradition has long stressed that civil law should be founded on moral values. But it also stresses that civil law need not seek to abolish all immoral activities in society."[63] Indeed, Murray scoffed at efforts in the nineteenth century to make illegal all that was immoral, and he noted in particular that "efforts to promote virtue in sexual matters through civil coercion are particularly unlikely to succeed."[64] Echoing Aquinas and recognizing America's pluralism and the religious freedom of citizens and groups who differ on moral matters, Murray argued that civil law may promote only *public* morality—on which there is consensus—which is tied to the common good of the whole of society.

In Catholic thought, all civil society—every person, every group, and every institution—is tasked with promoting the common good. Government promotes the common good in a particular way, through law, by ensuring the public order: comprised not only of public morality but also the rights of citizens and the civic peace. These three pillars serve as the fundamental framework, as Hollenbach and Shannon note, "that protects the most basic prerequisites of social life." While church leadership—together with many religious conservatives—have argued that abortion and same-sex marriage threaten social life, and therefore warrant a legal solution, many other citizens disagree. The resulting polarization in political and legal discourse has impeded efforts to promote the common good, which is "the overriding standard of both social morality and civil law in the Catholic tradition."[65]

As the bishops focus renewed attention on the immigration crisis in America, perhaps a different balance of moral-political advocacy will begin to emerge. Perhaps some nonlegal avenues for addressing the vast array of moral concerns will be explored. And perhaps new energy will be dedicated to a robust commitment to the common good in a social environment in which citizens of differing views, in Murray's words, "might live together in peace." Lay Catholics who understand the institutional church's advocacy and its impacts will be essential to those efforts.

NOTES

1. Christopher White, "U.S. Bishops Head to Border to Protest Trump Immigration Policy," *Crux*, June 29, 2018. Available at https://cruxnow.com/church-in-the-usa/2018/06/u-s-bishops-head-to-border-to-protest-trump-immigration-policy/.

2. This triad has become prominent in the church's description of moral-political issues, see United States Conference of Catholic Bishops, Call to Prayer. Available at http://www.usccb.org/issues-and-action/take-action -now/call-to-prayer/index.cfm (accessed January 3, 2020).

3. Edge of life issues include abortion, contraception, sterilization, assisted reproduction, embryonic stem cell research, euthanasia, physician-assisted suicide, and the death penalty. Angela C. Carmella, "When Businesses Refuse to Serve for Religious Reasons: Drawing Lines between 'Participation' and 'Endorsement' in Claims of Moral Complicity" (Newark, NJ: Rutgers Univ. Law. Rev. 1593 [2017]), 69.

4. David Hollenbach and Thomas Shannon, "A Balancing Act: Catholic Teaching on the Church's Rights and the Rights of All," *America*, March 5, 2012. Available at https://www.americamagazine.org/politics-society/2012/03/05/balancing-act-catholic-teaching-churchs-rights-and-rights-all (hereinafter, "A Balancing Act").

5. Interview with E. J. Dionne, "Shopping Period: Religion and America's Political Conscience," *Harvard Divinity School News*, September 6, 2018. Available at https://hds.harvard.edu/news/2018/09/06/ej-dionne -religion-and-americas-political-conscience# (hereinafter "Interview with E. J. Dionne").

6. Gregory A. Kalscheur, "Moral Limits on Morals Legislation: Lessons for U.S. Constitutional Law from the Declaration on Religious Freedom," *So. Cal. Interdisc. L. J.* 16 (2006): 1.

7. "I grew up in a time when one of the most powerful public expressions of religion was the Civil Rights Movement. Martin Luther King, Jr.'s book *Strength to Love* had an enormous impact on the way that I saw the world, and it was clearly the case that King used the gospels, the Old Testament prophets, and America's founding documents to make a case for reform and equality. In that era, other religious thinkers such as Reinhold Niebuhr and Paul Tillich got on the cover of *Time* magazine, which, in its day, was a pretty good test of presence in the mainstream of the culture. But for the last 30 years, and probably even more so in the last 15 years, religion in the public mind has been almost entirely associated with the political right, and with issues like gay marriage and abortion. This is probably saying it in a bit of an extreme way, but the public conversation in the United States has gone from Niebuhr to Falwell. And that's a very different public voice for religion, and that is a major reason why some young people look at religion and walk away." Interview with E. J. Dionne. Note, too, that Catholics were heavily involved in the Civil Rights Movement and, along with Niebuhr and Tillich, Catholic theologian and public philosopher John Courtney Murray, SJ, discussed below, also appeared on the cover of *Time*.

8. Fr. James Martin, *Building a Bridge: How the Catholic Church and the LGBT Community Can Enter into a Relationship of Respect, Compassion, and Sensitivity* (San Francisco: HarperOne, 2017).

9. Sharon Otterman and Elisabetta Povoledo, "Vatican Calls Abuses by Pennsylvania Priests 'Criminal and Morally Reprehensible,'" *New York Times*, August 16, 2018 (quoting Cardinal DiNardo). Available at https://www.nytimes.com/2018/08/16/us/catholic-church-abuse-vatican-statement.html.

10. Vatican II, Declaration on Religious Freedom (*Dignitatis humanae*), §4, (hereinafter Declaration; my emphasis), available at http://www.vatican.va/archive/hist_councils/ii_vatican_council/documents/vat-ii_decl_19651207_dignitatis-humanae_en.html.

11. Euthanasia is also mentioned as part of the church's commitment to life "from conception to natural death," but no states permit this. Physician assisted suicide, which is also considered an intrinsic evil, is permitted in a number of states.

12. William V. D'Antonio, "Catholic Bishops and the Electoral Process in American Politics," in *Voting and Holiness: Catholic Perspectives on Political Participation*, ed. Nicholas P. Cafardi, (Mahwah, NJ: Paulist Press, 2012).

13. Cathleen Kaveny, *Law's Virtues: Fostering Autonomy and Solidarity in American Society* (Washington, DC: Georgetown University Press, 2012), 225–36. Hereafter, *Law's Virtues*.

14. *Griswold v. Conn.*, 381 U.S. 479 (1965).

15. John Courtney Murray, "Memo to Cardinal Cushing on Contraception Legislation," in *Bridging the Secular and Sacred: Selected Writings of John Courtney Murray, SJ*, ed. Leon Hooper (Washington, DC: Georgetown University Press, 1995), 82.

16. Murray, *Bridging the Secular and Sacred*, 82.

17. Murray, *Bridging the Secular and Sacred*, 83.

18. Murray, *Bridging the Secular and Sacred*, 85.

19. Linda Greenhouse and Reva B. Siegel, *Before* Roe v. Wade*: Voices That Shaped the Abortion Debate before the Supreme Court's Ruling* (New Haven: Yale Law School, 2012), 282.

20. 410 U.S. 113 (1973).

21. Jesse Ryan Loffler, "Catholicpac: Why the United States Catholic Conference of Bishops Should (Probably) Lose Its 501(c)(3) Tax Exempt Status," *Rutgers J. L & Rel.* 14 (2012): 69, 129 [hereinafter, "Catholicpac"].

22. Angela C. Carmella, "Catholic Institutions in Court: The Religion Clauses and Political-Legal Compromise," *W.Va. L. Rev.* 120, no. 1 (2017): 318 (citing briefs) [hereinafter "Catholic Institutions"].

23. "Counseling and Waiting Periods for Abortion," Guttmacher Institute, https://www.guttmacher.org/state-policy/explore/counseling-and

-waiting-periods-abortion (accessed January 3, 2020); "State Bans on Abortion throughout Pregnancy," Guttmacher Institute, https://www.guttmacher.org/state-policy/explore/state-policies-later-abortions (accessed January 3, 2020).

24. Loffler, "Catholicpac," 129–30.

25. Elected officials could have an impact on the social conditions that affect women's decisions to have an abortion. "Even though the overall abortion rate has declined in the past three decades, it has risen by 18% among poor women. Catholic voters might conclude that the Democratic platform of social and economic aid could help alleviate the conditions that are motivating poor women to seek abortion in the first place.

Even though a particular candidate might want abortion to remain legal, this candidate might also support policies to lessen hunger and homelessness, improve education and healthcare, and strengthen the economy....A Catholic is not obligated to ignore the vast majority of a candidate's political platform and public behavior and vote solely based on whether he or she wants to criminalize abortion—especially if there's good reason to believe that said candidate doesn't have the ability (or the intention) to do anything of the sort." Fr. Paul Keller, "Can a Catholic Vote for a Democrat? Moral Considerations," *U.S. Catholic*, Blogpost March 11, 2016, https://www.uscatholic.org/blog/201603/can-catholic-vote-democrat-moral-considerations-30587.

26. 135 S. Ct. 2584, 2604–5 (2015).

27. Carmella, "Catholic Institutions," nos. 325, 326, 330, 333 (citing briefs); Loffler, "Catholicpac," 123.

28. See generally, Carmella, "Catholic Institutions," 61–62; Loffler, "Catholicpac," 121–25.

29. No hospital could be required to "make its facilities available for the performance of any sterilization procedure or abortion if the performance of such procedure or abortion in such facilities is prohibited by the entity on the basis of religious beliefs or moral convictions." 42 U.S.C. § 300a–7(b)(2). See also *Chrisman v. Sisters of St. Joseph of Peace*, 506 F.2d 308 (9th Cir. 1974) (district court lacked power to compel sterilization procedure).

30. United States Conference of Catholic Bishops, *Ethical and Religious Directives for Catholic Health Care Services*, 6th ed. (2018).

31. Angela C. Carmella, "For-Profit v. Non-Profit: Does Corporate Form Matter? The Question of For-Profit Eligibility for Religious Exemptions under Conscience Statutes and the First Amendment," in *Symposium Proceedings: Is a For-Profit Structure a Viable Alternative for Catholic Health Care Ministry*, ed. Kathleen M. Boozang (2012), 77–80.

32. Brief for U.S. Conference of Catholic Bishops as Amicus Curiae Supporting Respondents, *Obergefell v. Hodges*, 135 S. Ct. 2584 (2015) (Nos. 14-556, 14-562, 14-571, 14-574), 2015 WL 1519042, *23–27.

33. *Obergefell*, 135 S. Ct. 2584, 2626 (2015) (Roberts, C.J., dissenting).

34. *Masterpiece Cakeshop v. Colo. Civil Rights Comm.*, 138 S. Ct. 1719 (2018).

35. United States Conference of Catholic Bishops, "U.S. Catholic Bishops Conference Chairmen Urge Support for the 'First Amendment Defense Act,'" March 14, 2018. Available at http://www.usccb.org/news/2018/18-050.cfm.

36. Lawrence Hurley, "Gay Adoption Fight Looms after U.S. Supreme Court's Cake Ruling," *Reuters*, June 5, 2018. Available at https://www.reuters.com/article/usa-court-baker-adoption/rpt-gay-adoption-fight-looms-after-us-supreme-courts-cake-ruling-idUSL2N1T61PY.

37. Angela C. Carmella, "The Protection of Children and Young People: Catholic and Constitutional Visions of Responsible Freedom," *B.C. Law Rev.* 44 (2003): 1031; Carmella, "Catholic Institutions," 43–54.

38. "Catholic Dioceses and Orders That Filed for Bankruptcy and Other Major Settlements," *National Catholic Reporter*, May 31, 2018. Available at https://www.ncronline.org/news/accountability/catholic-dioceses-and-orders-filed-bankruptcy-and-other-major-settlements. See also the Reconciliation and Compensation Program for Victim-Survivors of Abuse of the New York Archdiocese, described at https://archny.org/ircp (accessed January 3, 2020).

39. Dan Levin, "Why the Explosive Report on Catholic Church Abuse Is Unlikely to Yield Criminal Charges," *New York Times* (August 15, 2018). Available at https://www.nytimes.com/2018/08/15/us/pennsylvania-sex-abuse-statute-of-limitations.html; Kenneth Lovett, "Exclusive: Catholic Church Spent $2M on Major N.Y. Lobbying Firms to Block Child-Sex Law Reform," *New York Daily News* (May 30, 2016). Available at http://www.nydailynews.com/news/politics/catholic-church-hired-lobby-firms-block-n-y-kid-rape-laws-article-1.2655010#.

40. *Catholic Charities of Diocese of Albany v. Serio*, 859 N.E.2d 459 (N.Y. 2006); *Catholic Charities of Sacramento, Inc. v. Superior Court*, 85 P.3d 67 (Cal. 2004).

41. See Sharon Otterman, "Archdiocese Pays for Health Plan That Covers Birth Control," *New York Times* (May 26, 2013). Available at http://www.nytimes.com/2013/05/27/nyregion/new-york-archdiocese-reluctantly-paying-for-birth-control.html.

42. *Burwell v. Hobby Lobby Stores, Inc.*, 134 S. Ct. 2751, 2762–63 (2014).

43. *Burwell*, 134 S. Ct. at 2763, discussing 45 C.F.R. § 147.131(a). See also Julie Rovner, "Rules Requiring Contraceptive Coverage Have Been in Force for Years," *NPR* (February 10, 2012). Available at http://www.npr.org/sections/health-shots/2012/02/10/146662285/rules-requiring-contraceptive-coverage-have-been-in-force-for-years.

44. Carmella, "Catholic Institutions," 83.

45. Hollenbach and Shannon, *A Balancing Act*.

46. Brief for Petitioners at 51, *Zubik v. Burwell*, 136 S. Ct. 1557 (2016) (Nos. 14–1418, 14–1453 & 14–1505), 2016 WL 93988 at *51.

47. *Id.*

48. *Id.*, 43 (quoting from a bishop's affidavit).

49. United States Conference of Catholic Bishops Ad Hoc Committee for Religious Liberty, "Our First, Most Cherished Liberty: A Statement on Religious Liberty," April 12, 2012. Available at http://www.usccb.org/issues -and-action/religious-liberty/our-first-most-cherished-liberty.cfm.

50. Editors, "Religious Freedom and the U.S. Catholic Bishops," *Commonweal*, April 12, 2012. Available at https://www.commonwealmagazine .org/religious-freedom-us-catholic-bishops.

51. For lists of cases, see https://www.becketlaw.org/research-central/ hhs-info-central/hhs-case-database/ (accessed January 3, 2020).

52. Douglas Laycock, "Religious Liberty and the Culture Wars," 2014 U. Ill. L. Rev. 839, 853 (2014) [hereinafter, "Culture Wars"].

53. *Burwell v. Hobby Lobby Stores, Inc.*, 134 S. Ct. 2751 (2014).

54. *Zubik v. Burwell*, 136 S. Ct. 1557 (2016).

55. White House Statement, "President Donald J. Trump Stands Up for Religious Freedom in the United States," accessed January 3, 2020, https:// www.whitehouse.gov/briefings-statements/president-donald-j-trump-stands -religious-freedom-united-states/ (summarizing protective measures during presidency).

56. Carmella, "Catholic Institutions," 70–76, 87–88 (describing efforts to promote the following: abortions as part of emergency services; gender transition services as part of health-care nondiscrimination; health insurance coverage for abortions, gender transition, and assisted reproduction).

57. United States Conference of Catholic Bishops, Call to Prayer, available at http://www.usccb.org/issues-and-action/take-action-now/call-to -prayer/index.cfm. "The U.S. bishops invite the faithful to join a movement of prayer and sacrifice for the protection of life, marriage, and religious liberty in our country. Serious threats to each of these have raised unprecedented challenges to the church and the nation. When confronted with challenges, our Lord calls us to sacrifice and pray. Follow the links below to learn more about how you can answer the Call."

58. Laycock, *Culture Wars*, 839, 865.

59. John Courtney Murray, *We Hold These Truths: Catholic Reflections on the American Proposition* (Lanham, MD: Rowan & Littlefield, 2005), 62.

60. *Id.*

61. *Id.*, 69.

62. Kaveny, *Law's Virtues*, 225–36.

63. Hollenbach and Shannon, *A Balancing Act*.

64. Hollenbach and Shannon, *A Balancing Act*.

65. Hollenbach and Shannon, *A Balancing Act*. ("Action that threatens the common good should be taken only when the justification for the action is entirely clear.")

Questions for Further Reflection

1. What does the author mean by the "life-marriage-religious liberty" activism of the American bishops and what have its consequences been for political discourse in our nation? What have its effects been on young people? What have its effects been on the teachings of the church?

2. What does the author say is the "moral catastrophe" of *Faithful Citizenship*?

3. How does the author say that the American bishops have been politically active in efforts to restrict abortion and same-sex marriage? What allies have the bishops sought in these activities?

4. Can the law abolish what is immoral in society? Should it even try? Are legal solutions the best response to moral issues?

5. What was John Courtney Murray's position on challenges to laws that prohibited the sale of contraceptive devices or medicines in the 1960s? What did he think the position of the bishops should be on these laws? What was his reasoning? Do you agree or disagree with Murray's position? Could you imagine a law today prohibiting the sale of contraceptive devices or medicines? How likely is it that such a law would be followed? What does this tell you about the difficulty of legislating morality?

6. The author says that abortion is a different moral issue than contraception. How? What is the Human Life Amendment? What is the Hyde Amendment? What is the Religious Freedom Restoration Act? What positions did the bishops take on each of these? Why?

7. According to the bishops, can Catholics vote for pro-choice candidates in good conscience? Why or why not?

8. What has been the bishops' role in opposing the legalization of same-sex marriage? What was their legal strategy? What other religious groups did the bishops link up with in their fight? What position does *Faithful Citizenship* take on "redefining" marriage? Should the bishops care about how the state defines civil marriage? Can Catholics support same-sex marriage laws in good conscience?

9. The bishops have fought for exemptions against recognizing the right to an abortion or the right to same-sex marriage for Catholic institutions and Catholic individuals. What have these efforts been and how successful have they been? Do you agree with this strategy? Why or why not?

10. The bishops have also argued against state scrutiny of internal church decisions in their defense of lawsuits for clergy sexual abuse of children. Do you agree with this strategy? Do you see this as a matter of religious liberty?

11. With the passage of the Affordable Care Act (sometimes called "Obamacare") most employers (excluding churches and their close affiliates) must provide contraceptive coverage to their female employees as a matter of normal preventive health care. Many church-related organizations, such as Catholic nursing homes, fought this requirement. Why? What accommodation did the government offer to them? Why was this accommodation rejected? Do you agree with this strategy? Why or why not?

12. What is the bishops' Committee for Religious Liberty? Why was it formed? What document has it published? How has its approach been broadened in recent years? Do you think this is something that the bishops should be doing? Why or why not?

13. Would a fair topic for the bishops' Committee for Religious Liberty be to address the unfair treatment of the predominantly Catholic migrant and refugees attempting to cross our southern border? Has this committee ever dealt with that issue?

14. As an American Catholic, do you believe that your civil rights are under threat by any laws or actions of the government? Explain.

15. What has the Catholic teaching on civil law been? Do Catholics have a moral obligation to try to make civil law conform to Catholic beliefs? Should wanting civil law to reflect Catholic beliefs affect the way Catholics vote?

15

The Transatlantic Catholic Gap

Pope Francis and the U.S. Catholic Church

Massimo Faggioli

Introduction

From the beginning of his pontificate, the Catholic Church in the United States has represented a particularly complex situation for Pope Francis. The ideological polarization of the country does not exempt the Catholic Church. The rift created in the church during the 1970s has become deeper since the mid-eighties, due to a policy of episcopal appointments that, for three decades, favored prelates whose culture and language was considered by the Vatican and by American Catholic power brokers, in Rome and in the United States, as necessary for fighting the "culture wars." During Francis's papacy this rift has become so pervasive to the point of potentially endangering the bond of communion of the church within the United States of America and between the church in the United States and Rome.

The pontificate of Francis, welcomed by liberal Catholics and criticized, if not sometimes openly rejected, by neoconservative and neotraditionalist Catholics, has brought out and revealed the depth of this preexisting rift. The potential honeymoon effect that Francis's visit to the United States of America in September 2015 could have had was neutralized by the shock felt by some U.S. bishops (appointed and promoted by John Paul II and by Benedict XVI) in their synodal experience of October 2015 (the second part of the Synod on the Family opened by the Synod of 2014) and in the post-synodal exhortation, "On Love in the Family," *Amoris laetitia*, published by Francis in April 2016. Additional elements that diminished this potential honeymoon effect were, first, the impact of Donald Trump's rise in the Republican party and the presidential election in November 2016 on the American Catholic Church and on transatlantic relations, and next, the beginning of the second phase of the sex abuse crisis in the spring and summer of 2018.[1]

The peak in this difficult relationship was reached during the unprecedented crisis of the summer of 2018 when, with the allegations made through the press by former nuncio to the United States (2011–16), Archbishop Carlo Maria Viganò, against Pope Francis (indirectly involving also his two predecessors, John Paul II and Benedict XVI) of having neglected the clerical sexual abuse crisis and having covered up the misconduct of (former) Cardinal Theodore McCarrick. These allegations were mixed up with an attempt to present other explosive allegations against individual members of the Vatican and American hierarchy as a moral crusade against homosexuality. Archbishop Carlo Maria Viganò concluded his "testimony" with a request for Pope Francis's resignation. In those tumultuous weeks, a significant portion of the United States episcopate and the Catholic conservative intelligentsia failed to signal their communion with Rome and actually took a public position about Francis's papacy that can be described as evasive and flirting with schism—at least until the truce represented by the audience granted by Francis to the leadership of the USCCB on September 13, 2018.[2]

The complex and dramatic picture of the relationship between the pontificate of Francis and the U.S. Catholic Church, and in particular with its hierarchical leadership, compels the church historian who tries to understand Pope Francis to follow the news cycle with his gaze on church history as a "history of present time"—which presents church historians with methodological challenges that are brought to the fore by the new media environment that Catholicism lives in today. Without writing a chronicle of the relations between Francis and the U.S. episcopate, this essay will attempt to identify four elements that are at the heart of this crucial aspect of Francis's pontificate: (1) the reception of Pope Francis's teaching in the context of an understanding of the historical development of tradition; (2) the different geopolitical views that exist between Francis and U.S. Catholicism about the role of Catholicism and of the United States; (3) a different approach to church politics; and (4) the different views of politics and of the role of government in Catholic social teaching.

Francis and the Continuity-Discontinuity Paradigm—The Reception of Francis's Teaching

The tensions between a majority of U.S. bishops and the minority of U.S. Catholic laity on one side, and Pope Francis on the other, must be understood in the context of the transition, within U.S. Catholic intellectual circles during the last decade, between two different paradigms: from the generation of Catholic neoconservatism of the 1980s–1990s to a younger generation of Catholic journalists and intellectuals that are closer to anti–Vatican II traditionalism than to a legitimate cultural and theological critique of some aspects of the post–Vatican II period. Setting aside here the relevant differences between the political cultures of neoconservatives and of neotraditionalists, this transition from one to another kind of theological conservatism is an important factor for understanding the resistance against—or simple disregard for—Pope Francis's teaching that is visible among some U.S. bishops. The transition from neoconservatism to neotraditionalism is not limited to intellectual circles, but one could argue that it has found an audience in the milieu composed by part of the U.S. episcopate, by some U.S. Catholic clergy, intellectual, and academic circles, and by some seminaries for the formation of priests.

If Catholic neoconservatism in the 1980s and 1990s had limited itself to contesting "the spirit of Vatican II" by identifying it with theological and political liberalism, during the pontificate of Benedict XVI, the second generation of anti-conciliar *revanche* assumed the traits of neotraditionalism: from the delegitimization of the event or the spirit of Vatican II, to the delegitimization of the Council itself.[3] For some Catholics, liturgical traditionalism was only the beginning of a larger movement trying to bracket or even expel Vatican II from the Catholic tradition.

This transition to neotraditionalism has one of its roots in U.S. conservatives' lack of nuance, and in some cases extremism, in the interpretation of Pope Benedict XVI's speech of December 22, 2005, on the hermeneutics of the Second Vatican Council.[4] In that famous and most consequential speech, Benedict XVI sought to find a middle ground between the classic traditionalism of the Lefebvrite schism of the Society of St. Pius X, which sees in Vatican II "the French Revolution" and a rupture in the Catholic Church, and the postmodernist antitraditionalism, which sees Vatican II as the last council of a never-ending Catholic medievalism. But in the clerical hierarchies of U.S. Catholicism, this *via media Ratzingeriana* really never took root: despite its best intentions, Pope Benedict XVI's speech helped Catholic neo-traditionalism to prosper in the United States. The neglect of parts of postconciliar progressive Catholicism in the United States to claim Vatican II as part of a tradition dynamically understood has inadvertently let Vatican II fall into traditionalist language on the subject: this helped pave the way for the traditionalists' seizure of the language of "tradition" in an anti–Vatican II fashion.

This has had huge consequences for Francis's pontificate in the United States, but also for some issues particularly sensitive in U.S. Catholicism, such as the development of Catholic teaching on Jews and Judaism, on religious freedom and freedom of conscience that had been approved by Vatican II, confirmed, and further developed by all popes of the post–Vatican II period. More and more, neotraditionalist Catholics in the United States have come to the conclusion that the Catholic magisterial tradition developed at Vatican II is not authentic Catholic teaching. One revealing episode of a deep fault line within U.S. Catholicism about the theology of Vatican II, and about one of its most critical developments, that is, the theology of the relations between Judaism and the church, was the "Cessario case" at the beginning of 2018.[5]

This debate on the interpretation of Vatican II has never been purely theoretical. For the political culture of the U.S. bishops, one must note that among the consequences of this rejection of the theology of Vatican II there is also the revisionist interpretation of the conciliar and postconciliar magisterium on social and political issues (for example, on social and economic justice), which is one factor in the revival of Catholic antiliberalism in the United States: political liberalism is identified with an alleged liberalism of the documents of Vatican II, and both political liberalism and the alleged liberalism of Vatican II are associated with and blamed for failed globalization and failed multiculturalism.

The consequences of this new wave of traditionalism with respect to Vatican II have been important for the relationship between conservative Catholicism and Pope Francis, who speaks—albeit often indirectly and in a way mediated through the documents of the post–Vatican II magisterium (especially that of Paul VI)—the language of Vatican II.[6] There is a set of particular issues that puts Pope Francis's fidelity to Vatican II in tension with the theological culture of the U.S. bishops. The first is that of the magisterium on *moral-theological issues*. Francis has tried since the beginning of his pontificate to encourage a truce between the church's ideological factions, especially on "life issues" and "sexual morality," key issues for the self-understanding of Catholicism in the United States. Francis is an anti-ideological Catholic who has made no secret of wanting to disarm the assumptions of the "culture wars." This was immediately perceived, as early as the summer of 2013, by some bishops as incompatible with the challenges of the church in the United States.[7] Some American bishops have repeatedly declared in public their discomfort for a pope who is changing the parameters of the relationship between the magisterium of the church and issues of sexual morality. During the most significant initiative of Pope Francis in terms of collegiality in the church on the issue of family and marriage, that is, the Bishops' Synods of October 2014 and October 2015, the majority of the U.S. bishops gathered in Rome for the synodal debates were clearly part of the "synodal minority," skeptical about Francis's attempt for a new, more pastoral language on "irregular situations."[8] The same phenomenon was unmistakable during the preparation of the Bishops' Synod on Youth, held in October 2018.[9]

No less problematic is the perception of the *social and political message* of Pope Francis. The cultural and theological background of the Jesuit pope must be looked at in Father Bergoglio, who witnessed of the fruits of the Cold War in the outskirts of the world far from the northern hemisphere, and of Bishop Bergoglio, ordinary of Buenos Aires during the Argentine default and the economic depression of 2001–2002. The centers of formation and expression of Catholic free-market

301

and libertarian thought in the United States made no secret of considering Pope Francis's teaching in social and economic matters incompatible with American capitalism.[10] Looking at the work of the USCCB since 2013, it is clear that the U.S. bishops as a whole have not received Francis's theological view of social and political priorities.

The parallel, rarely convergent courses between the USCCB and Francis should not be identified with the outright rejection of this pontificate by some conservative and traditionalist circles in the U.S. church. One example is Francis's decision to amend the *Catechism* about the death penalty, announced on August 2, 2018, with the appeal launched by a group of seventy-five Catholic intellectuals (the vast majority of them U.S.-based) to the cardinals and published on August 15, 2018, against Pope Francis's change in the *Catechism*.[11] The U.S. bishops have not identified with these critiques of Pope Francis's teaching on the economy and on the death penalty; one could actually make the argument that the activism of the U.S. Catholic Church on the death penalty since the time of John Paul II is one of the factors that made that change by Pope Francis in the *Catechism* possible in 2018. On the other hand, the U.S. bishops' lukewarm reception of some teaching (for example, the encyclical *Laudato si'* [2015] on the care of creation and the environment) must be seen in the context of a theological-political complex in the United States—made up not only of the bishops, but also by a powerful and wealthy elite of Catholic laity—that is distant from Francis's theological view of social and political issues.

Two Different Americas: Conflicting Geopolitical Views

The relationship between Francis, the United States, and the Americas, from both the geopolitical and the geo-religious point of view, is one of the keys to interpret Francis's mind.[12] A geopolitical analysis of Pope Francis is essential for relativizing the usual framing of this pontificate within the narrow scope of "right vs. left" or "conservative-traditionalist vs. liberal-progressive" categories. The geopolitics of Pope Francis contain some clear challenges for U.S. Christianity's geopolitical sense of self, which is linked to a set of ideas about the role of the United States in global history. Francis called his global look at the world a "Magellan's gaze," which invites us to look at the center from the periphery: this constitutes a challenge for all the geopolitical atlases of Americans, U.S. Catholics included.[13]

Pope Francis has placed his pontificate and the Roman papacy in a new position with respect both to the global political scene and to the universality of the Catholic Church in the global world, thanks to an inculturation of the papacy that goes well beyond the logistical and most visible aspects such as, for example, the choice to live in a hotel for the clergy in the Vatican (Santa Marta) and not in the papal apartment. From this point of view, the election of Donald Trump to the presidency of the United States in November 2016 helped clarify a misunderstanding often part of the narrative about Francis on the other side of the Atlantic, namely that Pope Francis would be a "pan-American pope," an expression of the whole American continent from Alaska to la Tierra del Fuego, and for this reason supposed to have better relations with U.S. Catholicism than his predecessors did.[14] Even without entering into the question of the complex relations between different cultural and national identities within Latin and South America and the specificities of Argentina within Latin America, it is evident that both Trump's and Pope Francis's leadership speak of a continent crossed by tensions, which makes it more difficult, from a religious and Catholic point of view, to speak about pan-Americanism.

There are a few elements that are necessary to understand the relationship between the geopolitical vision of Francis and Catholicism in the United States today. The first element is that of a "Catholic Pangea" in movement: the global pontificate of Francis is characterized not only by the effort to decentralize the Roman Catholic Church, but also by the decentralization of other "centers" of gravity in the church—including North America and U.S. Catholicism—one from the other. The image of the "Catholic Pangea" describes the redefinition of distances and trajectories in relations between the different geographical components of the Catholic *orbis* in their cultural, political, theological, and spiritual components. With respect to this, the pontificate of Francis places him at the service of and listening to the global church. But the same attempt by Francis to redefine the idea of the "center" of Catholicism has a great impact on a church, like the one in the United States, which thinks of itself as the center of the world—consciously or unconsciously, both in its conservative component (with its agenda of reaction against theological liberalism, against the pluralization of

the religious world, against secularization) and in the progressive component (with its agenda of universalization of same-sex marriage, of a
feminist theology of women's empowerment, of the theologization of
identity politics). In other words, the fracture that became more evident
within U.S. Catholicism during the pontificate of Francis is not just a
North American problem in its relationship with Rome: it is the most
visible fracture among the many fractures or fault lines in the globalization of Catholicism.[15]

A second element is that of a pontificate that has an insight on the
parallels and the convergences between the trajectories of the church
and the world, according to the ecclesiology of the pastoral constitution
Gaudium et spes of the Second Vatican Council. The pontificate of Francis
contradicts some recent tendencies of Catholic ecclesiology in the
United States, especially those attempts to brand the option of a radical
retreat from the public scene in order to found neo-monastic Christian
communities in which to rebuild small majority universes, away from
contemporary cultural and religious moral pluralism, in an acknowl-
edgment of the epochal defeat suffered by conservative Christianity in
the "culture wars" from the 1970s to today. On the one hand, from the
beginning of his pontificate, Francis proposed a far wider agenda than
that of "culture wars" on the theology and teaching on sexuality; on the
other hand, the Vatican II ecclesiology of Francis rejects any form of
medieval political Augustinianism, which presupposes a superior and a
legitimizing role of the church with respect to secular politics and the
secular state. The rejection of "the Benedict Option" by intellectual
Catholic circles in the Rome of Francis is a revealing element in the
relationship between U.S. Catholicism and this pontificate.[16]

A third element of tension between the worldview of Francis and
that of the United States and of some U.S. Catholics lies in the theological and social reflection about the epochal crisis of migrants and refugees. There is no question that on the issue of migrants and refugees
there is little difference, and actually a visible convergence, between the
positions of the U.S. bishops and Francis, except for the implications
of the kind of support tacitly given by some bishops to Donald Trump
in the elections of 2016. But there are deep and subtle cultural differences. For Francis as a priest and a Jesuit, the church and the world are
in a process of global "resettlement." If the U.S. imagination is that of
a world for settlers and of a nation settled by Christians, for Francis it is a
world for resettlers, for the displaced: in Francis's moral imagination, the

language of "dialogue" is more important than "identity." The acceptance of migrants and refugees for Francis also means the acceptance of some other kinds of "migrations" (cultural, theological, and moral) in the church and in the public square, with important consequences on the framing of other theological and "public" issues, such as the meaning of "religious liberty" in a multicultural and multireligious world.

The fourth element of tension has to do with a radical difference between the North American and the Latin American religious world in their relationship with the urban and megacity worlds in respect to the suburban and rural world. Francis speaks of the world as a global city, in which God and faith live in a complex and multifaceted, multicultural and multireligious environment, traversed by secular and composite identities.[17] The social and religious imagination of Francis is essentially urban, cosmopolitan, secular, and pluralist. If in the American imagination the city assumes the identity of a place of alienation between faith and life, Pope Francis sees the urbanization of religious life as a challenge and an opportunity for the church. This is one of the factors in the crisis of the ethos of citizenship in Catholic culture, at risk of falling into the image of the church as a village or a monastery to be defended from pluralism and the secular.

Finally, there is a long-term element of geopolitical and geo-religious change that Pope Francis embodies. The pope from Argentina, who decided to arrive in Washington, DC, via Cuba during his visit to the United States in September 2015, represents a reference to the demographic and cultural future of the United States, with the end of the control of Anglo-European whites in the U.S. Catholic Church. In a United States now grappling with the geopolitical shift from an Atlantic to a Pacific axis, the Vatican must be credited with an understanding of the global world that the American establishment seems to ignore or deny. The Vatican mediation, thanks to Pope Francis, between the United States and Cuba in the year 2014, and the provisional agreement between the Vatican and the People's Republic of China announced in September 2018, reminded the centers of American power of the resilience of papal "soft power" even in a secularized world.

Francis's geopolitical challenge to U.S. Catholicism and to the U.S. bishops' worldview must be seen in the context of other geopolitical shifts. Both Pope Francis and Donald Trump have helped to make the Atlantic wider and the United States and Europe more distant from one another. From the point of view of the cultural and institutional history of Catholicism, the relationship between the Roman Catholic Church in the United States and Europe, Italy, and the Vatican has always been revelatory of the profound movements within this immigrant religion (especially from Europe, from Latin America, from Asia).[18] In the United States of Donald Trump, Roman Catholicism still proposes itself as a form of internationalism that no longer finds an important interlocutor in the American presidency. On the other hand, the support offered by some Catholics (including some bishops) to the Trump presidency is one way to create a distance from the internationalism of the Catholic Church's social doctrine, starting in the first half of the twentieth century to Vatican II to the postconciliar magisterium.

A Shift in the Politics of the U.S. Catholic Church—A Different Approach

Pope Francis's pontificate did not mean only a challenge to the theological and geopolitical views of the U.S. Catholic Church that is represented by its bishops, but also—and much more tangibly—a shift in the politics of the church. Francis inverted some of the tendencies that had become normative for the shaping and maintaining of a certain balance of power in the U.S. episcopate.

This is not just a consequence of Francis's pontificate, but also of a more general shift in the alignments between Rome and the United States. The alignments between John Paul II and Ronald Reagan and between Benedict XVI and George W. Bush, for example, were an expression of a United States and of a Catholic Church significantly different from the ones in the relationship between Francis and Obama between March 2013 and November 2016, and between Francis and Trump after the elections of November 2016. The election of John Paul II had created a particular kind of political and cultural alignment between the papacy, the U.S. episcopate, and the United States as a country. This alignment survived in a different context during the time of Benedict XVI, and it underwent a metamorphosis in the sense of a growing rift within the U.S. church between a majority of the hierarchy close to the culture of neoconservatives and neotraditionalists and a majority of the laity close to a theological and political culture that could be called liberal-progressive.

With the persistence of this intra-ecclesial U.S. Catholic rift, some of the political dynamics of the rift changed between 2013 and 2016, with the election of Pope Francis and, three years later, of Donald Trump to the U.S. presidency. Pope Francis's pontificate coincided and in part contributed to the transformation of a transatlantic ecclesial bond, between the papacy and American Catholicism, in the sense that neoconservative and neotraditionalist voices within the U.S. episcopate no longer found a papacy that shared and inspired their postliberal or antiliberal theological culture.

This transatlantic tension within Catholicism that developed under Francis must be seen in the context of other shifts. On the one hand, there was the preexisting alignment of part of the U.S. episcopate with the Republican Party created by the "life issues" at first; on the other hand, there is the political and ideological trajectory of the Republican Party that part of the U.S. episcopate has followed especially during the years of the Obama administration. This growing identification between the political views of the U.S. episcopate and the Republican party has played a major role in the rift between the Vatican and the U.S. Catholic Church since the election of Pope Francis.

Much more could be said about the chronological overlap between the end of the Obama presidency and the beginning of Francis's pontificate and the way the U.S. bishops interacted with both Obama and Francis. What can be said here is that the tensions between the USCCB and the Obama presidency can be seen also as a *political* prelude to the *ecclesial* reaction of the U.S. bishops to the election of Pope Francis. If the Obama presidency was for many bishops and the leadership of the American bishops' conference a period of struggle against the assault of secular liberalism on the religious freedom of the Catholic Church in America, the pontificate of Francis is perceived by important centers of thought as a pontificate culturally and politically unfit to understand the extent of the challenges posed by liberalism and secularism to Christianity and Catholicism in the United States.

On this point, we cannot underestimate the rise in these last few years of the role of conservative Catholic media based in the United States—a media system that is an expression of the culture of wealthy Catholic donors whose political networks and agenda have been on the opposite side of Pope Francis's social and political message. It is a media system in which some of the U.S. bishops have a role, in the sense that media outlets like EWTN, for example, cannot really be considered an "independent" Catholic news organization, but rather a semiofficial voice expressing the views of some important U.S. bishops.

This alienation between the papacy in Rome and hierarchical Catholicism in America has consequences on both sides of the Atlantic. Compared to the period of John Paul II and Benedict XVI, the voice and presence of American Catholicism in Rome has been ostensibly reduced by Francis: a decline in the prominence of the voice of American prelates in key personnel appointments (especially bishops' appointments and cardinals), and in the management of particular dossiers (such as the two different doctrinal investigations of American religious women that were initiated by the Roman curia during the pontificate of Benedict XVI and brought to a conclusion by Francis in 2015). Francis's pontificate has paused the growth of American conservative Catholicism in Rome, which increased significantly under John Paul II and Benedict XVI. The departure or reassignment of influential American cardinals in Rome (especially Cardinal Raymond Burke with his removal from the position of Prefect of the Apostolic Signatura in the Roman curia in 2014) is an example of this shift.[19]

Different Political Theologies— Politics and the Role of Government in Catholic Social Teaching

An important gap between Francis and the U.S. episcopate exists in terms of political philosophy and theology. While Francis is rooted in the theology of Vatican II and especially in the ecclesiology of "the church in the world" from the pastoral constitution *Gaudium et spes*, in these last few decades the U.S. bishops as a group have grown distant from this pastoral constitution of the Council. The reception of *Gaudium et spes* in the United States has been interrupted.[20]

Francis is the first post–Vatican II pope. This has caused a gap in theological references between Francis and the U.S. bishops, which is an important element in the difference between Bergoglio and clerical culture in the United States today, where the "culture wars" have created a particularly negative memory of the post–Vatican II period. So, too, Ratzinger-Benedict XVI's *lectio* of the pastoral constitution, *Gaudium et spes*, represents a substantial challenge for Catholics of the strict "continuity vs. discontinuity" mindset.[21] One novelty of *Gaudium et spes* is the inclusion of the social realm not as an issue *ad extra*, but as one with ecclesiological consequences within the Catholic Church. The pastoral dimension of the Council's teaching is framed in *Gaudium et spes* through the theological assumption of the history of humankind and of the world in which *Gaudium et spes* operates: there is a new relevance for a theology of the world *ad extra*, including the secular, that is not part of the shared theological culture in the United States.

The place of "the secular" in *Gaudium et spes* is one of the problems for its reception in the current American ecclesial and ecclesiological context, in which the relations between religion and politics in the United States are substantially different from the relations between religion and politics in the culture of those who drafted this pastoral constitution between 1964 and 1965. But it is not just a difference of context, but of fundamentally different understandings of the role of religion. There is clearly a transatlantic "God gap" between America and Europe.[22] But there is also something like a transatlantic "City of God gap" between America and the political culture of Vatican II.[23] The Augustinianism of "radical orthodoxy" comes from the incompatibility of their political theology with the post-Augustinian and post-Christendom political ecclesiology of Vatican II: "Vatican II, which quotes Augustine abundantly, managed to liberate the church from 'political Augustinianism' thanks to *Gaudium et spes* and *Dignitatis humanae* on religious liberty....The revolution of Thomas Aquinas and Albert the Great had already produced theologically a decisive break in the system of political Augustinianism."[24]

Pope Francis's philosophy and theology of politics and of the state is at odds with the view of politics shaped by the Catholic reception of the culture wars in the United States. The conservative clerical opposition to Francis in the United States is expressed through a "political" criticism of the pope's message on mercy and discernment, on economic and social inequalities and injustices. It is a more complex and deeper gap than the usual "liberal vs. conservative." Francis's rejection of neo-Constantinianism and of the view of Catholicism as a refuge for the neoconservative and neotraditionalist ideologies is rooted in a much different understanding of the role of religion and of the church in secular modernity and in the "earthly city" than many American bishops and conservative American Catholics have.

Conclusions—Pope Francis, the U.S. Church, and the Disruption of Global Catholicism

From the beginning of his pontificate, there has been a complicated relationship between the U.S. episcopate and the Jesuit pope from Argentina. But nobody would have predicted that in the summer of 2018 the reverberations of the clerical sexual abuse crisis would lead some representatives of the U.S. episcopate close to a rupture of their bond of communion with the Bishop of Rome.

This part of the story of Francis's pontificate is important not only for U.S. Catholicism. The relations between Francis and the U.S. bishops have become an integral part of the global picture of the Catholic Church, not just for those who want to understand American Catholicism, but also for those who want to understand the papacy. It is no secret that the most important centers of the political and theological opposition to the papacy of Francis are symbolically and physically located in the United States. The opposition to Francis has been the attempt to resist a new course for the Catholic Church. But it should be clear that the tensions within American Catholicism about Francis have little to do with the reception of one particular point of papal teaching, for example: *Amoris laetitia* on marriage and family, or on the death penalty. The tension is about the awareness that the election of Francis has signaled—more than caused—a crisis in the theological and political paradigm shaped in U.S. Catholicism by the previous two popes.

The relationship between the U.S. episcopate and the papacy of Francis is larger than a simply national issue (concerning the United States only) and concerning this particular period only (Francis's pontificate). Rather it will play an important role in the future of Catholicism because it is a complex relationship that has to do not with two different cultural and theological individualities, but with the larger picture of different tectonic plates moving in different directions in the Pangea of Catholic globalization: the North American plate and the Roman papacy. What happens after Francis in U.S. Catholicism will tell us whether the strong alignment between Rome and the United States in the second half of the twentieth century was an exception. Certainly, the tense relationship between the U.S. episcopate and the Bishop of

Rome under Francis's pontificate has been exceptionally difficult by modern church history standards. It remains to be seen if this tense relationship will become part of the transatlantic Catholic relations for the next pontificate and the next decades, and if it is one of the signs of a Roman Catholic Church where the role of Bishop of Rome will be remodeled and redefined also because of the assertiveness of local episcopates.

NOTES

1. About this, see Massimo Faggioli, *Liminal Papacy: Francis on the Threshold of Global Catholicity* (Maryknoll, NY: Orbis, 2019).

2. For some journalistically accurate chronicles of those tumultuous weeks between August and September 2018, see, for example, Brian Roewe, "Who Is Archbishop Carlo Maria Viganò?," *National Catholic Reporter*, August 28, 2018, https://www.ncronline.org/news/accountability/who-archbishop-carlo-maria-vigano and Joshua McElwee, "US bishops Say Meeting with Francis on Clergy Abuse Was 'Lengthy, Fruitful,'" *National Catholic Reporter*, September 13, 2018, https://www.ncronline.org/news/accountability/us-bishops-say-meeting-francis-clergy-abuse-was-lengthy-fruitful.

3. One recent example of the pushback against the "spirit" of Vatican II that becomes though an accusation against the Council itself is the book *Slaying the "Spirit" of Vatican II with the Light of Truth*, eds. Robert J. Araujo, SJ, and the Bellarmine Forum, foreword by Bishop Thomas J. Paprocki (Hudson, WI: Wanderer Forum Foundation, 2017). This kind of position can be found in intellectual magazines like *First Things*, but also in the Catholic media system that reaches a very wide audience in the United States.

4. For a meticulous analysis of the speech of December 22, 2005, see Joseph A. Komonchak, "Novelty in Continuity. Pope Benedict's Interpretation of Vatican II," *America*, February 2, 2009; Joseph Komonchak, "Benedict XVI and the Interpretation of Vatican II," *Cristianesimo nella Storia* 28, no. 2 (2007): 323–37.

5. The article by Romanus Cessario, OP, published in *First Things* in February 2018, see https://www.firstthings.com/article/2018/02/non-possumus, was a review of the book *Kidnapped by the Vatican? The Unpublished Memoirs of Edgardo Mortara* by Italian journalist Vittorio Messori, in which Cessario praised the behavior of Pope Pius IX and justified the kidnapping of a Jewish boy in Bologna in 1858 (back then, still part of the Papal States) in order to baptize him. Cessario's position caused a significant reaction in mainstream media in the United States and elsewhere; the editor of *First Things*, R. R. Reno, published a clarification of his own personal position a few days later:

"Judaism, Christianity, and *First Things*," accessed January 6, 2020, https://www.firstthings.com/web-exclusives/2018/01/judaism-christianity-and-first-things.

6. See Massimo Faggioli, *A Council for the Global Church: Receiving Vatican II in History* (Minneapolis: Fortress Press, 2015), 329–35; Id., "'Evangelii Gaudium' as an Act of Reception of Vatican II," in *Pope Francis and the Future of Catholicism:* Evangelii Gaudium *and the Papal Agenda*, ed. Gerard Mannion (Cambridge: Cambridge University Press, 2017), 38–54.

7. See John L. Allen Jr., "Right Wing 'Generally Not Happy' with Francis, Chaput Says," *National Catholic Reporter*, July 23, 2013, https://www.ncronline.org/blogs/ncr-today/right-wing-generally-not-happy-francis-chaput-says.

8. Among the thirteen cardinals who signed the letter accusing Pope Francis of manipulation of the Synod's agenda and debates, leaked by the Italian journalist Sandro Magister on October 12, 2015, two were cardinals from the United States (the archbishop of New York, Timothy Dolan, and the archbishop of Galveston-Houston, Daniel DiNardo).

9. For example, Charles J. Chaput, "Thoughts on the 'Instrumentum Laboris,'" *First Things*, September 21, 2018, https://www.firstthings.com/web-exclusives/2018/09/thoughts-on-the-instrumentum-laboris; Charles J. Chaput, "From the Heart of a Young Father," *First Things*, April 18, 2018, https://www.firstthings.com/web-exclusives/2018/04/from-the-heart-of-a-young-father.

10. Just one example is Samuel Gregg, "Does Pope Francis Really Believe That 'Communists Think Like Christians'?" on the Acton Institute website (originally published in the Christian libertarian magazine *The Stream*, November 14, 2016), https://acton.org/pub/commentary/2016/12/07/does-pope-francis-really-believe-communists-think.

11. See "An Appeal to the Cardinals of the Catholic Church," in *First Things*, August 15, 2018, https://www.firstthings.com/web-exclusives/2018/08/an-appeal-to-the-cardinals-of-the-catholic-church; Edward Feser, "The New Catechism Text on the Death Penalty Will Damage the Church," *The Catholic Herald*, August 8, 2018, http://www.catholicherald.co.uk/commentandblogs/2018/08/08/the-new-wording-on-the-death-penalty/.

12. See Massimo Borghesi, *Jorge Mario Bergoglio: Una biografia intellettuale* (Milan: Jaca Book, 2017); English translation: *The Mind of Pope Francis* (Collegeville, MN: Liturgical Press, 2018).

13. See Antonio Spadaro, "Lo sguardo di Magellano. L'Europa, papa Francesco e il premio Carlo Magno," *Civiltà Cattolica* 3983 (2016): 469–79.

14. This is the thesis, for example, of Manlio Graziano, *In Rome We Trust: L'ascesa dei cattolici nella vita politica degli Stati Uniti* (Bologna: Il Mulino, 2016; English translation Stanford University Press, 2017).

15. For a deeper look at the geopolitics of Francis's pontificate, see *Il nuovo mondo di Francesco. Come il Vaticano sta cambiando la politica globale*, ed. Antonio Spadaro (Padua: Marsilio, 2018).

16. It is interesting to note that Rod Dreher's best-selling book *The Benedict Option* (New York: Sentinel, 2017), embraced by important U.S. bishops (such as Charles Chaput and Robert Barron), was negatively reviewed during the author's Italian tour in September 2018 in the pages of the official newspaper of the Holy See, *L'Osservatore Romano*, and a few months earlier, by the Jesuit-run magazine (approved by the Holy See) *Civiltà Cattolica* and by the large-circulation Catholic newspaper owned by the Italian bishops, *L'Avvenire*.

17. See Carlos Maria Galli, *Dio vive in città. Verso una nuova pastorale urbana* (Vatican City: Libreria Editrice Vaticana, 2014); Andrea Riccardi, *Periferie. Crisi e novità per la Chiesa* (Milan: Jaca Book, 2016). English translation: *To the Margins: Pope Francis and the Mission of the Church* (Maryknoll, NY: Orbis, 2018).

18. See Peter R. D'Agostino, *Rome in America: Transnational Catholic Ideology from the Risorgimento to Fascism* (Chapel Hill, NC: University of North Carolina Press, 2004).

19. One important example is the redeployment of Peter Wells, under Benedict XVI "assessor for General Affairs of the Secretariat of State," who in February 2016 was appointed by Pope Francis as nuncio to South Africa. On December 16, 2013, Pope Francis's appointments for the Roman Congregation for the Bishops saw the departure of Cardinal Justin Rigali and the new entry of Cardinal Donald Wuerl.

20. See Massimo Faggioli, *Catholicism and Citizenship: Political Cultures of the Church in the Twenty-First Century* (Collegeville, MN: Liturgical Press, 2017), 94–122.

21. For Joseph Ratzinger's approach to *Gaudium et spes*, see his introduction to the first of the two volumes dedicated to Vatican II, in the series of his complete works: "Vorwort," in *Zur Lehre des Zweiten Vatikanischen Konzils: Formulierung–Vermittlung–Deutung*, Joseph Ratzinger Gesammelte Schriften, vol. 7/1 (Freiburg i.B.: Herder, 2012), 5–9, esp. 6–7.

22. See Thomas Albert Howard, *God and the Atlantic: America, Europe, and the Religious Divide* (New York: Oxford University Press, 2011).

23. One recent example is John Hittinger, "*Gaudium et Spes* and the Importance of Political Philosophy," *Josephinum* 20, no. 2 (Summer/Fall 2013): 279–306, esp. 302–4.

24. Yves Congar, "Église et monde dans la perspective de Vatican II," in *L'Église dans le monde de ce temps*, ed. Yves Congar and Michel Peuchmaurd (Paris: Cerf, 1967), 31.

Questions for Further Reflection

1. The author believes that the appointment of "culture warrior" bishops in decades past threatens the unity of the church in the United States and the unity between Rome and the American church and within the American church. What is a "culture warrior" bishop? Do you think that is a fair or unfair description? Why? Do you agree or disagree that the unity of the American church or its unity with Rome is threatened by them?

2. What effect do you think the clergy child sex abuse crisis has had on this unity?

3. What does the author mean by the "continuity-discontinuity" paradigm? Who are the parties on either side of this paradigm? What effect does the author say that this divide has had on the church in the United States?

4. What is the difference between neoconservatism and neotraditionalism? How did Pope Benedict XVI's speech on the hermeneutics of the Second Vatican Council affect the neotraditionalists in the United States? According to the author, what effect has "misunderstanding" had on the reception of Pope Francis's papacy in the United States?

5. What is the Cessario case? What point about anti-Semitism in the church in the United States is the author trying to make by using it as an example? Do you agree or disagree? Why?

6. The author says that Pope Francis wants to disarm the assumptions of the culture wars. What are these assumptions? Why do you suppose that Pope Francis would want to challenge them? Is this a change in church teaching that Pope Francis is proposing or merely a change in emphasis?

7. The author says that free-market and libertarian Catholics think that Pope Francis's teaching on social and economic justice is incompatible with American capitalism. What are Pope Francis's views on economic and social justice? Do you think they are incompatible with

free-market capitalism? Why or why not? What have the American bishops said about this?

8. What has been the reaction of American Catholics to the change that Pope Francis has made in the *Catechism of the Catholic Church* on the impermissibility of capital punishment? Do you agree or disagree with this change? Explain.

9. What does the author say is Pope Francis's geopolitical view? What has formed this view?

10. What are the five elements that the author says are necessary to understand the relationship between the geopolitical vision of Pope Francis and of U.S. Catholicism today? Explain what the author means by each of these elements. Do you agree or disagree with the author on any or all of these five elements? Explain.

11. The author says that the election of Pope Francis changed the relationship between the U.S. church and American politics. How and why does the author claim this relationship has changed? Do you agree or disagree? He also says that it changed the relationship between the papacy and American Catholics overall. How? Do you agree or not? Why?

12. What does the author say about the rise of conservative Catholic media in the United States? Can media with a blatantly political agenda or purpose call itself Catholic? Who determines whether such media are Catholic or not?

13. The author attributes some of the disconnect between the U.S. Catholic Church/hierarchy and Pope Francis to the failure of the church in the United States to accept the teachings of the Second Vatican Council, particularly *Gaudium et spes* on the value/place of the secular in the church. How does the author articulate this disconnect? Do you think that such a disconnect exists? Why or why not?

Afterword

David Gibson

At a meeting of the U.S. Conference of Catholic Bishops in early June 2019, San Diego Bishop Robert McElroy rose to speak during what seemed like an otherwise perfunctory discussion of *Faithful Citizenship*—perfunctory largely because the USCCB leadership had already decided not to redraft the document to highlight the priorities of Pope Francis, nor to address the more emergent issues of the day. In his brief remarks, however, McElroy still sought to cut to the heart of the political drama facing voters at the ballot box in November 2020, and to make a larger point about what was at stake.

"I feel there are two essential questions that really supersede any specific issue in this election coming up," McElroy told the more than two hundred prelates in a cavernous hotel meeting room in Baltimore. "One is the nature of the sickness in our society politically, and in our culture. And thus I think the primary obligation of a faithful citizen is, before any other issue comes into play, to try to heal and downplay the divisions in our culture."

"And the second thing that comes up," he continued, "is the issue of character."

McElroy is a genial pastor with one of the sharpest minds in the American hierarchy; the latter is an attribute that, along with his clear empathy for the inclusive approach of Pope Francis, doesn't always win him friends among his more conservative brethren. Yet he persisted. McElroy stressed that the issue of character is one "I feel we underattended to" in all the previous iterations of *Faithful Citizenship* and he

317

asked that, at the least, a proposed introductory letter for the 2020 edition would "note the issue of character" and would ask "why people aren't doing what their conscience calls them to do. Character is important in terms of faithful citizenship."

It is, indeed, as the volume you have just read makes clear throughout. That these articles address underlying questions of character is good and important for many reasons. One is that the bishops didn't change *Faithful Citizenship* much at all, despite the ongoing deterioration under President Trump of our civil discourse and civic traditions—the very traditions that make citizenship possible. The bishops in June decided that their introductory letter would consist of just 750 words, hardly enough room to expand on any new issues with much depth or force. They also voted to supplement that letter with four ninety-second videos designed to reflect the teachings of Pope Francis. It's unlikely such videos will go viral.

Of greater import is the reality that the Catholic bishops were meeting under the still-lengthening shadow of the clergy sex abuse scandal. Their agenda in Baltimore was focused on adopting, belatedly, policies aimed at tightening anti-abuse efforts and, for the first time, taking steps to hold themselves accountable for shielding abusers and failing to protect children. Given the nature and scope of the story, the growing global impact of abuse revelations, and the reverberations that led to Pope Francis and back out to the rest of the church, this angle was the almost exclusive focus of the media coverage, when the media covered the meeting at all.

The discussion of *Faithful Citizenship* itself received almost zero coverage. Not that media coverage of the document would have had much impact. Even before the recrudescence of the clergy scandal in the summer of 2018, voters paid little heed to what the bishops said on political issues, and the USCCB's Crusade-level focus on battling gay rights and the Obama administration's contraception policy over the previous decade look irrelevant in the wake of the abuse revelations. The election of Donald Trump, with the critical help of white Catholics in key swing states, thrust the question of character and leadership and national identity to center stage at the very moment when the American hierarchy's credibility was at its ebb. A March 2019 Pew Research survey showed more Catholics than ever were considering leaving the church over the abuse stories, and those who remained were donating less.

Yet the reemergence of the abuse crisis also reignited the push for greater lay involvement in the church, while the impending election of 2020, and the wider political crisis in the country, highlighted the critical role that lay Catholics could, and must, play in redirecting the nation's moral and social life toward the greater good and the common good.

So here is the reality, and the stakes: lay Catholics—not priests, not bishops, not cardinals, not even the pope, but laypeople—now have an opportunity to bear witness to the power and efficacy of our faith not just inside the church but in the political matrix where our actions, for the wider world, will be the most obvious and convincing measure of our belief. The credibility of the bishops is shot. Laymen and women have long said that the church should not be judged solely by its ordained class, and that laypeople should have a greater role. This is their chance. *Faithful Citizenship* is about what Catholic citizens can do as Catholic believers in the United States of America, and the character that Bishop McElroy spoke of is not exclusively about the character of the bishops, or even the character of President Trump, God help us. It is above all about the character of Catholic voters.

Make no mistake about the difficulty of this challenge. As the late Andrew Breitbart, rightwing controversialist and founder of the eponymous news service that continues his corrosive legacy, famously put it, "Politics is downstream of culture."

And religion? Well, it's downstream of politics. "Most Americans choose a political party before choosing whether to join a religious community or how often to attend religious services," writes Michele Margolis, author of *From Politics to the Pews: How Partisanship and the Political Environment Shape Religious Identity.* "Research shows that it's not just that our religious beliefs affect our politics—it's that our politics affect our religious choices. We don't just take cues about politics from our pastors and priests; we take cues about religion from our politicians."

In the case of too many Republicans, the political leaders they look to are Trump and his enablers. Too many Democrats, on the other hand, have been turned off by the right's use, and misuse, of faith, and have abandoned religion and its moral traditions and communal dynamic. Religion becomes politics, and politics becomes religion. That is an injustice to both. A healthy balance ought to be our goal. Unfortunately, the distortion of faith and the vacuum of disaffiliation, combined with malfeasance and nonfeasance by our political class, have created openings for all manner of backward-looking demagoguery and self-indulgent theorizing.

One such example is the resurgence of interest in "integralism," a reactionary longing for old altar-and-throne alliances that would see the State formally support and implement as policies the doctrines of the church, "the church" meaning of course the Catholic Church. This was essentially putting the church at the service of a political platform, and it was the fever dream of rightwing nostalgists like Charles Maurras and *Action Française* of the last century, a project that was decisively condemned by Rome. (Pope Pius XI forced Cardinal Louis Billot, a Jesuit who supported *Action Française*, to resign from the College in 1927, the only cardinal to face such a penalty until our own day and the revelations of the abuse scandal.)

The opposite of the integralist impulse is found in the appeal of the so-called Benedict Option, Rod Dreher's bespoke version of a monastic tradition tailored to the contemporary tastes of a white suburban gated community. Dreher's proposal continues to draw much ink and various iterations and admirers, though there seems to be little chance that such futuristic nostalgia can work in the real world, nor would the Catholic tradition say that it should. Catholics are not just responsible for the sins we commit but also for what we fail to do, and engagement with the world and on behalf of people and our society is a *sine qua non* of being Catholic. A retreat from responsibility is also an encouragement to the growing threat of tribalism.

This clan-based worldview, which is in essence ethnic and racial and religious nationalism dressed up as patriotism, is at the heart of the populist movement that is surging in so many countries, including the United States, and which poses a much greater threat than such boutique ideologies like integralism and the Benedict Option.

No matter their origin or importance, they all take aim at everybody's current favorite punching bag, the political and cultural framework of modern democratic life known as "liberalism." What is liberalism? That's a good question, since everyone, on the left and the right, seems to have a preferred definition that tends to highlight their own bête noir—crony capitalism, moral individualism, representative democracy. Vladimir Putin has written liberalism's epitaph (which conveniently coincides with the death of the United States) while liberals decry the version known as "neoliberalism" for aggravating all sorts of social ills.

Afterword

Samuel Moyn, a professor of law and history at Yale University, has offered a good and succinct definition:

> In these discussions, "liberalism" refers not to the philosophy of one American political party, but rather to the turn after the Protestant Reformation to a secular politics that allowed individuals and groups to coexist while they pursued their own goals in their own way. Over centuries, state enforcement of Christianity waned in Europe in exchange for greater pluralism and tolerance, and more citizens got more freedom to pursue their own visions of the best life. But such a system, critics have long said, breeds not autonomy but atomism, not fairness but inequality, not fulfillment but emptiness, not culture but anarchy. It also, many conservatives say today, promotes hedonism, nontraditional sexuality, abortion on demand and an unhealthy focus on self-expression.

Writing in the *Washington Post* in June 2019, Moyn dismissed most of the fashionable alternatives to liberalism, noting how such alternatives—besides tilting toward an authoritarianism that suppresses freedom and dignity—tend to be simplistic, and thus illusory, shortcuts to a genuine working out of our differences: "Liberalism is not a dogma: It is a set of dilemmas about how to balance freedom and the common good, economic liberty and social fairness, the search for meaning and the desire to be left alone."

Political liberals and conservatives have in recent years failed miserably at this process of debate and discernment. Yet the Catholic tradition, as *Faithful Citizenship* and the essays in this volume demonstrate, encourages such a working out of differences, and provides not only an ethical framework for such a process but also a spiritual attitude that can—contrary to common perceptions—show religion to be an ally of civil discourse, not an enemy of social peace. Pope Paul VI called politics "the highest and most effective form of charity," a view that seems like it comes from some other universe rather than the one we are living in.

Yet Catholics are not political Puritans or partisan fanatics. As Pope Francis has said, Catholics should not be ideologues and should reject "angelic forms of purity…empty rhetoric, objectives more ideal than real, brands of ahistorical fundamentalism." Francis has repeatedly underscored that point, not only in the way he governs the church, but in the advice he gives Catholics about the role they ought to play in our political life. Politics, Francis says, "is a daily martyrdom: seeking the common good without letting yourself be corrupted." But, he told a group of young Italians about the importance of Catholics going into politics, "Seek the common good by thinking of the most fitting ways for this, the most fitting means. Seek the common good by working for the little things….It gives little return, but one does it. Politics is important: small politics and big politics."

"In the world it's difficult to do good in a society without getting your hands or your heart a little dirty," Francis told them. "But that is why you go ask for forgiveness, you ask for pardon and continue to do it. Don't allow this to discourage you."

Character is central to this perseverance. It is not perfectionism. Rather, it is about doing one's best, recognizing our mistakes, admitting our errors, and moving forward toward a more perfect union—not a perfect union. That is unattainable in this life. It is, however, the goal toward which our common journey must be directed.

Right now, Catholics are seen as politically "homeless," or as Massimo Faggioli has put it, Catholics are wandering in "a political wilderness." That's not such a bad thing. The Catholic vote continues to be the critical swing vote, which means that Catholic voters have a chance to be both prophetic and pragmatic—true to their calling as believers and as citizens.

The wilderness is a place to take stock, a test of one's faith and character, and of communal unity and identity. If we stay true to the path of pilgrimage, we can emerge as a stronger community, a stronger witness, a stronger church.

David Gibson, director of the Center on Religion and Culture at Fordham University in New York, is a longtime journalist who has covered Catholicism from Rome to Washington and is the author of several books on the church.

Contributors

Christina Astorga is professor and chair of the Theology Department of the University of Portland. Among her many publications is *Catholic Moral Theology and Social Ethics: A New Method*, which was named best book by the College Theology Society in 2014 and by the Catholic Press Association of America in 2015.

Gerald J. Beyer is associate professor of Christian Ethics at Villanova University. His publications include *Recovering Solidarity: Lessons from Poland's Unfinished Revolution* (University of Notre Dame Press, 2010) and articles in outlets such as *Journal of Catholic Social Thought*, *Horizons*, *Political Theology*, *Journal of Religious Ethics*, *National Catholic Reporter*, and *America*. Beyer coedited and contributed a chapter to the critical edition of Karol Wojtyła, *Katolicka etyku społeczna* (Lublin: Wydawnictwo KUL, 2018). His forthcoming book is tentatively entitled *Solidarity or Status Quo? Catholic Social Teaching and Higher Education in the Age of the Corporatized University* (Fordham University Press). Beyer is vice president of the Villanova AAUP Chapter, and executive committee member of Catholic Scholars for Worker Justice.

Nicholas P. Cafardi is a civil and canon lawyer. He is Dean Emeritus and former Professor of Law at Duquesne University in Pittsburgh. He is the author of *Before Dallas*, a history of the child sex abuse crisis in the American church; *Understanding Nonprofit and Tax Exempt Organizations* (with J. Cherry); *Church Property, Church Finances and Church-Related Corporations* (with A. Maida); and *Priests without People*, a novel. He was also the editor and chapter author of *Voting and Holiness* (Paulist Press, 2012).

Lisa Sowle Cahill is J. Donald Monan, SJ, Professor at Boston College. She earned her BA at Santa Clara University, and her PhD at the University of Chicago. She is past president of the Catholic Theological Society of America, and the Society of Christian Ethics, and a fellow of the American Academy of Arts and Sciences. Her books include *"Blessed Are the Peacemakers": Just War Theory, Pacifism and Peacebuilding* (Fortress Press, 2019); *A Theology and Praxis of Gender Equality* (Bangalore: Dharmaram Publications, 2019); *Global Justice, Christology and Christian Ethics* (Cambridge, 2013); and *Theological Bioethics: Participation, Justice and Change* (Georgetown, 2005).

Charles Camosy is an associate professor of Theological and Social Ethics at Fordham University. He is the author of five books, most recently *Resisting Throwaway Culture* (New City Press, 2019). A board member of Democrats for Life, he was recently awarded the St. Jerome Award for academic excellence in theology from the Catholic Library Association.

Angela C. Carmella teaches at Seton Hall University School of Law where she is Professor of Law and The James B. and Anita L. Ventantonio Board of Visitors Research Scholar. She has written extensively on religion and the First Amendment, religious land use, Catholic Church-state litigation, and Catholic social teaching, and coedited *Christian Perspectives on Legal Thought* (with Michael W. McConnell and Robert F. Cochran Jr.).

Robert G. Christian, III, is the founding editor of *Millennial*, an online periodical featuring millennial Catholic writers on religion, politics, and culture. He has master's degrees in International Security from the University of Leicester (UK) and American Politics from the Catholic University of America, where he was also a PhD candidate, lecturer, and graduate fellow at the Institute for Policy Research & Catholic Studies. He is a columnist for the *Messenger of Saint Anthony* magazine. He and his wife, Sarah, have three children: Avery, Bob, and Emma Kate.

Nancy A. Dallavalle is special assistant to the Provost and associate professor of Religious Studies at Fairfield University. Her recent presentations are on theologians as institutional partners for Catholic higher education (at the 2019 meeting of the Catholic Theological Society of America), and the role of gender and sexuality in Catholic theology (at the 2018 meeting of the College Theology Society). She serves on the Advisory Board for the Liturgical Press, and writes for its monthly prayer publication, *Give*

Us This Day. She is interested in gender questions, Catholics in public life and social institutions.

David E. DeCosse is director of Campus Ethics Programs at the Markkula Center for Applied Ethics at Santa Clara University, where he is also adjunct associate professor of Religious Studies. He has written articles on Catholicism and democracy for *Theological Studies*, *Political Theology*, *America*, and the *National Catholic Reporter*. He is also the coeditor of *Conscience and Catholicism: Rights, Responsibilities, and Institutional Responses* (with Kristin Heyer) and *Conscience and Catholic Health Care: From Clinical Contexts to Government Mandates* (with Thomas Nairn). He is completing a book that articulates a Catholic public theology of freedom for the American social and political context.

Massimo Faggioli (PhD, University of Turin) is professor of theology and religious studies at Villanova University, Philadelphia, PA. He is contributing writer for *Commonweal* magazine. His most recent books published in English are *Catholicism and Citizenship: Political Cultures of the Church in the 21st Century* (Liturgical Press, 2017) and *The Rising Laity: Ecclesial Movements since Vatican II* (Paulist Press, 2016). His latest book is *The Liminal Papacy of Pope Francis: Moving toward Global Catholicity* (Orbis, 2020).

John Gehring is Catholic program director at Faith in Public Life, and a contributing writer for *Commonweal* magazine. He is author of *The Francis Effect: A Radical Pope's Challenge to the American Catholic Church*. His analysis and commentary have been featured in the *Washington Post*, the *New York Times*, CNN, and other media outlets. A former associate director for media relations at the U.S. Conference of Catholic Bishops, Gehring has been a staff writer at the *Catholic Review*, the *Frederick Gazette*, and *Education Week*. He has contributed essays to *Pope Francis and the Future of Catholicism in the United States: The Challenge of Becoming a Church for the Poor* (University of San Francisco, Lane Center) and *Voting and Holiness: Catholic Perspectives on Political Participation* (Paulist Press).

M. Cathleen Kaveny is the Darald and Juliet Libby Professor of Law and Theology at Boston College. She held the Cary and Ann Maguire Chair in Ethics and American History at the Library of Congress in 2018. Her work lies at the intersection of law, religion, and morality. Her most recent books are *Prophecy without Contempt: Religious Discourse in the Public Square* (Harvard, 2016) and *Ethics at the*

Edges of Law: Christian Moralists and American Legal Thought (Oxford, 2018). She is currently working on a manuscript on complicity with the wrongdoing of others.

Bernard G. Prusak is professor of philosophy and director of the McGowan Center for Ethics and Social Responsibility at King's College in Wilkes-Barre, Pennsylvania. His research focuses in moral and political philosophy, in recent years with special attention to moral formation, conceptions of conscience, and conscientious objection. He is the author of *Parental Obligations and Bioethics: The Duties of a Creator* (Routledge, 2013) and *Catholic Moral Philosophy in Practice and Theory: An Introduction* (Paulist Press, 2016).

Bishop John Stowe, OFM Conv, has been bishop of the Diocese of Lexington since May 2015. He served as a priest in the Diocese of El Paso, including as vicar general from 2002 to 2010 and at the Basilica and National Shrine of Our Lady of Consolation in Carey, Ohio, while also serving as vicar provincial for the Conventual Franciscans. In addition, he currently serves as bishop-president of Pax Christi USA, the National Catholic Peace movement.

Tobias Winright is a theological ethicist. He is associate professor with joint appointments in the Department of Theological Studies and the Center for Health Care Ethics at Saint Louis University in St. Louis. He is the coauthor of *After the Smoke Clears: The Just War Tradition and Post War Justice* (with M. Allman); coeditor and chapter author of *Can War Be Just in the 21st Century? Ethicists Engage the Tradition* (with L. Johnson); coeditor of *Environmental Justice and Climate Change: Assessing Benedict XVI's Ecological Vision for the Catholic Church in the United States* (with J. Schaefer); coeditor of *Violence, Transformation, and the Sacred* (with M. Pfeil); and editor of *Green Discipleship: Theological Ethics and the Environment*.